I0894801

Ecological Sustainability and the Law: The European Green Deal and the New Frontiers of Sustainability

This book is about the emergence of ecological sustainability as a new EU policy and legal objective, distinct and autonomous from sustainable development. It argues that sustainability can no longer be conflated into sustainable development only, but should be rather represented as a plural construction, in which ecological sustainability coexists next to sustainable development. While the latter orientates most of the regulatory measures stemming from the Green Deal, the former is playing an increasing relevant role in a number of legislative initiatives.
The purpose of the volume is to discuss whether and how the EU legislator is exploiting the new opportunities brought forth by the redefinition of sustainability. To do so, a thematic approach has been adopted and the inquiry has been organized in five different parts, each devoted to one specific transition triggered by the European Green Deal.
Navigating the dynamics of the many transitions occurring in the horizon of European climate neutrality, key chapters shed light on the EU regulatory schemes through which ecological sustainability is in the process of being operationalized and critically discuss their points of strength, weaknesses and underlying tensions. In doing so, they provide an overview of the of legal changes occurring in areas of topical interest such as agri-food, energy, digitalization, corporate governance and intellectual property, as well as a number of insights on the relevance of ecological sustainability for the internal dynamism of the European Green Deal.

Edoardo Chiti is Professor of Administrative Law at the Sant'Anna School of Advanced Studies, Pisa. In the editorial board of a number of academic journals and member of various public law societies, he holds an LL.M. from the University College London (UCL) and a Ph.D. from the European University Institute (EUI). He has authored five monographs, co-edited various books and published several articles in international journals in the fields of EU, global and comparative administrative law, all approached from a 'law in context' perspective.

Andrea Giorgi is a Ph.D. Candidate in Administrative Law at the Sant'Anna School of Advanced Studies, Pisa. He has been a Visiting Doctoral Researcher at the Faculty of Law of the University of Oxford. He holds a Master's Degree in Law from the Sapienza University of Rome. He has authored articles and chapters on national and European administrative law, EU economic law and the European Green Deal.

Ecological Sustainability and the Law: The European Green Deal and the New Frontiers of Sustainability

Edited by

Edoardo Chiti and Andrea Giorgi

Routledge
Taylor & Francis Group
LONDON AND NEW YORK

G. Giappichelli Editore

First published 2025
by Routledge
4 Park Square, Milton Park, Abingdon, Oxon OX14 4RN

and by Routledge
605 Third Avenue, New York, NY 10158

Routledge is an imprint of the Taylor & Francis Group, an informa business

and by G. Giappichelli Editore
Via Po 21, Torino – Italia

British Library Cataloguing-in-Publication Data
A catalogue record for this book is available from the British Library

ISBN: 978-10-328-7471-5 (hbk-Routledge)
ISBN: 978-10-035-6518-5 (ebk-Routledge)
ISBN: 978-10-329-3280-4 (pbk-Routledge)
ISBN: 979-12-211-0883-5 (hbk-Giappichelli)
DOI: 10.4324/9781003565185

Typeset in Simoncini Garamond
by G. Giappichelli Editore, Turin, Italy

Research Project PRIN 2022, D.D. No. 104 of 2 February 2022 – 'Shifting Paradigms: Biodiversity Law, Ecological Primacy and the Redefinition of Sustainability in the Eu-ropean Green Deal' - Project Code 2022PPLTLJ, CUP J53D23005820006.

The manuscript has been subjected to a peer review process prior to publication.

CONTENTS

page

Part 1: The Agri-Food Transition

CONTRIBUTORS

Beatrice Baldini, doctoral candidate in Law at the Sant'Anna School of Advanced Studies.

Michela Biscosi, doctoral candidate in Law at the Sant'Anna School of Advanced Studies.

Edoardo Chiti, Professor of Administrative Law at the Sant'Anna School of Advanced Studies.

Georgios Christou, doctoral candidate in Law at the Sant'Anna School of Advanced Studies.

Giulia Corsini, doctoral candidate in Human Rights, Global Politics and Sustainability at the Sant'Anna School of Advanced Studies.

Michele Di Vita, doctoral candidate in Sustainable Development and Climate Change at the Scuola Universitaria Superiore IUSS – Pavia.

Emanuele Fazio, doctoral candidate in Law at the Sant'Anna School of Advanced Studies.

Andrea Giorgi, doctoral candidate in Law at the Sant'Anna School of Advanced Studies.

Matteo Greco, doctoral candidate in Law at the Sant'Anna School of Advanced Studies.

Antonio Manzoni, PhD in Human Rights, Global Politics and Sustainability at the Sant'Anna School of Advanced Studies.

Enrico Mezzacapo, doctoral candidate in Human Rights, Global Politics and Sustainability at the Sant'Anna School of Advanced Studies.

Federica Montanaro, doctoral candidate in Law at the Sant'Anna School of Advanced Studies.

Luisa Nenci, doctoral candidate in Sustainable Development and Climate Change at the University of Genova.

Licinia Pascucci, doctoral candidate in Sustainable Development and Climate Change at the University of Cassino.

Stefano Porfido, PhD in Law at the Sant'Anna School of Advanced Studies.

Camilla Signoretta, doctoral candidate in Law at the Sant'Anna School of Advanced Studies.

Roberto Talenti, doctoral candidate in Human Rights, Global Politics and Sustainability at the Sant'Anna School of Advanced Studies.

Antonio Taurelli, doctoral candidate in Law at the Sant'Anna School of Advanced Studies.

Emmalucia Virardi, doctoral candidate in Law at the Sant'Anna School of Advanced Studies.

ABBREVIATIONS

ABLJ	American Business Law Journal
Agr. ist. merc.	Agricoltura Istituzioni Mercati
AJDA	L'Actualité Juridique Droit Administratif
Alb LJ Sci & Tech	Albany Law Journal of Science & Technology
Am U Int'l L Rev	American University International Law Review
Annu. Rev. Ecol. Evol. Syst.	Annual Review of Ecology, Evolution, and Systematics
Antitrust LJ	Antitrust Law Journal
BAE	Bio-based and Applied Economics journal
BTLJ	Berkeley Technology Law Journal
CMLRev	Common Market Law Review
CNS	Capitalism Nature Socialism
Colum. J. Eur. L.	Columbia Journal of European Law
Competition Pol'y Newsl.	Competition Policy Newsletter
Conserv. Biol.	Conservation Biology
Corp Soc Resp. Env Ma.	Corporate Social Responsibility and Environmental Management
Curr Leg Probl	Current Legal Problems
DePaul L Rev	De Paul Law Review
Dir. Pen. Cont. Riv. Trim.	Diritto Penale Contemporaneo – Rivista trimestrale
Dir Pubbl	Diritto Pubblico
ECLR	European Competition Law Review
Ecol. Ind.	Ecological Indicators

Ecol. Soc.	Ecology & Society
EIPR	European Intellectual Property Review
ELJ	European Law Journal
Enc. Dir.	Enciclopedia del diritto
Energy Convers. Manag.	Energy Conversation Management
Environ. Dev. Sustain.	Environment Development and Sustainability
Environ. Law Rev.	Environmental Law Review
Environ. Res. Lett.	Environmental Research Letters
Environ. Sci.	Environmental Science
Environ. Sci. Technol.	Environmental Science & Technology
Eur. Bus. L. Rev.	European Business Law Review
Eur. Bus. Org. L. Rev.	European Business Organization Law Review
Eur. Energy Environ. Law Rev.	European Energy and Environmental Law Review
Eur. L. Rev.	European Law Review
Eur. Papers	European Papers
Fed Cir BJ	Federal Circuit Bar Journal
Fordham Intell. Prop. Media & Ent. L.J.	Fordham Intellectual Property Media & Entertainment Law Journal
Front. Ecol. Evol.	Frontiers in Ecology and Evolution
Front. Microbiol.	Frontiers in Microbiology
Geo Envtl. L Rev	Georgetown Environmental Law Review
Geo Int'l Envtl L Rev	Georgetown International Environmental Law Review
Geo. J. Int'l L.	Georgetown Journal of International Law
Geo Mason J Int'l Com L	George Mason Journal of International Commercial Law
Geo Wash L Rev	The George Washington Law Review
Glob. Ecol. Conserv.	Global Ecology and Conservation
Global Environ. Change	Global Environmental Change

Harv L Rev	Harvard Law Review
Hastings LJ	Hastings Law Journal
HBS Working Papers	Harvard Business School Working Papers
IDEA	The Law Review of the Franklin Pierce Center for Intellectual Property
IIC	International Review of Intellectual Property and Competition Law
Int. J. Sustain. Dev. World Ecol.	International Journal of Sustainable Development & World Ecology
Int. Spect.	The International Spectator
Int'l L & Mgmt Rev	International Management & Law Review
IPR	Internet Policy Review
Ist. del Fed.	Istituzioni del Federalismo
J Antitrust Enforc	Journal of Antitrust Enforcement
J Compet Law Econ	Journal of Competition Law & Economics
J High Tech L	Journal of High Technology Law
J Int'l Econ L	Journal of International Economic Law
J Pat Off Soc'y	Journal of the Patent and Trademark Office Society
J. Agric. Econ.	Journal of Agricultural Economic
J. Big Data	Journal of Big Data
J. Clean. Prod.	Journal of Cleaner Production
J. Ecol.	Journal of Ecology
J. Econ. Geo.	Journal of Economic Geography
J. Env. L.	Journal of Environmental Law
J. Environ. Policy Plan.	Journal of Environmental Policy & Planning
J. Eur. Integr.	Journal of European Integration
J. Eur. Public Policy	Journal of European Public Policy
J. Ind. Ecol.	Journal of Industrial Ecology
J. Law & Soc.	Journal of Law and Society
J. Socio Econ.	The Journal of Socio-Economics
J. Urban Technol.	Journal of Urban Technology

J. World Bus.	Journal of World Business
JECLP	Journal of European Competition Law & Practice
JEEPL	Journal for European Environmental & Planning Law
JEMI	Journal of Entrepreneurship, Management and Innovation
JETL	Journal of European Tort Law
JIPITEC	Journal of Intellectual Property, Information Technology and Electronic Commerce Law
JIPLP	Journal of Intellectual Property Law & Practice
JL & Econ	The Journal of Law & Economics
JPP&M	Journal of Public Policy & Marketing
Ky LJ	Kentucky Law Journal
Law & Critique	Law and Critique
Maast. J. Eur. & Comp. L	Maastricht Journal of European and Comparative Law
Marq Intell Prop L Rev	Marquette intellectual Property Law Review
McGill L J	McGill Law Journal
Mich. J. Int. Law	Michigan State University College of Law Journal of International Law
Mich Telecomm & Tech L Rev	Michigan Telecommunications and Technology Law Review
Minn JL Sci & Tech	Minnesota Journal of Law Science & Technology
Mod. L. Rev.	Modern Law Review
Nat Cli Ch	Nature Climate Change
Nat. Commun.	Nature Communications
Nat. Food	Nature Food
Nat. Sustain.	Nature Sustainability
New J. Eur. Crim. Law	New Journal of European Criminal Law
Nw J Tech & Intell Prop	Northwestern Journal of Technology and Intellectual Property

Organ Environ	Organization & Environment
OWID	Our World in Data
Oxf. J. Leg. Stud.	Oxford Journal of Legal Studies
Perspect. Fed.	Perspectives on Federalism
PLoS Pathog	PLoS Pathogens
Polish YBInt'l Law	Polish Yearbook of International Law
RD rur.	Revue de Droit Rural
REA	Italian Review of Agricultural Economics
RECIEL	Review of European, Comparative & International Environmental Law
Reg. Stud.	Regional Studies
Regul. Gov	Regulation and Governance
Renew. Sustain. Energy Rev.	Renewable and Sustainable Energy Reviews
Resour. Conserv. Recycl.	Resources, Conservation & Recycling
Riv Dir Comp	Rivista di Diritti Comparati
Riv reg mer	Rivista della Regolazione dei Mercati
Riv. dir. Agr	Rivista di Diritto Agrario
Riv. It. dir. proc. pen.	Rivista italiana di diritto e procedura penale
Riv. Tri. dir. pen. econ.	Rivista trimestrale di diritto penale dell'economia
RQDA	Rivista Quadrimestrale di Diritto dell'Ambiente
SAJELP	South African Journal of Environmental Law and Policy
Sci. Total Environ.	Science of the Total Environment
SCS	Sustainable Cities and Society
SMJ	Strategic Management Journal
Smu L Rev	Southern Methodist University Law Review
Stan Intramural L Rev	Stanford Intramural Law Review
Sustain. Dev.	Sustainable Development
Sustain. Sci.	Sustainability Science
TEL	Transnational Environmental Law

TulLRev	Tulane Law Review
U Pitt L Rev	University of Pittsburgh Law Review
UCLA L Rev	UCLA Law Review
Utah L Rev	Utah Law Review
Utrecht L Rev	Utrecht Law Review
Va L Rev	Virginia Law Review
VELJ	Virginia Environmental Law Journal
Waste Manage.	Waste Management
World Comp	World Competition
Yale L J	Yale Law Journal
Yearb. Eur. Law	Yearbook of European Law

FOREWORD

The European Green Deal is reshaping the traditional construction of sustainability in the EU legal order. It does so by gradually articulating, next to sustainable development, a new and more ecological understanding of sustainability, aimed at ensuring ecosystem integrity and ecological primacy. This book explores ways in which the new policy objective of ecosystem sustainability is actually penetrating European Union (EU) legislation, how ecological sustainability is shaped in different regulatory frameworks, the tensions between ecological sustainability and sustainable development, and the relevance of regulation for their composition.

The perspective from which such process is observed is dynamic and evolutionary, sensitive to legal change and to the transformations of EU law in the overall horizon of climate neutrality. Five main transitions triggered by the Green Deal are considered: agri-food, energy, ecological, digital, and economic. Navigating the dynamics of such transitions, we aim at illuminating the complex combination of innovation, resistance and adaptation accompanying the rise of ecological sustainability.

This extensive appraisal of the field is designed for academics, researchers and advanced students interested in the new ecological law stemming from the Green Deal, the changing features of sustainability and the relevance of the Green Deal as a regulatory project. Given the extent and variety of the cases discussed in the chapters, this book is also aimed at EU and domestic policy-makers and regulators who wish to engage with the ongoing debates in the field of ecological transition and the Green Deal.

The book is the result of a collective research project carried out within the context of the Ph.D. programme in Law at the Sant'Anna School of Advanced Studies. All authors are promising Ph.D. candidates in the final stretch of their research projects. We have tried to combine scientific passion, legal creativity and intellectual rigour. Working together in this project has been a privilege.

Edoardo Chiti
Andrea Giorgi

Introduction

SUSTAINABILITY IN TRANSITION

Edoardo Chiti and Andrea Giorgi

ABSTRACT: *This Introduction aims at providing the basic parameters of the inquiry, which approaches sustainability from a legal-evolutionary perspective. It defines the research questions, illustrates the main findings of the study, and clarifies its relevance. After presenting the structure of the book and explaining its rationale, it introduces the other Chapters and provides some interpretative keys emerging from the issues dealt with therein. The main argument of this Introduction is as follows: the European Green Deal is revising the traditional understanding of sustainability in the EU order. A potentially important but still under-explored process of legal change is now taking place. Next to sustainable development, the Commission is gradually articulating a different and promising understanding of sustainability aimed at ensuring ecosystem integrity and ecological primacy. Like any transition process, however, this one is also marked by tensions and contradictions, certainties and ambiguities.*

KEYWORDS: *Ecological sustainability – Sustainable development – European Green Deal – Climate neutrality – Transition – Regulation.*

1. Sustainability and the Green Deal

Multiple and challenging transitions have been triggered by the Green Deal, the multifaceted strategy for climate neutrality launched in 2019 by the European Commission.[1] This is hardly surprising when considering climate neutrality as a highly transformative target, pushing for a rethinking

[1] See The European Green Deal, COM (2019) 640.

of a wide array of key policy areas capable of deeply impacting the legal, economic, social, and cultural construct of the European Union (EU).[2] Equally unsurprisingly, sustainable development is put by the Commission at the centre of all those transitions, which can be appropriately managed only by taking into consideration and balancing economic, social and environmental interests.

While such explicit reference to sustainable development is coherent with the macro-objective of climate neutrality, as well as clearly in line with a deeply rooted EU political and legal culture, this book argues that the European Green Deal is revising the traditional understanding of sustainability in the EU order. A potentially important but still under-explored process of legal change is now taking place.[3] Next to sustainable development, the Commission is gradually articulating a new and promising understanding of sustainability, one aimed at ensuring ecosystem integrity and ecological primacy.

The ongoing process of redefinition of sustainability raises several significant questions, all revolving around the ability of the new policy objective of ecosystem sustainability to penetrate the EU legal order and orientate the multiple transitions undergoing its regulatory space. How is sustainability precisely shaped in the different policies and legislations stemming from the Green Deal? To what extent do such policies and legislations integrate the goal of biodiversity protection and ecosystem restoration within their respective logics and mechanisms? What model of sustainability is promoted by the EU legislator in each policy field, and through which options and regulatory schemes is it constructed and operationalized? How consistent and reasonable are the overall regulatory strategies in light of the specific objectives of each transition? And what are the potential implications of the emergence of ecological sustainability for the overall construction of the Green Deal?

---

[2] *Ibidem*, 4; in the legal scholarship the transformative force of climate neutrality is explored by Chiti E., "Managing the ecological transition of the EU: the European Green Deal as a regulatory process", in *CMLRev*, 2022, 59, 19-48, discussing the impact of the European strategy for climate neutrality on the EU substantive constitution.

[3] On the need for a dynamic understanding of law and a perspective attentive to the evolution of legal paradigms, see the seminal article by Pound R., "Law in Books and Law in Action", in *American Law Review*, 1910, 44(1),12-36. In European legal scholarship, the importance of exploring the transformations of (administrative) law is underscored by Cassese S., "Le trasformazioni del diritto amministrativo dal XIX al XXI secolo", in *Riv. trim. dir. pubbl.*, 2002, 1, 27-40; Auby J.-B., "La bataille de San Romano. Réflexions sur les évolutions récentes du droit administrative", in *AJDA*, 2001, 11, 912-926; and D'Alberti M. (ed.), *Le nuove mete del diritto amministrativo*, il Mulino, 2010, 1-187.

These are the relevant research questions that this book aims at addressing, by navigating the dynamics of the many transitions occurring in the overall horizon of European climate neutrality. As the various Chapters will show, these dynamics are not always as harmonious and linear as one might assume, but are rather characterized by tensions, conflicts, and underlying ambiguities.

This Introduction aims at providing the basic parameters of the inquiry, presenting its main findings and clarifying its relevance. It opens by discussing the meaning of the ongoing articulation of sustainability as an EU objective. In particular, it asks how ecological sustainability has been formulated as a policy and legal objective in the framework of the Green Deal (§ 2) and discusses the distinction between ecological sustainability and sustainable development (§ 3). Coherently with such premises, this book aims at exploring the ways in which the EU legislator is in the process of actually shaping sustainability in the context of the multiple transitions triggered by the Green Deal: the structure and main findings of the inquiry are then presented (§ 4). Finally, the Introduction provides four overall interpretative keys emerging from the case-studies and issues dealt with in the various Chapters (§ 5).

2. Basic parameters: ecological sustainability as a policy and legal objective

Ecological sustainability is an indispensable component of any sound strategy against climate change, especially one aimed specifically at achieving climate neutrality. Indeed, ecosystem health is as important as technological innovation in reaching a balance between anthropogenic emissions by sources and removals by sinks of greenhouse gases, as it allows forests, soils and other fundamental ecosystems to operate as carbon sinks, storage and substitution. In the academic debate surrounding the Green Deal, this is recognized both by those who promote and those who oppose the EU strategy for climate neutrality. In spite of deep disagreements about the possibility to reduce absolute emissions of carbon dioxide while attempting to grow economically in the temporal horizon of 2050, most positions converge on the idea that protecting and restoring nature is to be a component of any credible action against climate change.

The same point has been openly made by the Commission in the three main strategies developing the ecological dimension of the Green Deal, namely, the Biodiversity Strategy, the Soil Strategy and the New Forest Strategy,[4]

[4] See, respectively, the EU Biodiversity Strategy for 2030, COM (2020) 380; the EU

where nature is presented as a «vital ally» in adapting to and fighting against climate change and it is stressed that nature-based solutions are essential for emission reduction and climate adaptation. It has also been formalized in the European Climate Law, which stipulates that restoration of ecosystems should «assist in maintaining, managing and enhancing natural sinks and promote biodiversity while fighting climate change»,[5] and recently reasserted by the European Environment Agency (EEA) and the European Scientific Advisory Board on Climate Change (Advisory Board).[6]

It is appropriate to consider the way in which the Commission has developed ecological sustainability as a new policy objective. To begin with, ecological sustainability features as part of a wider framework of assumptions of ecosystem ecology, starting with the idea that biological diversity has many different components, from species and genetic diversity to the variety of the energy processes internal to each ecosystem. Moreover, ecological sustainability requires two complementary activities, namely preservation and restoration of ecosystems: the former tackles a number of key drivers of biodiversity loss, such as changes in land and sea use and overexploitation, while the aim of the latter is to reverse biodiversity loss. In addition to this, and most importantly, ecological sustainability is defined in a clearly functional way: ecosystems are healthy, and therefore sustainable, when they are capable of providing their ecosystem services. A clear illustration of this understanding is provided by the Commission's Communication on Managing climate risks, where ecosystem health is unambiguously associated to the provision of «life-supporting services such as freshwater, food and biomaterial, carbon sequestration, soil and coastal erosion control, flood and drought prevention, cooling of densely populat-

Soil Strategy for 2030, COM (2021) 699; and the New EU Forest Strategy for 2030, COM (2021) 572.

[5] Regulation (EU) 2021/1119 of the European Parliament and of the Council of 30 June 2021 establishing the framework for achieving climate neutrality and amending Regulations (EC) 401/2009 and (EU) 2018/1999 (European Climate Law), O.J. 2021, L 243/1, Whereas 23.

[6] See, respectively, EEA, Report 01/2024, presenting the first European Climate Risk Assessment (EUCRA); and European Scientific Advisory Board on Climate Change, Towards EU climate neutrality. Progress, policy gaps and opportunities. Assessment Report 2024, Luxembourg, Publications Office of the European Union, 2024, 181-207. For a discussion on the challenging relationship between the EEA and the Advisory Board, and the risks of regulatory conflicts between these two technical bodies assisting the Commission in achieving climate neutrality, see Giorgi A., "The EU Green Deal and the Transformations of the European Administrative System: Does the 'Epistemic Leadership' of the Scientific Advisory Board Push the Agency Model Over the Sunset Boulevard?", in *Eur. Papers*, 2023, 8(2), 879-900.

ed urban areas».[7] In the same vein, the Soil Strategy argues that soils can be considered to be healthy ecosystems «when they are in good chemical, biological and physical condition, and thus able to continuously provide as many ecosystem services as possible», such as, for example, providing food and biomass production, absorbing, storing and filtering water, providing the basis for life and biodiversity, acting as a carbon reservoir and as a source of raw materials.[8] The key concept is that of «resilience», elaborated in a large and deep scientific debate[9] and used by the Commission in the specific sense of «resilience of ecosystem functions».

The Commission's ecological view is highly demanding. The new objective of ecosystem health implies a duty to protect and restore the «integrity» of ecological systems. Integrity is essential to the capability of an ecosystem to provide its basic services. The objective of protecting and restoring healthy and resilient ecosystems may only be achieved by ensuring their functional integrity. This is strictly connected, in the line of reasoning followed by the Commission, to the search for mechanisms to support ecosystem recovery, including those imposing limitations on economic and social concerns. Taken seriously, the very idea of ecological integrity, on which the goal to protect and restore healthy and well-functioning ecological systems is based, opens the way to a potentially radical understanding of the ecological concerns in the Green Deal.

When moving from policy documents to legislations, however, the ecological approach taken by the Commission seems less straightforward and more nuanced: the way in which the policy objective of ecological sustainability has been legally shaped in particular areas suggests that the EU legislator is applying it in a rather relaxed way.

Consider, for example, the main ecological legislation stemming from the Green Deal, namely the «Nature Restoration Law».[10] It is designed to ensure the recovery to biodiverse and resilient nature across the EU territory and it encapsulates a strong understanding of ecological sustainability. More precisely, the Nature Restoration Law expressly sets out the «over-

---

[7] COM (2024) 91, 15.

[8] See e.g. COM (2021) 699, cited *supra* fn. 3, 4.

[9] See e.g. Capdevila P. et al., "Reconciling resilience across ecological systems, species and subdisciplines", in *J. Ecol.*, 2021, 109, 3102-3113; and Chambers J.C, Allen C.R. and Cushman S.A., "Operationalizing Ecological Resilience Concepts for Managing Species and Ecosystems at Risk", in *Front. Ecol. Evol.*, 2019, 7, Article 241, 1-27.

[10] Regulation (EU) 2024/1991 of the European Parliament and of the Council of 24 June 2024 on nature restoration and amending Regulation (EU) 2022/869, O.J. 2024, L 29.07.2024.

arching objective» to contribute to «the long-term and sustained recovery of biodiverse and resilient nature across the Member States' land and sea areas through the restoration of degraded ecosystems».[11] Restoring ecosystems to good conditions requires their full functionality, that is their capability to provide a range of essential ecosystem services: biodiverse ecosystems «deliver, if in good condition, a range of essential ecosystem services».[12] Moreover, the goal of ecosystem health is directly associated to climate neutrality, coherently with the overall construction of the Green Deal. In particular, it is stressed that healthy, biodiverse agroecosystems, forests and marine ecosystems provide an important contribution both to a number of economic sectors, such as agriculture, forestry and fisheries, and to the long-term objective of mitigating climate change. Crucially, ecosystem health is given priority over economic and social concerns: it is not insulated from such concerns, as it is presented as functional to the social and economic activities of human beings; but it is designed as a pre-condition for human activities, a goal which is important to achieve in order to have a number of socio-economic benefits. Healthy ecosystems are considered essential both for our long-term survival and for our well-being, prosperity and security, as they «contribute to a broad range of socio-economic benefits, depending on the economic, social, cultural, regional and local characteristics».[13]

Yet, this clearly formulated ecological objective, implying a strong understanding of ecosystem health, is not accompanied by an equally well-defined set of implementing measures. Actually, the Nature Restoration Law sets several binding restoration targets and obligations concerning a broad range of ecosystems, leaving to Member States the task to identify the measures through which such objectives should be achieved. The key instrument is that of planning. Member States are asked to strategically plan the appropriate restoration measures and to organize them in «national restoration plans».[14] Such a regulatory technique is obviously reasonable, given the technical complexity of the issues at stake, as well as the need to consider the diversity of national situations. Unsurprisingly, the Nature Restoration Law stresses the fact that national restoration plans should be based on the best available scientific evidence and take account of the specific needs in the relevant territories. The choice for national planning, though, is also highly problematic. It assumes that domestic authorities will

[11] *Ibidem*, Article 1. See also Recitals 14 and 65.

[12] *Ibidem*, Recital 14.

[13] *Ibidem*.

[14] *Ibidem*, Articles 14-19.

be able not only to ensure the consistency of the identified restoration measures with those laid down in other plans required by the Green Deal legislation, including the adaptation plan and the integrated national energy and climate plans, but also to cooperate with other Member States to ensure restoration across borders. Moreover, and most importantly for our purposes, the EU legislator, in spite of all procedural and substantive details laid down in the relevant provisions, leaves unaddressed the key problem of explaining when and how exactly the priority of ecosystem health over economic and social concerns should be operationalized. This is a task entirely left to Member States' administrations.

Another example is provided by the Regulation to curb EU-driven deforestation and forest degradation.[15] Forest health, presented as a crucial nature-based opportunity for climate mitigation, is specifically described as the resilience of ecosystems and their services.[16] Unlike the Nature Restoration Law, however, the objective of the Regulation is not that of restoring the integrity of forests as functionally healthy ecosystems and to give it priority over economic and social interests. More modestly, the Regulation aims at «sustainably using» forests, that is at restoring forests as ecosystems at the same time healthy and providing subsistence and income to human beings. The functional integrity of forests is not a pre-condition for social and economic well-being. Rather, it is a desired outcome that the EU legislator aims at achieving by orienting the cycle of production and consumption. Coherently with such perspective, the Regulation lays down a set of instruments which should both minimize «consumption of products coming from supply chains associated with deforestation or forest degradation» and increase EU demand for 'deforestation-free' commodities and products.[17] In this case, the regulatory framework aims at promoting forest integrity and health without at the same time prioritizing it over economic and social concerns.

---

[15] Regulation (EU) 2023/1115 of the European Parliament and of the Council of 31 May 2023 on the making available on the Union market and the export from the Union of certain commodities and products associated with deforestation and forest degradation and repealing Regulation (EU) 995/2010, O.J. 2023, L 150/206.

[16] See e.g. the first Recital, stating that forests provide a broad variety of environmental, economic and social benefits, maintain ecosystem functions, help protect the climate system, provide clean air and play a vital role for the purification of waters and soils as well as for water retention and recharge.

[17] *Ibidem*, 1.

3. Redefining the balancing exercise: ecological sustainability and sustainable development

If ecological sustainability is gradually emerging as an EU objective, what is its relationship with the fundamental declination of sustainability under EU law, sustainable development?

The starting point to address this uneasy question may be the Commission's view. While formulating ecological sustainability as a demanding policy objective, calling for the functional integrity of ecosystems and inevitably responding to the logic of ecological primacy, the Commission is not explicitly arguing that ecological sustainability is a goal distinct from sustainable development. On the contrary, it seems to maintain a unitary narrative, one in which ecological sustainability and sustainable development are part of the same political and legal discourse. This is in line with the overall Treaty framework, in which sustainability is clearly formulated in the terms of sustainable development,[18] as well as with Article 37 of the Charter of Fundamental Rights, requiring Member States to «integrate» and «ensure» a high level of environmental protection and the improvement of the quality of the environment in the policies of the Union, «in accordance with the principle of sustainable development».[19]

---

[18] See the Preamble of the Treaty on the European Union (TEU, where Member States reaffirm their determination «to promote economic and social progress for their peoples, taking into account the principle of sustainable development»; and Article 2 TEU. On the legal relevance of sustainable development in the EU order, which has been conceptualized either as a legal principle or as an objective, see Bándi G., "Principles of EU Environmental Law Including the (Objective) of Sustainable Development", in Peeters M. and Eliantonio M. (eds.), *Research Handbook on EU Environmental Law*, Elgar, 2020, 36-53; Barral V., "The principle of sustainable development", in Krämer L. and Orlando E. (eds.), *Principles of Environmental Law*, Elgar, 2017, 103-114; and Verschuuren J., "The growing significance of the principle of sustainable development as a legal norm", in Fisher D. (ed.), *Research Handbook on Fundamental Concepts of Environmental Law*, Elgar, 2016, 276-305.

[19] For a particularly clear formulation of such understanding of sustainable development see Case C-371/98, *First Corporate Shipping Ltd*, ECLI:EU:C:2000:600, as well as the Opinion of Advocate General Léger, ECLI:EU:C:2000:108. In particular, Advocate General Léger argues that «[t]he concept 'sustainable development' does not mean that the interests of the environment must necessarily and systematically prevail over the interests defended in the context of the other policies pursued by the Community in accordance with Article 3 of the EC Treaty [...]. On the contrary, it emphasises the necessary balance between various interests which sometimes clash, but which must be reconciled» (para. 54). The reasoning goes on by clarifying that «[t]o reconcile these diverse interests in the context of 'sustainable development', the Treaty on European Union introduced the principle of 'integration' in Article 130r(2) in fine» (para. 57).

Such position seems to reflect the view that the goal of ecosystem health simply represents an articulation of the traditional understanding of environmental protection as «social regulation».[20] By referring to biodiversity, in other terms, the EU is modernizing and updating its understanding of environment, now presented as a multiplicity of ecosystems. However, this does not change the overall idea, inspired by the rationale and conceptual framework of ecological modernization,[21] that the protection of the environment should be internalized in the market and conceived as a set of legal tools to address a specific type of market failures. According to this view, the new focus on ecological sustainability simply reconceptualizes environment as nature and ecosystems, while confirming that environmental concerns should be balanced with economic and social interests and integrated in the definition and implementation of other policies and actions, as required by sustainable development under EU law.

Our reading of the ongoing legal process, however, is different. We observe that ecological sustainability redefines the balancing exercise between environmental, social and economic interests, which is at the very heart of sustainable development. This is a consequence of the ecological construction followed by the Commission when articulating the policy objective of ecosystem health: as previously highlighted, such construction is rooted on the integrity of ecosystems and their capability to provide their essential services, two functional features that are determined by scientific parameters, laid down by ecology as a scientific discipline, and that require approaches for supporting ecological recovery.

In its most radical version, the search for ecosystem integrity necessarily implies «ecological primacy». Taken seriously, the very idea of ecological integrity assumes that ecological limits must have primacy over social and economic regimes, when this is necessary to protect and restore ecosystems in danger or in bad conditions.[22] In this understanding, ecosystem integrity

[20] For a discussion of the distinguishing features and rationale of social regulation see Joerges C., "Bureaucratic Nightmare, Technocratic Regime and the Dream of Good Transnational Governance", in Joerges C. and Vos E. (eds.), *EU Committees: Social Regulation, Law and Politics*, Hart, 1999, 3-18; and Majone G., *Regulating Europe*, Routledge, 1996, 1-61.

[21] On the ability of ecological modernization prescriptions to influence and shape European environmental legal and political discourse from the mid-1980s, see Chalmers D., "Inhabitants in the Field of EC Environmental Law", in Craig P. and de Búrca G. (eds.), *The Evolution of EU Law*, OUP, 1999, 672-684; Andersen M.S. and Massa I., "Ecological modernization – origins, dilemmas and future directions", in *J. Environ. Policy Plan*, 2000, 2(4), 337-345; and Gouldson A. and Murphy J., "Ecological modernization in the European Union", in *Geoforum*, 1996, 27(1), 11-21.

[22] This is a point made by the legal scholarship articulating a normative vision of a

cannot be subject to negotiation or balancing with social and economic interests, but it operates as an autonomous goal.

Such approach is exemplified by the Nature Restoration Law. As already highlighted, in such legislation ecosystem health is given priority over economic and social concerns, in line with the logic of ecological primacy. Ecosystem health is certainly presented as functional to the social and economic activities of human beings. But it is also clearly designed as a precondition for human activities. A further example is the «strict protection» regime for primary and old-growth forests envisaged in the New EU Forest Strategy. Admittedly, such regime has not yet been made legally binding, but only indirectly reaffirmed by the legislative proposal on a monitoring framework for resilient European forests.[23] What is important, however, is the underlying rationale of the envisaged regime. Primary and old-growth forests are ecosystems of particular importance, given their exceptional biodiversity value and capability to store significant carbon stocks and to provide critical ecosystem services. For this reason, they require a particularly strict protection, leaving the dynamic of the forest cycle to natural processes and limiting human activities.

This is not, however, the only possible understanding of ecological sustainability. In a second version, ecological sustainability promotes the idea that regulation should enable economic and social activities that may positively contribute to ecosystem recovery, rather than to economic development. Such version of ecological sustainability implies some kind of balancing, as in the sustainable development paradigm, but it stipulates that the balancing exercise should be specifically oriented toward identifying measures that attenuate anthropogenic pressures responsible for ecosystem degradation and enable ecological recovery.

The EU regulatory measures offer many examples of this second regulatory approach, from biodiversity protection in the agri-food sector to mitigation of biodiversity risks in the energy and economic transition. One example is provided by Commission Regulation (EU) 2023/334, prohibiting the use of some pesticides to protect pollinators, including bees.[24] By

---

new «ecological law»: see Anker K. et al., *From Environmental Law to Ecological Law*, Routledge, 2021, 1-284; Sbert C., *The Lens of Ecological Law: A look at Mining*, Elgar, 2020, 1-240; Bosselmann K., "The Rule of Law Grounded in the Earth: Ecological Integrity as a Grundnorm", in Westra L. and Vilela M. (eds.), *The Earth Charter, Ecological Integrity and Social Movements*, Routledge, 2014, 3-12; and Garver G., "The Rule of Ecological Law: The Legal Complement to Degrowth Economics", in *Sustainability*, 2013, 5, 316-337.

[23] COM (2023) 728.

[24] Commission Regulation (EU) 2023/334 of 2 February 2023 amending Annexes II

adopting that Regulation, the Commission has widened the rationale of Regulation (EC) 178/2002 and Regulation (EC) 396/2005, which were primarily focused on the protection of human health and consumers' interests, to take into account the health of agro-ecosystems. Moreover, it has adopted measures aimed at tackling ecosystem degradation, recognizing that agro-ecosystem health depends on the protection of pollinator populations from the risks posed by active substance.

4. The structure and findings of the inquiry

This book aims at exploring and discussing whether and how the EU legislator is exploiting the new opportunities brought forth by the redefinition of sustainability. It does so by presenting and discussing five main transitions triggered by the Green Deal: agri-food, energy, ecological, digital, and economic. Transitions, indeed, rather than just policy sectors. The language employed is not neutral, it reveals a clear preference and heuristic approach. The purpose of this collective effort is not to provide a sectional, static, and updated perspective on sustainability. Rather, this book aims at exploring the ongoing process of legal adaptation and change triggered in key policy areas by the pluralisation of the sustainability discourse in the EU.

While the approach is not entirely conventional, the rationale behind this work is quite simple. Moving from the formulation and articulation within the Green Deal of a genuine ecological understanding of sustainability, it is possible to measure the resistance opposed by each discipline to the penetration of such alternative declination of sustainability; the elements of continuity and discontinuity with previous legal regimes; or the pushes towards the transformation of well-established and defined regulatory frameworks. Thus, the perspective from which this process of legal change is observed is dynamic and evolutionary, sensitive to the transformations of European law[25] and concerned with the effects of Europeanisation on domestic law.[26]

---

and V to Regulation (EC) 396/2005 of the European Parliament and of the Council as regards maximum residue levels for clothianidin and thiamethoxam in or on certain products, O.J. 2023, L 47/29.

[25] For an outstanding example of this approach, see Craig P. and de Búrca G. (eds.), *The Evolution of EU Law*, OUP, 2021, 1-977.

[26] On the Europeanisation phenomenon see, among others, Snyder F. (ed.), *The Europeanisation of Law: The Legal Effects of European Integration*, Hart, 2000, 1-376; Ladeur K.-H. (ed.), *The Europeanisation of Administrative Law. Transforming National Decision-Making Procedures*, Ashgate, 2002, 1-159; Sedelmeier U., "Europeanization",

The inquiry is organized in five different parts.

4.1. The agri-food transition

Part I discusses the agri-food transition, placing the resilience and sustainability of food systems at the forefront of the reform agenda outlined in the Green Deal.[27] This constitutes a topical and challenging field of inquiry, given the multiple and competing economic, social, environmental, and ethical concerns at stake within current agri-food systems. Policy-makers and regulators are increasingly required to give due consideration to the multifaceted interactions among the various components of the food system, as part of a strong advocacy for a systemic view and holistic approach to the agri-food discipline.

The first contribution by Enrico Mezzacapo and Antonio Manzoni delineates the evolutionary trajectory of the Common Agricultural Policy (CAP) across different historical phases, each characterized by specific objectives and priorities. The aim is twofold: on the one hand, to ascertain whether and to what extent the final outcome of this evolutionary path – i.e. the new CAP – effectively embraces the principles of agri-food sustainability advocated by the Green Deal, which calls for the adoption of a genuine food system approach; on the other, to assess the role and capabilities of the Member States to design and implement sustainable food systems at a national level. A nuanced depiction emerges. The new CAP undeniably advances the promotion of a fairer and greener agri-food sector, adopting a holistic perspective that considers the intricate network of interactions and interdependencies among the numerous components of the food system. The positive aspects include the development of new instruments and financial options to support the sustainability of the agricultural sector, as well as the increased involvement of Member States in the bottom-up attainment of common objectives. However, as the authors underscore, the current framework shows inconsistencies and gaps in outlining how to achieve a sustainable EU food system: a concept and objective that risks remaining not fully substantiated, yet still rooted in the rationale of sustainable development.

The new CAP 2023-2027 is also the focal point of the second Chapter by Roberto Talenti and Giulia Corsini, aimed at understanding which of

in Jones E., Menon A. and Weatherill S., *The Oxford Handbook of the European Union*, OUP, 2012, 823-837; and Bobek M., "Europeanization of Public Law", in Cassese S., von Bogdandy A. and Huber P. (eds.), *The Max Planck Handbooks in European Public Law. The Administrative State*, OUP, 2017, 1, 631-673.

[27] See A Farm to Fork Strategy, COM (2020) 381.

the various interpretations of the polysemic and multifaceted concept of sustainability aligns most closely with the new approach of the EU legislator. In doing so, the focus is placed on two case studies of significant environmental and ecological impact and mitigation potential: the livestock sector and food waste. The analysis reveals an attempt to place the concept of sustainability at the center of the transformation process of the European food system. However, despite commendable efforts to curtail environmental degradation, the introduction of new regulatory tools to incentivize sustainable agricultural practices, and the favour for a preventive and circular approach to food waste, the new CAP falls short of expectations. At least for the two sectors examined, it misses the opportunity to adopt, implement, and operationalize a scientifically grounded ecological idea of sustainability, one that prioritizes the protection and restoration of agro-ecosystems. Rather, as the authors argue, the European legislator still aims to reconcile productivity and economic growth (even in the short term) with environmental protection and social benefits, following the balancing rationale of the sustainable development paradigm.

4.2. The energy transition

Part II is dedicated to the energy transition. The energy sector plays a pivotal role in the EU overarching strategy for climate neutrality and is currently undergoing a deep transformation. Due to the undeniable significance of energy production and consumption in influencing pollutant emissions, the decarbonization of the energy sector and the shift toward a secure, efficient, clean, and sustainable energy system stand as focal points on the policy agenda of the European institutions. The EU regulatory efforts have gained increased momentum, particularly in the aftermath of the Russian war in Ukraine, which has underscored the urgent necessity for a structural energy transformation.[28]

The first contribution by Matteo Greco delves into the realm of bioenergy, serving as a litmus test to assess the penetration of an ecological dimension of sustainability in the regulatory framework for renewable energy. While bioenergy stands as a valuable ally in the decarbonization of the energy sector, precautions must be taken to prevent its production and utilization from adversely affecting the health and equilibrium of ecosystems, depleting biodiversity, and irreversibly harming ecological processes. The evolutionary analysis of the sustainability criteria mandated by the European legislator, essential for categorizing bioenergy as a renewable source,

[28] See REPowerEU Plan, COM (2022) 230.

underscores progress compared to the previous legal regime. Within the recently adopted EU regulatory framework, there is an enhanced awareness of the need for ecologically sustainable bioenergy production. As the author argues, the legislative reform attests to the progressive infusion of an ecological understanding of sustainability into the domain of renewable energy, following a gradual and incremental approach. The new sustainability criteria for bioenergy partially succeed in mitigating conflicts among different regulatory objectives of the Green Deal, pushing towards a reconciliation of the energy transition with the ecological one.

Emmalucia Virardi authors the second Chapter of this Part, focusing on the main regulatory measures adopted by the EU to foster the energy transition process and overcome administrative barriers hindering its implementation. The emphasis is on two key concepts of administrative law: procedure and administrative discretion. These notions are significantly influenced by the EU prioritization of the decarbonization goal and the presumption of renewable energy as an overriding public interest. The implications of this prioritization go beyond streamlining and simplifying the rules governing the permitting process for renewable energy plants. This process shapes and reorients the discretionary power of domestic administrations, aligning its exercise with a singular, preeminent public interest – that of decarbonization – overshadowing other competing concerns. As the author claims, the outcome is twofold: on the one hand, these dynamic limits the room for administrations to balance the various competing interests in individual cases; on the other hand, it indirectly challenges the underlying rationale of sustainable development, which in energy realm requires to balance between economic, social, environmental, and security needs.

In the third contribution by Michele Di Vita the perspective of the investigation shifts, moving from the regulatory level to an analysis of the case-law within a specific Member State, namely Italy, in the context of energy transition. Building on the constitutional principle of widest distribution of renewables, the Chapter reconstructs the evolution of constitutional and administrative jurisprudence regarding the siting of renewable energy plants, highlighting the diverse interpretations given to the concept of sustainability over time. These interpretations are contingent upon the interests and objectives that the courts, at each instance, have been tasked with assessing and balancing. The reconstruction paints a picture that underscores the courts' tendency to identify and tether sustainability to the principle of sustainable development. Although an autonomous notion of ecological sustainability has not yet emerged in relevant jurisprudence, and sustainable development is still the reference paradigm, the concrete application of the latter reveals a series of fluctuations, tensions, and uncertainties. As the author claims, these ambiguities lead the case-law to characterize sustainable development alternately as an (implicit) overarching objective and as a concern to be balanced with other potentially conflicting interests, such as the protection of the cultural landscape.

Part II concludes with a Chapter by George Christou, focusing on the role played by European Smart Cities in the energy transition and exploring the sustainability model that the EU fosters for these local actors. This urban level analysis introduces a different perspective, shifting the focus to a subject – Smart Cities – with a significant impact on energy consumption and, consequently, the production of harmful emissions. The contribution discusses a series of recent initiatives that are particularly noteworthy within the broader, multifaceted EU strategy for Smart Cities. This strategy employs a diverse array of regulatory instruments aimed at encouraging greater sustainable energy consumption. These tools include leveraging binding legislative sources (hard law), plans and communications (soft law), voluntary bottom-up initiatives (such as partnerships between local and regional authorities), market instruments (in the form of public funding), and, last but not least, behavioural changes. The analysis of this loose legal material leads the author to conclude that the energy regulatory framework promotes an idea of sustainability deeply rooted in sustainable development for the latest generation of Smart Cities. This model attempts to balance and amalgamate multiple public, private, and community interests (economic, social, and incidentally environmental). However, it ultimately leaves little or no room for ecological concerns.

4.3. The ecological transition

In Part III, the spotlight shifts to the ecological transition, and ecosystem sustainability takes centre stage. Among the multiple transitions triggered by the Green Deal, the ecological one stands out as the most subversive for the EU legal order. By strongly advocating for ecosystem integrity, it pluralises and complicates the legal construction of sustainability in the EU, historically rooted in the paradigm of sustainable development and its balancing rationale. And by promoting the idea of ecological primacy, it challenges the logic that has traditionally underpinned environmental protection in EU law, aimed at reconciling the environment with market principles and exigencies.[29]

The initial Chapter by Michela Biscosi investigates the protection of European biodiversity, providing an evolutionary perspective on EU legisla-

[29] *Supra*, paras. 2 and 3.

tion for ecosystem restoration and examining the case-law of the Court of Justice related to the conservation of natural habitats. The historical reconstruction of EU sectoral disciplines for nature and biodiversity protection (the so-called Nature Directives: Habitats and Birds) sets the stage for the analysis of the Nature Restoration Law, to evaluate its elements of continuity and discontinuity and test its overall ecological potential. The Nature Restoration Law is depicted in a positive light: despite some ambiguities, it embraces a genuine ecological understanding of sustainability. The landing point of EU ecosystems legislation addresses the main shortcomings of the previous discipline, which was criticized for a narrow geographic scope of protected areas and a lack of specific enforceable restoration obligations. As noted by the author, the EU legislator establishes an ambitious goal for ecosystem restoration, supported by binding targets for national authorities and an appropriate governance structure. Yet, the intense negotiations leading up to the approval of the Nature Restoration Law partially undermined its ecological substance and diminished its innovative reach, as many key obligations from the original proposal were compromised by the EU legislator in the final text.

The second contribution by Licinia Pascucci further delves into the Nature Restoration Law. Such legislation is a key element of the overall regulatory patchwork assembled by the EU for biodiversity protection goals. At the same time, it represents one of the most intriguing juridification pathways of the new policy objective of ecological sustainability. The Nature Restoration Law aims at protecting and restoring the health and resilience of ecosystems across the EU territory. Specifically, it couples a general goal of restoring European nature and biodiversity with a set of mandatory targets for Member States to recover specific ecosystems, thus formulating a twin-track strategy. From the analysis of the legislative text, it emerges that the main aspiration driving the EU legislator is to prioritize and substantiate an ecological dimension of sustainability. As the author remarks, this ecological understanding is strictly related to ecosystem integrity and resilience, the latter being understood as the capacity of healthy ecological systems to continuously provide a range of fundamental ecosystem services. While these regulatory objectives are clearly instrumental to the EU climate ambitions, they are also the precondition for the health, prosperity, safety, and ultimately the survival of human beings.

The third and final Chapter by Antonio Taurelli shifts the focus from European legislation protecting biodiversity to the challenging and somewhat ambiguous relationship between sustainability and Criminal Law. To assess the capacity of sustainability to shape some of the foundational structures of contemporary Criminal Law, the analysis proceeds along two levels. After an examination of Italian Environmental Criminal Law and its criminalization techniques, the discussion explores recent EU regulatory initiatives on environmental crimes to measure their transformative potential for European criminal policy and discuss their implications for the domestic criminal system. Despite the absence of a solid foundation for sustainability in positive law, defining its boundaries and substantiating its relevance in criminal matters, there is room to investigate whether and to what extent the concept of sustainability might influence Criminal Law, its temporal horizon, and underlying rationale. Indeed, as argued by the author, within the realm of Criminal Law, there is a tendency for the concept of sustainability to overlap with that of the environment. By dynamically and evolutionarily analysing how the legislator conceives the environment as a legally protected interest, it becomes feasible to assume which declination of sustainability – whether ecological (ecocentric) or grounded in sustainable development (anthropocentric) – is endorsed and safeguarded by Criminal Law from time to time.

4.4. The digital transition

The digital transition is the focus of Part IV. Its centrality is evident from a dual and complementary perspective: first, as a transformative objective in itself, for which the EU is deploying significant regulatory efforts to build a "human centred, sustainable and more prosperous digital future" [30]; and second, as an enabling factor for European climate ambitions. Achieving climate neutrality inevitably involves the development of new digital technologies and infrastructures to support both decarbonization and the protection of EU natural capital. A mutually reinforcing relationship ties the green and digital transitions, although potential frictions, such as the energy-intensive use of digital technologies, should not be overlooked.

The first Chapter by Emanuele Fazio delves into the relationship between sustainability and digitization, focusing on data-driven ecosystems as a significant enabling factor for the EU digital and green transition. The interface between the twin transitions is challenging: to effectively contribute to a zero-emission circular economy, digital systems and technologies must internalize a genuine understanding of sustainability. Among the policies undergoing a profound reorientation as part of the EU digital and green transformation, competition policy undoubtedly holds a prominent position. It is increasingly expected to consider environmental, climate, social,

[30] See 2030 Digital Compass: the European way for the Digital Decade, COM (2021) 118, 1.

and privacy aspects in competitive assessments on data-related practices. To tackle the challenges of the data economy, a shift from a monocentric to a polycentric competition law is advocated, exploring the full potential of this new conceptual framework for sustainability purposes. As the author argues, a polycentric approach enables a comprehensive assessment of the multiple and multifaceted interactions within the data-driven ecosystem. By doing so, it allows antitrust enforcers to appreciate potential social and sustainability benefits of anticompetitive behaviours and, accordingly, to enhance the qualitative dimension of competition.

With the second Chapter by Beatrice Baldini, the attention returns to the urban context. The local level reaffirms its crucial role in the EU mitigation efforts, and Smart Cities stand as intriguing laboratories for experimenting with innovative solutions for decarbonization and testing models of urban sustainability. The evolutionary reconstruction of Smart Cities – from their origins in Western thought to their current physiognomy – shows an interesting shift from a technology-driven to a human rights-based approach. In the former, the emphasis was mainly on economic competitiveness and growth linked to investments in technological infrastructures, while the latter places technology at the service of citizens, assigning it an instrumental role in meeting their essential needs. The goal is to ensure, through technological innovation, a series of public services (e.g., urban transport, water supply, waste disposal) that are not only efficient but also sustainable in terms of natural resource management. Digital solutions are leveraged for the community's well-being, to be understood in a holistic sense: as a harmonious combination of economic prosperity, social development, and environmental protection. As the author points out, the dominant paradigm in the multidimensional urban context is still that of sustainable development, and despite the increasing weight of environmental concerns over time, the protection of biodiversity and ecosystem integrity struggles to be truly prioritized.

4.5. The economic transition

Finally, Part V explores the economic transition, one of the axes around which the overall EU reform project triggered by the challenge of climate neutrality revolves. The need to transform the European economy by putting it on the path of sustainability is recognised by the EU from the very beginning. The Commission ambitiously portrays the Green Deal as "a new growth strategy" that aims at providing the EU with "a modern, resource-efficient and competitive economy", based on decoupling emissions from economic growth and on circular production and consumption systems.[31] The transition to a new model of market economy inspired by sustainable growth is a clear objective of the Green Deal from the outset, supported and articulated by a range of different strategies, public policies, and regulations.

The first Chapter by Camilla Signoretta explores the increasingly central role assumed by Intellectual Property (IP) Law in greening the European economy. This discipline stands at the intersection of two conflicting exigencies: the inherent need to protect patents and promote innovation, and the need not to hinder the diffusion of environmentally sound technologies that contribute to emissions reduction and environmental protection. The call for an interpretation of IP Law that is sensitive to sustainability goals and instrumental to the fight against climate change becomes even more urgent in the context of the Green Deal. The challenge is to develop or refine legal instruments that encourage the transfer and dissemination of innovative green technologies (e.g., clean hydrogen, Lithium-ion batteries, carbon capture, utilization and storage) at reasonable prices while curbing the trend of over-enforcement of intellectual property rights on such technologies. As pointed out by the author, one effective remedy, in line with the TRIPS Agreement, to limit the over-exclusionary exercise of patent rights is the essential facilities doctrine, whose functioning is investigated from a comparative perspective between the US and the EU. This doctrine, characterized by its flexibility and open texture, can be shaped and leveraged to pursue environmental protection within a comprehensive green industrial policy.

Among the tools that the EU aims at leveraging for the climate neutrality target, a significant one is represented by sustainable finance, which is the subject of the second contribution by Luisa Nenci. The financial sector is tasked with promoting investments in sustainable economic activities and projects that positively impact the environment, nature, and society. The relevant policy objective is clearly an economic one: supporting sustainable economic growth and stable financial markets by integrating Environmental Social and Governance (ESG) criteria into financial investments decisions. An intriguing relationship links sustainable and climate finance, the latter originating within the global governance institutional discourse and now central to the Green Deal project. While climate finance, in principle, endorses a carbon-free economy and addresses both mitigation and adaptation, it does not fully leverage its strong transformative potential and largely replicates the traditional sustainable finance pattern. This is illustrated by the implementation of the EU Taxonomy, the main regulatory instrument

[31] See COM (2019) 640, 1.

of the EU sustainable finance framework. The analysis of such market transparency tool paints a nuanced picture. The EU Taxonomy defines the criteria for qualifying an economic activity as sustainable, creating a shared language that enhances certainty for investors and businesses. However, while including climate-related and ecological concerns, the actual relevance of biodiversity protection is still limited. As the author argues, several issues risk undermining its effectiveness and operationalization, such as the exclusion of key industries and the inclusion of some green harmful sectors on a transitional basis. Yet, one should not lose sight of the direction of the process, which pushes towards increased recognition of potential financial risks associated with ecosystem degradation.

The shift towards sustainable finance goes hand in hand with the need to develop effective rules and mechanisms to make companies accountable for their impact on the environment and society.

With the third Chapter by Federica Montanaro, another key actor enters the stage for the transition towards a sustainable and resilient economic system. Corporations, especially larger ones, significantly contribute to polluting emissions, and their business models play a relevant role in shaping the balances (or imbalances) between the market and the environment. Within the broader EU regulatory mosaic for assessing the sustainability performance of corporations, a crucial piece is undoubtedly represented by the recent Corporate Sustainability Reporting Directive (CSRD). Through this discipline, the EU legislator aims at improving and strengthening the rules concerning the social and environmental information that companies are required to report and disclose to the market. The new regulatory framework takes decisive steps forward compared to the previous regime: it transforms the reporting mechanism from optional to mandatory, laying the groundwork for a desirable future standardization; it extends the obligation to report on sustainability to a broader range of companies; and it enhances the reliability, consistency, and accessibility of information for investors and consumers. As the author points out, this sectoral intervention should be interpreted within the context of establishing a new sustainable corporate governance throughout the entire EU market. This process involves the full recognition of corporate social responsibility and aims to foster a more balanced relationship between business, society, and the environment, in line with the rationale of sustainable development.

The fourth and final contribution by Stefano Porfido keeps grappling with the transition to sustainable models of corporate governance, offering a different yet complementary perspective on the role of the private sector. The focus is on the EU strategy for addressing, minimizing, or neutralizing environmental damage caused by corporations, which includes two interconnected directives: one on Environmental Protection through Criminal Law (ECP) and the other on Corporate Sustainability Due Diligence (CSDD). These regulatory initiatives, formulated under the Green Deal, tackle corporate damage with distinct logics and instruments. The first focuses on enhancing the harmonization of criminal offenses and related sanctions to ensure effective deterrence against environmental crimes. The second mandates sustainability due diligence for a range of EU and non-EU companies – especially those operating in sectors with a high risk of adverse environmental impact – to promote corporate social responsibility throughout the whole supply chain. As argued by the author, the most intriguing distinction concerns the approach to sustainability in the two directives. While the first still conveys a weak understanding based on the compromise between environmental protection and other socially valuable interests, the second endorses a distinct conception of sustainability, seen as a pre-condition for corporate thriving. This understanding is grounded in the concept of sustainable profit within ecological limits and the close convergence of private and public interests.

5. Sustainability in transition: four interpretative keys

The analyses carried out in the five Parts of the book present a colourful and nuanced picture of the multiple transitions triggered by the Green Deal. The issues addressed in the various Chapters span and intersect a number of policies and legislations central to the European integration project, its current arrangements, and future developments. When assembled, the individual pieces give rise to an intricate and complex puzzle. In this paragraph, four interpretative keys are provided that might be of some help to the reader in navigating the different transitions taking place under the umbrella of climate neutrality.

5.1. Regulatory entanglement

To begin with, as it has been pointed out, the decision to structure the volume around transitions has its specific rationale. The aim is to provide, from a legal-evolutionary perspective, an overview of the process of legal change, adaptation, or resistance that key disciplines stemming from the Green Deal are undergoing as a result of the redefinition of sustainability in the EU.[32] However, this division should not be understood in a rigid

[32] *Supra*, § 6.

and monolithic sense but rather as flexible and fluid. While policies and legislations adopted under the Green Deal form a somewhat cohesive mosaic, the boundaries demarcating individual tiles are mobile and porous. Among the various transitions, there are explicit or tacit dialogues, allegedly peaceful coexistences, or more often conflicting relationships, spill-over processes, and cross-fertilization phenomena. The multiple transitions fuelled by the Green Deal do not proceed in parallel along linear trajectories and harmonious dynamics; rather, their relationships are characterized by a number of tensions, ambiguities, frictions, and eventual collisions.

From this perspective, the pluralization of the sustainability discourse brings to the forefront old regulatory conflicts (e.g., promotion of renewable energy vs environmental and landscape protection) and gives rise to different and partly new ones (e.g., decarbonization priorities vs protection and restoration of ecological integrity). Conflicts arising from the competing regulatory objectives of the Green Deal ultimately fall on administrations, tasked with imaging, developing, and implementing legal solutions that can balance the various interests at stake. While the outcome is open to a variety of operational arrangements, this process serves as a laboratory for public powers to explore the potential of the law, by testing the effectiveness of consolidated principles and regulatory techniques, as well as experimenting with the possibilities offered by emerging ones.

5.2. Resistance: the enduring relevance of sustainable development

Second, in the relationship between ecological sustainability and sustainable development, the scale decidedly tips in favor of the latter. Sustainable development continues to shape the majority of legislation and measures stemming from the Green Deal. Admittedly, this is hardly surprising. While its elasticity is broad enough to embrace different conceptualisations of the environment,[33] ranging from its representation as a non-living physical space to a dynamic and autopoietic system based on complex interactions between living and non-living components,[34] its rationale proves well-

[33] This inherent elasticity has led some authors to argue that sustainable development lacks a sufficiently precise definition in the EU legal order, resulting in excessive vagueness and difficulty in operationalisation: see van Hees S.R.W., "Sustainable Development in the EU: Redefining and Operationalizing the Concept", in *Utrecht L Rev*, 2014, 10(2), 60-76.

[34] For a clear formulation of this systemic conception see Capra F. and Luisi P.L., *The Systems View of Life. A Unifying Vision*, CUP, 2014, 1-510.

suited for balancing the conflicting interests at stake and reconciling the different objectives of each transition. The integration of environmental concerns, or at most ecological ones, in the formulation of EU policies and actions remains the preferred regulatory option for legislations that substantiate and implement the various transitions.

The explanation for this prevalence is rather simple both in functional and normative terms. It is the technique most consistent with the overall goal of balanced, responsible, and sustainable growth; more functional for the stability of the financial system and the profitability of corporate activity; more in line with the ideal of a competitive, circular, and resource-efficient economy; and more suitable for multidimensional institutional contexts (e.g., Smart Cities) and policy sectors characterized by strong interdependencies and the need to reconcile a plurality of competing interests (e.g., agri-food systems).

5.3. Innovation: the penetration capacity of ecological sustainability

Third, while the rationale of sustainable development is particularly useful in supporting the path towards climate neutrality, it is important to recognize the capacity of ecosystem sustainability to gradually penetrate and shape the dynamics of transitions other than the ecological one. Admittedly, this process is not uniform; it occurs with varying intensity and yields different implications.

In some cases, the outcome is to mitigate regulatory conflicts generated by the Green Deal, fostering almost complete reconciliation among the objectives of different transitions (e.g., decarbonization through renewable energy and preservation of ecosystem health) or, at the very least, a notable convergence (e.g., economic growth and biodiversity protection). Examples of the former include the necessity for ecologically sustainable bioenergy production, while instances of the latter involve efforts to align financial activities with ecological concerns and pursue sustainable corporate profit within ecological limits. In other scenarios, the process of colonization of other transitions occurs only on the surface. That is, there is a transmigration of concepts proper to ecology, endowed with normative force and explanatory power, into disciplines other than the former. These concepts are borrowed, readapted, and functionalised to serve the (sustainability) purposes and the objectives of other transitions, as is the case, for example, with data-driven ecosystems in the context of the digital transition.

5.4. The significance of ecological sustainability for the Green Deal

Finally, the potential implications of the emergence of ecological sustainability for the Green Deal should be recognized. As already observed, ecological sustainability is an essential component of a sound strategy for climate neutrality. Of course, it is not and should not be seen as an alternative to sustainable development. Instead, it is a complementary and additional policy and legal objective. While there is no reason to renounce to sustainable development, provided that balancing is a fundamental and inevitable technique to manage the multidimensional issues at stake, ecological sustainability should play a role in the Green Deal as a distinct objective, coexisting with sustainable development and contributing on its part to the achievement of climate neutrality.

The possibility to rely on two different sustainability rationales certainly gives the Commission some flexibility in shaping the Green Deal regulatory measures. In particular, it allows the Commission and the EU political institutions to differentiate goals and instruments in relation to the diversity of situations, within the overall framework of the macro-objective of climate neutrality. The complication and articulation of the legal construction of sustainability, in other terms, provide the Commission and the EU legislator with a variety of policy and regulatory options, ranging from strict protection of specific ecosystems to nuanced balances between environmental, economic and social interests.

At the same time, one should acknowledge that the choice between different versions of sustainability and their operationalisation in coherent legislative schemes raises uneasy issues. A first problem is how to appropriately design ecological legislation: far from being a straightforward task, identifying the appropriate instruments for ecosystem recovery may prove to be highly contentious, given the variety of theoretical approaches, specific goals and possible actions. On a more profound level, managing the interaction between ecology and law requires reflection about the regulatory force of ecology, the prescriptive nature of many of its key propositions and the role played by law, which is not necessarily a purely instrumental one. A second issue is how to contain the economic and social costs associated to the ecological transition. The prioritisation of ecological concerns may be politically and socially acceptable in certain specific cases, exemplified by the protection and restoration of primary and old-growth forests. In most situations, though, rule-makers are called to prioritise ecosystem integrity while managing the social impact of the planned measures. A third issue is how to develop ecological sustainability in a regulatory framework which is overall committed to growth through economic freedoms. The making of a body of ecological law is likely to imply a reconsideration of the internal logic of sustainable development, which should be revised in such a way to become fully coherent with the timing and requirements of climate change. This might be the most challenging political and regulatory task of the Green Deal process.

Part 1

THE AGRI-FOOD TRANSITION

Chapter 1

SUSTAINABILITY IN THE AGRI-FOOD SECTOR: THE TORTUOUS PATH OF COMMON AGRICULTURAL POLICY TOWARDS A FOOD SYSTEM APPROACH

Enrico Mezzacapo and Antonio Manzoni

ABSTRACT: *This Chapter analyses the past and present of the EU Common Agricultural Policy (CAP). After reconstructing its evolutionary trajectory, it examines the characteristics, limitations, and gaps of this key instrument in the context of the Green Deal actions aimed at fostering the transition to a sustainable food system, with a particular focus on the Farm to Fork strategy.*

KEYWORDS: *Common Agricultural Policy – Farm to fork – Agri-food transition.*

1. Introduction

The European Union (EU)'s Common Agricultural Policy (CAP) has undergone a remarkable transformation since its beginning in 1962. From the narrowly-productivist approach of its origins, aimed at reaching market stability and food security, the CAP has gone through several reforms that have progressively introduced measures to protect environmental and social interests. This Chapter asks whether such evolution has aligned the CAP with a broader 'food system approach', as envisioned by the Green Deal (GD) strategy for the EU agri-food sector. The GD and its related strategies, such as the Farm to Fork (F2F) and the EU Biodiversity Strategy for 2030, have set the stage for a substantial shift in the EU's conception of agri-food sustainability. By focusing on the agri-food and agri-environmental sector, this Chapter aims to dissect the nature of the CAP's evolution, scrutinize how the new CAP (2023-2027) intends to embrace the principles of agri-food sustainability established by the GD through a *food system approach*, and assess the role of Member States in implementing these changes through their CAP National Strategic Plans (CSPs). In doing so, it seeks to elucidate the innovative elements introduced by the new CAP for a sustainable agri-food sector while also addressing the inconsistencies that may challenge its overarching objectives.

The Chapter is structured as follows. First, it traces the evolution of the CAP from its inception, highlighting the shift in its goals and priorities, particularly its growing responsiveness to environmental and social concerns (paras. 2-6). Second, it delves into the impact of the GD and its strategies on the transition to sustainable food systems, with a particular focus on the F2F and the Biodiversity Strategy for 2030. Since the CAP plays a crucial role in the transition, the Chapter evaluates the structure, characteristics, and targets of the new CAP 2023. To analyse the effectiveness of the new CAP, it turns its attention to Member States and their CSPs, evaluating how sustainability concepts are being translated into action at a national level (paras. 7-11). The inquiry shows the progress made by the new CAP in fostering a fairer, greener, and more systematic agri-food sector, while also underlining the challenges and inconsistencies that may hinder the realization of its intended goals.

2. «Mountains of milk and butter»: the overproduction of the first two decades of the CAP

Behind the emergence of the CAP in 1962 there was the dramatic situation in which Europe was at the time due to the WWII aftermath. It was a starving Europe that before anything else was trying to be self-sufficient in terms of agri-food needs. Considering this critical situation, coordination between European States was deemed necessary to re-establish economic relations among each other and to restart the agricultural sector, namely the primary source of employment and livelihood for the entire EU population. The first important step in the creation of the CAP was the entry into force of the Treaty of Rome in 1958, which still contains nowadays its legal foundations.[1] Notably, Article 39 sets out the objectives of the CAP:

> "(a) to increase agricultural productivity by promoting technical progress and by ensuring the rational development of agricultural production and the optimum utilization of the factors of production, in particular labor;
> (b) thus, to ensure a fair standard of living for the agricultural community, in particular by increasing the individual earnings of persons engaged in agriculture;
> (c) to stabilize markets;
> (d) to assure the availability of supplies;
> (e) to ensure that supplies reach consumers at reasonable prices".

Therefore, the first phase of the CAP was characterized by a strong accent on *productivity* to ensure a fair standard of living for farmers, more stable markets, and a secure supply chain with reasonable prices for producers and consumers. Agriculture and farming were mostly considered as any other industrial sector to be enhanced while concrete concerns for the environment were almost totally absent from the EU agenda. However, the CAP was seen as an overall success by European farmers: the market started to find greater stability, the technological advancements began to show their results, and the rate of agricultural production and food self-sufficiency for most of the population increased as well.[2]

The 1970s marked a phase in which, as it was reported later, the CAP was a "victim of its own success".[3] The boost in production was achieved by means of substantial subsidies to European farmers based on how much they could produce for the market – these subsidies are referred to as direct coupled payments.[4] This articulated payment system worked

---

[1] The original name of the Treaty of Rome (signed on March 25th, 1957) was "Treaty establishing the European Economic Community" (or EEC Treaty). See Sotte F., *La Politica Agricola Europea. Storia e Analisi*, Agriregionieuropa, 2021.

[2] Loyat J. and Petit Y., *La Politique Agricole Commune (PAC): Une Politique En Mutation*, Documentation Française, Reflexe Europe, 2008; Cardwell M.N., *The European Model of Agriculture*, Oxford University Press, 2004.

[3] Frascarelli A., "L'evoluzione Della PAC e le Imprese Agricole: Sessant'anni di Adattamento", in *Agriregionieuropa*, 2017, 50, 1; Bianchi D. and Fischer Boel M., *La Politica Agricola Comune (PAC): Tutta La Pac, Niente Altro Che La PAC: Compendio Di Diritto Agrario Comunitario*, Felici, 2007.

[4] Coupled direct payments are granted to farmers based on the amount produced, e.g., per ton of wheat produced or per Liter of milk, or linked to production inputs, e.g., hectares of arable crops or number of livestock. A decoupled payment is linked to the area farmed, but there is no requirement for a farmer to produce.

within a scheme of institutional prices also known as intervention prices.[5] The strong accent on the maximization of production soon started to show its inherent shortcomings: the market was struggling to re-absorb the excess of production, and this of course entailed huge costs to re-absorb and eliminate the products in excess. Ironically, Europe went from a condition of food scarcity to a situation where the offer was structurally exceeding the demand (the famous "mountains of milk and butter" phase of the CAP).[6] However, there were even further downsides to this trend. For instance, there were great imbalances between MSs regarding agricultural productivity, especially due to the ratio underlying the subsidies received by farmers, that favoured those regions with larger farms. On top of this, intensive farming methods were causing huge damage to the rural environment, biodiversity habitats, and farmland ecosystems. In other words, the CAP approach to agriculture during these first decades was still *sector-specific* and *linear*, since it was still mainly – if not only – focused on increasing the value chain productivity and on stabilizing the common market, while environmental and social concerns were almost absent.

3. Reforming the CAP in the light of sustainable development (1980-1999)

The first realization that a deep change was needed to regulate all the multiple facets and interactions of the agricultural sector occurred during the 1980s. Notably, environmental and social concerns began to acquire growing importance within the CAP agenda, alongside the all-absorbing market-oriented targets of the origins. On the environmental side, it is worth mentioning the 5th Environmental Action Program "Towards Sustainability", which marked an important step in the progressive inclusion of sustainable development principles in the CAP, especially after the landmark Brundtland Report "Our Common Future" (published in 1987).[7] This Program

[5] Intervention prices were those prices at which public bodies withdrew unsold products from the market through export refunds (subsidies to exporters) and import levies (taxes on imported products). The mechanism was intended to keep production high without driving down the price of goods.

[6] Bianchi D. and Fischer Boel M. (fn. 3).

[7] European Commission, *'Towards Sustainability' (5th EC Environmental Action Program) – The European Community Programme of policy and action in relation to the environment and sustainable development*, 1993. The themes touched by this document were numerous: the achievement of a good quality of life for everybody, the access to natural resources, the avoidance of environmental damages by human activities, and

was aimed at setting long-term goals for the EU, adopting a more global approach that would enhance the integration of environmental sustainability concerns in all the future European policies – especially the CAP, given the strict interconnection between agriculture and the environment. Besides, even *social* concerns started to acquire more importance in the mind of the EU agri-food legislator. For example, in 1988 the EU Commission published the report "The Future of rural society", which constitutes the first text calling for the CAP to extend its scope to cover rural development issues and pave the way for the creation of the CAP Rural Development Program a few years later.[8] This document moves from the observation that the economic and social evolution after WWII has produced a profound change in rural areas, to the point of requiring a conceptual update in their consideration. Thus, a proper political agenda specifically devoted to the European rural areas was needed. The CAP itself needed to adapt, integrating "the traditional *sectoral* dimension, relating to the problems and prospects of the primary sector, with a territorial dimension aimed at supporting, *with a systemic approach*, integrated development of the rural economy and society".[9]

At the beginning of the 1990s, the EU legislator realized that a simple "restyling" of the CAP was not enough to face the increasingly pressing internal and external challenges that the agricultural sector was undergoing. Not to mention that the so-called Uruguay Round of negotiations within the WTO (launched in 1986 and concluded in 1992), determined that the excessively protectionist policy of the European Economic Community (EEC) was hindering the global market due to the unfair competition of European prices. Following these negotiations' conclusions, the EU legislator acknowledged the necessity of lowering the prices of agricultural products – for them to be more in line with the global market -, and of providing support in a manner that does not affect production nor distorts the market (*decoupling*).[10] Therefore, in 1992 the CAP saw its first *structural*

---

others. See also Brundtland G.H., *Report of the World Commission on Environment and Development: "Our Common Future"*, United Nations, 1987.

[8] COM (88) 501 (1988) 198; COM (85) 333 final 1985.

[9] Sotte F. (fn. 1) 16.

[10] Under these conditions, the supply of agricultural products would have been determined exclusively by market convenience. See Sotte F. (fn. 1); Alabrese M., *Il Regime Della 'Food Security' Nel Commercio Agricolo Internazionale. Dall'Havana Charter al Processo Di Riforma Dell'Accordo Agricolo WTO*, Giappichelli, 2018; Castellano-Álvarez F.J. and Robina Ramírez R., "Relevance of the Uruguay and Doha Rounds in the Evolution of International Agricultural Trade: The Case Study of Latin American Countries and Continental Products", in *Economies*, 2023, 11, 2.

revision: the so-called *MacSharry Reform*. From this moment, environmental and social concerns become an integral (albeit still marginal) part of the CAP. In fact, not only the first regulation on organic agriculture of the EEC was enacted in 1991, [11] but also several other agro-environmental concerns and greening of existing measures started to officially be encompassed by the CAP. [12]

4. The need for a fairer and environmentally-sound CAP: multifunctionality, rural development and eco-conditionality

A pivotal turning point occurred at the threshold of the new millennium's eve when the EU needed a structural CAP reform to face its high costs and the rapid geo-political and economic changes that were taking place in those years. The *Agenda 2000 reform* (introduced in 1999) is the reform that launched the CAP into the new millennium. [13] The main objective was to set up a new agricultural model for the EU, namely a system where agriculture is an integrated sector embedded into an open market economy, but which also addresses extra-economic issues such as the protection of the environment and endorses the principles of sustainable development. In other words, it seemed the EU legislator had gained an increased awareness that, to achieve sustainable and prosperous agriculture, there was a vital need to *systematically* tackle a wide array of aspects that affect each other in a complex web of interconnections. In this context, the issue of agriculture's *multifunctionality* became pivotal in the new CAP. [14] Namely, the

[11] Regulation EEC 2092/1991.

[12] For instance, the Council Regulation (EEC) 2078/92 (so-called "agri-environmental regulation") introduced farming methods more compatible with the environment, the protection of landscapes, soil, and biodiversity by the farmers as "custodians" of the territory, the Council Regulation (EEC) 2079/92 (setting a scheme for farmers' early retirement, the Council Regulation (EEC) 2080/92, enacting a scheme for forestry measures in agriculture, and the afore-mentioned 5th Environmental Action Program, which was officially launched in 1993.

[13] COM (97) 2000.

[14] Di Nuccio A. and Monteduro M., "Multifunctional Agriculture for the Regeneration of Rural Areas at Risk of Demographic, Economic and Socio-Cultural Desertification", in *Ist. del Fed.*, 2020, 2, 365; Bodiguel L., "La Multifonctionnalité de l'activité Agricole et Sa Reconnaissance Par Les Politiques Publiques Actes Du Colloque International de La Société Française d'économie Rurale", in *Actes du colloque international de la Société française d'économie rurale*, 21-22 mars 2002, Versailles Cedex, Editions Quae, 2003; Bodiguel L., "La Multifonctionnalité de l'agriculture: Un Concept d'avenir?", in *RD rur.*, 2008, 365, 35; Henke R., *Multifunzionalità Agraria e PAC*, Edizioni Scientifiche Italiane, 2004.

European legislator finally acknowledged that agriculture did not only constitute an economic sector devoted to mere food production but, on the contrary, agriculture was *also* a sector that provides a wide array of additional material and immaterial (and many times *not commodifiable*) benefits to society: the provision of public goods and ecosystem services, social cohesion and inclusion in rural areas, environmental and landscape protection, food security, cultural heritage, just to name a few. In this sense, the main innovation brought by the Agenda 2000 reform is the official launch of the Rural Development Program (RDP). The RDP encompassed various pre-existing rural development measures, and it acquired proper financial autonomy thanks to the institution of a dedicated fund, the European Agricultural Fund for Rural Development (EAFRD).[15] The launch of the RDP marked a crucial step in the EU agricultural policymaking, since a relevant part of the CAP budget from that moment on began to be spent to ensure adequate esteem and sustain to this part of agriculture that was not necessarily focused on the mere production and market exchange as it was at the origins. The CAP was slowly, but steadily, steering from a substantially industrial and sectoral program towards a *food system policy*, namely an agricultural policy which embeds the regulation of food production within a larger spectrum of other inter-related *activities* (processing, transport, retail, consumption, etc.) and *outcomes* (mostly environmental and social, to complement the economic ones that were already largely present from the beginning).

This trend kept on going even in the subsequent years. Indeed, just after the Agenda 2000 reform, another restyling of the CAP was deemed necessary. That is why a "mid-term review" was adopted in 2003, under the name of *Fischler reform*. The reform started the transition from the coupled direct payment system to decoupled farmer support. This meant that the EU subsidies to farmers became linked to eligible hectares of agricultural land regardless of the intensity of agricultural activity. This reform allowed the redistribution of resources to reach all farmers, especially the smallhold producers, and also to comply with the pressure of the WTO competition requirements. Among the most pressing issues at stake, in addition to the main motivation of enhancing European agriculture competitiveness, there was the claim that, in addition to sustaining farmers' incomes, the CAP had to set higher targets in its delivery of environmental protection,

---

[15] Until that moment, the CAP financial needs were satisfied by one fund, the European Agricultural Guidance and Guarantee Fund (EAGGF), which was dedicated to the CMOs and market measures for the agricultural products, and which constituted the 1st Pillar of the CAP. From the Agenda 2000 onwards, the RDP became the CAP 2nd Pillar.

landscape preservation, food quality, animal welfare, just to name a few. Regarding an increased concern for the environment, it is worth highlighting that the Fischler reform made the so-called *eco-conditionality* of direct payments to farmers compulsory (which was first introduced a few years before and which will be further enhanced in later reforms). This innovation entailed that those farmers who were not complying with certain agro-environmental, ecological, food safety, and animal welfare standards in their work could see their payments reduced or even cleared. [16] Alongside the increased environmental concerns, even the social ones related to enhancing the EU rural development were advancing. Indeed, after the mid-term review, even the subsequent 2007-2013 CAP reform continued the path towards a further enlargement of its scope towards environmental and social issues related to agriculture.

When comparing the novelties brought by these reforms with the early stages of the CAP, it is evident how a less "productivist-oriented" approach was establishing itself as the guiding perspective of the EU agri-food legislator. The CAP regulatory measures started to confirm a renewed awareness of the crucial importance of the environmental and social issues related to the agricultural sector, alongside the economic ones. In other words, it appears that the EU agri-food regulatory framework started to show a shift in its scope, from a regulation that was mainly focused on the food value chain, to an approach that started to consider the larger spectrum of deeply interconnected issues that affect – and are affected, in return – by all the activities necessary to produce food (e.g., outcomes such as environmental depletion, climate change mitigation, employment, rural development, etc.).

5. A further attempt for a "greener" CAP: the 2014-2020 reform

The subsequent CAP reform was designed to cover the 2014-2020 period. [17] Regarding the main novelties of this reform, the greening of direct payments is probably the main innovation that marks another step in the enlargement of the scope of the CAP towards environmental and social issues over the years. Indeed, in addition to the basic payments that corre-

[16] See Sotte F. (fn. 1).

[17] Even though its validity has been extended until the end of 2022, mostly due to the difficulties in finding a political agreement for the subsequent CAP reform 2023-2027 within the "trilogue" process (that is, the negotiate involving the Commission, the Parliament, and the Council) and due to the complications brought by the outbreak of the Covid-19 pandemic.

sponded to farmers for their compliance with the compulsory obligations of conditionality, the green direct payments constitute an additional layer of payments for those farmers who "go beyond" these compulsory measures, by providing essential public goods – e.g., clean air, water, ecosystems, soils health, landscapes – with their work. If farmers want to receive these payments, they need to comply with specific practices that are beneficial to the environment (crop diversification, maintaining permanent grassland, and the so-called Ecological Focus Areas (EFA).

Another important novelty along these lines is the so-called *cross-compliance*. As mentioned, especially from the Agenda 2000 reform onwards, the farmers' consideration of the environment, animal welfare and health, plant health, and, more generally, sustainable agricultural practices have acquired considerably more relevance for the disbursement of CAP income support. According to *cross-compliance*, there could be a reduction in farmers' payments (even to zero) when they do not comply with the prescribed environmental measures. Most notably, the farmers might see not only their direct payments reduced for not complying with these rules but also with different RDP payments (e.g., area-based payments including agri-environmental measures, areas with natural constraints, NATURA 2000 measures, afforestation measures, forest environmental payments, agroforestry, organic farming). In other words, the institution of *cross-compliance* is designed as an incentive for European farmers, by rewarding them when they meet higher standards for what regards sustainable agricultural practices. *Cross-compliance* is compounded by a two-tiered set of rules. The first set is the so-called *Statutory Management Requirements* (SMRs) – The SMR rules regard issues such as public, animal, and plant health, animal welfare, and the environment. The second one is *Good Agricultural and Environmental Conditions* (GAEC) – The GAEC standards have a wide array of agri-environmental goals, such as preventing soil erosion, maintaining a certain amount of permanent grassland, protecting farmland biodiversity and ensuring the retention of landscape features, protecting and managing water, and others.

Looking at the bigger picture, this CAP reform marked the first true shift towards the embracement of the United Nations Sustainable Development Goals (UN SDGs) into its objectives. The Regulation (EU) 1306/2013 explicitly stated that the CAP performance had to be monitored in relation to three main objectives which mirror the three axes of sustainability: (a) viable food production, with a focus on agricultural income, agricultural productivity, and price stability; (b) sustainable management of natural resources and climate action, with a focus on greenhouse gas emissions, biodiversity, soil, and water; and (c) balanced territorial development, with a focus on rural employment, growth and poverty in rural areas.[18]

Overall, with this CAP reform, the EU legislator has tried to merge two conflicting souls living within this pluri-annual European policy. On the one hand, the attainment of a higher degree of farms' competitiveness, thanks to the strengthened market orientation and farmers' income support. On the other, the remuneration of public goods produced by agriculture, thanks to an enhanced conditionality (the above-described greening of direct payments), and a stronger rural development policy.[19] The former objective aimed to enhance the capacity of European farmers to "stay in the market" and thus conduct their activity more competitively, within the framework of a free market. To favor this situation, the selected measures adopted a less stringent approach to pricing and supply control mechanisms, along with the removal of production quotas, for instance. The second goal, instead, aimed at providing compensation for public goods produced by farmers, such as farmland biodiversity, rural landscapes, domestic food security, and clean drinking water, which are not typically remunerated by the market due to their status as externalities. This was primarily achieved through the greening of direct payments and other agro-environmental measures envisioned by the RDP.

Despite the good intentions and initiative of this reform, the results analyzed have been rather discouraging, especially in terms of environmental impacts. Among the most frequently criticized aspects of this CAP,[20] there is undoubtedly the choice of concentrating most of the resources on the development of measures aimed at environmental protection in the European Agricultural Guarantee Fund (EAGF), rather than in the European Agricultural Fund for Rural Development (EAFRD). The possibility of developing more targeted measures allows for a greater adaptation of the intervention to the specific characteristics of the agricultural target.[21] The "greening measures", like, for example, the one dedicated to crop diversifi-

---

[18] See Article 110, para. 2.

[19] See Frascarelli N. (fn. 3). Even though the environmental efforts of this CAP reform was criticized for their complexity and for their weak effectiveness. See European Court of Auditors, *Greening: A More Complex Income Support Scheme, Not yet Environmentally Effective*, Special Report No. 21/2017.

[20] Hart K. and Baldock D., "Greening the Cap: Delivering Environmental Outcomes Through Pillar One", Institute for European Environmental Policy papers, 2011; Matthews A., "Greening Agricultural Payments in the EU's Common Agricultural Policy", in *BAE*, 2013, 2.

[21] Cardwell M., "European Union Agricultural Policy and Practice: The New Challenge of Climate Change", in *Environ. Law Rev.*, 2013, 13.

cation, have had minimal impact, especially compared to the increased costs and labor required to implement them, as shown by data released by the European Union itself.[22] Indeed, the Commission 2016 published a report focused on the assessment of these measures one year after their implementation, where it seems to admit between the lines that in several respects, the results achieved have been less than expected.[23]

Among the most emblematic passages, the Commission stated that "the actual impact on environmental outcomes depends – for certain aspects – on the choices made by MSs and farmers".[24] However, one of the most critical aspects of the measures in question is precisely the lack of foresight in the creation of the prerequisites for good environmental management at the central level.[25] Many of these observations seem to be reflected in the European Court of Auditors (ECA) Special Report 21/2017[26] which encourages the European institutions to work on a more ambitious CAP and points out that it has never been clearly demonstrated the real benefits of the proposed greening practices and that it is highly unlikely that they would lead to appreciable climate-environmental results.[27]

6. Assembling the pieces: channelling sustainability into the agri-food sector through a food system approach

The previous analysis shows a rather clear trajectory in the CAP evolution over the years. What emerges is a long, constant evolution from mostly sectoral and production-oriented agri-food policies to a more unitary "food system approach". This trend is illustrated by the various CAP reforms described earlier, which constantly enlarged the spectrum of environmental and social measures in the regulation of the agri-food sector, adding up to the narrowly productivist outlook of the origins.

---

[22] The Farm Accountancy Data Network (FADN) shows that only 1.4 percent of the Union's territory is affected by this measure, as in the vast majority of cases crop diversification is implemented spontaneously by farmers and is therefore part of business as usual.

[23] SWD (2016) 218.

[24] *Ibidem.*

[25] Ferraris L., "La Protezione dell'ambiente nella Pac che verrà. Commento alla Comunicazione della Commissione sul futuro dell'alimentazione e dell'agricoltura", in *Agr. ist. merc.*, 2016, 175.

[26] European Court of Auditors (fn. 19).

[27] To know more, See Strambi G., "Condizionalità e Greening nella PAC: è abbastanza per il clima?", in *Agr. ist. merc.*, 2016, 2, 64.

The "food system" concept emerged several decades ago within the context of food security studies,[28] due to the main need to systematically analyze the complex framework of the food value chain, which spans from the agricultural inputs production, through the harvesting, production, distribution, processing, retail, packaging, consumption and disposal. In contrast to models focalizing merely on some specific aspects of food security, the food system concept endorses a multi-disciplinary and trans-disciplinary approach that posits food within its various social, environmental, and economic implications as intertwined with each other in a complex web of interrelations. In other words, other mono-sectorial approaches to food security "do not sufficiently recognize that food security outcomes have multiple causes and are the result of a complex set of activities, interactions, and interdependencies among different aspects of food systems".[29] On the contrary, the food system concept can be thought of as a model that embraces all the combinations of the activities ('what we do') together with the outcomes of these activities ('what we get').[30] It aims at framing and analyzing the ultimate goal of food security with all the food chain activities and all the social, economic, environmental, and political aspects that are involved in carrying out these activities. The conceptualization of the food system, in other words, "entails defining systems boundaries and systems building blocks and linkages among them, while simultaneously being connected to neighboring systems such as health, ecological, economy and governance, and the science and innovation systems".[31]

By embracing such a view, where the environmental, economic, and social outcomes of the agri-food sector are systematically taken into account in their intricate web of inter-relations, the output in policymaking will def-

---

[28] Ingram J., "A Food Systems Approach to Researching Food Security and Its Interactions with Global Environmental Change", in *Food Security*, 2011, 3, 417; Ericksen P.J., "Conceptualizing Food Systems for Global Environmental Change Research", in *Global Environ. Change*, 2008, 18, 234.

[29] UNEP, *Food Systems and Natural Resources. A Report of the Working Group on Food Systems of the International Resource Panel*", ed. by? Westhoek H., Ingram J., Van Berkum, S., Özay, L. and Hajer M., United Nations Environment Programme, 2016, 31; Alabrese M., "Food Security: Different Systems, Different Notions", in *Perspect. Fed.*, 2019, 11, 3, 1; Alabrese M., *Il Regime Della 'Food Security' Nel Commercio Agricolo Internazionale. Dall'Havana Charter al Processo Di Riforma Dell'Accordo Agricolo WTO*, Giappichelli, 2018.

[30] UNEP (fn. 29) 31.

[31] Von Braun J. et al., "Food Systems – Definition, concept and application for the UN Food Systems Summit. A paper from the Scientific Group of the UN Food Systems Summit", Sci. Innov 27, 2021.

initely change accordingly, steering towards a more integrated and holistic conceptualization of *food* which is not only narrowed down to the mere supply and production issues. Therefore, this necessary entanglement between the environmental, social, and economic dimensions gave birth to the conceptualization of a *sustainable food system* by the Food and Agriculture Organization (FAO), which defines it as "a system that delivers food security and nutrition for all in such a way that the economic, social and environmental bases to generate food security and nutrition for future generations are not compromised".[32] Drawing upon these considerations, thus, a *food system approach* embraces "a complex socio-ecological system perspective in the research and decision-making processes of food".[33] Such an approach aims at encompassing the complex web of inter-relations, feedback loops, and synergies that characterize food systems, adopting a *holistic*, trans-disciplinary, and coordinated vision that would embrace all these components.

Considering the afore-described CAP reforms, through the progressive decoupling of farmers' support, the greening of direct payments, the introduction of the RDP, and through environmental and social conditionality, the CAP has continuously attempted to embed perhaps the most crucial agricultural activity – food production – within the larger context represented by all those closely-related activities and outcomes that compound our *food systems*. As further evidence of this trend, it is noteworthy to observe a significant upsurge in the usage of the term "food system" within the lexicon of EU legislative texts, particularly since 2015. Indeed, performing an advanced search on EUR-Lex – the official repository for EU law – within all the domains and using the "food systems" AND "food system" search string, the database shows 288 results. If we filter these results by year, out of 288 results, 272 (94%) are just from 2016 onwards, clearly highlighting how the food system (and *sustainable* food system) terminology has begun to consistently enter the EU law lexicon only after the elaboration of the UN SDGs in 2015.

---

[32] Group of Chief Scientific Advisors – SAM EGE, *Towards a Sustainable Food System – Moving from Food as a Commodity to Food as More of a Common Good*, Brussels, European Commission, 2020, 14; FAO, *Developing Sustainable Food Value Chains – Guiding Principles*", Rome, 2014.

[33] SAPEA Science Advice for Policy by European Academies, *A Sustainable Food System for the European Union*, SAPEA, 2020, 67.

7. The bumpy road of the EU agri-food sustainability: the new "Green" CAP

The GD plays a critical role in shaping the relevance and role of sustainability in the European agri-food sector. Indeed, it sets out the unpaved path to make Europe the first climate-neutral continent by 2050. It maps a new strategy that has the ambition to reach this ambitious goal while boosting the economy, improving health and quality of human life and nature, and leaving no one behind.[34] To advance in this course and to reach this objective, in 2019 the EU issued two key communications, namely the F2F[35] and the "EU Biodiversity Strategy for 2030" (EBS30).[36] Among all the sectors and interventions highlighted by the GD as targets for a radical green transition, these strategies cast the light on the agri-food sector and its ecosystems. Among these strategies, the F2F addresses the challenges of creating sustainable food systems, it acknowledges the indissoluble relations between the health of people, societies, and environment, and it tries to facilitate the shifting to healthier and sustainable diets, while advancing in the direction of bringing nature back into our lives. For the first time in the history of the EU food law, the "food sustainability" issue is addressed comprehensively and systematically, from production to consumption. Arguably, the notion of sustainability developed by the GD and its associated strategies (first and foremost, the F2F Strategy) for the agri-food realm is the one the new CAP must comply with.

It is imperative to emphasize the scale of the venture that the EU has chosen to undertake. It is equally important to specify that the F2F does not define the specific "sustainability" it is going to pursue, nor it explicitly acknowledges its multidimensional nature. Instead, the strategy seems to focus more on the output and promising results of enforced sustainable food systems, describing the range of environmental, social, and economic benefits that these would bring. It also establishes clear and determined goals to arrive at the chased sustainability. These objectives revolve around the reduction of dependency on pesticides and antimicrobials; the reduction of the excess of fertilization; the increase of organic farming; the improvement of animal welfare; the reverse biodiversity loss by 2030. The fact of not defining *how* to reach a certain "sustainability model" is certainly a deficiency that is familiar to the whole GD project, and the agri-food context is undoubtedly no exception to this trend. Here we have a situation

[34] COM (2019) 640 final 2019.

[35] COM (2020) 38.

[36] COM (2020) 380.

that has paradoxical characteristics: a concept that is so central to the ultimate goal of the strategy remains undefined and appears as a panacea without clear conceptual boundaries.[37] However, to depict the F2F as a mere list of desirable goals and outputs to achieve an unsolved knot called a "sustainable food system" would be unfair. It has been widely recognized[38] the reformist attitude of the strategy is expressed in the form of 27 regulatory actions presented in the Annex to the Communication.[39] The nature of reformist interventions has three different faces: the first one aims to the revision of the current regulatory framework according to the new objective and sub-objectives on pesticides, fertilizers, organic farming, antimicrobial use, etc. The second one proposes new regulatory instruments such as the eagerly awaited "proposal for a legislative framework for sustainable food systems." This regulation proposal, which is a flagship output of the F2F strategy, has the core objective of promoting agri-food policy coherence at the EU and national level, delivering "sustainability" in all food-related policies and strengthen the resilience of food systems making the transition to sustainable food systems easier. Eventually, among these 27 actions, there is a cross-cutting initiative that is fundamental for its horizontal impact along the entire EU agri-food chain. This is the "use" as an instrument for sustainability of the new CAP foreseen for the period 2023-2027 and, notably, the direction and control of its CSPs. The latter are prepared by Member States according to the abovementioned strategies' vision. At the time the F2F was published, the new CAP proposal was still under difficult negotiations that were far from finding their conclusions. This created already a first major issue at the roots of this CAP which should work towards the direction of a vague sustainability vision expressed in a communication rather than a legislative framework not yet finalized. The CAP, after all, has its cycle of life that cannot be disregarded. The latest circumstances, as we will see afterward in this work, brought the last CAP 2014-2020 to a period of extension, or rather a transition period of two years that brought to light the new CAP only in 2023. Despite the delay, the new CAP is still the first adopted instrument in the direction of the "EU sustainable food system" conceived as a goal of the GD and the Farm to Fork Strategy. These years of delay triggered by many events, and the lack of conceptual boundaries on sustainability matters create a cogni-

[37] As argued in Schebesta H. and Candel J., "Game-Changing Potential of the EU's Farm to Fork Strategy", in *Nature Food*, 2020, 1, 586.

[38] Group of Chief Scientific Advisors – SAM EGE (fn. 32).

[39] These are divided into the 4 main policy areas, accompanied by the indication of the range of the years (between 2021 and 2024) in which they will be probably implemented.

tive space where there is a real concern for the emergence of policy incoherencies, as policy actions that contribute to realizing some of the underlying objectives of the strategy may impede or result in a step backward for others.

8. The tortuous path for the reform of the CAP 2021-2027

Considering these premises and expectations, it is now worthwhile to reconstruct the life of this new CAP, so that we can assess its characteristics gaps, and opportunities. The EU's first step of the path for the definition of the new CAP 2021-2027 took place under the Junker administration in February 2017. Afterward, in November 2017, the Commission presented a communication called "The future of food and agriculture" [40] setting the new ideas for the new delivery model of the CAP. [41] The new model provided a mechanism where States are called to prepare a single CSP that must include their direct payments to farmers, support for rural development, and agricultural markets. On 1st June 2018, the Commission presented the legislative proposals for the CAP 2021-2027 characterized by this a *new delivery model* that leads the CAP toward a more results-based policy with greater flexibility in its implementation. With essentially no time available for a comprehensive discussion and proficient impact assessment, the project was left as a legacy to the new parliament elected in May 2019. But in this year, the reformist driving force due to the establishment of the new Commission together with the GD proposal [42] signed by Ursula Von der Leyen, changed all predictions of a new reformed CAP promptly finalized. The new Commission has undoubtedly played a crucial role, not only proposing and mediating but also playing a political role of urging and guiding the Junker CAP proposal pushing for a more pronounced environmentalist and sustainability ambition. Since the publication in December 2019, in fact, it was made clear that the environmental and climate crisis were at the core of the new Commission's plans. During 2020, in line with the GD's roadmap, the F2F and biodiversity strategies had been disclosed. Last, but not least, 2020 is a well-known year for the disruption of the Covid-19 pandemic and its holistic cascade effect on EU life and its priorities. [43] That is why, with the absence of an agreement on

---

[40] See more on Bolognini S., "La comunicazione della Commissione "Il futuro dell'alimentazione e dell'agricoltura", in *Riv. Dir. Agr.*, 2018, 1, 110.

[41] COM (2017) 713.

[42] COM (2019) 640.

[43] The EU efforts during the pandemic were focused on the NextGenerationEU

the future CAP, a transitional regulation[44] was delivered, extending in the meantime most of the previous CAP rules until the end of 2022. After a series of amendments to the EU Parliament and extensive negotiations, the Parliament and Council agreed on the 2023-2027 CAP legislative framework[45] and adopted it at the end of the year.[46] The long-awaited regulations changed the CAP significantly from the administration point of view thanks to its new delivery model.

9. Enhanced subsidiarity at the service of sustainability targets: the new CAP delivery model

Since the first communication presented under the Junker administration in 2017[47], the new CAP has been conceived with a delivery model that leads the CAP towards a more results-based and performance-oriented policy with greater flexibility in its implementation, while trying to preserve its common dimension. Through a bottom-up policy exercise, Member States are called to prepare one CSP[48] through the guidance and assessment of the EU Commission to contribute and reach the common objectives of the CAP. This creates an important change from a centralized, compliance-based (CAP 2014-20) to a decentralized management and evaluation of results and performance based on specific targets and outcome indicators. In this regard, the Commission has a fundamental role in evaluating the CSPs, carrying out a novel co-management relationship with MSs in the concrete implementation of the CAP. At the end of 2020, in fact, the Commission published its recommendations[49] for each MS on the preparation of their national CSP.[50] The aim of the new delivery model is to enable a simplifica-

(NGEU) recovery plan. This temporary instrument forms the largest stimulus package ever financed in Europe. A total of €2.018 trillion were located helping rebuild a greener, more digital and more resilient Europe. Additional €8 billion from the NextGenerationEU were assigned to the European agricultural fund for rural development (EAFRD).

[44] Regulation (EU) 2020/2220.

[45] Regulation (EU) 2021/2116, Regulation (EU) 2021/2115, Regulation (EU) 2021/2117.

[46] European Commission – Press release, "Political agreement on new Common Agricultural Policy: fairer, greener, more flexible", Brussels, 25 June 2021, available at https://agriregionieuropa.univpm.it/sites/are.econ.univpm.it/files/2021_political_agreement_on_new_common_agricultural_policy.pdf.

[47] See fn. 41.

[48] With the sole exception of Belgium where Flanders and Wallonia will each have a CSP.

[49] COM (2020) 846.

[50] The European Commission provided a total of 402 recommendations covering

tion[51] of the current system, which will be achieved through more subsidiarity, increasing MSs' responsibilities in implementing the policy through their CSPs while reducing EU-level bureaucracy in the management of the measures.[52]

First, all the CSPs must be based on an evaluation and identification of needs (Regulation 2021/2115, Article 108) according to the CAP objectives (Article 6). Regarding the monitoring and evaluation mechanism, after the already mentioned ex-ante recommendation for the CSP, the European Commission carried out two rounds of evaluation of the CSPs by means of observation letters.[53] The observation letters were an interim step in the Commission's overall assessment and approval process for the CSPs. Each EU country addressed the observations made and submitted a revised version of the plans. In addition to this evaluation, every year each MS is going to schedule in accordance with the Commission an "Annual review meeting" (Article 136). The review meeting is aimed at analyzing the effectiveness of the implementation of each CSP. In 2025 and 2027, it is foreseen that, on the basis of the annual reports of each MS, the Commission prepares a "Biennial performance review" (Article 135). Moreover, The Commission shall submit to the European Parliament and to the Council a summary report of national CSPs by 31 December 2023. The report shall include an analysis of the joint effort and collective ambition of MSs to address the specific CAP objectives set out in Article 6 and the contribution to the GD objectives.[54]

---

key policy parameters to assist Member States in the drafting of their CSPs. The Country-specific and differentiated assessments were structured around the nine specific objectives of the future CAP and on the GD Objectives.

[51] In countries with a regional system applied to the CAP these seems to relax the administrative burden for the EC. Taking the example of Italy, a single CSP instrument replaces the 21 regional rural development programs, the one for second-pillar national measures, and the notifications for direct payments and sectoral interventions. In this sense, the European Commission is freed from a great deal of preliminary, negotiation and control work and the role of the regions and local institutions in partnership and governance is recognized and made more explicit.

[52] Sotte F. (fn. 1).

[53] The European Commission Observation letters and the MSs Comments are available online on the European Commission website: https://agriculture.ec.europa.eu/cap-my-country/cap-strategic-plans/observation-letters_en.

[54] The objectives of these two strategies can be summarize in: 50% reduction in the use and risk of chemical pesticides, and use of more hazardous pesticides; 50% reduction in sales of antimicrobials for farmed animals and in aquaculture; 100% access to fast broadband internet in rural areas by 2025; 25% of the EU's agricultural land dedicated to organic farming; 10% of agricultural area under dedicated to high diversity landscape features, 50% reduction in nutrient losses while ensuring no deterioration in

10. Policy strategies and sustainability objectives

These ambitious objectives have important and unprecedented attention devoted to the health of agri-food ecosystems. This attention is present as a legacy of the GD project and, more specifically, in the F2F and Biodiversity strategies. These two reflect the crucial interrelation between biodiversity and food production, which is considered a crucial step for the macro-goal of the much sought-after climate neutrality. Since it is now clear that humanity cannot avoid producing GHG emissions, the solution seems to be to reduce these emissions and absorb as much of them as possible, or at least to reach a degree of sustainability where no more emissions are generated than can be absorbed. Therefore, it is necessary to gradually and significantly reduce emissions while at the same time trying to enlarge and empower carbon sinks. In this double action, it is of fundamental importance the incorporation of biodiversity protection into the strategy.[55] In this sense, the Biodiversity strategy 2030 shares some objectives and targets of the F2F strategy. It adds other more nature-related targets and counts on the CSP for setting certain agricultural practices that are seen as drivers of biodiversity decline. There is considerable attention to the enlargement of protected natural sites (many of which are farmland) and an extensive plan for nature restoration, which of course involves agriculture among other sectors. The safeguarding of biodiversity, the reduction of the use of agrochemicals and synthetic fertilizers, and the nutritional quality of production accessible to all are presented as essential links of the same chain which is the ultimate goal of climate neutrality by 2050.[56] Consequently, one of the most important objectives seems to be "Do not harm" in the first place. This means, at least in a theoretical framework, that all the measures of the new CAP that stimulate harmfully and therefore "unsustainable" production practices should be phased out. A second important principle suggests allocating "public money for the public good". This means that EU taxpayers' money should not be used anymore just for the support of the production of marketable goods or services. Farmers cannot be economically supported for business-as-usual traditional production practices. Practices that, moreover, do not allow them to be paid sufficiently and fairly for their

---

soil fertility; Contribution to the 55% greenhouse gas emission reduction target by 2030 and to climate neutrality by 2050.

[55] To see more about this line of reasoning see Chiti E., "Oltre la disciplina dei mercati: la sostenibilità degli ecosistemi e la sua rilevanza nel Green Deal europeo", in *Riv. Reg. Merc.*, 2, 2022.

[56] De Castro P., Miglietta P.P. and Vecchio Y., "The Common Agricultural Policy 2021-2027: a new history for European agriculture", in *REA*, 2020, 75, 3, 5-12.

work. Agricultural aid should be based on the production of common (or private) goods enjoyed by society as a whole, namely ecosystem services, investment in the health of ecosystems and biodiversity assets.[57]

Albeit without making it explicit, the objectives of these strategies suggest and give us a trace of the European legislator's desire to prioritize the health of the environment and ecosystems in its policy choices or at least as a common denominator to implement its objectives. What we find, however, in the objectives of the new CAP described in Regulation 2115/2021, Article 6, already at first glance does not seem to bring anything new compared to the old CAP, nor does not seem to add a different interpretation to the classical structure of sustainability recognized in the principle of sustainable development that has been utilized since post-Brundtland report era. There are in fact nine objectives,[58] equally divided and balanced into the three typical spheres of actions of sustainable development: economic, environmental, and social objectives. Moreover, some of these objectives seem to address matters related to "the economic sustainability of agricultural production" or to "improve market orientation" and "increase the competitiveness" of farms. All these points seem to go against what is observed in strengthening public good instead of the market orientation of the agricultural sector.

11. The sustainable food system transition in the hands of Member States

In this section, we aim to outline certain reflections on the vision and potential impact of the new CAP instruments and available financial options, as well as the decisions made by Member States in their CSPs regarding the utilization of these financial resources. We should start by observing that one of the fundamental governance issues concerning the unbalanced allocation of funds between the two pillars of the CAP, previously highlighted among the shortcomings of the CAP 2014-2020, remains unaltered. The

[57] Peeters A. et al., "A Green Deal for implementing agroecological systems: Reforming the Common Agricultural Policy of the European Union", in *Landbauforschung*, 2020, 70, 83.

[58] According to Article 6 of the Regulation 2115/2021, the economic objectives are: ensuring a viable income for farmers; strengthening EU agriculture's market orientation through more competitiveness and productivity; enhancing farmers' position in the value chain. The environmental objectives are: climate change action; environmental care; preserve landscapes and biodiversity. The socio-economic objectives are: support generational renewal; vibrant rural areas; protect food and health quality.

fund for rural development (the above-described "Pillar II" of the CAP) has about one-third of the total budget at the expense of the first pillar.[59] Of this, 51.1% is still dedicated to the "Basic Income Support for Sustainability (BISS)" which are the major payment dedicated to the EU farmers and is based on the payment of titles (eligible hectares). This unchanged "income support" logic is still based on hectares, which still have the majority of the financial allocation available, which means that large and intensive-wise polluting forms of agriculture continue to have too easy and generous access to European pockets (including intensive livestock).

The first move toward a greener CAP in this regard is undertaken through an "enhanced cross-compliance" on environmental requirements, the SMRs, the GAECs and the new social conditionality to receive these payments.[60] The SMRs[61] for sure do not change the sustainability direction of the CAP since these apply to all farmers whether or not they receive income support. Regarding the GAECs,[62] despite the reinforcement of these conditionalities, there are already several criticisms regarding the lack of effectiveness of these measures.[63] According to the ECA,[64] greening has historically improved practices on just the 5% of agricultural land, and fundamentally remains "an income support scheme". Moreover, it has been noticed how certain standards such as the GAEC number 8, which stipulates a minimum allocation of 4% of the arable land to non-productive areas, can easily be evaded for a number of reasons.[65] Together with GAEC 7 (obligation on crop rotation) which is clearly linked to the 2030 Biodiversity Strategy's objectives, this conditionality effectiveness has been further

---

[59] The European agricultural guarantee fund (EAGF), which has been set at €291.1 billion (in current prices); and the European agricultural fund for rural development (EAFRD), which will amount to €95.5 billion.

[60] See *supra*, p. 37.

[61] *Supra* p. 11, these are a series of rules coming from 13 directives and regulations on water (SMR1-2), Nature Conservation (SMR3-4), Food Safety (SMR 7-8) Plants protection (9-11) Animal welfare (SMR9-11). See more details on Annex II of REG 2115/2021.

[62] Supra p.11, the Good Agricultural and Environmental Conditions (GAECs), are a set of specific practices related to environmental protection that farmers must respect.

[63] To know more, see Russo L., "Le "nuove" misure agroambientali della Pac 2023-27: quali novità?", in *Riv. Dir. Agr*, 2022, 2; Alabrese M. and Cristiani E., "Clima e impegni internazionali nell'attuazione della Pac", in *Riv. Dir. Agr.*, 2022, 2.

[64] European Court of Auditors (fn. 19).

[65] Farmers could be exempted from the obligation, like for limited dimension of arable land. All Member States but Denmark, Estonia and Ireland are making use of these exemptions.

undermined by the general European Commission derogation in 2023 and 2024, applied by most Member States after the outbreak of war between Russia and Ukraine and the new growing concerns for supplies in the European agri-food sector, the energy sector crisis and increasing costs and the recent protests of European farmers in Brussels.[66]

The other important innovation in terms of environmental measures is the "new green architecture" regulated by Regulation 2115/2021, Article 31 and 97. These are a series of environmental measures and practices called "Eco-schemes" to reward and compensate farmers (in addition to the BISS payment) for contributing to public goods via sustainable practice and going beyond the baseline. These practices must necessarily include at least two areas of the main climate and biodiversity objectives.[67] The Eco-scheme regime is compulsory for states and voluntary for farmers. As a basic rule, States are required to allocate 25% of the budget for direct payments (Pillar I) and identify the list of eco-schemes they intend to propose to their farmers. It is entirely at the discretion of individual farmers whether or not to adopt one or more eco-schemes. This new provision raised several perplexities about the future environmental impact. The regime is seen to be a soft measure:[68] there are no eco-schemes directly dedicated to the reduction of industrial intensive livestock farming, and only 8 eco-schemes are linked somehow to the result indicator to address livestock emissions designed by seven MS. Among the 158 eco-schemes presented to the Commission, 18% provide payments that go beyond the BISS ('top-up' to BISS). The remaining 82% provide payments intended to offset or compensate the additional costs and income loss.[69] The eco-schemes regime has been criticized[70] also for lacking transparency and accountability, and

---

[66] Providing for derogations from Regulation 2021/2115 of the European Parliament and of the Council as regards the application of the standards for good agricultural and environmental conditions of land (GAEC standards) 7 and 8 for claim year 2023.

[67] These objectives are gathered in the following categories: 1) Climate Change mitigation 2) Climate Change adaptation 3) Water quality 4) Soil quality 5) Biodiversity 6) Pesticide use reduction 7) Animal welfare 8) Antimicrobial resistance the European Commission list of potential agricultural practices that eco-schemes could support is available here https://agriculture.ec.europa.eu/system/files/2021-01/factsheet-agri-practices-under-ecoscheme_en_0.pdf.

[68] BirdLife Europe & EEB report, Nemcová T. and Nyssens-James C. et al., *New CAP unpacked and unfit*, December 2022, https://eeb.org/wp-content/uploads/2022/12/New_CAP_Unpacked-6.pdf.

[69] EC, Approved 28 CAP Strategic Plans, 2023 text available here: https://agriculture.ec.europa.eu/system/files/2023-06/approved-28-cap-strategic-plans-2023-27.pdf.

[70] Some of these early considerations have been published by ARC, Willard M. et al.,

unclear methodologies on the evaluation of these practices and how to reach the budget allocated for that. While this flexibility for MSs and farmers to express their own choices is certainly an added value for addressing context-specific solutions, it was empirically observed how up to this new CAP a scarcity of clear requirements and evaluation criteria encourages a "race to the bottom" where MS "compete" for the lowest requirements for their farmers' Direct Payments.[71]

Another major criticism being leveled against the new CAP is the maintenance of the status quo against the most polluting sectors of the agri-food industry. We can observe unchanged support for intensive livestock farming through the use of the above-mentioned instrument of the coupled payments. In fact, coupled aid has not disappeared altogether. It is a voluntary instrument that can be used for interventions in specific sectors to address needs that require particular interventions, with a maximum budget allocation of 15% of direct payments (Pillar I). Despite the problematic nature of this instrument, all analyzed Member States (except the Netherlands) plan to offer coupled income support. Over 70% of coupled payments are dedicated to the livestock sector.[72] Intensive livestock production causes the most severe environmental and health impacts in the agri-food sector which include GHGs, air and water pollution, antimicrobial resistance, and direct and indirect deforestation via feed imports. On these points, the lack of systemic vision is once again evident. Indeed, to reach the systemic and integrated sustainable food system steps it is urgently needed to move towards a lower animal per hectare production process, to diversify production in a way that cycles nutrients and reuses waste flows, and to reduce severe dependencies on imported feed.

There has been progress regarding socio-economic goals to promote employment, growth, and gender equality. There is an important mandatory allocation (3% of direct payments) that will bring incentives to activities run by "Young Farmers" to fight the aging of European farming. Besides,

---

Project Report CAP Strategic Plans: Reforming the CAP in wartime, December 2022, https://www.arc2020.eu/wp-content/uploads/2022/12/ARC2020_CAP_Strategic_Plans_Reforming_the_CAP_in_war_time.pdf and Prof. Alan Matthews (European Agricultural Policy in the Department of Economics at Trinity College, Dublin, Ireland) https://capreform.eu/author/alan-matthews/.

[71] See more on this point in the work of Pe'er G. et al. "Action needed for the EU Common Agricultural Policy to address sustainability challenges", in *People and Nature*, 2020, 2.2, 305-316.

[72] Approved 28 CAP Strategic Plans (2023-2027) Summary overview for 27 Member States Facts and figures https://agriculture.ec.europa.eu/system/files/2023-04/approved-28-cap-strategic-plans-2023-27.pdf.

social conditionality has been added as a complementary layer to the already present "environmental" conditionality. For the first time, in fact, income support from CAP and rural development funds will be linked to the respect for the social and labor rights of farm workers. Farmers will have to provide their workers with a written description of the agreed working conditions and will have to guarantee a safe and healthy working environment. If farmers violate the regulations, their CAP payments will have to be reduced and, in the most serious case, excluded completely from the direct payment system. In terms of redistribution and fairness of payments, the external and internal convergence processes to reduce differences in the unitary level of direct payments within Member States have been enhanced.[73] These processes aim to progressively equalize the value of decoupled direct payment entitlements among Member States (external convergence) and within each Member State or region (internal convergence). The willingness of states reflected in the preparation of strategic plans, however, once again confirmed the reluctance, in redistributive terms, to use instruments such as capping and *degressivity* (gradual reduction). These are additional instruments that Member States may use to reduce payments of larger beneficiaries – on the ground of economies of scale – to better target income support, thus increasing farms' viability and competitiveness. Among MSs, will 17 are not going to use this voluntary instrument.

12. The interrupted evolution of the CAP and the unfulfilled promises of a food system approach

This Chapter has discussed whether the CAP has aligned to the 'food system approach' endorsed by the GD and its associated strategies. It has shown the radical reforms of the CAP throughout the decades. From a sectoral policy almost exclusively focused on increasing productivity, the CAP

[73] Internal convergence: EU countries that still make direct payments based on historical references for payment entitlements will need to continue reducing the differences between payments per hectare in their Member State. This process, called internal convergence, must ensure that all payment entitlements have a value of at least 85% of the average in 2026. External convergence: Countries that receive a level of direct payments per hectare (ha) of agricultural land that is below 90% of the EU average per hectare payment will see an increase of their budget up to half of the difference to 90% of the average. Payments will be at least €200/ha in 2022 and increase to €215/ha in 2027. This process is called external convergence and continues the trend of bringing average levels of payments in EU countries closer together. Source: European Commission website: https://agriculture.ec.europa.eu/common-agricultural-policy/cap-overview/cap-2023-27/key-reforms-new-cap_en.

has been forced by internal and external contingencies to continuously enlarge the scope of its concerns. Indeed, it has progressively embraced environmental and social concerns related to the agricultural sector. This process culminated in the recent mainstreaming of the UN SDGs into the CAP objectives and with the synergic collaboration of this policy agenda with the ambitious targets of the GD.

First in the 2014-2020 reform, albeit quite timidly, and then with the recent 2023 reform, with a proper official endorsement, the pursuit of a *sustainable food system* has finally replaced the obsolete goal of production maximization as the only possible goal of a European agricultural policy. In other words, the various souls compounding the EU apparatus have eventually acknowledged the importance of a systemic, integrated, and holistic approach to the regulation of the agri-food sector. Climate neutrality cannot be achieved without shorter food supply chains, preserving biodiversity without healthier consuming habits, or viable rural development without cleaner energy sources.

However, despite the progress made, which owes much to the long and fundamental process that led to the approval of the new CAP beginning under a different European Commission with other priorities, the CAP 2023-27 does not seem to be in line with the relevance given to environmental and biodiversity concerns by the GD, the F2F, and 2030 Biodiversity strategy. Furthermore, this new CAP does not provide the necessary tools for the desired transition to integrated and systematic sustainable food systems. While there is a clear inclination towards balancing economic, social, and environmental dimensions in line with the sustainable development path, the ecological considerations emphasized after the GD (see § 2.4) are present in the basic ideas but are inadequately reflected in the instruments that the CAP offers. Even more critically, these ecological priorities are poorly echoed in the commitments of the States.

A large proportion of the CSP budget is still spent on poorly targeted and concentrated payments like the one allocated in the first pillar dedicated to basic payments, and sometimes even harmful payments such as the coupled payments concentrated on the livestock sector case. Nevertheless, the governance of the CAP has an adaptive nature, which includes a series of future summits and consultations to evaluate results and identify possible areas for improvement. Strategic plans can be changed and amended. This flexibility offers hope and creates a scenario where this CAP could be a potential game changer, placing the European agri-food system on a more consistent and coherent sustainable path.

Chapter 2

THE NEW COMMON AGRICULTURAL POLICY APPROACH TOWARDS THE LIVESTOCK SECTOR AND FOOD WASTE. LYING AT WHICH POINT OF THE SUSTAINABILITY *CONTINUUM*?

Roberto Talenti and Giulia Corsini

ABSTRACT: *Understanding that sustainability exists within a continuum, this Chapter seeks to identify which declination of sustainability aligns most closely with the objectives, targets, and mechanisms of the new Common Agricultural Policy (CAP). It does so by specifically addressing two case studies that play a pivotal role in the transition towards sustainable European food systems: the livestock sector and food waste.*

KEYWORDS: *Sustainability – Sustainable development – Sustainability of ecosystems – Common Agricultural Policy – Livestock sector – Food waste.*

1. The new CAP: understanding its relationship with the multifaceted sustainability concept

As underlined by scholars such as Du Pisani, Bosselman, Caradonna, and Purvis, the concept of sustainability is as complex as fuzzy, and it has assumed different meanings in different times and contexts.[1] It may be ob-

[1] See Du Pisani J.A., "Sustainable development – historical roots of the concept", in *Environ. Sci.*, 2007; Bosselmann K., *The Principle of Sustainability: Transforming Law and Governance*, Routledge, 2008; Caradonna J.L., *Sustainability: a History*, Oxford University Press, 2014; Purvis B., Yong Mao and Robinson D., "Three pillars of sustainability: in search of conceptual origins", in *Sustain. Sci.*, 2018.

served that sustainability exists within a *continuum* which ranges from the definition of 'sustainable development' to the definition of 'sustainability of ecosystems'.

On the one hand, the sustainable development paradigm is closer to the development discourse than to the pure sustainability discourse,[2] it has its origins in the IUCN Strategy of 1980, and it has been further worked-out, *inter alia*, in the Brundtland Report of 1987 and in the Rio Declaration of 1992, but also in the Johannesburg Declaration of 2002, and in the 2030 Agenda for Sustainable Development of 2015.[3] Sustainable development relies on a strongly anthropocentric approach,[4] it is underpinned by the assumption that it will be economic development (declined as economic growth) to trigger environmental and social benefits,[5] and it therefore depicts economic, social, and environmental elements as interacting into an optimistic win-win scenario.[6] Indeed, as the Brundtland Report famously claims, 'if large parts of the developing world are to avert economic, social, and environmental catastrophes, it is essential that global economic growth be revitalized. In practical terms, this means more rapid economic growth in both industrial and developing countries'.[7] It is also the case of highlighting that the theoretical soundness of the concept of sustainable development has been put into question by a large number of scholars. Indeed, while Castro argues sustainable development to 'sound suspiciously like plain old development', Lorenzini has defined sustainable development as 'the most famous oxymoron in the history of international relations', and Kotzé and Adelman, have described sustainable development as 'a legally sanctioned ideological palli-

---

[2] Castro C., 'Sustainable Development – Mainstream and Critical Perspectives", in *O&E*, 2003.

[3] IUCN, *World Conservation Strategy – Living Resource Conservation for Sustainable Development* (IUCN, 1980); Gro Harlem Brundtland, *Our Common Future: Report of the World Commission on Environment and Development*, UN-Document A/42/427 (1987); United Nations Rio Declaration on Environment and Development (13 June 1992), 31 I.L.M. 874 (1992); United Nations, *Report of the World Summit on Sustainable Development*, A/CONF.199/20 (2022); UN General Assembly, *Transforming our world: the 2030 Agenda for Sustainable Development*, A/RES/70/1 (2015).

[4] Pierri M., "Il limite antropocentrico dello sviluppo sostenibile nella prospettiva del personalismo costituzionale. Riflessioni a margine della riforma degli articoli 9 e 41 della Costituzione italiana", in *RQDA*, 2022.

[5] See IUCN, *World Conservation Strategy – Living Resource Conservation for Sustainable Development*, 1980, 62; United Nations, *Our Common Future*, 1987, 7.

[6] Purvis B., Yong Mao and Robinson D., "Three pillars of sustainability: in search of conceptual origins", in *Sustain. Sci.*, 2018.

[7] Brundtland (fn. 8) 66.

ative at the centre of environmental law and governance that enables its proponents to rationalize continuing destruction of the fragile earth system, rather than safeguarding planetary integrity'.[8]

On the other side of the spectrum, the 'sustainability of ecosystem approach' has never been explicitly referred to in any legal document, but it has deeper roots in the history of the concept of sustainability, since the publication of Elton's *Animal Ecology,* Odum's *Fundamentals of Ecology*, and Carson's *Silent Spring.*[9] The sustainability of ecosystems approach is less optimistic about the synergies existing among the three traditional dimensions of sustainable development (*i.e.*, the environmental, social and economic ones) and,[10] according to it, when a tension arises among these three different dimensions, the environmental one shall ultimately prevail. More specifically, while a sustainable development documents frame the different dimensions encompassing it (*i.e.*, economic, social, and environmental) as mutually reinforcing,[11] the sustainability of ecosystems approach puts the accent on the necessity of balancing between these different dimensions, as well as of the importance of prioritizing environmental protection and conservation objectives over short-term economic considerations.[12] On this regard, it might be observed that further works implicitly upholding a sustainability of ecosystems approach, from '70s works such as 'A Blueprint for Survival' and *The Limits to Growth,* to more recent ones such as 'The 'Anthropocene'' and 'Planetary boundaries: Guiding human development on a changing planet', while putting the accent on the immanent constrains on human action on Earth, have traditionally debunked the typically Western growth-oriented developmental narrative.[13] Indeed, as

---

[8] Castro (fn. 7); Lorenzini S., *Global Development a Cold War History,* Princeton University Press, 2019; Kotzé L.J. and Adelman S., "Environmental Law and the Unsustainability of Sustainable Development: A Tale of Disenchantment and of Hope", in *Law&Critique,* 2023.

[9] See Elton C., *Animal Ecology*, The Macmillan Company, 1927; Odum E., *Fundamentals of Ecology*, Saunders, 1953; Carson R., *Silent Spring*, Houghton Mifflin, 1962.

[10] See, among the others, Zeng Yiwen, Maxwell S., Runting R.K., Venter O., Watson J.E.M. and Roman Carrasco L., 'Environmental destruction not avoided with the Sustainable Development Goals", in *Nat. Sustain.*, 2020; Hickel J., *The contradiction of the sustainable development goals: Growth versus ecology on a finite planet*, Wiley, 2019.

[11] See, among the others, Rio Declaration (1992); Johannesburg Declaration (2002); Agenda 2030 (2015).

[12] Chiti E., "Managing The Ecological Transition Of The EU: The European Green Deal As A Regulatory Process", in *CMLRev.*, 2022.

[13] "A Blueprint for Survival", in *The Ecologist*, 1972; Meadows D., Randers J. and Behrens III W.W., *The Limits to Growth*, Universe Books, 1972; Crutzen P.J. and Stoermer E.F., "The 'Anthropocene", in *Global Change Newsletter*, 2000; Rockström J.,

the introductory section of 'A Blueprint for Survival' strongly stated, 'indefinite growth of whatever type cannot be sustained by finite resources. This is the nub of the environmental predicament'.[14]

Against this background, this Chapter will discuss which declination of sustainability more closely aligns with the objectives, targets, and mechanisms of the new Common Agricultural Policy (CAP). It will do so by specifically addressing two case studies, namely the case of the livestock sector and the case of food waste. In the light of the several possible ways to (legally) construct sustainability, it will try to understand which choices have been made, on this regard, by the European legislator when it came to the establishment of the CAP 2023-2027.

The focus on these two case studies is justified not only by the significant environmental impact they bring about, but also by their great mitigation potential, and by the fact that they have long been ignored by the European Union (EU) legislator.[15] On this regard, it is also the case of highlighting that, in spite of the great consequences that the livestock sector and the food waste issue cause, *inter alia*, in terms of economic and social impact, this study will mainly focus on the environmental dimension. This is the case because the EU legislator's way of approaching the environmental dimension constitutes a major element of discrimination between the two ideal typical conceptualizations of sustainability. Indeed, on the one hand, any aprioristic depiction of the pursuit of environmental objectives as achievable through path-dependent and incremental improvements and as, *ipso facto*, generating economic gains (*e.g.*, green growth, green jobs, etc.), will reveal the proximity to the sustainable development paradigm. On the other hand, acknowledging both the constraints of efficiency-oriented solutions to environmental challenges and the necessity of making economic

---

Steffen W., Noone K., Persson Å., Stuart III C.F., Lambin E., Lenton T.M., Scheffer M., Folke C., Schellnhuber H.J., Nykvist B., De Wit C.A., Hughes T., Van der Leeuw S., Rodhe H., Sörlin S., Snyder P.K., Costanza R., Svedin U., Falkenmark M., Karlberg L., Corell R.W., Fabry V.J., Hansen J., Walker B., Liverman D., Richardson K., Crutzen P. and Foley J., "Planetary Boundaries: Exploring the Safe Operating Space for Humanity", in *Ecol. Soc.*, 2009.

[14] *The Ecologist*, cit., 3.

[15] See, among the others, van der Veen R., de Vries M., van de Pol J., van Santen W., Sinke P., de Vries J., Kampman B. and Bergsma G., "Methane reduction potential in the EU Between 2020 and 2030", in *CE Delft*, 2022; Westhoek H., Lesschen J.P., Rood T., Wagner S., De Marco A., Murphy-Bokern D., Leip A., van Grinsven H., Sutton M.A. and Oenema O., "Food choices, health and environment: Effects of cutting Europe's meat and dairy intake", in *Global Environ. Change*, 2014; Scherhaufer S., Moates G., Hartikainen H., Waldron K. and Obersteiner G., *Environmental impacts of food waste in Europe*, Elsevier, 2018.

trade-offs in pursuit of environmental interests highlights the affinity with the sustainability of ecosystems approach.

To address the issue at stake, this Chapter will be structured as follows. Bearing in mind that there is more than one possible conceptualization of sustainability, § 2 and § 3 will be devoted, respectively, to analysing whether and how the new CAP has addressed both the livestock sector and the waste management issue. More precisely, § 2 will introduce the livestock sector with the aim of providing a glimpse into its massive ecological footprint. Afterwards, it will look at how the EU legislator has addressed the livestock sector with the aim of mitigating its environmental impact. In this context, after analysing whether and how the Farm to Fork Strategy Communication (F2F) refers to the role of the livestock sector,[16] the CAP 2023-2027 will be considered, with the aim to ascertain at which point of the sustainability *continuum* it lies. Subsequently, § 3 will shed light on the environmental impacts of food waste and focus on the analysis of the relevant European legal framework with the aim of both underscoring the missed opportunities and identifying the sustainability approach adopted with regard to food waste. § 4 will present the final remarks and findings of this work.

The inquiry is relevant for at least two reasons. Firstly, in the light of the widespread usage of the word 'sustainability' in environmental discourses, policies, and pieces of legislation, it becomes particularly urgent to acknowledge and value the range of meanings that this concept can assumes. Secondly, provided the heinous threats that environmental degradation poses to both human and non-human life on Earth,[17] and considering that the sustainability of ecosystem approach appears to be better tailored to operate in the respect of environmental boundaries,[18] detecting the eventual closeness of the new CAP to this approach would, *per se*, constitute a remarkable information. Importantly, as we recognize that the application of the sustainable development paradigm might be particularly functional in specific contexts,[19] this research refrains from reducing the dis-

---

[16] The Farm to Fork Strategy is the Communication providing guidelines for reducing 'the environmental and climate footprint of the EU food system' (2020) p 5.

[17] World Economic Forum, *Global Risk Report,* 18th ed., 2023. According to the Report, the four most severe long-term risks that humanity faces are, from the first to the fourth one: failure to mitigate climate change, failure of climate-change adaptation, natural disasters and extreme weather events, biodiversity loss and ecosystem collapse.

[18] See, *inter alia*, Bosselmann K., *The Principle of Sustainability: Transforming Law and Governance*, Routledge, 2008; Ross A., "Modern Interpretations of Sustainable Development", in *J. L: & Soc.*, 2009; Chiti (fn. 16); Kotzé, Adelman (fn. 12).

[19] *I.e.*, mainly in less industrialized countries where standards of living lie below the sufficiency threshold.

tinction between sustainable development and sustainability of ecosystem to a Manichean "bad vs good" sustainability dichotomy. However, in the light of the massive environmental impact of the EU food production system, and provided that European food consumption patterns far outweighs the sufficiency threshold,[20] this work also argues that an approach of the new CAP which stands close to the sustainability of ecosystem paradigm would be not only appropriate, but necessary. Indeed, this rapprochement would indicate that the new CAP is equipped with a suite of features that significantly increase its ability to operate safely in today's environmentally compromised natural surroundings.

What the study observes is that, as far as the regulation of both livestock and food waste is concerned, the new CAP continues missing the opportunity to adopt an eco-centric and scientifically sound sustainability approach which could be declined in terms of ecosystem sustainability.

2. Addressing the livestock sector

2.1. Animal farming and its environmental impact

The livestock sector encompasses all those activities which contribute to the production of terrestrial animal food products, and the ways through which it impacts the environment are numerous and diversified. At the global level, the livestock sector alone emits more GHGs than the entire transport sector, and it is the single biggest cause of habitat loss[21]. Farmed animals alone nowadays constitute 60% of the Earth's mammal biosphere,[22] and intensive livestock farming is a main source of risk when it comes to both antibiotic resistance and the spread of zoonosis.[23] At the EU level, the situation does not get better. Indeed, the livestock sector produc-

---

[20] van der Veen R., de Vries M., van de Pol J., van Santen W., Sinke P., de Vries J., Kampman B. and Bergsma G., "Methane reduction potential in the EU", in *CE Delft*, 2022.

[21] FAO, *Tackling Climate Change Through Livestock*, 2013; Machovina B., Feeley K.J. and Ripple W.J., "Biodiversity conservation: The key is reducing meat consumption", in *Sci. Total Environ.*, 2015.

[22] Bar-Ona Y.M., Phillips R. and Milo R., "The biomass distribution on Earth", in *PNAS*, 2018. On this regard, it could also be relevant to observe that humans constitute 36% of the mammal biosphere, and wild animals only the remaining 4%.

[23] Hickman R.A., Leangapichart T., Lunha K., Jiwakanon J., Angkititrakul S., Magnusson U., Sunde M., Järhult J.D., "Exploring the Antibiotic Resistance Burden in Livestock, Livestock Handlers and Their Non-Livestock Handling Contacts: A One Health Perspective", in *Front. Microbiol.*, 2021.

es more than half of EU methane emissions[24] and it constitutes 'between 73% (water quality) to about 80% (biodiversity, air quality, soil acidification and global warming) of the overall agricultural impact'.[25]

Even though the range of consequences the livestock sector produces on the environment is evidently wide, it is possible to reduce them to one single cause, i.e., the intrinsic inefficiency of livestock production. As a matter of fact, livestock production is terribly consuming both in terms of land use and water consumption, and this is due to the particularly low conversion rate of feed into animal food. It might be useful to highlight that, to produce one kilogram of poultry meat, pig meat, or beef, you respectively need more than four, six, and thirty-six kilograms of feed.[26] As a consequence of its inefficiency, while the livestock sector occupies four fifths of global agricultural land, it contributes to less than one fifth of global calories supply.[27] Moreover, it is because of animal food production's inefficiency that a global dietary transition which goes in the direction of 'favouring plant-based diets over less efficient animal-based ones can potentially feed more humans than complete elimination of conventional food losses'.[28]

As far as remedies to livestock-related environmental pollution are considered, there is little doubt that any of them entails a significant reduction of animal food production and consumption patterns. As the European Court of Auditors has observed, there are 'no effective and approved practices that can significantly reduce livestock emissions from feed digestion without reducing production. [...]. Some of these practices encourage production expansion, and may thus increase net emissions'.[29] In addition, the reduction of livestock related GHG emissions (and thus the reduction of livestock production) also has a central role to play when it comes to the achievement of climate change targets. As a matter of fact, Eisen and

---

[24] Van der Veen et al. (fn. 23).

[25] Leip A., Billen G., Garnier J., Grizzetti B., Lassaletta L., Reis S., Simpson D., Sutton M.A., de Vries M., Weiss F. and Westhoek H., "Impacts of European livestock production: nitrogen, sulphur, phosphorus and greenhouse gas emissions, land-use, water eutrophication and biodiversity", in *Environ. Res.* Lett., 2015, 11.

[26] Shepon A., Eshel G., Noor E. and Milo R., "Energy and protein feed-to-food conversion efficiencies in the US and potential food security gains from dietary changes", in *Environ. Res. Lett.*, 2016.

[27] Ritchie H. and Roser M., "How much of the world's land would we need in order to feed the global population with the average diet of a given country?", in OWID, 2019, Link to the website: https://ourworldindata.org/agricultural-land-by-global-diets.

[28] Shepon A., Eshel G., Noor E. and Milo R., "The opportunity cost of animal-based diets exceeds all food losses", in *PNAS*, 2018, 3807.

[29] European Court of Auditors (fn. 5) 22.

Brown have calculated that the rapid global phaseout of animal food consumption and production could stabilize GHG levels for 30 years, and it would offset 68 per cent of carbon dioxide emissions this century.[30] When it comes to the European level, 'land-based mitigation commitments for achieving the Paris target require considerable expansion of forest areas, yet large-scale afforestation or reforestation conflicts with other land use objectives'.[31] Therefore, in order to expand European forest land area and making the EU in line with the Paris targets without compromising EU food security, a 'drastic reduction in meat demand is required; 57.5% and 56.7% of the ruminant and non-ruminant meat demand, respectively'.[32]

On a positive note, such a reduction in animal food production and consumption would not only occur to the advantage of the environment, but also to the benefit of human health. In fact, lowering meat consumption would also reduce the risk of cardiovascular diseases, strokes, and colorectal cancer. Moreover, further health benefit would arise out of the improved quality of water, air, and the reduced use of antibiotics.[33] It emerges, then, that for 'human health, the environment, and animal welfare, a win-win-win can best be realized by strongly reducing animal product consumption'.[34]

2.2. Livestock regulation at the EU level – the Farm to Fork Strategy

Despite the presence of extensive scientific literature on the issue at stake, both legal scholars and policymakers have traditionally disregarded the role that the livestock sector must play when it comes to contrasting environmental degradation[35]. Against this background, and with the aim of filling

[30] Eisen M.B. and Brown P.O., "Rapid global phaseout of animal agriculture has the potential to stabilize greenhouse gas levels for 30 years and offset 68 percent of CO2 emissions this century", in *Plos Climate*, 2022.

[31] Lee H., Brown C., Seo B., Holman I., Audsley E., Cojocaru G., and Rounsevell M., "Implementing land-based mitigation to achieve the Paris Agreement in Europe requires food system transformation", in *Environ. Res. Lett.*, 2019, 8.

[32] *Ibidem*, 4.

[33] Westhoek H. et al. (fn. 17).

[34] Scherer L., Behrens P. and Tukker A., "Opportunity for a Dietary Win-Win-Win in Nutrition, Environment, and Animal Welfare", in *One Earth*, 2019, 355.

[35] See, among the others, Donahue D.L., "Elephant in the Room: Livestock's Role in Climate and Environmental Change", in *Mich. J. Int. Law*, 2008; Bailey R., Froggatt A. and Wellesley L., *Livestock – Climate Change's Forgotten Sector*, Chatham House, 2014; Bas-Defossez F. and Lake S., "The biggest climate solution missing from COP27: meat reduction", in *IEEP*, 2022, link to the article: https://ieep.eu/news/the-biggest-climate-solution-missing-from-cop27-meat-reduction.

the current literature gap, both the current and the next sub-paragraph (§ 2.2-§ 2.3) will try to understand whether the EU has recently implemented measures for the regulation of the livestock sector which may fall under any definition of sustainability. In order to do so, while sub-paragraph § 2.2 will carefully address the F2F Strategy, sub-paragraph § 2.3 will move to the analysis of the CAP 2023-2027.

The F2F Strategy Communication is the agenda-setting document launched in 2020 through which the European Commission traces the path that EU food systems will have to follow to become sustainable and thus contribute to the achievement of the climate and environmental objectives enshrined in the GD.[36] The analysis of the F2F Communication is indeed relevant given the scope of this research, as it represents one of the main policy documents launched by the Von Der Leyen Commission contributing to the shaping of the new CAP.[37] In this context, while some researchers as Boer and Aiking welcome the sustainability approach adopted by the Strategy,[38] law scholars as Mowlds adopt a more critical stance towards it and claim that, despite setting ambitious targets, 'the strategy falls short of recognising key links in and between the food system', and it ultimately does 'not adequately consider the importance of transforming agricultural practices for environmental outcomes'.[39]

When it comes to its relationship with the livestock sector, the F2F Strategy does not seem to take a particularly net position. In fact, on the one hand, the Strategy does not identify any livestock-emission reduction target, it does never explicitly mention the importance to reduce European livestock production and, on the contrary, it states that the Commission will promote 'the placing on the market of sustainable and innovative feed additives' and will 'support the most sustainable, carbon-efficient methods of livestock production'.[40] On the other hand, the Communication also underlines that the livestock sector constitutes a challenge for the Europe-

---

[36] European Commission, COM (2020) 381 final. In particular, the Communication states that 'the Farm to Fork Strategy will strengthen their [*i.e.*, farmers and fishermen] efforts to tackle climate change, protect the environment and preserve biodiversity' (p.12).

[37] European Commission, *Farm to Fork strategy*, (last accessed in 2023) (link to the website: https://food.ec.europa.eu/horizontal-topics/farm-fork-strategy_en).

[38] de Boer J. and Aiking H., *Exploring food consumers' motivations to fight both climate change and biodiversity loss: Combining insights from behavior theory and Eurobarometer data*, Elsevier, 2021.

[39] Mowlds S., "The EU's farm to fork strategy: missing links for transformation", in *Acta Innovations*, 2020, 17.

[40] European Commission (fn. 2) 7-8.

an food system sustainability, and it explicitly reminds that it is responsible for 70% of EU agricultural GHG emissions, and for occupying '68% of the total agricultural land'.[41] Furthermore, the F2F identifies a quite diversified portfolio of measures going in the direction of a reduction of animal food consumption patterns. Indeed, beyond explicitly stressing the importance of moving 'to a more plant-based diet with less red and processed meat', it pushes for the introduction of price and tax incentives for the promotion of healthy diets (*i.e.*, fiscal measures), and it takes effort to examine the possibility of creating a sustainable labelling framework to 'empower consumers to make informed, healthy and sustainable food choices' (*i.e.*, consumers-empowerment measures).[42] Furthermore, the Strategy envisages a reduction of 'overall EU sales of antimicrobials for farmed animals and in aquaculture by 50% by 2030',[43] the enhancement of animal welfare legislation, and the introduction of trade policy reforms aimed at obtaining ambitious commitments in the areas of 'animal welfare, the use of pesticides[,] the fight against antimicrobial resistance' and 'global deforestation and forest degradation' (*i.e.*, animal welfare and health measures).[44]

It emerges, therefore, that the F2F Strategy is surely aware of the importance of addressing the environmental impact of the livestock sector. Nonetheless, two elements need to be highlighted. Firstly, despite identifying several environmental targets (e.g., in terms of reduction of pesticides and antibiotics use), the F2F Strategy does not set any GHG emission reduction target either for the livestock or the overall agriculture, forestry and other land use (AFOLU) sector. Provided that the F2F should be, at least in theory, strictly related to the realization of the GD (whose main aim is the achievement of climate neutrality by 2050) the existence of such an empty space in the Strategy remains particularly problematic, and it can be reconducted to the Commission's willingness not to create discontent among European agricultural lobbies and producers.

Secondly, the Strategy acknowledges that 'current food consumption patterns are unsustainable from both health and environmental points of view' as, 'in the EU, average intakes of [*inter alia*] red meat [...] continue to exceed recommendations'.[45] Nonetheless, while underscoring the necessity to decrease animal food consumption both in the name of environmental and healthcare considerations, the Strategy is not only reluctant to iden-

[41] *Ibidem,* 7.

[42] *Ibidem,* 13.

[43] *Ibidem,* 8.

[44] *Ibidem,* 17.

[45] European Commission, COM (2020) 381 final, 13.

tifying the animal food reduction levels to be achieved (both in terms of consumption and production), but also to acknowledge that a reduction in animal food consumption must necessarily be mirrored, in order to achieve any kind of environmental improvement, by a reduction in animal food production. Such an ambiguous posture evidently echoes what Schebesta and Candel define as one of the main vulnerabilities of the F2F, i.e., the vagueness gravitating around central concepts which underpin the whole Strategy.[46] In fact, as the two scholars observe, concepts as 'food sustainability' or 'sustainability of food systems', despite being at the heart of the Strategy, remain ill-defined, they are framed as fancy catchphrases which avoid displeasing any stakeholder, and they finally fall short of identifying any legal guideline or policy direction. Some of these shortcomings were expected to be addressed with the announced launch of the legislative framework for sustainable food systems. However, the Von der Leyen Commission failed to present the widely awaited proposal during its first mandate, and it appears even less likely to do so during its second.

In the light of these considerations, it emerges that the line followed in the F2F Strategy strongly reflects the EU legislator difficulty to balance between scientific evidence on the (ecological) unsustainability of specific economic activities and the political cost to make short-term economic sacrifices in the name of long-term environmental benefits. As a matter of fact, although it frames the livestock sector as particularly problematic in the light of its massive environmental impact, and it also acknowledges that a transition towards more plant-based diets in the EU will be necessary, the Strategy fails to envisage any pathway for the reduction of European animal-food production, probably in order not to undermine the economic interests of European farmers.

2.3. Which sustainability approach from the new CAP?

Entered into force in January 2023, the (allegedly) green CAP has received the attention of a number of experts, especially since the final CAP agreement has been reached in December 2021. Actually, already before its entrance into force, scholars as Alabrese underlined the necessity of greater coordination, both at the international and at the European level, between climate change and agricultural policies.[47] Nonetheless, as it has been not-

[46] Schebesta H. and Candel J.J.L., "Game-changing potential of the EU's Farm to Fork Strategy", in *Nat. Food.*, 2020.

[47] Alabrese M., "Politiche climatiche, politiche agricole e il bisogno di coordinamento", in *Riv. Dir. Agr.*, 2020.

ed in the introductory paragraph of this Chapter, the new CAP did not obtain a particularly warm reception from most ecology-conscious scholars, journalists, and NGOs, and it disappointed the expectations of several field experts. In fact, while researchers as Heyl et. al noted that the general architecture enshrined in the proposal for the new CAP was 'not groundbreaking' in terms of environmental commitments,[48] Hannes Lorenzen, president of the Agricultural and Rural Convention, came to define the CAP 2023-2027 as 'an aberration with regard to the climate and environmental impact of agriculture'.[49] Against this background, it is useful to understand how does the new CAP address livestock sector emissions, so to figure to which conceptualization of sustainability its approach may be closer.

The new CAP identifies three general objectives, broken into nine specific objectives, which shall be achieved at the EU level through Member States' drafting and implementation of their CAP Strategic Plans.[50] Out of nine specific objectives, three of them concern environmental issues and specifically relate to: 'climate change mitigation and adaptation', fostering 'sustainable development and efficient management of natural resources', and 'halting and reversing biodiversity loss, enhance ecosystem services and preserve habitats'.[51] Interestingly enough, despite being labelled as 'specific', these objectives do not include any precise target goal or commitment. Nevertheless, on a positive note, result indicators defined at Article 7 and listed in Annex I of Regulation 2021/2115 (*i.e.*, the indicators which shall keep track of the achievement of CAP specific objectives) include 'reducing emission in the livestock sector' and 'environmental performance in the livestock sector'. It emerges, therefore, that although the new CAP does not introduce any specific environmental target for the livestock sector, it is not completely blind to its impact on the environment.

To achieve its objectives, the CAP can rely over two funds, i.e., the European agricultural guarantee fund (EAGF) and the European agricultural fund for rural development (EAFRD), respectively set, for the 2023-2027

---

[48] Heyl K., Döring T., Garske N., Stubenrauch J. and Ekardt F., "The Common Agricultural Policy beyond 2020: A critical review in light of global environmental goals", in *RECIEL*, 2020, 104.

[49] Lorenzen H., "The Common Agricultural Policy is an aberration with regard to the climate and environmental impact of agriculture", in *Le Monde*, 2023 (link to the website: https://www.lemonde.fr/en/opinion/article/2023/02/25/the-common-agricultural-policy-is-an-aberration-with-regard-to-the-climate-and-environmental-impact-of-agriculture_6017260_23.html).

[50] European Commission, Regulation (EU) 2021/2115, Articles 5-6.

[51] *Ibidem,* Article 6(1).

period, at €291.1 billion and €95.5 billion. Specifically, the EAGF focuses primarily on providing income support to farmers through direct payments, while the EAFRD is dedicated to rural development measures, which are often funded through annual payments.[52] Importantly, both forms of payments can be granted only when farmers and other beneficiaries have respected conditionalities, to be identified in the good agricultural and environmental conditions (GAEC) and statutory management requirements (SMRs). Provided the scope of this Chapter, it is particularly interesting to investigate over the content of both GAECs and SMRs, whose *raison d'être* is to better address 'environmental and climate challenges',[53] and to discover that none of them is related to the regulation of the livestock sector. In fact, while SRM9 and SRM10 only include the duty to respect the rules enshrined in the directives laying down minimum standards for the protection of calves and pigs,[54] no GAEC or SMR ever refers to the importance of reducing livestock production, livestock intensity, and not even livestock-related pollution.

However, one of the novelties introduced with the New CAP is the establishment of the schemes for the climate, the environment and animal welfare, the so-called eco-schemes. Being an evolution of the Greening instruments enshrined in the previous CAP,[55] eco-schemes are financed through the EAGF, and they shall receive a minimum of 25% of the funds destined to direct payments. Eco-schemes are mostly addressed at Article 31 of Regulation 2021/2115, and their adoption is voluntary for farmers but mandatory for Member States, as specified in their CAP Strategic Plans. Furthermore, when it comes to their establishment, States must consider that each eco-scheme shall cover at least two out of a series of seven 'areas of action'.

The general idea underpinning eco-schemes is to incentivize agricultural practices which are particularly ambitious in terms of environmental, climate, or animal welfare protection. In fact, in order to be granted, eco-schemes shall envisage agricultural standards which 'go beyond [...] GAEC standards', 'go beyond [...] relevant minimum requirements' related to the use of fertilizers, plant and animal protection, and 'go beyond the

[52] *Ibidem,* Article 85.

[53] *Ibidem,* Preamble, para. 41.

[54] See Council Directive 2008/119/EC and Council Directive 2008/120/EC.

[55] Cuadros-Casanova I., Cristiano A., Biancolini D., Cimatti M., Sessa A.A., Yeraldin Mendez Angarita V., Dragonetti C., Pacifici M., Rondinini C. and Di Marco M., "Opportunities and challenges for Common Agricultural Policy reform to support the European Green Deal", in *Conserv. Biol.*, 2023.

conditions established for the maintenance of the agricultural area in accordance with Article 4(2)'.[56] Notwithstanding this, none of the areas of actions identified at Article 31 and which must be covered in eco-schemes ever refers to the necessity to tackle intensive animal farming, nor to the importance of mitigating its environmental impact.

Still, it would be wrong to infer that Article 31 presents no reference to livestock. In fact, Article 31(7) states that, while eco-schemes will take the form of annual payments which will depend on all eligible hectares covered in farmers' commitments, a derogation will take place for 'animal welfare commitments, commitments combatting antimicrobial resistance and, [...] commitments for agricultural practices beneficial for the climate [which] may also take the form of an annual payment for the livestock units'.[57] While incentivizing the establishment of eco-schemes related to the regulation of the livestock sector, such a provision could end up benefiting both large-scale breeders and all those breeders who adopt intensive animal farming techniques. In fact, Article 31 does not identify any area of action focused on contrasting intensive farming. Furthermore, Article 31(7) makes eco-scheme payments proportional to the number of livestock units while remaining blind on the surface of the grazing land, and thus directly incentivizing, given the same surface area, higher intensity factory farms. Evidently, tying an environmental and climate protection payment with the number of livestock unknit contrasts all scientific evidence on the impossibility of decoupling livestock production from its environmental impact, and thus risks going against the very (environmental and climate) objectives of the eco-scheme.

Similar to eco-schemes are the agri-environment-climate commitments (AECMs) enshrined in Article 70. As it is the case for eco-schemes, also the adoption of AECMs shall be included in Member States' CAP Strategic Plans, their adoption is voluntary for farmers, and their rationale is, again, to go beyond minimum environmental targets set up by GAECs and SMRs. AECMs are financed under the EAFRD, and it is mandatory for Member States to adopt AECMs which differ from eco-schemes.[58] Furthermore, while each eco-scheme must cover at least two of the areas of action identified under Article 31, AECMs must be considered beneficial for the achievement of at least one out of the nine CAP specific objectives enshrined in Article 6.[59] However, provided that none of the CAP specific

---

[56] European Commission (fn. 48), Article 31(5).

[57] *Ibidem*, Article 31(7).

[58] *Ibidem,* Article 70(3)(d).

[59] *Ibidem*, Article 70(2).

objectives directly refers to the livestock sector, it emerges that not even AECMs are directly related to the necessity to mitigate livestock environmental footprint.

At this point, it might also be relevant to address the content of CAP Strategic Plans drawn by individual Member States. On this regard, scholars as Alabrese and Cristiani, but also Scheid and Ittner, and Midler and Pagnon, have respectively focused on the analysis of the National Strategic Plans of Italy, Germany, and France, and they have identified a 'number of shortcomings', [60] in plans which still 'fall short of expectations', [61] and finally result 'insufficient to trigger the shift in farming systems and practices needed to respond to the scale and urgency of the climate and biodiversity crisis'. [62] When it comes to the role attributed to the livestock sector in NSPs, it must be noted that, out of the fifty schemes related to animal agriculture analysed by the EEB, the most common focus area was animal welfare, followed by rearing of indigenous breeds, and grazing. [63] Moreover, according to national experts, most schemes are not being promoters of virtuous change, and they are rather benefiting breeding systems which were already extensive before the establishment of the new CAP. [64] Evidently, having the possibility to choose between environmental protection and animal welfare measures, national legislators have preferred focusing on the latter. This has probably been the case because the promotion of animal welfare-measures does not necessarily undermine livestock final production and breeders' revenues and it hence turns up being more politically (and economically) acceptable than any effective measure focusing on environmental protection at the cost of reducing the supply of animal food.

There are two further elements of the new CAP which it is important to address in relation to livestock regulation. First, it must be observed that the new CAP grants a special level of protection for livestock activities, and this both emerges from Article 3 of Regulation 2021/2116 and Article 12 of Regulation 2021/2017. As a matter of fact, when it comes to the obligation to implement CAP Strategic Plans, Article 3 recognizes just six circumstances as force majeure, out of which two are specifically related to the

[60] Alabrese M. and Cristiani E., "Clima e impegni internazionali nell'attuazione della Pac", in *Riv. Dir. Agr.*, 2022, 246.

[61] Scheid A. and Ittner S., "Environment and climate assessment of Germany's CAP Strategic Plan", in *IEEP*, 2023, 7.

[62] Midler E., Pagnon J., "Environment and climate assessment of France's CAP Strategic Plan", in *IEEP*, 2023 51.

[63] European Environmental Bureau (fn. 6).

[64] *Ibidem*.

livestock sector.[65] On the same wavelength, Article 12 allows public intervention, i.e., interventions which allow products to be 'bought in by the competent authorities of the Member States and stored by them',[66] for only five categories of products, among which there are both beef and veal, and butter and skimmed milk powder.[67] The exceptional attention showed towards the safeguarding of animal food-related activities and products, while indisputably having a positive impact on the economic resilience of the livestock sector (*i.e.*, they make more stable both costs and revenues associated with it), surely enshrines no environmental-protection intent. On the contrary, by continuing to *tout court* ignoring the necessity to scale down livestock production levels, these measures continue promoting the (artificial) solidity of the European livestock sector, while also making it more attractive as a destination for both workforce and capital investments.

Second, when it comes to coupled income support, it must be noted that the CAP 2023-2027 just allows it when directed to a handful of products, among which it is worth mentioning milk and milk products, sheep meat and goat meat, and beef and veal.[68] The possibility to allocate coupled payments for animal food production led fourteen out of the sixteen countries which included coupled payments in their CAP Strategic Plans to spend the largest share of it to support livestock production.[69] Nonetheless, coupled payments provide a strong incentive to increase the supply of associated products, and the relationship between coupled payments and products' overallocation has long been demonstrated.[70] In the light of the environmental damage associated with a further expansion of the livestock sector, it can be stated that the CAP's introduction of coupled payments for animal food products represents a blatant demonstration of the EU legislator's will to prioritize European farmer's revenues over environmental sustainability considerations.

---

[65] Force Majeure is, *inter alia*, recognized in the case of 'the accidental destruction of livestock buildings on the holding' (Regulation 2021/2116, Article 3(1)(b)), and in the case of 'an epizootic, a plant disease outbreak or the presence of a plant pest affecting part or all of the beneficiary's livestock or crops' (Article 3(1)(c)).

[66] European Commission, Regulation (EU) 1308/2013, Article 8(a).

[67] European Commission, Regulation 2021/2117, Article 12(d)-12(e).

[68] European Commission, Regulation 2021/2115, Article 33.

[69] European Environmental Bureau (fn. 6). For more information on CAP Strategic Plans, look at E. Mezzacapo, "Mind the Gap: Assessing Member States' Implementation of Farm to Farm-to-Fork Targets within the 2023–2027 Common Agricultural Policy", in *Eur. J. Risk Regul.*, 2024.

[70] Balkhausen O., Banse M. and Grethe H., "Modelling CAP Decoupling in the EU: A Comparison of Selected Simulation Models and Results", in *J. Agric. Econ.*, 2008.

As it has been shown, despite its green claims, the CAP2023-2027 is particularly disappointing when it comes to the mitigation of livestock sector's environmental impact. As a matter of fact, not only basic conditionalities for direct payments (*i.e.*, GAECs and SRMs) do not enshrine any direct connection to the livestock sector, but also the allegedly more ambitious eco-schemes and AECMs miserably fail to do so. A further proof of the lack of environmental efficacy of the new CAP can be found once having analysed Member States' CAP Strategic Plans. Indeed, the lion's share of the schemes destined to the livestock sector has pointed at increasing animal welfare and it has mostly benefited those companies which were adopting extensive livestock practices already before the introduction of the new CAP, while largely ignoring the necessity to mitigate livestock-associated environmental damage.

Furthermore, the new CAP has not only disregarded the necessity to reduce livestock-related environmental pollution, but it has also introduced measures which aim at making the livestock sector economically more attractive and can finally result in an expansion of European animal food supply. Indeed, the special level of protection guaranteed to livestock sector-activities and products, as well as the possibility to maintain coupled payments for animal food production (which brough most EU States to direct the largest part of coupled payments towards the livestock sector) go in the direction of stimulating the economic development of the livestock sector, while definitely turning the back to the environmental sustainability objective.

Finally, it can be stated that it would be particularly hard to define the CAP's approach towards the livestock sector as sustainable, especially if the definition of sustainability of ecosystems is taken into consideration. Instead, the sustainability approach adopted by the EU legislator in this matter seems to be more oriented towards the prioritization of (short-term economic) development. Indeed, despite introducing parameters which are sensible to the livestock sector's GHG emissions and performance, the new CAP introduces no pollution reduction target associated to animal farming, neither when it comes to CAP specific objectives, conditionalities, or eco-schemes. It appears, then, that the new CAP does never turn environmental protection into a pre-requisite for livestock-related regulation. Instead, it results more focused on the sector's economic solidity, as it provides Member States with a number of instruments which are tailored for both securing the sector's stability and even making livestock production more profitable. Apparently, the new CAP does not favour a transition towards reduced animal food production levels, thus ignoring the impossibility to decouple livestock production from environmental degradation, and the necessity to lessen the environmental footprint of the European livestock sector.

It emerges that, in line with the conceptualization of sustainable development enshrined, *inter alia*, in the Brundtland Report, the new CAP does never acknowledge the impossibility to conciliate economic expansion with environmental sustainability, and it rather (implicitly) frames economic development as a precondition for the achievement of environmental recovery. The adoption of such an approach, however, might result particularly short-sighted when it comes to the regulation of the livestock sector. As a matter of fact, the prioritization of larger breeders' short-term economic interests over environmental considerations will not only undermine the sustainability of natural ecosystems, but it is also likely to impact the long-term economic sustainability of the European livestock and agri-food sector, whose productivity strongly depend on the health and resilience of those same ecosystems that, in a business-as-usual scenario, livestock sector activities might continue jeopardizing.

3. Addressing food waste

3.1. Food waste and its environmental impact

We shall now turn our attention to the issue of food waste and loss (hereafter, "food waste"), looking first and foremost at its environmental impact. Although this issue also affects the economic and social dimensions, it is the environmental dimension that should be considered as the parameter for understanding the sustainability approach adopted by the European legislator in the new CAP. On this regard, it is important to be aware that food waste is associated to direct and indirect environmental costs. The former is linked to methane (a particularly powerful greenhouse gas) produced by the food which is disposed of in landfills, which then pollutes natural resources such as water and soil, causing as well the loss of biodiversity. The latter, instead, refers to the resources needlessly used throughout the entire product's life cycle (*i.e.*, energy, water and land). Therefore, the later the food is wasted along the chain, the greater its environmental impact since more resources (both energy and natural ones) have been used in processing, transporting, storing, and cooking. Before getting to the core of the matter, it is necessary to make some qualitative and quantitative preliminary considerations so to value the reasons why the issue of food waste must be tackled.

Firstly, a single definition for food waste is still missing since it finds different declinations in international, EU and national legal frameworks. At the international level it is common to refer to the definition elaborated by the Food and Agricultural Organisation (FAO) (2011) according to which food loss (what occurs in the food supply chain prior to consumption) is distinct from food waste (retail-consumer level). At the EU level, instead, a highly general declination has been given which, interestingly enough, mainly tackles the environmental aspect.[71] In other terms, it is possible to observe the establishment of two different approaches: respectively, the *food*-focused approach and the *waste*-focused approach.[72] By avoiding the 'sharp demarcation of outlines or limits'[73] of this issue it comes without saying that it is not possible to adopt a single and efficient policy strategy. For instance, which phase of the food supply chain should be addressed? Which impacts have to be reduced? In which way?

The reason behind these uncertainties may be found in the fact that there is great disagreement on which elements are to be considered when talking about food waste. For example, some studies take into account edible and non-edible parts of food (*i.e.*, coffee grounds and egg shells)[74] while others only focus on the edible parts[75]; some distinguish between avoidable, possible avoidable, and unavoidable food waste originating from edible food parts,[76] while others also consider over-

---

[71] Article 3, Directive 2018/851/EU (the so-called "Waste Framework Directive", which amends the Directive 2008/98/EC) defines food waste as "all food as defined in Article 2 of Regulation (EC) 178/2002 of the European Parliament and of the Council that has become waste" and, according to the same article, waste is "any substance or object which the holder discards or intends or is required to discard". This definition has not been modified in the current consolidated version of the Directive (18.02.2024, available at https://eur-lex.europa.eu/legal-content/EN/TXT/PDF/?uri=CELEX:02008L0098-20240218. Accessed 2/09/2024).

[72] Maccioni G., *Spreco Alimentare – Regole e limiti nella transizione verso modelli agroalimentari sostenibili*, Giappichelli, 2018.

[73] Definition of 'definition' in Merriam-webster online dictionary, available at https://www.merriam-webster.com/dictionary/definition.

[74] Östergren K., Gustavsson J., Bos-Brouwers H., Timmermans T., Hansen O.-J., Møller H., Anderson G., O'Connor C., Soethoudt H. and Quested T. et al., *FUSIONS Definitional Framework for Food Waste*, Full Report, The Swedish Institute for Food and Biotechnology, 2014; Scherhaufer S., Moates G., Hartikainen H., Waldron K. and Obersteiner G., "Environmental impacts of food waste in Europe", in *Waste Manag.*, 2018, 77, 98-113; Caldeira C., De Laurentiis V., Corrado S., van Holsteijn F. and Sala S., "Quantification of food waste per product group along the supply chain in the European Union: A mass flow analysis", in *Resour. Conserv. Recycl.*, 2019, 149, 479-488.

[75] Thyberg K.L. and Tonjes D.J., "Drivers of food waste and their implications for sustainable policy development", in *Resour. Conserv. Recycl.*, 2016, 106, 110-123; Food and Agriculture Organization of the United Nations (FAO), *Global Food Losses and Food Waste. Extent, Causes and Prevention*, 2011.

[76] Monier V., Mudgal S., Escalon V., O'Connor C., Gibon T., Anderson G., Montoux H., Reisinger H., Dolley P. and Ogilvie S. et al., *Preparatory Study on Food Waste*

consumption.[77] Having said that, it becomes clear how challenging will be, for the European Union, to halve its *per capita* food waste (according to FUSIONS project (2016), FW amounts at 173 kg/year/capita[78]).[79] Indeed, the plethora of definitions makes food waste measurement particularly hard, and this prevents countries, companies and people from programming their investments and from taking sustainable decisions.

Secondly, nearly one third of the food produced for human consumption is lost or wasted globally.[80] This data is strictly linked to the following consideration (population growth) in the sense that the hunger issue can be addressed starting (and maybe ending) by preventing food to be discarded and equally distributing it throughout the world population. In fact, it has been assessed that halving food waste could meet the demand for food of the growing population.[81] Moreover, besides the social and economic impacts, food production requires the use of resources which, in the case of food waste, are employed inefficiently, further exaggerating the environmental problems related to agricultural production (*e.g.*, biodiversity loss, land use changes, greenhouse gas emissions).[82] In a glimpse, food loss and

Across EU 27: Final Report, European Commission (DG ENV), 2020; Quested T. and Johnson H., *Household Food and Drink Waste in the UK*, Final Report, 2009, WRAP.

[77] Alexander P. et. al., "Losses, inefficiencies and waste in the global food system", in *Agricultural Systems*, 2017, 153, 190-200; Smil S., "Improving Efficiency and Reducing Waste in Our food System", in *Environ. Sci.*, 2004, 1, 17-26.

[78] EU FUSIONS, Estimates of European food waste levels, 2016. https://www.eufusions.org/phocadownload/Publications/Estimates%20of%20European%20food%20waste%20levels.pdf.

[79] The EU is committed to the (legally non-binding) UN Sustainable Development Goal 12.3, according to which, "By 2030, halve per capita global food waste at the retail and consumer levels and reduce food losses along production and supply chains, including post-harvest losses"; see United Nations (UN). A/RES/70/1, Resolution adopted by the General Assembly on 25.09.2015. Transforming our World: The 2030 Agenda for Sustainable Development; United Nations, 2015.

[80] FAO, *The future of food and agriculture: trends and challenges*, 2017.

[81] Garske B. et. al., "Challenges of Food Waste Governance: An Assessment of European Legislation on Food Waste and Recommendations for Improvement by Economic Instruments", in *Land*, 2020, 9, 231.

[82] Intergovernmental Panel on Climate Change (IPCC). Climate Change and Land. An IPCC Special Report on Climate Change, Desertification, Land Degradation, Sustainable Land Management, Food Security, and Greenhouse Gas Fluxes in Terrestrial Ecosystems; Summary for Policymakers; IPCC Secretariat: Geneva, Switzerland, 2020 and European Commission. Communication from the Commission to the European Parliament, the Council, the European Economic and Social Committee and the Committee of the Regions: A Farm to Fork Strategy for a Fair, Healthy and Environmentally-Friendly Food System; COM (2020) 381 final from 20.05.2020; European Commission: Brussels, Belgium, 2020.

food waste globally cause the emission of 3.3 Gt CO_2 eq. every year (excluding emissions from land use change), they consume 250 km^3 of surface water and groundwater, and occupy 1.4 billion hectares of land, which is around one third of the global agricultural land area.[83]

Finally, there is the issue the population growth. Indeed, according to the FAO, the world's population is projected to grow to 9.7 billion by 2050.[84] Evidently, feeding the growing world population will constitute a global challenge, but the solution does not necessarily lie in increasing food production. Indeed, as previously stated, prevention of food waste and loss, redistribution, and fair accessibility to food represent the very solution to this worldwide dilemma.

In one word, fighting food waste is a triple win: it lowers the environmental and climate impact of food production and consumption, it saves food for human consumption, and it brings savings for primary producers, companies and consumers.

That being said, it should be clear that food waste does not only hinder the achievement of food security, but it also has several direct/indirect implications for multiple interlinked environmental impacts. In fact, a huge emission of GHGs, as well as a large use of fertile soil, fresh water, fertilisers and energy, are needed in order to produce food. Specifically, the IPCC estimates that more than one quarter of the anthropogenic greenhouse gas emissions are caused by agriculture, forestry, and other land use.[85] Therefore, the implementation of an efficient food waste management policy – alternative to an increase in food production – would highly decrease these negative environmental effects. According to the FAO, 4.4 Gt of CO_2 equivalents were related to food waste, (including land use change associated with the food wastage) which accounts for 8% of the total global anthropogenic greenhouse gas emissions.[86] If food waste were a country, it would be the third largest emitter in the world after China and the USA.[87] Globally, the major contributors to the carbon footprint of food waste are cereals (34%) and animal-derived products (21%), while the GHG emis-

---

[83] FAO, *Food wastage footprint. Impacts on natural resources. Food wastage footprint Impacts on natural resources*, 2013.

[84] FAO, *The future of food and agriculture: alternative pathways to 2050*, 2018.

[85] Intergovernmental Panel on Climate Change (IPCC), *Climate Change and Land. An IPCC Special Report on Climate Change, Desertification, Land Degradation, Sustainable Land Management, Food Security, and Greenhouse Gas Fluxes in Terrestrial Ecosystems*, Summary for Policymakers, IPCC Secretariat, 2020, 10.

[86] UNEP, *Food Waste Index Report 2021*, https://www.unep.org/resources/report/unep-food-waste-index-report-2021, 20.

[87] FAO, *Food Wastage Footprint & Climate Change*, 2017, 1.

sions per kilogram of product are particularly high for meat products.[88] In fact, as previously mentioned (§ 2.1.), animal-derived products have been associated with considerable resource wastage. A plethora of scientific studies highlight the resource-intensive production (in terms of land, fertilisers, and freshwater) of meat products. Therefore, even though meat products only account for a small share of the wasted food, their resource-intensity gives them a leading role in the context of food waste.[89] Conclusively, it is clear enough that key elements in the fight against climate change could be represented by the reduction of animal-derived food production[90] and the decrease of food waste.

3.2. Food waste regulation at the EU level: the role of the Green Deal

Food waste represents a global threat which therefore requires global action. The European effort can have a great impact in this regard since the EU plays a particularly active role in international environmental fora. In fact, the EU may generate an important change in the global volume of food waste thanks to the several policies it elaborates and implements (*i.e.*, the CAP, the Common Fisheries Policy, the waste policy and the food safety policy).

To understand what conception of sustainability the new CAP is closest to, it might be helpful to start by analyzing the European strategies stemming from the GD. Indeed, the GD and the CAP are linked by a close connection, as the CAP represents the instrument through which several GD's objectives may be achieved.[91]

As previously stated (§ 1), the GD resets the Commission's commitment to tackle climate and environmental challenges, while aiming to achieve climate neutrality by 2050, *inter alia*, by decoupling economic growth from re-

---

[88] Istituto Superiore per la Protezione e Ricerca Ambientale (ISPRA), *Spreco alimentare: un approccio sistemico per la prevenzione e la riduzione strutturali*, 2018, 122.

[89] FAO, *The State of Food and Agriculture 2019. Moving Forward on Food Loss and Waste Reduction*, 2019.

[90] Garnett T., "Where are the best opportunities for reducing greenhouse gas emissions in the food system (including the food chain)?", in *Food Policy*, 2011, 36 (Suppl. 1), S23-S32, 29 and Vanham D. et. al., "Lost water and nitrogen resources due to EU consumer food waste", in *Environ. Res. Lett.*, 10, 2015, 1-16; Weishaupt A. et al., "Land Use, Livestock, Quantity Governance, and Economic Instruments – Sustainability Beyond Big Livestock Herds and Fossil Fuels", in *Sustainability*, 2020, 12, 2053, 7-8.

[91] Analysis of links between CAP Reform and Green Deal, Commission Staff Working Document, 20th of may 2020, SWD (2020) 93 final.

source use. It is a regulatory project with high ambitions that promotes the sustainable development rationale and approach [92], aiming to implement the Agenda 2030. [93] Within the GD Communication, the Commission's awareness of the need to tackle food waste clearly emerges. In fact, it is stated that 'Food production still results in air, water and soil pollution, contributes to the loss of biodiversity and climate change, and consumes excessive amounts of natural resources, while an important part of food is wasted'. The Commission is also concerned about the fact that 'A sustainable product policy also has the potential to reduce waste significantly. Where waste cannot be avoided, its economic value must be recovered and its impact on the environment and on climate change avoided or minimized'. [94]

Having said that, among the several strategies set by the GD, the most relevant for the analysis of the food waste case are the Farm to Fork Strategy (F2F) [95] and the New Action Plan for Circular Economy (CEAP) [96]. More precisely, only the former strategy shyly tackles food waste, while the latter directly refers to the F2F, being the tool addressing the food system.

The fact that the CEAP avoids from facing in a structured way the food waste issue might be considered as a bizarre gap. In fact, the very idea of circularity may be considered as sharing its rationale with the issue of food waste. More precisely, an integral and groundbreaking concept within circular economy, rooted in industrial ecology, emphasizes the incorporation of waste into the industrial process, either as a material or energy flow, at the end of its life. Otherwise stated, different scenarios can be described which take into consideration agricultural by-products or food waste in general so to transform it into biogas and energy. [97] This integration in

---

[92] In Part One of the Communication, the Commission declares that "The Green Deal is an integral part of this Commission's strategy to implement the United Nation's 2030 Agenda and the sustainable development goals". Furthermore, in Part Three, the one promoting the EU as a global leader, it is often stated the will to enhance the sustainable development. For instance, in the very first paragraph of this Part it is said that "It will develop a stronger 'green deal diplomacy' focused on convincing and supporting others to take on their share of promoting more sustainable development".

[93] Resolution A/RES/70/1, adopted by the General Assembly of the United Nations on 25th of September 2015. This plan of action is made up of 17 goals and 169 targets among which there is the aim to tackle food waste. Specifically, within the goal n. 12 (Responsible consumption and production) there is the target 12.3 which states that '*By 2030, halve per capita global food waste at the retail and consumer levels and reduce food losses along production and supply chains, including post-harvest losses*'.

[94] COM (2019) 640 final.

[95] COM 381/2020.

[96] COM 98/2020.

[97] Hoehn D., Margallo M., Laso J., García-Herrero I, Bala A., Fullana-I-Palmer P.,

product and process design aims to create a closed material and energy cycle, maximizing the utilization of waste while minimizing reliance on virgin materials and the release of environmentally harmful substances [98].

Additionally, the very circularity approach is to be achieved not only by improving circularity, but also by decreasing the resource use. [99] Otherwise stated, 'to achieve a more sustainable economy, it is insufficient to only increase recycling […], but it is essential to also achieve absolute reductions in resource extraction and consumption, that is, to downsize the socioeconomic metabolism'. [100] According to this rationale, food waste prevention and management represents, once again, the solution. In fact, referring to the Zero Waste Europe Report [101], it is visibly suggested the reduction of the size of the circle by adopting 'waste prevention targets (a general one but also a sector specific)' and 'legally binding food waste reduction targets in line with the farm to fork strategy'.

Moving to the analysis of the F2F, it may be interesting to highlight the focus of this Strategy on the social dimensions of sustainability, which is just one of the three dimensions taken into consideration by the European Commission. This narrow view can be considered peculiar if food waste needs to be addressed holistically, considering also the other negative impacts, specifically the environmental ones.

Moreover, the F2F Strategy is equally questionable when considering the Commission's commitment in 'halving *per capita* food waste at the *retail and consumer level* by 2030'. Indeed, when talking about the adoption of a

---

Irabien Á. and Aldaco R., "Energy embedded in food loss management and in the production of uneaten food: seeking a sustainable pathway", in *Energies*, 2019, 12 (4), 767; see also Gaglio M., Tamburini E., Lucchesi F., Aschonitis V., Atti A., Castaldelli G. and Fano E.A., "Life cycle assessment of maize-germ oil production and the use of bioenergy to mitigate environmental impacts: a gate-to-gate case study", in *Resources*, 2019,8 (2), 60.

[98] Martins de Oliveira M. et al., "Food loss and waste in the context of the circular economy: a systematic review", in *J. Clean. Prod.*, 2021, 294, 126284. For a literature review on the topic of circular economy, see Ghisellini P., Cialani C. and Ulgiati S., "A review on circular economy: the expected transition to a balanced interplay of environmental and economic systems", in *J. Clean. Prod.*, 2016, 114, 11-32.

[99] Zero Waste Europe, *Zero Waste Europe Response to the New Circular Economy Action Plan Consultation*, Position Briefing, 2020, 4, available at https://zerowasteeurope.eu/wp-content/uploads/2020/01/zero_waste_europe_policybriefing_response-to-the-new-ce-action-plan_en.pdf.

[100] Meyer A. et al., "Measuring Progress towards a Circular Economy: A Monitoring Framework for Economy-wide Material Loop Closing in the EU28", in *J. Ind. Ecol.*, 2019, 23, 1, 63.

[101] Zero Waste Europe, *Zero Waste Europe Response to the New Circular Economy Action Plan Consultation*, cit., 4.

holistic approach, it is important not only to tackle the problem considering all the dimensions affected by food waste (*i.e.,* economic, environmental and social), but also to keep into account the entire food supply chain. In other terms, in spite of the very title of this Strategy, food waste is not tackled from the farm to the fork, but only at the retail and consumer level, thus leaving aside the primary production level and the early stages of the supply chain. This gap seems to be inexcusable if considering the several studies revealing that 30% [102] to 59% [103] of Europe's total food waste occurs at the pre-retail stage.

Not only this restriction seems to be in contrast with the general *modus operandi* of the F2F Strategy, but also with further EU policies, missing the original purpose of ensuring a sustainable transition. Indeed, at least in theory, this very Strategy aims at realizing a sustainable food system which can be fulfilled only through a holistic approach. Moreover, what may really jump to the sight is the partial reference to the UN SDG 12.3 according to which the European Union committed to halve *per capita* food waste at the consumer level *and* to 'reduce food loss along production and supply chains, including post-harvest losses'. Finally, a lack of coherence may be found when comparing the F2F to Article 9(1)(g) of the Waste Framework Directive (WFD) [104] which, once again, promotes the reduction of food waste along the entire supply chain.

A further consideration referred to the F2F must be done in relation to the valorization of food waste. The Directive 2018/851/CE (WFD) establishes that food waste must be managed following the so-called waste hierarchy [105] according to which there has to be prevention of food waste, preparing for re-use, recycling, other recovery and, as a last option, disposal. The first step can be achieved both by encouraging 'food donation and other redistribution for human consumption' or by using food as an-

---

[102] EU FUSIONS, *Estimates of European food waste levels*, 2016 available at https://www.eufusions.org/phocadownload/Publications/Estimates%20of%20European%20food%20waste%20levels.pdf.

[103] FAO, *Global Food Losses and Food Waste*, 2011, available at http://www.fao.org/3/mb060e/mb060e.pdf.

[104] This concept has not been modified in the current consolidated version of the Directive (18.02.2024, available at https://eur-lex.europa.eu/legal-content/EN/TXT/PDF/?uri=CELEX:02008L0098-20240218. Accessed 2/09/2024).

[105] Though the five-level waste hierarchy has been considered as a revolutionary attempt, it is difficult not to observe that this tool focuses on waste, not on *food* waste. Therefore, the European Court of Auditors proposed a different hierarchy, structured on six levels and clearly referred to food waste: prevention, donation, use as animal feed (until this step, food still does not constitute waste), recycling (e.g., for industrial uses), other recovery (e.g., for energy production) and disposal.

imal feed (giving priority to 'human use over animal feed'). Focusing on the 'animal feed' solution, a study conducted by the European Environment Bureau[106] highlighted a change of strategy by the Commission. A first draft of the F2F Strategy proposed to 'review the feed ban rules for feed for non-ruminant animals (in particular pigs and poultry) as well as certain rules of the Animal By-Products Regulation in order to promote more circularity and better valorization of animal by-products while safeguarding animal and human health'. Unfortunately, this section was eliminated from the final version, thus canceling the vast benefits which would have risen from reducing the European reliance on soya driving deforestation 'to decoupling feed supply chain from global commodity markets to reducing feed costs driving ever more intensive and damaging livestock farming practices'.[107]

Finally, these overarching considerations surely suggest that food waste represents a global challenge that needs to be urgently tackled. Nonetheless, the tools implemented by the EU legislator do not seem to be so decisive and the obligations that Member States must take are still vague as if the underlying problem was not extremely crucial. Important steps still must be taken. For instance, provided that many years have passed since the implementation of a European waste policy, a stronger harmonization through the adoption of a Regulation – instead of the Directive – could be advisable, so to oblige every single Member State to adopt serious action. Moreover, a clear and precise definition of food waste still has to be elaborated and no sanctions are established in case of lack of achievement of fixed food waste reduction goals. Finally, only partial considerations can be done since the WFD is now going through a revision phase and the EU Commission has announced in the F2F Strategy the adoption, by the end of 2023, of the 'legally binding targets to reduce food waste across the EU'.[108] Specifically, in July 2023, the European Commission proposed a

---

[106] The European Environmental Bureau (EEB), *Tackling food waste in the Farm to Fork strategy*, NGO letter, 2020, 7.

[107] For more details on the GHG emissions savings, other benefits, and safety aspects, see Bowman M. and Luyckx K., *Avoiding food waste through feeding surplus food to omnivorous non-ruminant livestock*, 2019, EU Horizon 2020 REFRESH available at https://eu-refresh.org/avoiding-food-waste-through-feeding-surplus-food-omnivorous-non-ruminant-livestock.

[108] European Commission. Communication from the Commission to the European Parliament, the Council, the European Economic and Social Committee and the Committee of the Regions: A Farm to Fork Strategy for a Fair, Healthy and Environmentally-Friendly Food System; COM (2020) 381 final from 20.05.2020; European Commission: Brussels, Belgium, 2020. For further information, check https://food.ec.europa.eu/safety/food-waste/eu-actions-against-food-waste/food-waste-reduction-targets_en.

revision of the Waste Framework Directive, introducing legally binding targets for reducing food waste[109]. Under this proposal, Member States were required to achieve a 10% reduction in food waste at the processing and manufacturing levels, and a 30% reduction at the retail and consumption stages. However, in March 2024, the European Parliament voted to increase these binding targets to 20% for processing and manufacturing, and 40% for retail and consumer sectors.[110] Subsequently, in June 2024, the Council adopted its position on the revised Waste Framework Directive.[111] These targets will likely strengthen the European commitment, while awaiting the further steps to be taken by the EU.

3.3. Which sustainability approach from the new CAP?

The history and the context of the CAP have notably changed throughout the years due to several factors. Not only there has been a shift from the product support to the producer support, but also an important transformation in socio-economic, environmental, and institutional terms has occurred. For instance, only recently, there have been events as the Brexit, the significant budgetary cuts as proposed in the MFF 2021-2027, the changing composition of the European Parliament and Commission, the quickening of global warming with life-threatening temperatures and serious natural disasters over the course of the last years, the outbreak of the Covid-19 pandemic and, last but not least, the war in Ukraine.[112]

From a food waste perspective, some improvements have occurred since this issue is evidently taken into consideration. For instance, Article 6 of Regulation 2021/2115, states that 'The achievement of the general objec-

---

[109] Proposal for a Directive of the European Parliament and of the Council amending Directive 2008/98/EC on waste, COM(2023) 420 final, available at https://eur-lex.europa.eu/resource.html?uri=cellar:05b634bd-1b4e-11ee-806b-01aa75ed71a1.0001.02/DOC_1&format=PDF. Last access on 2/09/2024. Accessed 2/09/2024.

[110] https://www.europarl.europa.eu/news/en/press-room/20240308IPR19011/meps-call-for-tougher-eu-rules-to-reduce-textiles-and-food-waste#:~:text=They%20propose%20higher%20binding%20waste,households%20(instead%20of%2030%25). Accessed 2 September 2024.

[111] General Secretariat of the Council: *Proposal for a Directive of the European Parliament and of the Council amending Directive 2008/98/EC on waste - General approach, 11300/24,* available at https://data.consilium.europa.eu/doc/document/ST-11300-2024-INIT/en/pdf. Accessed 2/09/2024.

[112] Massot Marti A., *Research for AGRI Committee – The Farm to Fork Strategy Implications for Agriculture and the CAP*, European Parliament, Policy Department for Structural and Cohesion Policies, 2020.

tives (Article 5) shall be pursued through the following specific objectives[113]: […] *i)* to improve the response of Union agriculture […] to reduce food waste […]'. Furthermore, Article 201a, n.1 of Regulation 2021/2117 states that agreements, decisions, and concerted practices regarding agricultural products which aim to apply a sustainability standard higher than mandated by the Union or national law do not fall under the prohibition of the competition clause. At No. 3, it specifies that "sustainability standard" means a standard which aims to contribute to one or more of the listed objectives, among which there is the transition to a circular economy, including the reduction of food waste. Therefore, food waste management is concretely understood as a tool to achieve sustainability.

In addition, the transition to the producer-support system has decreased overproduction, probably contributing to the decrease in food waste. However, at the same time, coupled payments stimulate the production of specific products for which it may happen that there is no – or low – demand.[114] In contrast, the market intervention measures (*i.e.,* public intervention, private storage, market withdrawals, green harvesting and non-harvesting) may cause threats as well. In fact, products may either be stored until there is an increase in market price and then returned to the market for sale, donation or export, or may be placed differently (*e.g.*, destroyed). Also, not to be underestimated is the "price factor". Especially when talking about fruit and vegetables, their generally low price can lead to over purchasing[115]. Therefore, these measures may directly cause food waste and it would be convenient to assess their potential impact on the generation or prevention of food waste.[116]

In other terms, the CAP can help reduce food waste and loss by encouraging better production and processing practices (*e.g.*, through the use of technologies to extend the shelf life of perishable products) or by supporting initiatives that transform traditional production-use-disposal consumption patterns into a circular bioeconomy. Examples include the reuse of products that are still edible for feed use or no longer edible for self-composting, or

[113] According to the Regulation 2021/2115, there are 9 specific objectives which can be divided in three categories based on the dimension addressed: economic (letters a, b, c), environmental (letters d, e, f) and social dimension (letters g, h, i).

[114] European Court of Auditors (ECA), *Combating Food Waste: An Opportunity for the EU to Improve the Resource-Efficiency of the Food Supply Chain*, Special Report No. 34/2016; European Court of Auditors, 2016, 25.

[115] Caldeira C., De Laurentiis V., Corrado S., van Holsteijn F. and Sala S., "Quantification of food waste per product group along the supply chain in the European Union: A mass flow analysis", in *Resour. Conserv. Recycl.*, 2019, 149, 479-488.

[116] *Ibidem*, 29.

the adoption of the Product Environmental Footprint (PEF) method for determining the environmental footprint of products.[117]

In this regard, it is worth noting that Article 39, § 1, lett. a) of the TFEU[118] – which establishes that one of the CAP's objectives is 'to *increase* agricultural productivity [...] by ensuring the *rational development* of agricultural production and the *optimum utilisation* of the factors of production [...]' – has been interpreted in line with environmental exigencies. As Bolognini underlines,[119] the unamended version of this norm must be read in conjunction with Art. 11 TFEU, according to which the Union's policies and activities must be guided by environmental protection requirements. In the light of this, it seems possible to view food waste reduction as a tangible accomplishment of this need. At the same time, considering the following observations, it is questionable whether the new CAP has actually materialised this environmentally oriented interpretation.

In fact, another interesting consideration can be done referring to Article 7 of Regulation 2021/2115 which has to be read together with the Annex I of the same Regulation. As previously explained (§ 2.3), this Article rules common indicators which must be used to evaluate the achievement of the specific objectives (Article 6). In accordance with Article 6, 1(i), the reduction of food waste is one of these, together with the achievement of other food and health demands (*i.e.,* high-quality, safe and nutritious food). Though, when it comes to the Annex I, the impact and result indicators referred to the specific objective ruled in Article 6(1)(i) do not mention food waste but only refer to antimicrobial, quality food, and animal welfare. This points to the conclusion that the evaluation of food waste's impact is not fulfilled at all. A question arises: how can Members States be exhorted to pursue such an objective if there is no interest in evaluating the achievement of food waste reduction? This seems a missed opportunity.

A similar reflection may be done when it comes to the good agricultural and environmental conditions of land (GAEC standards) and the Statutory Management Requirements (SMR).[120] Also these instruments have been

---

[117] Voluntary national scheme for assessing and reporting the environmental footprint of products «Made Green in Italy», based on the PEF methodology as defined in the recommendation 179/2013/UE, https://www.minambiente.it/pagina/made-green-italy.

[118] European Union, *Consolidated version of the Treaty on the Functioning of the European Union*, 13 December 2007, 2008/C 115/01, available at: https://eur-lex.europa.eu/legal-content/EN/TXT/PDF/?uri=CELEX:12012E/TXT, accessed 2 September 2024.

[119] Bolognini S., "PAC, sostenibilità e bioeconomia", in Marini S. and Rubino V. (a cura di), *La sostenibilità in agricoltura e la riforma della PAC*, Cacucci, 2021, 85.

[120] Cfr. Annex III of Regulation 2115/2021.

previously described (§ 2.3.) as the tools that make up the system of conditionality under which farmers and other beneficiaries may receive direct payments for implementing practices aimed at achieving more ambitious environmental objectives. Among the three designated areas, food waste is not mentioned. Indeed, although the reader could *prima facie* believe that it is taken into consideration within the 'climate and the environment, including water, soil, and biodiversity of ecosystems', this is really not the case. Nonetheless, food waste management surely represents a viable path to achieve the mitigation of (and adaptation to) climate change. Finally, the same consideration may be done when dealing with the 'echo-schemes'. [121] Indeed, while this specific direct payment is issued when farmers voluntarily commit to achieving climate, environmental, and animal welfare objectives, food waste management is, again, a great absent.

From this analysis, two opposite possible explanations may arise. On the one hand, there could be a fake commitment from the EU legislator which randomly refers to food waste as to an issue to overcome, but without really believing in the potential of managing and preventing it. On the other hand, instead, addressing this global challenge could be seen as inherently aligning with the logic of the CAP. Arguably, by proving the implementation of food waste management practices, the farmers may in any case receive these direct/annual payments. Otherwise stated, if food waste management represents the key solution to reduce food production – and all the negative impacts coming from this activity – could the proof of its implementation be sufficient to become entitled to such payments? If this is not so, which are the tools that the European legislator adopts to encourage the prevention of food waste?

Following this short overarching assessment of the CAP related to food waste, a conclusive statement regarding the type of sustainability adopted by the EU can be expressed. In doing so, it is noteworthy that food waste is mentioned only in two out of the three Regulations ruling the CAP. In one case (Regulation 2021/2115, Article 6), this topic is treated with reference to the nine specific objectives which can be divided in three categories based on the three pillars of sustainable development and food waste is part of the social dimension. This setting seems to be confirmed also by reading the Whereas 35 according to which 'The CAP [...] should help to improve the response of Union agriculture to new *societal* demands on food and health, including sustainable agricultural production, healthier

[121] To deepen the study of the direct payments system, see de Meo E. et al., "Il nuovo Sistema dei pagamenti diretti nella riforma della PAC 2023-2027", in *Riv. Dir. Agr.*, 2022, 2, 274-288.

nutrition, animal welfare and reduction of food waste […]' (basically it repeats what is stated in the mentioned Article). In the second case (Regulation 2021/2117, Article 201a, n.3), food waste is addressed as an economic-environmental element in the sense that it is mentioned as something that guarantees the transition to a circular economy, within the context of the clause of competition. Conclusively, it seems that the European approach is still oriented on a sustainable development since food waste causes and is caused by economic, social and environmental drivers along the entire food supply chain. This means that the environmental dimension is not considered, once again, as something prominent. Nonetheless, by saying so, there is no intention to criticize this approach but only to highlight it. In fact, as it has been already stated throughout this study, the food waste issue affects several dimensions and, therefore, has to be tackled holistically.

In other terms, the structure outlined in the several legal acts and strategies, at least when dealing with food waste, still seems highly fragmentated and the environmental dimension of this issue does not even emerge in the new CAP, nor in the F2F Strategy. Indeed, food waste is considered as a social issue especially in the F2F and as a social-economic problem in the CAP. The only case in which the environmental sphere is considered (the WFD), it is still questionable, in the sense that there are no specific rules addressing *food* waste, but only waste. Thus, it might seem that the environmental dimension of food waste is only to be understood in an indirect and casual manner, not as something intentionally ruled as such by the EU legislator. In this sense, it currently may seem that the negative environmental consequences caused by a bad food waste management are not strongly addressed by the EU legislator. The environmental dimension seems the weak pillar of the sustainable development approach. While on the theoretical level we can be satisfied (in the legal framework analysed there is a clear awareness of the urge to tackle food waste), the same cannot be said when referring to the practical level, which is still lagging behind (Annex I, SMR, GAEC). This inevitably also has repercussions on the environment.

4. Conclusions: ecosystem sustainability is still *so far away, so far I just can't see*

The European legislation is a continuously evolving process characterized by the pursuit of often conflicting goals in which there is certainly an effort towards the achievement of climate objectives. However, it still (too) often comes to terms with market rules in a way that does not benefit the sustainability needs, especially when it comes to environmental ones.

Against this background, this study has adopted an EU wide scope of analysis to understand at which point of the sustainability continuum the new CAP, as delineated by EU legislators, can be situated. Arguably, the disciplines ruling the livestock and the food waste areas already underscore the urgency to implement a sustainability transition. Indeed, the EU legislator has acknowledged that the adverse environmental (together with the social and economic) impacts caused by these activities need to be reduced and that, accordingly, sustainability should be conceived as a main objective in the process of transformation of the European food system. Nonetheless, as this study has acknowledged, in the light of the wide array of declinations that the concept of sustainability can assume, the mere effort to classify the CAP 2023-2027 as either sustainable or not could scarcely contribute to a better understanding of its capacity to lessen the environmental impact of European food systems while dealing with the tensions existing between environmental, social, and economic issues.

Otherwise stated, the decoding key of the text is not to be found through a black and white approach (*i.e.*, whether the CAP approach is either sustainable or not, or whether the EU legislator is pursuing either the sustainable development or the ecological sustainability paradigm) but in a more nuanced question: what kind of sustainability is the EU pursuing? The sustainability discourse cannot be built in a dualistic manner, but rather in a pluralistic way. Sustainability is a multidimensional concept whose precise boundaries have never been made explicit in any legal or policy document either at the EU or international level.

What emerges from our analysis is that the CAP and the GD, at least when it comes to addressing both the livestock and food waste issues, are representative of this outlook: sustainability is the declared objective to be reached, but elements as ecological primacy and ecosystems safety still seem to be overshadowed. The need to establish environmentally sound and climate-oriented regulatory frameworks governing the agri-food sector is well recognized, but this awareness is not followed by the identification, design, and implementation of measures which could credibly contribute to the realization of the objectives at stake. Indeed, measures enshrined in the new CAP identify path-dependant, incremental, and growth-oriented instruments aimed at aligning livestock and food waste activities with the EU climate neutrality objective, in the name of the economic benefit that they will bring about, and in spite of the lack of scientific evidence about their environmental effectiveness.

The CAP 2023-2027 is particularly close to the sustainable development approach, at least when it comes to the way in which livestock and food waste are regulated. The pursuit of a European food system aligning with the sustainability of ecosystem paradigm still seems to be far: at best it has blurred boundaries and at worst it may lead to a backsliding.

Part 2

THE ENERGY TRANSITION

Chapter 3

THE QUEST FOR A SUSTAINABLE ENERGY TRANSITION: THE CASE OF BIOENERGY

Matteo Greco

ABSTRACT: *This Chapter explores the integration of ecological sustainability into the energy regulatory framework. It highlights the critical role of bioenergy in the energy transition, emphasizing its dual potential to contribute to decarbonization while posing ecological risks, particularly through habitat and biodiversity loss. The analysis of sustainability criteria, as outlined in European directives, examines their effectiveness in safeguarding ecosystem health while supporting climate neutrality. Despite progress, the Chapter underscores the necessity of further aligning renewable energy regulations with ecological sustainability to avoid conflicts between energy and ecological transitions.*

KEYWORDS: *Energy transition – Ecological sustainability – Bioenergy – Sustainability criteria.*

1. Integrating ecological sustainability in the energy regulatory framework

Decarbonizing the energy system is a key element of the European Green Deal:[1] it represents the core of the so-called energy transition, which requires an increase in energy efficiency and significantly higher shares of energy from renewable sources within an integrated energy system. Carbon-neutral solutions, however, may have negative impacts on ecosystem health and integrity. This is precisely the case of renewable energies. Their deployment contributes to operationalize and achieve climate neutrality within the energy sector, but it is not necessarily capable of preserving or restoring ecosystem chemical and bio-physical conditions, as well as their structural functions over time.[2]

---

[1] COM (2020) 640, 6.

[2] See, in particular, the New EU Forest Strategy for 2030, COM (2021) 572.

The challenge is thus to achieve an ecologically sustainable[3] energy transition, to reconcile the development of renewable energies with the health and integrity of ecosystems. This is particularly true in relation to bioenergy, which is a form of energy generated from biomass.[4] In fact, while bioenergy can be considered as climate-friendly – to the extent that produced taking into account the biomass carbon-cycle, as it will be better explained below – the extraction of biomass for energy purpose can obviously result in habitat and biodiversity loss, causing the disruption of ecological processes and affecting the ecosystem health. The issue is specifically addressed by the *sustainability criteria* set by Directive (EU) 2018/2001,[5] whose fulfillment is a precondition for qualifying bioenergy as renewable for the purposes of the energy transition.

By discussing such *sustainability criteria*, recently revised by Directive (EU) 2023/2413[6], as part of the Fit for 55 package, this Chapter aims at verifying the degree of penetration of ecosystem sustainability within the European energy regulatory framework. In particular, the following questions will be addressed: to what extent are the *sustainability criteria* actually capable of guaranteeing ecosystem health and integrity? What is the overall assessment of their design and functioning? The discussion is organized as follows. The Chapter opens with a brief discussion of bioenergy, its role for the energy transition and the ways in which its production can conflict with the objective of ecosystem sustainability (§ 2). Then, it focusses on the *sustainability criteria* and their recent normative development linked to the Green Deal implementation process (§ 3). Finally, some concluding remarks are presented (§ 4).

---

[3] On the relevance of *ecological sustainability* in the Green Deal, see Chiti E., "Managing the Ecological Transition of the EU: The European Green Deal as a Regulatory Process", in *CMLRev.*, 2022, 59, 34-35. The Biodiversity Strategy 2030 explicitly takes the issue into consideration by stating that "the EU will prioritize solutions such as ocean energy, offshore wind (which also allows for fish stock regeneration), solar-panel farms that provide biodiversity-friendly soil cover, and sustainable bioenergy".

[4] Biomass is any kind of biogenic materials, such as wood, food crops, waste from forests or farm, excluding material embedded in geological formations and transformed to fossils.

[5] Directive (EU) 2018/2001 of the European Parliament and of the Council of 11 December 2018 on the promotion of the use of energy from renewable sources (Red II).

[6] Directive (EU) 2023/2413 of the European Parliament and of the Council of 18 October 2023 amending Directive (EU) 2018/2001, Regulation (EU) 2018/1999 and Directive 98/70/EC as regards the promotion of energy from renewable sources and repealing Council Directive (EU) 2015/652.

2. Bioenergy: on the edge of two environmental crises

Bioenergy is an extremely broad term describing the form of energy, used for electricity, heat or transport, generated from biomass.[7] Bioenergy production is a type of bioeconomy, a term referring to all those economic activities whose productive cycle is mainly based on the use of renewable biological resources (animals, plants, micro-organisms, and derived biomass, including organic waste).[8] It plays a key role for the energy transition, since both the International Energy Agency (IEA) and the Intergovernmental Panel for Climate Change (IPCC) consider it an indispensable renewable for the effective achievement of the net-zero target by 2050, in line with the requirements of the UN Paris Agreement.[9] Actually, bioenergy produced from agricultural, forestry and organic waste feedstock continues to be the main source of renewable energy in the EU, accounting for about 59% of renewable energy consumption in 2021,[10] contributing to heat, power and fuel production. Additionally, "unlike many renewables, biomass provides a storable energy solution and can be used within the existing fossil infrastructure",[11]

---

[7] Article 2, paras. 1-24, of Directive (EU) 2018/2001. More specifically, biofuels are solid, liquid or gases fuel produced from biomass through advanced conversion technologies, like fermentation and gasification. For example, biodiesel is produced from vegetable oils and animal fats or waste. For an overview of the major technical aspects of biofuels, including the generations of biomass feedstocks, types of biofuels, and the main conversion technologies applied to generate the biofuels from biomass see Zaky A.S., Moirangthem K. and Wahid R., "Biofuels: An Overview", in Abomohra A. E., Wang Q. and Huang J. (eds.), *Waste-to-Energy*, Springer, 2022, 85-144.

[8] See EU Commission, *A bioeconomy strategy for Europe – Working with nature for a more sustainable way of living*, Publications Office, 2013, available at https://data.europa.eu/doi/10.2777/17708, and *A sustainable bioeconomy for Europe – Strengthening the connection between economy, society and the environment: updated bioeconomy strategy*, Publications Office, 2018, available at https://data.europa.eu/doi/10.2777/792130.

[9] United Nations, Framework Convention on Climate Change (UNFCCC) of 12 December 2015, UN Doc FCCC/CP/2015/L9/Rev/1 ('Paris Agreement').

[10] EU Commission, *Report from the Commission to the European Parliament, the Council, the European Economic and Social Committee and the Committee of the Regions – State of the Energy Union Report 2023*, SWD (2023) 646 final: "For bioenergy, primary solid biofuels represent the largest share at 70.3%. Liquid biofuels account for 12.9%, biogas/ bio-methane for 10.1% and renewable share of municipal waste for 6.6%. In the EU, woody biomass is the main feedstock reported for solid biomass production (labelled as "forest biomass" in the figure below), accounting for 66% of the total and followed by biomass from organic waste (26%) and agricultural biomass (8%)". See also the date presented in the *IEA Tracking reports*, available at https://www.iea.org/reports/bioenergy.

[11] Kouchaki-Penchah H., Levasseur A., Bahn O. and Vaillancourt K., "The contri-

which makes it extremely useful to accelerate the transition toward a carbon neutral energy system.

Despite its extreme versatility and widespread use, however, bioenergy poses several challenges to ecosystem health.

First, the extraction of biomass for energy can cause a reduction in natural carbon sinks and stocks, an ecosystem service essential for the purpose of climate neutrality. Indeed, unlike solar or wind power, bioenergy production is not an inherently zero-emission process. For example, when forest biomass is burned for heating or electricity, the carbon absorbed through photosynthesis is released into the atmosphere; the overall process can be considered carbon neutral provided that the amount of forest biomass harvested for energy is offset by the production of an equivalent amount of wood.

For this reason, bioenergy carbon neutrality is envisaged by the Land Use, Land Use Change and Forestry (LULUCF) regulation, [12] which specifically aims at protecting and strengthening the capacity of soil ecosystems to continuously provide their essential services, including the capacity to store and sink carbon. In particular, the LULUCF regulation considers biomass production as a reduction in natural carbon stocks. [13] Accordingly, accounting for the same amount of CO_2 as both an emission within the energy sector and a negative variation in natural carbon stocks would lead to unjustified duplication: "any additional wood harvested for bioenergy purposes (or a greater energy use of wood) may reduce fossil fuel emissions under the ETS or effort sharing sectors but will also generate a carbon debit in LULUCF if it brings emissions beyond the forest reference level (FRL)". [14] However, according to the fundamental "no debt"

---

bution of forest-based bioenergy in achieving deep decarbonization: Insights for Quebec (Canada) using a TIMES approach", in *Energy Convers. Manag.*, 2022, 252, 1.

[12] Regulation (EU) 2018/841 of the European Parliament and of the Council of 30 May 2018 on the inclusion of greenhouse gas emissions and removals from land use, land use change and forestry in the 2030 climate and energy framework and amending Regulation (EU) 525/2013 and Decision 529/2013/EU (LULUCF Regulation).

[13] This approach is adopted by the IPCC guidelines for national GHG inventories (IPCC 2006, 2019) and by the UNFCCC for the accounting under the Paris Agreement.

[14] Camia A., Giuntoli J., Jonsson K., Robert N., Cazzaniga N., Jasinevičius G., Avitabile V., Grassi G., Barredo Cano J.I. and Mubareka S., *The use of woody biomass for energy production in the EU*, Publications Office of the European Union, 2020, 9.

According to Article 3, paras. 1-7 of Regulation (EU) 2018/841, "Forest Reference Level" (FRL) means "an estimate, expressed in tonnes of CO_2 equivalent per year, of the average annual net emissions or removals resulting from managed forest land within the territory of a Member State". The acronym "ETS" stands for Emission Trading System, and it is a regulatory approach to control GHG emissions. The ETS works by as-rule, [15] which requires Member States to ensure that accounted greenhouse gas emissions from land use are fully compensated by an equivalent removal, the impact of GHG emissions caused by the use of bioenergy may never result in an increase that exceeds the related removals.

Furthermore, and most importantly, the expansion of bioenergy crops often leads to indirect land use change (ILUC), including the conversion of forests, grasslands, or wetlands. This can result in habitat and biodiversity loss, affecting ecosystem health and ultimately causing the disruption of ecological processes. After all, biomass is a soil ecosystem service and its uncontrolled use as raw material for bioenergy production can compromise ecosystem well-functioning. Admittedly, this might seem somewhat paradoxical: a renewable energy functional for decarbonizing the energy sector but at the same time threatening to the health of the ecosystem. Yet, this mismatch is not limited to bioenergy but characterizes the dynamics of the entire energy transition. [16]

In this perspective, the Commission has effectively pointed out that "bioenergy sits at the nexus of two of the main environmental crises of the 21st century, the biodiversity and climate emergencies", [17] highlighting that bioenergy may be part of the solution only if produced in an ecological sustainable way. Moreover, the New Forestry Strategy 2030 expressly requires producing biomass for energy "taking into account the Union's carbon sink and biodiversity objectives as well as the overall availability of wood within sustainability boundaries in 2030 perspective". [18] The revision of RED II, which is part of the wider Fit for 55 package, goes in the same direction:

---

signing emission allowances to specific companies or industries, limiting the total amount of emissions permitted. Companies can buy or sell these allowances based on their needs. This system creates a market for emissions where companies that reduce their emissions below their allocated allowances can sell the excess to those who exceed their limits.

[15] The "no debit" rule is provided by Article 4 of Regulation (EU) 2018/841 and requires each Member State to ensure that accounted CO_2 emissions from land use are entirely compensated by an equivalent accounted removal of CO_2 from the atmosphere through action in the LULUCF sector. If total emissions exceed total removals, Member States shall cover the resulting "carbon debt" by increasing CO_2 mitigation efforts under the "Effort Sharing Regulation" (Regulation (EU) 2018/842) that sets binding national GHG emission reduction targets for sectors not covered by the ETS. In case removals exceed emissions, part of the generated "carbon credit" can be used by the State to meet national emission reduction targets, thanks to the provision of a flexibility mechanism between LULUCF and the "Effort Sharing" regime.

[16] See Virardi E., "Reshaping Administrative Proceedings and Discretion for a Fast-Forwarded Energy Transition", in this volume.

[17] Camia et al. (fn. 14) 5.

[18] COM (2021) 572 final, 7.

Recital 76 of Directive (EU) 2023/2413 states that, in pursuing carbon neutrality, "it is essential to also contribute to wider environmental objectives, and in particular the prevention of biodiversity loss, on which the indirect land use change associated with the production of certain biofuels, bioliquids and biomass fuels has a negative impact".[19]

3. Sustainability criteria: a gradual juridification of ecological sustainability?

Article 29 of Directive (EU) 2018/2001 defines a set of criteria for all end-use sectors to establish the conditions under which bioenergy can contribute to the EU binding renewable energy targets[20] and receive financial support.

Its paragraph 10 sets the so-called "GHG emission saving criteria", which indicate a series of percentages of GHG emissions that should be saved by using different forms of bioenergy instead of energy produced from fossil fuels.[21] Such criteria are specifically aimed at ensuring that bioenergy contributes substantially to reduce the overall greenhouse gas emissions in the energy sector. Although bioenergy may be qualified as sustainable only provided that it complies with these criteria, they do not take into consideration the impact of bioenergy on biodiversity and soil ecosystem. They are exclusively aimed at decarbonization, that is the main rationale behind the energy transition.

This is not the case for the other criteria, which promote an ecological idea of sustainability.

The criteria laid down in Article 29, paragraphs 3 and 6, are aimed at preventing that the promotion of bioenergy turns in a stimulus to destroy

[19] Directive (EU) 2023/2413 of the European Parliament and of the Council of 18 October 2023, amending Directive (EU) 2018/2001, Regulation (EU) 2018/1999 and Directive 98/70/EC as regards the promotion of energy from renewable sources, and repealing Council Directive (EU) 2015/652.

[20] Article 3, para. 1, of Directive (EU) 2018/2001.

[21] More in details, for the post-2020 framework (2021-2030), the Directive 2018/2001 required at least 50% savings of GHG emissions compared to fossil fuels to be reached for biofuel, biogas and bioliquids produced in installations starting operation on or before 5 October 2015 and 60% for the ones produced in installation starting operation until 2020. Biofuel, biogas and bioliquids produced in installation starting operation from 2021 must reach at least 65% GHG emissions saving. Biomass fuels for electricity, heating and cooling production used in installations starting operation from 1 January 2021 until 31 December 2025 must reach at least 70% GHG emissions saving, and 80% for installations starting operation from 1 January 2026.

soil biodiversity. In particular, paragraph 3 defines no-go areas for agricultural feedstocks, in which production for bioenergy is not allowed, for the purposes of the Directive, from land that was classified as: (i) primary forest and other wooded land where there is no clearly visible indication of human activity and the ecological processes are not significantly disturbed; (ii) highly biodiverse forests or grasslands; (iii) areas designated for nature protection purposes. Moreover, raw materials may be used if their production "did not interfere with those nature protection purposes".[22] Crucially, this provision does not refer to "significant interference" but requires the absolute absence of any interference, a regulatory option which recalls the policy objective of "do no harm".[23]

While paragraph 3 refers to agriculture feedstocks, paragraph 6 regulates forest biomass production. Accordingly, all economic operators taking part in the EU market shall carry out a risk-based assessment, building on existing sustainable forest management legislation, including monitoring and enforcement systems, in force in country or region of origin (UE and extra-UE) of the forest biomass. More specifically, under the guidelines laid down by the Commission,[24] economic operators have to demonstrate whether or not the legislation of the country or region of origin of the forest biomass ensures the following elements: the legality of harvesting operations; the forest regeneration of harvested areas; the protection of that areas designated for nature protection purposes; and that harvesting is carried out minimizing negative impacts on soil quality and biodiversity, as well as maintaining or improving the long-term production capacity of the forest. In case such requirements are not met, bioenergy is excluded from public financial support, and its use does not contribute to national and European targets and obligations related to renewable energy deployment. By integrating the objective of ecosystem sustainability into the regulation of bioenergy production, these provisions promote ecosystem health.

The remaining criteria laid down in Article 29 also pursue the objective of ecosystem health, albeit indirectly. Paragraph 2 states that bioenergy produced from waste and residues derived from agricultural land should be considered for the purpose of the Directive only if operators or national authorities have monitoring or management plans in place to address the

---

[22] Article 29, para. 3, lett. b) and c).

[23] This imperative was first outlined in the Commission Communication on the Green Deal and later confirmed by the European Council Conclusions of 17-21 July 2020, point 18.

[24] EU Commission implementing Regulation (EU) 2022/2448 on establishing operational guidance on the evidence for demonstrating compliance with the *sustainability criteria* for forest biomass laid down in Article 29 of Directive (EU) 2018/2001.

impacts on soil quality and soil carbon. Moreover, paragraphs 4 and 5 envisage no-go areas also for agricultural feedstocks in which production for bioenergy is not allowed from land that was classified, in or after 2008, as land with high carbon stocks, while paragraph 7 sets specific LULUCF conditions for the use of imported forest biomass for energy. The main objective of these last criteria is to strengthen the link between RED II and the LULUCF regulation and minimize the negative impact on natural carbon sinks caused by bioenergy production. This is in line with the twofold nature of the Commission's strategy to achieve climate neutrality, which is based on the reduction of GHG emissions, on the one hand, and on the compensation of the emissions which cannot be avoided, through the removal of greenhouse gases, on the other.

Finally, as for the compliance with the "sustainability and greenhouse gas emissions saving criteria", this is ensured through national certification schemes that each Member State must establish. Alternatively, Member States may also use international voluntary certification schemes recognized by the EU.

The analysis carried out so far suggests that the aim of RED II was and remains the promotion of renewable energies as a privileged tool for the transition to a low-carbon society. The *sustainability criteria*, though, may be seen as an attempt to integrate the ecological concern within the energy legislation, well before the launch of the Green Deal in 2019.

Nevertheless, there is no shortage of critical elements. To begin with, not all bioenergy plants have to comply with these criteria, which must be applied only with reference to "installations producing electricity, heating and cooling or fuels with a total rated thermal input equal to or exceeding 20 MW in the case of solid biomass fuels, and with a total rated thermal input equal to or exceeding 2 MW in the case of gaseous biomass fuels".[25]

Member States can also derogate from the criteria laid down in Article 29, for a limited period and under certain conditions, in the case of installations located in the ultra-peripheral regions according to Article 349 TFEU, as long as these derogations serve to facilitate the gradual application of the *sustainability criteria*.[26] Furthermore, while bioenergy produced from agricultural biomass considered for the purposes of the Directive shall not be made from raw material obtained from land with especially biodiverse and carbon-rich habitats, the same does not apply to forest biomass. With regard to the greenhouse gas emissions saving criteria, they do not apply to existing biomass-based installations.

[25] Article 29, para. 1, of Directive (EU) 2018/2001.

[26] Article 29, para. 13, of Directive (EU) 2018/2001.

The amendments to Article 29 made by Directive (EU) 2023/2413 tackles many of such issues, trying to make bioenergy production more ecologically sustainable. This clearly emerges from Recital 74, which states that, in pursuing climate neutrality through the EU renewable energy policy, "it is essential to also contribute to wider environmental objectives, and particularly the prevention of biodiversity loss, on which the indirect land use change associated with the production of certain biofuels, bioliquids and biomass fuels has a negative impact".

To this end, the scope of application of *sustainability criteria* has been extended: the minimum threshold for their applicability in installations producing heating, electricity and cooling has been lowered from the current 20 MW to 7,5 MW and it has been set new specific thresholds also for biogas plants.[27] Special attention was given to the production of bioenergy from forest biomass. A number of exclusions and limitations have been introduced, in line with the approach for biofuels, bioliquids and biomass fuels produced from agricultural biomass.[28] Directive (EU) 2023/2413 has also introduced an obligation for Member States to consider the utilization of the "cascading principle".[29] That principle aims at achieving the resource efficiency of biomass use by prioritizing, wherever possible, the material use of biomass over its energy use.[30] Woody biomass should be used according to its highest economic and environmental added value in the following order of priority: (1) wood-based products, (2) extension of their life cycle, (3) re-use, (4) recycling, (5) bioenergy and (6) waste disposal. Furthermore, Member States shall not grant any new support or renew any existing support to produce electricity from forest biomass in electricity-only installations, unless such installation is located in a just transition territory, is equipped with carbon capture and storage technology or is located in an ultra-peripheral region where forest biomass is the only available re-

[27] Article 1, para. 19, of Directive (EU) 2023/2413.

[28] Article 1, para. 19, lett. e), of Directive (EU) 2023/2413.

[29] For an overview about the cascading principle of woody biomass see Olsson O., Bruce L., Hektor B., Roos A., Guisson R., Lamers P., Hartley D., Ponitka J., Hildebrandt J. and Thrän D., *Cascading of woody biomass: definitions, policies and effects on international trade*, 2016, available at urly.it/3a577; EU Commission, *Guidance on cascading use of biomass with selected good practice examples on woody biomass*, Publications Office, 2018, available at https://data.europa.eu/doi/10.2873/68553.

[30] Article 3 of Directive (EU) 2018/2001 now expressly states that Member State "shall take into account the waste hierarchy set out in Article 4 of Directive 2008/98/EC and shall ensure the application of the principle of the cascading use of biomass, with a focus on support schemes and with due regard to national specificities" (Article 1, para. 2, lett. b) of Directive (EU) 2023/2413).

source. Finally, Member States must include new "bioenergy plans" as part of their national energy and climate plans (NECPs).

These novelties further integrate the policy objective of ecosystem sustainability in the regulatory framework of renewable energy. They do so by strengthening the consistency of the *sustainability criteria* with the emerging ecological paradigm. Nevertheless, such legislative development also reflects the gradualism and incrementalism that characterize the *modus operandi* of the EU legislator in the implementation the Green Deal.[31]

4. Conclusions: avoiding conflicts between transitions

Bioenergy plays a crucial role in the energy transition process launched by the Green Deal. Its use is subordinated to the so-called *sustainability criteria*, which serve a twofold function: they ensure that bioenergy effectively contributes to the decarbonization process, on the hand, and the ecological sustainability of bioenergy production, on the other. As argued in this Chapter, these criteria can be seen as an attempt, albeit partial and limited, to minimize the conflict between different objectives of the Green Deal and to juridify the goal of ecological sustainability in the renewables' regulatory framework. The analysis carried out in the previous pages has also shown that ecological sustainability has been formulated as a policy and legal goal before the Green Deal. The relevant discipline dates back to 2018 and was adopted, *inter alia*, to strengthen the *sustainability criteria* introduced in 2009.[32] Nonetheless, the Green Deal has given new emphasis to ecological sustainability as an EU policy objective. It has specified its meaning and extended its scope to those sectors in which ecosystem health is not immediately perceived as an indispensable condition, like in the case of bioeconomy.

The relevance given to ecological sustainability in the field of bioenergy is far from surprising. Ecological sustainability is particularly important in this sector because bioenergy production, as a form of bioeconomy, is mainly based on the use of renewable biological resources. In other words,

---

[31] The same approach is also endorsed with reference to the implementing process of the Forestry Strategy 2030 and the Soil Strategy for 2030, as underlined by Chiti E., "In motu. L'Unione Europea e la trasformazione della costruzione giuridica della sostenibilità", in *La riforma costituzionale in materia di tutela dell'ambiente*, Editoriale Scientifica, 2022, 183-210.

[32] Article 17 of Directive (CE) 2009/28 of the European Parliament and of the Council of 23 April 2009 on the promotion of the use of energy from renewable sources and amending and subsequently repealing Directives 2001/77/EC and 2003/30/EC.

well-functioning ecosystems directly influence the productive cycle. However, ecological sustainability is not only about bioenergy. It is relevant for all renewable energy sources. This should be acknowledged by the Commission, which should incorporate ecological sustainability into the regulatory framework of other renewable energy sources. Without such development of the regulatory framework, the objectives of the energy transition are destined to clash with those of the concurrent ecological transition. Such a risk is confirmed by recent research:[33] for example, the presence of huge offshore wind farms could turn in a barrier to the movement of certain species or could affect the ecosystem well-functioning, due to the production of vibration or electromagnetic fields. The same applies to photovoltaic power plants (PV) due to their best-known negative impact on the soil ecosystems. Reconciling the two transitions – or at least managing the possible conflicts between their goals – is an uneasy but inescapable regulatory task.

[33] Galparsoro Iza I., Menchaca I., Seeger I., Nurmi M., McDonald H., Garmendia J., Pouso S. and Borja A., *Mapping potential environmental impacts of offshore renewable energy*, Report 2, European Topic Centre on Inland, Coastal and Marine waters, 2022, available at https://l1nq.com/zy3dN; Li C., Coolen J. W.P., Scherer L., Mogollón J.M., Braeckman U., Vanaverbeke J., Tukker A. and Steubing B., "Offshore Wind Energy and Marine Biodiversity in the North Sea: Life Cycle Impact Assessment for Benthic Communities", in *Environ. Sci. Technol.*, 2023, 57, 6455-6464.

Chapter 4
RESHAPING ADMINISTRATIVE PROCEEDINGS AND DISCRETION FOR A FAST-FORWARDED ENERGY TRANSITION

Emmalucia Virardi

ABSTRACT: *This Chapter investigates the impact of the European Green Deal on administrative proceedings and discretion in relation to the energy transition. The increasing urgency of implementing renewable energy has resulted in the adoption of provisions aimed at addressing and overcoming administrative barriers. Although explicitly directed at modifying procedural rules, the analysed provisions imply a set of political values and preferences that ultimately affect the powers of national administrations.*

KEYWORDS: *Energy transition – Regulatory conflicts – Administrative discretion.*

1. Energy transition and the issue of streamlined administrative proceedings

The process of transformation triggered by the 2019 Communication on the European Green Deal[1] has pervaded the structure of the energy system, aiming at the establishment of a society grounded on clean, affordable and secure energy and reinvigorating the need to use renewable sources. This has resulted in a series of measures to implement and facilitate the energy transition,[2] including an ever-increasing focus on streamlining the related administrative proceedings.

---

[1] COM (2019) 640 (The European Green Deal), 6. Such process is to be understood as a «deep and holistic transformation of our society and our economy»: see COM (2023) 410, 1.

[2] For a general overview, Woolley O., "Regulating the promotion of renewable elec-

The interconnection between the Green Deal and the energy transition is complex and multifaceted. On the one hand, the energy system's decarbonisation is pivotal to achieving the Green Deal's objective of climate neutrality. According to the Commission, more than 75% of the EU's greenhouse gas emissions can be traced back to the energy sector.[3] Therefore, the Green Deal project also entails a progressive increase in the targets concerning the implementation of renewable energy.[4] On the other hand, the transformative capacity of the Green Deal redefines some key components of the EU substantive constitution.[5] In the case of the energy transition, in particular, one must assess its impact on economic regulation,[6] both at the level of identification of the relevant objectives and at that of the design of the regulatory model.[7] Indeed, while the sectoral regulatory framework has been traditionally oriented to the liberalisation of the market, regulation is now opening to a plurality of public interests.[8] For exam-

---

tricity consumption and production: a European Union case study", in Roggenkamp M.M., de Graaf K.J. and Fleming R.C. (eds.), *Energy Law, Climate Change, and the Environment*, Edward Elgar Publishing, 2021, 388-398; Penttinen S., "Regulatory and Policy Instruments to Promote Decarbonization in the Energy Sector", in Reins L. and Verschuuren J. (eds.), *Research Handbook on Climate Change Mitigation Law*, Edward Elgar Publishing, 2022, 338-362.

[3] The European Green Deal, 6.

[4] To visually envision the progressive evolution in renewable energy targets, see the graph available at https://energy.ec.europa.eu/topics/renewable-energy/renewable-energy-directive-targets-and-rules/renewable-energy-targets_en (last access 30 April 2024). In this regard, it should be differentiated between the 2030 targets (which underwent a process of amendment) and the 2050 target (which, as will be highlighted, entails the achievement of climate neutrality). In particular, Directive (EU) 2023/2413 of the European Parliament and of the Council of 18 October 2023 amending Directive (EU) 2018/2001, Regulation (EU) 2018/1999 and Directive 98/70/EC as regards the promotion of energy from renewable sources, and repealing Council Directive (EU) 2015/652 (Red III), OJ 2023 L 2413, Article 1 para. 2 has introduced a binding target of at least 42.5% and a collective endeavour to reach 45%.

[5] Chiti E., "Managing the Ecological Transition of the EU: The European Green Deal as a Regulatory Process", in *CMLRev*, 2022, 59, 29.

[6] The relation between pro-competitive regulation and the EU substantive constitution is the subject of an extensive and varied reflection. With specific regard to the energy sector, see Cameron P. and Heffron R. (eds.), *Legal Aspects of EU Energy Regulation*, 2nd ed., Oxford University Press, 2016.

[7] Chiti (fn. 5) 31-32.

[8] See the overall perspective provided by Schneider J., "Energy and Trans-European Networks", in Hofmann H.C.H., Rowe G.C. and Türk A.H. (eds.), *Specialized Administrative Law of the European Union: A Sectoral Review*, Oxford University Press, 2018, 378-403; Talus K., *EU Energy Law and Policy: A Critical Account*, Oxford University Press, 2013. On the principle of solidarity, see Boute A., "The Principle of Solidarity

ple, the Commission argues that a *principle* of *energy efficiency first* is in the process of emerging[9] together with a *principle* of *renewable energy as an overriding public interest.*[10] This development has been crucially affected by the macro-objective of climate neutrality.[11]

The measures to implement the energy transition, in any case, meet several obstacles, including administrative barriers. This is particularly true for certain renewable sources, such as photovoltaic and wind power.[12] Administrative barriers may be classified according to three main criteria, namely *how*, *what* and *who*.[13] As for the first criterion, it refers to the rules governing administrative proceedings for the authorisation and operation of renewable sources plants, which may suffer, for instance, from the lack of a transparent framework.[14] The second criterion deals with the presence of competing interests, that need to be taken into consideration by the competent authority and may be considered to outweigh the interest to renewable

---

and the Geopolitics of Energy: Poland v. Commission (OPAL Pipeline)", in *CMLRev*, 2020, 57, 889-914; Galicz K., "Solidarietà nel settore energetico: Prospettive e strumenti dell'Unione europea per contrastare la povertà energetica", in *Dirittifondamentali.it*, 2023, 2, 497. This also intercepts the need to deliver a just transition, Heffron R., "Applying Energy Justice into the Energy Transition", in *Renew. Sustain. Energy Rev.*, 2022, 156, 111936.

[9] On this principle, refer to Commission Recommendation (EU) 2021/1749 of 28 September 2021 on Energy Efficiency First: from principles to practice – Guidelines and examples for its implementation in decision-making in the energy sector and beyond [2021], OJ L 350/9. See also Fazio E., "Le "eccezioni" del diritto della concorrenza per contrastare la povertà energetica", in *Dirittifondamentali.it*, 2023, 2, 418.

[10] COM (2022) 230 (RepowerEU Plan), 11; Red III, Recital 44.

[11] Such policy objective has been identified in The European Green Deal, 4, and has been legally formalised in Regulation (EU) 2021/1119 of the European Parliament and of the Council of 30 June 2021 establishing the framework for achieving climate neutrality and amending Regulations (EC) 401/2009 and (EU) 2018/1999 (European Climate Law), OJ 2021 L 243, Article 1.

[12] RepowerEU Plan, 11.

[13] Such classification, although partially different, is also present in DG Energy European Commission, "Technical support for RES policy development and implementation – Simplification of permission and administrative procedures for RES installations (RES Simplify): Interim report", 2022 (RES Simplify Report). Under the RES Simplify Report, the borders of the identified categories do not overlap with those utilised in this Chapter. Moreover, it also takes into consideration obstacles stemming from the grid process which, although essential for the operation of renewable energy plants, is outside the scope of this Chapter.

[14] In the RES Simplify Report, the reference here is to process-related issues, consisting of the execution of the administrative process and being grouped in: (i) bureaucratic issues; (ii) non-transparent processes; (iii) staffing problems; and (iv) insufficient spatial planning. *Ibidem*, 38-40.

energy. [15] The final criterion pertains to the lack of acceptance by different stakeholders, both public and private, which may also result in judicial proceedings aggravating the authorisation process. [16]

Admittedly, the outlined classification is somewhat artificial. Indeed, the identified obstacles often characterise simultaneously more than one group and are difficult to place in a clear-cut manner. [17] Moreover, the structure of the *how*, *what* and *who* reinforces each other's characteristics. Subsequently, any modification aimed at affecting one of such spheres also impacts the others.

Nevertheless, this classification can still serve as a useful lens for the purposes of the inquiry carried out in this Chapter, [18] as it allows to shed some light on the need to rely on shorter and faster procedures in the implementation of the energy transition. To investigate the implications that the provisions addressing administrative barriers have on administrative proceedings and discretion, the analysis is structured as follows. First, we will analyse some recent modifications dealing with the identified issues, focusing on the introduction of the presumption of renewable energy as an *overriding public interest*. Afterwards, we will address some of the challenges posed by these provisions related to the underlying political values and functional preferences they express. In particular, we will investigate their implications on the regulatory tension between renewable energy and environmental protection, the balancing process regarding the components of the energy transition, and administrative proceedings and discretion. Finally, some conclusions will be drawn concerning the re-articulation of public power in the context of the Green Deal.

[15] In relation to this category, the RES Simplify Report takes into consideration conflicting public goods, which, in most cases, are to be identified in: (i) environmental issues; (ii) land use conflict; and (iii) aviation and military conflicts. *Ibidem*, 40-42.

[16] The RES Simplify Report sheds light on how the plant developers interact with different stakeholders. Barriers in this regard may arise from: (i) a lack of political and public interest in certain typologies of projects (*e.g.*, offshore wind farms); (ii) public resistance; (iii) third-party complaints. *Ibidem*, 42-44.

[17] For instance, spatial planning equally intercepts the three categories. Firstly, it is explicitly classified by the RES Simplify report in the *how* group, regardless of its existence. Secondly, spatial planning often encapsulates the competing interests of the *what* group. Finally, regarding the *who*, two profiles can be easily identified: (i) on the one hand, it may be the expression of the lack of acceptance of local communities connected to the territories where the renewable energy plants are to be located; and (ii) on the other hand, it may ground judicial proceedings or its legitimacy may therein be the contested object.

[18] The focus will be mainly on what has been identified as the *how* and the *what*.

2. How to address administrative barriers?

The idea of considering the specificities of renewable sources for the evaluation and readjustment of permitting procedures is not at all new.[19] However, this *leitmotiv* has been strengthened and reshaped in the context of the Green Deal implementing measures. In this regard, particular attention should be paid to certain parts of the RepowerEU Plan,[20] which try to address and overcome administrative barriers.[21] The regulatory understructure is laid down by the Red II,[22] that had already established

[19] Directive 2001/77/EC of the European Parliament and of the Council of 27 September 2001 on the promotion of electricity produced from renewable energy sources in the internal electricity market, OJ 2001 L 283, Recital 20 and Article 6. See also Peeters M. and Schomerus T., "An EU Law Perspective on the Role of Regional Authorities in the Field of Renewable Energy", in Peeters M. and Schomerus T. (eds.), *Renewable Energy Law in the EU*, Edward Elgar Publishing, 2014, 21-24; Peeters M. and Schomerus T., "Regional renewable energy: A string of legal and financial challenges", in Peeters and Schomerus (fn. 19) 308.

[20] RepowerEU Plan, 6-7; and COM (2022) 108 (RepowerEU Communication), 9-10.

[21] In particular, regarding the measures related to RepowerEU Plan, the analysis deals with: (i) the Commission Recommendation (EU) 2024/1343 of 13 May 2024 on speeding up permit-granting procedures for renewable energy and related infrastructure projects (Updated Permit-granting Procedures Recommendation), C/2024/2660 final, laying down guidance for Member States to speed up procedures relating to renewable energies, which replaced the Commission Recommendation (EU) 2022/822 of 18 May 2022 on speeding up permit-granting procedures for renewable energy projects and facilitating Power Purchase Agreements (Permit-granting Procedures Recommendation), OJ 2022 L 146; and (ii) the Red III, aiming to expand the recommended mechanisms. Due to the energy emergency caused by the geopolitical turmoil following Russia's invasion of Ukraine, moreover, some of these provisions have been anticipated on the ground that they have been deemed to be useful contributions to the crisis in the short term, Council Regulation (EU) 2022/2577 of 22 December 2022 laying down a framework to accelerate the deployment of renewable energy (Regulation to Accelerate RES), OJ 2022 L 335. In relation to the application period of the Regulation to Accelerate RES, see also Council Regulation (EU) 2024/223 of 22 December 2023 amending Regulation (EU) 2022/2577 laying down a framework to accelerate the deployment of renewable energy, OJ 2024 L 223. It should be noted that the Regulation to Accelerate RES applies in relation to proceedings having a starting date within this timeframe (the Member States may also include pending proceedings where this results in a shorter process and provided the preservation of pre-existing third-party legal rights). Additionally, the Regulation to Accelerate RES does not affect national rules establishing shorter deadlines. More generally, on the geopolitical implications of the decarbonization of the energy system, see Giuli M. and Oberthür S., "Assessing the EU's Evolving Position in Energy Geopolitics under Decarbonisation", in *Int. Spect.*, 2023, 3, 152-170.

[22] Directive (EU) 2018/2001 of the European Parliament and of the Council of 11 December 2018 on the promotion of the use of energy from renewable sources (recast) (Red II), OJ 2018 L 328.

some requirements[23] for Member States to converge towards a simplified and streamlined permitting process in light of the energy efficiency first principle.[24]

One might wonder whether such modifications can be considered a mere reiteration of the pre-existing framework, its development along the same lines or something at least partially novel. Indeed, some of the provisions may be traced back to the same rationale and scope of the previous ones, finding their *raison d'être* in incomplete or unsatisfactory implementation and enforcement at the national level. Needless to say, the need to further the progress towards the revised renewable energy targets inevitably fuels this concern. However, a new – and potentially disruptive – stance is in the process of emerging.

A general underlying requirement is that the *how* of the proceedings is to benefit from the most favourable procedure available in each national framework.[25] Several additional requirements build upon this base and pursue this rationale. Namely, as per the Updated Permit-granting Procedures Recommendation, Member States should include in each national framework the following: (i) the establishment of precise and as short as possible maximum deadlines;[26] (ii) the creation of a single unified application process;[27] (iii) the designation of single contact points;[28] and (iv) rules to attribute consequences for any delays or lack of action from administrative authorities.[29] The Red III better delineates this groundline, also taking into account the particularities of certain projects (*e.g.*, repowering).[30]

These mechanisms can be regarded as legal responses to concerns with the permitting decision-making process,[31] aiming to enhance the predictability of the proceeding (both in relation to the procedure to be followed and the outcome) and to lessen the perceived risk for project developers.

---

[23] *Ibidem*, Articles 15-17.

[24] *Ibidem*, Article 15, para. 1.

[25] Updated Permit-granting Procedures Recommendation, para. 2.

[26] *Ibidem*, para. 3.

[27] *Ibidem*, para. 5.

[28] *Ibidem*, para. 14.

[29] *Ibidem*, para. 17.

[30] Red III, Article 1, para. 7, in relation to the insertion of Article 16 (organisation and main principles of the permit-granting process), Article 16a (permit-granting procedure in renewables acceleration areas), Article 16b (permit-granting procedure outside renewables acceleration areas), Article 16c (repowering), Article 16d (solar energy equipment) and Article 16e (heat pumps).

[31] Woolley O., *Renewable Energy Law*, Bloomsbury Hart Publishing, 2023, 160-163 and 168-175.

In order to identify the applicable administrative procedure,[32] it is also necessary to draw attention to a *discrimen* posed by this framework to ensure faster deployment of renewables where the environmental risk is to be considered lower. The governing rules of the proceeding would depend, in this view, on the localisation of the plant and entail prior spatial planning, with which Member States are entrusted.[33] The Red III provides for a set of criteria to be respected, relating both to the area's specificities and to the plant's technology,[34] and a requirement to establish mitigation measures.[35] This results in the differentiation between renewables acceleration areas and other areas, for which different procedures are envisaged.[36]

In between the *how* and the *what* is the compliance of the projects with the obligations stemming from EU environmental law.[37] For the purpose of simplifying such assessment, the Red III takes into consideration the derogations procedures provided for under the Habitats Directive,[38] the Water Framework Directive[39] and the Birds Directive.[40] In such cases,[41] Member States are entrusted to ensure that renewable plants are to be considered as being in the overriding public interest and serving public health and safety

---

[32] Although directly concerning the identification of the *how*, this can be regarded as a point of overlapping with the *who* sphere.

[33] Red III, Article 1, para. 6 in relation to the part where it introduces Articles 15b and 15c. See also SWD(2024) 333 final.

[34] Red III, Article 1, para. 6 in relation to the part where it introduces Article 15c, para. 1a.

[35] *Ibidem*, Article 1, para. 6 in relation to the part where it introduces Article 15c, para. 1b.

[36] *Ibidem*, Articles 1, para. 7, in relation to the part where it introduces Article 16a and Article 16b.

[37] Updated Permit-granting Procedures Recommendation, para. 30.

[38] Council Directive 92/43/EEC of 21 May 1992 on the conservation of natural habitats and of wild fauna and flora (Habitats Directive), OJ 1992 L 206.

[39] Directive 2000/60/EC of the European Parliament and of the Council of 23 October 2000 establishing a framework for Community action in the field of water policy (Water Framework Directive), OJ 2000 L 327.

[40] Directive 2009/147/EC of the European Parliament and of the Council of 30 November 2009 on the conservation of wild birds (Birds Directive), OJ 2009 L 20.

[41] In particular, the reference is to Articles 6, para. 4 and 16 para. 1c of Habitats Directive, Article 4, para. 7 of the Water Framework Directive and Article 9, para. 1a of the Birds Directive. See also Ruge R., "The Reality Gap: Simplification of Environmental Law as Key for the Acceleration of Permit Procedures for Europe's Green Deal", in *Eur. Energy Environ. Law Rev.*, 2022, 31, 258. As for the requirement of 'imperative reasons of overriding public interest' (IROPI), see Case C-182/10, *Solvay and others*, EU:C:2012:82; and Case C-43/10, *Nomarchiaki Aftodioikisi Aitoloakarnanias and others*, EU:C:2012:560.

until the achievement of climate neutrality.[42] The introduction of this presumption is mitigated by giving Member States the possibility to limit its scope in relation to parts of the territory, certain types of renewables or in the presence of specific characteristics.[43] It is in this mechanism that the new approach is most prominently perceivable. While such provision is expressly presented as the operationalisation of the principle of renewable energy as an overriding public interest,[44] further considerations may also be drawn up.

3. The impacts of a fast-forwarded energy transition

As already stressed, the analysed modifications are explicitly oriented to fast-forward the energy transition. They aim at doing so by streamlining administrative procedures. However, an approach merely focusing on this objective would be too narrow and short-sighted. Indeed, the RepowerEU Plan and the related measures go beyond what meets the eye. For the purpose of our analysis, at least three different profiles are relevant.

3.1. False friends? Reconciling renewable energy and environmental protection

To begin with, it is appropriate to point to the nature of the modifications. By specifying the procedural requirements to be embedded in the national legal texture in order to simplify and streamline the permitting process,[45] this framework encapsulates a set of political values and preferences that need to be considered by national administrations. Far from being neutral, these provisions express a clear functional rationale and provide guiding criteria on the interests involved in the permitting process.

By relaxing the procedure for renewable energy plants, the revisions un-

[42] Red III, Article 1, para. 7, in relation to the part where it introduces Article 16f.

[43] It should be stressed that such restriction is possible only in duly justified and specific circumstances with a view to the priorities provided under national integrated energy and climate. Moreover, in this regard, there is also a duty of information and justification of Member States to the Commission. *Ibidem*, Article 1, para. 7, in relation to the part where it introduces Article 16f.

[44] RepowerEU Plan, 11.

[45] It should be noted that a merely procedural dimension of the mechanisms simplifying and streamlining administrative procedures is difficult to isolate. Indeed, «unnecessarily' and 'delay' are not objective terms. Rather, they are informed by the commentator's perspective», Woolley (fn. 31) 157.

veil the approach endorsed by the Commission with reference to the characteristics and the prioritisation of the interests. This can be observed both from a perspective within and outside the energy sector. On the one hand, the energy transition in itself is grounded on a plurality of rationales which may need to be reconciled.[46] On the other hand, potential conflicts may also arise from the interaction between the energy transition and other Green Deal policies and objectives. The most prominent example is, unsurprisingly, environmental protection.[47] Indeed, while renewable energy and environmental objectives are regarded as closely interlinked, there are several situations in which they may actually clash.[48] For instance, this is the case for the localisation of renewable energy plants,[49] which may entail a negative effect on the environmental and ecological matrices of the territory where they are to be built.[50] Typically, in such situations, use has been made of mechanisms aimed at reconciling the possible tension between energy and environmental protection and at identifying harmonised options (*e.g.*, spatial planning, strategic environmental assessment and environmental impact assessment).[51]

---

[46] Talus (fn. 8) 175-211. See also Giuli M. and Oberthür S., "Third Time Lucky? Reconciling EU Climate and External Energy Policy during Energy Security Crises", in *J. Eur. Integr.*, 2023, 45, 395.

[47] Woolley O., "Climate Law and Environmental Law: Is Conflict between Them Inevitable?", in Zahar A. and Mayer B. (eds.), *Debating Climate Law*, Cambridge University Press, 2021, 398-411; Gasparatos A. et al., "Renewable Energy and Biodiversity: Implications for Transitioning to a Green Economy", in *Renew. Sustain. Energy Rev.*, 2017, 70, 161; Hilson C., "It's All About Climate Change, Stupid! Exploring the Relationship Between Environmental Law and Climate Law", in *J. Env. L.*, 2013, 25, 359; Jackson A.L.R., "Renewable Energy vs. Biodiversity: Policy Conflicts and the Future of Nature Conservation", in *Global Environ. Change*, 2011, 21, 1195.

[48] The emergence of this scenario has been anticipated in relation to 2020 renewable energy targets by Peeters M. and Schomerus T., "Modifying Our Society with Law: The Case of EU Renewable Energy Law", in *Climate Law*, 2014, 4, 135-136.

[49] Another example can be found in the utilisation of bioenergy, Giljam R.A., "Towards a Holistic Approach in EU Biomass Regulation", in *J. Env. L.*, 2016, 28, 95; Red III, Recital 10.

[50] The most prominent example of this is in relation to wind energy farms. In this respect, see DG Environment European Commission, "Guidance document on wind energy developments and EU nature legislation", 2020. The case of localisation of renewable energy plants has been frequently addressed in case law, especially at the national level. See, in relation to an Italian case, Baldini B., "Transizione energetica, ambiente e tutela del patrimonio culturale: un recente orientamento del Consiglio di Stato", in *Ist. del Fed.*, 2023, 2, 417. The European Court of Justice has also dealt with this issue. See *e.g.* Case C-727/17, *ECO-WIND Construction*, ECLI:EU:C:2020:393; Case C-2/10, *Azienda Agro-Zootecnica Franchini e Eolica di Altamura*, EU:C:2011:502; Case C-244/05, *Bund Naturschutz in Bayern e a.*, ECLI:EU:C:2006:579.

[51] Woolley (fn. 46) 405.

Under the mentioned provisions, however, such tools are somewhat forfeited (or, at least, relaxed) to bring about an expedited implementation of renewables.[52] This is not to say that the ecological element is disregarded in the analysed framework. Indeed, as will be seen, the simplification and shortening of the permitting process is to be conducted taking into account the do no harm principle.[53]

This type of development shows that the Green Deal is increasingly producing situations where conflicts between different objectives become unavoidable or where the identification of intermediate solutions is rendered useless due to the urgency of the measures to be taken. In the context of the revisions adopted under the RepowerEU Plan, this general dilemma seems to be addressed, once again, in the light of climate neutrality, which serves as the fundamental objective to orientate the arising conflicts.[54]

3.2. The components of the energy transition through the lens of the ongoing process of (re)definition of sustainability

As already noted, potential conflicts can also be observed from an internal point of view. Indeed, the energy sector itself is specifically characterised by the coexistence of different rationales, which pertain to affordability, security and sustainability.[55] While in some instances it may be possible to identify mechanisms to unwind any possible tension, the diverging claims may not always be reconciled. Needless to say, completely forfeiting one of the components would not be feasible.[56] However, these aspects may be

---

[52] In parallel, the same approach seems to be endorsed also in Regulation (EU) 2024/1991 of the European Parliament and of the Council of 24 June 2024 on nature restoration and amending Regulation (EU) 2022/86 (Nature Restoration Law), OJ 2024 L 1991.

[53] Red III, Recital 22.

[54] For instance, *ibidem*, Article 1, para. 7, in relation to the part where it introduces Article 16f, expressly provides for the presumption of renewable energy as an overriding public interest «until climate neutrality is achieved».

[55] This is often depicted as the *energy trilemma*. The components to be considered and their denominations often differ in the literature, also depending on the time frame of the analysis. In this regard, Fleming R.C., "The Energy Trilemma", in Roggenkamp M.M., de Graaf K.J. and Fleming R.C. (eds.), *Energy Law, Climate Change and the Environment*, Edward Elgar Publishing, 2021, 31-40. For the sake of clarity, the wording here adopted is the one generally used by the Commission (*e.g.*, see RepowerEU Communication).

[56] This is in contrast to Green Deal measures specifically focusing on biodiversity; see *e.g.* the EU Biodiversity Strategy for 2030, COM (2021) 699.

held in different regards and the balancing process may be conducted by giving preference to one of them. Understanding the way in which such conflicts are managed contributes to unveiling the identification of the political values and preferences encapsulated by the analysed modifications, which are then reflected in the phase of the administrative proceeding.

In this regard, it is also necessary to consider that this is affected by the process of (re-)definition of the legal construction of sustainability in the EU. Indeed, the pluralization of the sustainability discourse brought about by the Green Deal influences and is strictly connected to the way the energy sector manages its own regulatory conflicts. Accordingly, the influence of the Green Deal can be measured by its impact on the substantive components of the energy transition and on the balancing process to be conducted, so as to untangle regulatory tensions. This may also contribute to shaping the phase of administrative decision-making, which will be analysed in the next paragraph.

In this sense, it is necessary to assess the characteristics of the energy transition endorsed by the RepowerEU Plan and the sustainability model that is in the process of emerging. In the set of actions to be taken, the rationale of sustainability (which, in terms of objectives to be met, is declined as «a massive speed-up and scale-up in renewable energy» in the context of the RepowerEU Plan)[57] is understood as also serving and reinforcing both security and affordability.[58] Therefore, the importance of implementing renewables is stressed for the purpose of providing secure and affordable energy. Moreover, the measures adopted to overcome administrative barriers contribute to emphasizing the attention to the sustainability aspect, given that their scope does not directly concern the other ones. In this context, particularly significant is also the reference to the do no harm policy principle, which needs to be considered while further simplifying and shortening the renewables' permitting process.[59]

This may lead one to believe that the current energy transition is characterised by the preponderance of the sustainability sphere. While it may hold some truth, it would also be too simplistic. Indeed, it is certainly pos-

---

[57] RepowerEU Plan, 6.

[58] This is clearly stated in *ibidem*, where it is stressed the link of the implementation of renewables with, on the one hand, «our phasing out of Russian fossil fuels» and, on the other hand, «lower electricity prices». Moreover, it is also noted that «the green transformation of Europe's energy system will strengthen economic growth, reinforce its industrial leadership, and put Europe on a path towards climate neutrality by 2050», *ibidem*, 20.

[59] Red III, Recital 22. The significance of such green oath is stressed by Chiti (no. 5), 37.

sible to observe a different quality in the approach, which involves a general and progressive prioritisation of environmental needs. However, while this preference has been strengthened in the analysed framework, it is not a prevalence *stricto sensu* and the energy transition, at least in relation to the specific objective of speeding up the implementation of renewables, seems to remain under the traditional sustainability model. In fact, the other components are still present in the RepowerEU Plan: on the one hand, it is deeply influenced by security concerns following the energy crisis [60] and, on the other hand, the need to ensure «fairness» and «solidarity» is regarded as a guiding parameter. [61] In this sense, the legal adaptation which is required in the analysed context seems to still be anchored to sustainability requirements and not to ecosystems as such.

3.3. Reshaping administrative discretion

The quest to speed up the permitting process may also carry significance in terms of the powers vested in national administrations in relation to the renewables' permitting process. It has already been noted that part of the mission of EU administrative law consists of a power-redirecting function in light of the EU's objectives. [62] Similarly, while the modifications are clearly aimed at streamlining the administrative proceedings, they are also capable of reshaping the public power involved.

This calls into play the notion of administrative discretion. This concept has had many conceptualisations over the years and jurisdictions. [63] At its

---

[60] RepowerEU Plan, 1-2.

[61] *Ibidem.* See also Kaschny L., "Energy Justice and the Principles of Article 194(1) TFEU Governing EU Energy Policy", in *TEL*, 2023, 12, 270.

[62] Chiti E., "Is EU Administrative Law Failing in Some of Its Crucial Tasks?", in *ELJ*, 2016, 22, 584.

[63] The literature on the concept of discretion is too wide to be appropriately recalled here. See however Galligan D.J., *Discretionary Powers: A Legal Study of Official Discretion*, Clarendon, 1986; Mendes J., "Administrative discretion in the EU: comparative perspectives", in Rose-Ackerman S., Lindseth P.L. and Emerson B. (eds.), *Comparative Administrative Law*, 2nd ed., Edward Elgar Publishing, 2017, 632-649; Caranta R., "On Discretion", in Prechal S. and van Roermund B. (eds.), *The Coherence of EU Law: The Search for Unity in Divergent Concepts*, Oxford University Press, 2008, 185-216; Craig P., *EU Administrative Law*, 3rd ed., Oxford University Press, 2018, 436-483; Giannini M.S., *Il potere discrezionale della Pubblica Amministrazione. Concetto e problemi*, Giuffrè, 1939; Mattarella B.G., "Discrezionalità amministrativa", in Cassese S. et al. (eds.), *Dizionario di diritto pubblico: Vol. III*, Giuffrè, 2006, 1993-2003; Prek M. and Lefèvre S., ""Administrative Discretion", "Power Of Appraisal" And "Margin Of Appraisal" In Judicial Review Proceedings Before The General Court", in *CMLRev*, 2019, 56, 339;

very core is the idea that public administrations, when deciding an issue,[64] are involved in a balancing process to be performed in relation to the relevant interests in different ways.[65] The identification of this room for administrative manoeuvre is strictly connected to the rules that embed public power. In order to evaluate the effect that the framework has on the exercise of administrative discretion, some broader considerations are in order. In general terms, law can be regarded as serving a dual function of attribution and delimitation in respect of administrative discretionary powers.[66] In this last regard, there is a first – and more blatant – layer, which concerns the establishment of boundaries enclosing the area of discretion.[67] Yet, an additional layer can be grasped in relation to the pre-identification of the weight to be given to the relevant interests,[68] which ought to orientate the exercise of discretion. It is within this mechanism that the analysed framework is affecting public power. Indeed, the provisions may be regarded as collectively contributing to the definition of a sort of blueprint of the decision to be adopted, by imprinting on the procedure a series of mechanisms intended to expedite the clean transition of the energy system.

As already noted, both the *how* and *what* of the permitting process are undergoing a process of modification to tackle administrative barriers hindering the energy transition. Regarding the *how*, modelling the permitting process with a view to ensure the most favourable procedure available implies a set of preferences, which contribute to corroding the availability of choice by introducing constraints to the scope of the exercise of discretion.[69] More strikingly, the meddling with the *what* sphere sheds further

Fritzsche A., "Discretion, Scope of Judicial Review and Institutional Balance in European Law", in *CMLRev*, 2010, 47, 361.

[64] In order to fully grasp this, it might be useful to recall the visual and spot-on representation of discretion as «the hole in the doughnut», Dworkin R., *Taking Rights Seriously*, 2nd ed., Duckworth, 1978, 31.

[65] Galligan (fn. 63) 6-7, which, while focusing on the central features of discretion, refers to the possibility to «choose amongst different courses of action for good reasons».

[66] Mendes J., "Discretion, Care and Public Interests in the EU Administration: Probing the Limits of Law", in *CMLRev*, 2016, 53, 419.

[67] Mattarella B.G., "Law and Discretion: A Public Law Perspective on the EU", in Mendes J. (ed.), *EU Executive Discretion and the Limits of Law*, Oxford University Press, 2019, 30.

[68] Mendes J., "Law, Public Interest and Interpretation: Prolegomena of a Normative Framework on Administrative Discretion in the EU", in *Yale Law & Economics Research Paper Series*, 2014, 519.

[69] On the general capacity of procedural rules of limiting discretion, Mattarella (fn. 67) 26-27.

light on this interaction. In this respect, the existence of competing interests is clearly regarded as a potential obstacle to the implementation of renewables. But the power to decide on competing (and potentially conflicting) claims is the very essence of what discretion is about. With the permitting process of renewable plants being at the crossroads of several interests, we are facing a shift to a situation in which administrative implementation involves one single public interest, pre-determined by the EU level. Such prioritisation brings about a qualitative change of national administrations' powers, basically stripping them of discretionary powers in such proceedings, or, at the very least, a piercing bounding of the balancing process. Moreover, and under a complementary perspective, this process also affects the very nature of administrative proceedings, which turns from the ideal forum to evaluate competing interests and concretely address regulatory tensions into a mechanism serving a single, predetermined, public interest. In this sense, the analysed provisions of the RepowerEU Plan and its related measures are reshaping national administrations' powers in the permitting process for renewable energy plants.

4. Towards a re-articulation of public power for the achievement of climate neutrality?

The implementation of the energy transition is becoming more and more urgent, due to both the achievement of climate neutrality and energy security concerns. Indeed, the Green Deal regulatory project envisages a society grounded on clean, affordable and secure energy, which requires increasing use of renewables. Moreover, the need to phase out dependency on Russian fossil fuels has enhanced the importance of fast-forwarding this process.

This has resulted in the adoption of a series of regulatory measures aimed at achieving this objective, including provisions to address and overcome administrative barriers. In this last regard, the overall rationale is to ensure the best procedure available for the permitting process of renewable plants. Such aim is pursued by trying to streamline and simplify the governing rules of the proceeding to be undergone and, strikingly, by introducing the presumption of renewable energy as an overriding public interest.

By analysing the relevant provisions, this Chapter has assessed their significance in terms of the values expressed (taking into specific consideration regulatory tensions external and internal to the energy sector) and the effect that they have on national administrations' powers. First, the approach endorsed brings light to the role that climate neutrality may serve in relation to possible arising conflicts between Green Deal's objectives. Moreover, it is also possible to observe a modification of the characteristics of the components of the energy transition and the way they interact with one another, with an expansion of the importance given to the sustainability sphere. Finally, the framework has a qualitative impact on the exercise of discretion, by orientating the permitting process conducted by national administrations as to progressively serve a single public interest.

These observations are in line with the transformative force held by the political objective of climate neutrality. However, this is far from being the end of the story and at least two other scenarios open up. On the one hand, the evolving configuration of the energy transition may require the establishment of additional discretionary powers in relation to different types of authority or procedure. On the other hand, national administrations' powers in other sectors may undergo a similar process in light of achieving climate neutrality.

Chapter 5

ENERGY TRANSITION AND SUSTAINABILITY BEFORE COURTS: THE EVOLUTION OF THE CASE-LAW OF ITALIAN ADMINISTRATIVE COURTS

Michele Di Vita

ABSTRACT: *This Chapter focuses on the concept of sustainability as articulated by the administrative courts of an EU Member State, namely Italy, within the context of the energy transition. Specifically, it illustrates the evolving notion of sustainability that has emerged in judgments concerning the development and construction of renewable energy power plants.*

KEYWORDS: *Energy – Renewable energy plants – Sustainability – Case-law – Italy.*

1. Energy transition and sustainability before Italian courts

The purpose of this Chapter is to identify and assess the ways in which the concept of sustainability has been used by the constitutional and administrative courts of a European Union (EU) Member State, namely Italy, within the context of renewable energy and the energy transition.

More precisely, the inquiry focusses on litigation in the topical sector of renewable energy plants' location (i.e., wind and solar farms) and seeks to explore the evolving judicial representation of sustainability in this specific field. By concentrating on one single Member State and focussing on case-law, instead of regulation, this Chapter differs from the previous ones. It shares with them, however, a basic assumption: the legal use of the concept of sustainability has been evolving over time and one may now detect different and perhaps conflicting meanings of sustainability.

The changing features of sustainability in the Italian case-law on renewable energy plants deserve our attention for two main reasons. First, given the abundance of constitutional and administrative judgements, it is now appropriate to reconstruct the historical evolution of case-law in this area and discuss whether the concepts of sustainable development and sustainability, as applied by constitutional and administrative Courts, have changed over time. The manner in which these policy goals are combined and the relevant (public and private) interests are balanced is emblematic of the different meanings that the term sustainability may assume in a given legal context [1]. Second, the legislation in this field is undergoing sharp changes, particularly after the Russian-Ukrainian conflict. Energy security reasons are becoming a major and urgent concern of the legislator [2]. Environmental concerns may become even more deeply intertwined with economic and security-related motivations, in turn influencing the very concept of sustainability. [3]

By examining a number of key judgments, this Chapter will argue that

---

[1] Concurrent with judicial decisions, there has been an increasing interest in scholarly circles regarding the concepts of sustainable development and sustainability. See, among the most recent contributions, Pieraccini M. and Novitz T. (eds.), *Legal Perspectives on Sustainability*, 1st ed., Bristol University Press, 2020 and Mauerhofer V., Rupo D. and Tarquinio L. (eds.), *Sustainability and Law – General and Specific Aspects*, Springer, 2020.

[2] See Directive (EU) 2023/2413 of the European Parliament and of the Council of 18 October 2023 amending Directive (EU) 2018/2001, Regulation (EU) 2018/1999 and Directive 98/70/EC as regards the promotion of energy from renewable sources, and repealing Council Directive (EU) 2015/652 [2023] OJ L2413. Such Directive specifically refers to climate ambitions and energy security as main concerns in the EU. The same goals are set in the so called "RePowerEU" Plan, Communication from the Commission to the European Parliament, the European Council, the Council, the European Economic and Social Committee and the Committee of the Regions (COM (2022) 230).

[3] In this context, Italy is undergoing a process of simplification/deregulation of the environmental impact assessment and authorization procedures. An example is provided by the legislation over solar panels' installation: see e.g. Law-Decree 77/2021, on the Governance of the National Recovery and Resilience Plan and first measures to strengthen administrative structures and accelerate and streamline procedures; Legislative Decree 199/2021, on the implementation of Directive (EU) 2018/2001 on the promotion of the use of energy from renewable sources; Law 34/2022, conversion into law, with amendments, of the Law-Decree 17/2022, containing urgent measures for the containment of electricity and natural gas costs, for the development of renewable energies, and for the relaunch of industrial policies; Law-Decree 50/2022, laying down urgent measures regarding national energy policies, enterprise productivity, and investment attraction, as well as on social policies and the Ukrainian crisis; Law-Decree 13/2023, containing urgent provisions for the implementation of the National Recovery and Resilience Plan (NRRP) and the National Plan for Investments complementary to the NRRP (PNC), as well as for the implementation of cohesion policies and the common agricultural policy; Law-Decree 181/2023, containing urgent provisions for the energy security, the promotion of the use of renewable energy sources.

the use of the concept of sustainability made by Italian administrative courts has evolved over time, largely depending on how different interests at stake in the development of renewable energy facilities have been balanced among them. Moreover, even if the concept of sustainability has been changing in administrative case-law and is still in a process of transition, ecological sustainability[4] has not yet emerged in the case-law as an autonomous notion. Sustainability remains strongly embedded within sustainable development.

The Chapter is structured as follows. First, the relevant case-law of the Constitutional Court will be analysed, with the specific aim of outlining the European-derived principle of "widest distribution" of renewable energies, which has strongly influenced Italian administrative courts in assessing the balance of the interests at stake (§ 2). The evolution of the concept of sustainability in the case-law of administrative courts is then examined, starting with the "traditional" concept of sustainability (§ 2.1) and then reconstructing the most recent judicial developments (§§ 2.2 and 2.3). Eventually, some conclusions of the evolving features of the concept of sustainability will be drawn (§ 3).

2. The principle of "widest distribution" of renewable energy and the other interests at stake

The Italian Constitutional Court's case-law on the legislative competences concerning the location of renewable energy plants may be examined in the light of the principle of "widest distribution" of renewable energy sources,[5] developed in a series of rulings on the constitutionality of regional regulations which have been limiting the development of renewable energy plants.

It is appropriate to outline the constitutional framework within which such case-law is embedded. Under Article 117 of the Italian Constitution, both energy and land use planning are indicated as a shared competence between State and Regions. Accordingly, Regions can legislate in the field

[4] Ecological sustainability is here understood, in line with the overall approach of this book, as a concept of sustainability where ecological concerns may prevail over economic and social ones. For a philosophical declination of ecological sustainability, see Hattingh J.P., "Conceptualising ecological sustainability and ecologically sustainable development in ethical terms: issues and challenges" in *Annale: 2001/2. Department of Philosophy, Stellenbosch: Stellenbosch University*, 2001, 1-22.

[5] See e.g. Constitutional Court 25 March 2022, No. 77; 30 July 2021, No. 177; 5 April 2018, No. 69; 30 January 2014, No. 13.

of energy and the location of renewable energy plants, but their legislations cannot conflict with state law. The relevant state law is Legislative Decree 387/2003, implementing Directive 2001/77/EC on the promotion of electricity produced from renewable energy sources.[6] In this context, Regions have traditionally legislated restrictively under the framework laid down by Legislative Decree 387/2003, mainly for political and social reasons.[7] Indeed, subnational institutions and local communities often oppose the installation of energy production facilities in their areas, as it is widely believed that the local negative impacts of such facilities outweigh the associated benefits. Italy is one of the foremost countries in Europe experiencing such phenomenon, defined as NIMBY – Not In My Backyard by sociologists.[8]

In response, the Italian State has challenged before the Constitutional Court such restrictive laws issued by Regions that often minimize the areas suitable for the location of green power plants, both directly and indirectly. In particular, the Constitutional Court has scrutinized on several occasions regional provisions containing strict limits for the localization of plants under regional land use legislation[9], measures which set a quota to the number of new renewable plants, thus limiting the issuance of new authorizations[10], measures of compensation to the local municipalities for the instal-

---

[6] Directive 2001/77/EC of the European Parliament and of the Council of 27 September 2001 on the promotion of electricity produced from renewable energy sources in the internal electricity market [2001] OJ L 283. Directive 2001/77/EC was repealed by Directive 2009/28/EC of the European Parliament and of the Council of 23 April 2009 on the promotion of the use of energy from renewable sources and amending and subsequently repealing Directives 2001/77/EC and 2003/30/EC [2009] OJ L 140. This was, in its turn, repealed and replaced by Directive (EU) 2018/2001 of the European Parliament and the Council of 11 December 2018 on the promotion of the use of energy from renewable sources [2018] OJ L 328. Directive (EU) 2018/2001 is currently in force, as amended by Directive (EU) 2023/2413 of the European Parliament and of the Council of 18 October 2023 amending Directive (EU) 2018/2001, Regulation (EU) 2018/1999 and Directive 98/70/EC as regards the promotion of energy from renewable sources, and repealing Council Directive (EU) 2015/652 [2023] OJ L 2023/2413. At the national level, Legislative Decree 387/2003 is currently in force, as amended and complemented over time by subsequent legislative decrees.

[7] For an explanation of the different reasons underpinning subnational resistance to the diffusion of "green" power plants, see Fanetti S. and Pozzo B., "Subnational resistance against renewable energy: The case of Italy", in Peeters M. and Schomerus T. (eds.), *Renewable Energy Law in the EU*, Edward Elgar, 2014, and Cuocolo L., *Le Energie Rinnovabili tra Stato e Regioni, un equilibrio instabile tra mercato, autonomia e ambiente,* Giuffrè, 2011.

[8] Buffoli M. et al., "Not In My Back Yard (NIMBY), An endemic syndrome influencing Environmental Policies", in *Epidemiology, Biostatistics, and Public Health*, 2016, 13, 4.

[9] See e.g. Constitutional Court 30 January 2014, No. 13.

[10] Constitutional Court 1 April 2010, No. 124.

lation of plants[11], general suspension of authorization procedures to the issuance of authorizations for the installation and operation of plants at a regional level[12].

In its judgements, the Constitutional Court has generally conferred most of the competences, on the ground of Article 117(2) and Article 117(3) of the Italian Constitution, to State legislation, thus reducing the margin of discretion Regions had in adapting the State rules under Legislative Decree 387/2003. Within this context, the Court stressed that the limitations set by the regional legislation would be inconsistent with the principle of widest distribution of renewable energy. According to the Court, such principle stems from the EU Directives on the promotion of renewable energy sources and is given, as such, a constitutional status under Article 117(1) of the Constitution, according to which legislative power is exercised by State and Regions in compliance with the constraints deriving from EU law and international obligations. Most importantly, this principle has entered into the legal reasoning of the Constitutional Court. [13]

As for administrative courts, in many instances they have been called to decide over the diffusion of renewable energy plants. Litigation has mainly concerned measuring denying authorizations to build and operate plants[14], environmental impact assessment procedures[15] and the right to receive feed-in tariffs and other public incentives[16].

Judgments dealing with denials of authorizations and environmental impact assessment are particularly interesting in order to identify the underlying concept of sustainability. In such rulings, administrative courts are typically tasked with assessing the correctness of the balancing of competing interests carried out by the administration. As already observed, the interests involved in this field are usually numerous and tangled. Typically, they involve (i) energy transition and decarbonization under the principle of widest distribution, (ii) the protection of landscape, (iii) the protection of the cultural heritage, (iv) the right of private economic initiative protected under Article 41 of the Italian Constitution, (v) environmental protec-

---

[11] Constitutional Court 26 March 2010, No. 119.

[12] Constitutional Court 27 October 2022, No. 221.

[13] For a detailed analysis of the Constitutional Courts's line of reasoning, see Buratti V., "Il principio di massima diffusione delle fonti rinnovabili e l'illegittimità di divieti assoluti nella giurisprudenza costituzionale", in *Rivista Giuridica dell'Ambiente*, 2019, 3, 635-658.

[14] See e.g. Council of State, V, 12 November 2018, No. 6342.

[15] Council of State, IV, 30 June 2022, No. 5465.

[16] T.A.R. Lazio, Roma, III-ter, 4 November 2020, No. 11406.

tion, although rarely articulated in the administrative courts' judgments.[17] Importantly, the Council of State has hardly ever used the term "sustainability" expressly in its rulings. Nevertheless, it has inevitably assumed a certain meaning of sustainability when specifying, combining and eventually balancing such interests. Such concept has undergone various interpretations in the case-law over time. The discussion of a selected series of rulings given by the Council of State may illustrate the point.

2.1. A traditional concept of sustainability

According to a well-established case-law, the Council of State has considered that the principle of widest distribution involves the balancing between interests concerning, respectively, environmental protection, landscape and the energy transition. This line of reasoning is clearly formulated in judgement 1768/2016,[18] where the Council of State declares that Directive 2009/28/EC "required Member States to reduce obstacles to the increase of electricity production from renewable sources, including by streamlining and speeding up administrative procedures [...] but did not preclude the balancing, by Member States, of the interest in the promotion of energy production, in the forms indicated, with the safeguarding of other values of obvious domestic constitutional importance [...] protection of the territory, environment and landscape".

Administrative courts make use of a variety of terms indicating the different interests at stake in the field of environmental law: "environment", "landscape", "production of electricity from renewables", "protection of the territory". Such interests are considered to be on the same level, without any prioritization between them. They are also considered as distinct and potentially conflicting, as they relate to different constitutional principles.[19] Unsurprisingly, the balance of different interests is at the very core of the judgements of the Council of State, which refers to such activity as "reconciling" (*contemperare*).

---

[17] Environmental protection has been recently given a constitutional recognition under Article 9 of the Constitution of the Italian Republic. Before the constitutional reform, environment was only listed under Article 117 of the Italian Constitution regarding the share of competences between States and Regions.

[18] Council of State, VI, 5 May 2016, No. 1768.

[19] For an analysis of the interests and values typically in conflict in these judgments, Meli M., "Quando l'ambiente entra in conflitto con sé stesso: fonti energetiche rinnovabili e tutela del paesaggio" in *AmbienteDiritto.it,* 2021, 2, available at https://www.ambientediritto.it/dottrina/quando-lambiente-entra-in-conflitto-con-se-stesso-fonti-energetiche-rinnovabili-e-tutela-del-paesaggio/.

As for sustainability, the Council of State, while not expressly using the term, seems to understand it as implying a balance between different constitutional interests, none of which prevailing over the others. Most importantly, the meaning implicitly adopted by the Council of State can be traced back to the traditional and consolidated understanding of sustainability, namely sustainable development. Indeed, the balance involves, at the same time, economic concerns (the production of electricity as a privatized activity), less noticeable social interests (the protection of the territory) and environmental protection in its different facets, including landscape and the production of electricity from renewable energy sources.

2.2. A new concept of sustainability? The prioritization of green energy production

Such traditional understanding of sustainability has been modified in the case-law of the last few years. The Council of State's judgment 2983/2021[20] provides a telling example.

The case concerned an authorization procedure to build and operate a solar farm in the Italian Region of Lazio. The *Soprintendenza Archeologia, Belle Arti e Paesaggio*, subordinate to the Ministry of Culture, had issued a negative opinion regarding the construction of the photovoltaic plant on agricultural land, pointing to several critical issues, mainly regarding the environmental impact assessment of the relevant project. A steering committee was then convened by the proceeding administration[21] with a view to undertaking a comprehensive analysis of the public interests at stake in the authorization procedure. The steering committee stressed that the opinion of the *Soprintendenza Archeologia, Belle Arti e Paesaggio* was to be considered non-binding, given the absence of constraints on the project areas under the applicable land use laws. Moreover, that opinion did not envisage or suggest any design changes to the project in order to overcome the negative opinion itself.[22] Accordingly, the competent administrative authority, Lazio Region, issued the authorization (*provvedimento autorizza-*

[20] Council of State, IV, 12 April 2021, No. 2983.

[21] The proceeding administration was the Lazio Region. Typically, the Region is the public body entrusted with the issuance of the authorization to build a utility-scale renewable energy plant under Legislative Decree 387/2003, Article 12.

[22] In accordance with paragraph 3 of Article 14-ter of Law 241/90, a negative opinion can be overcome in case the public body which issues the opinion indicates specific requirements to be fulfilled.

torio unico regionale). Such measure was then challenged before the administrative court by the Ministry of Culture, which argued, among the other things, that the Region had given preference to a *private* interest – the production of electricity – over the relevant public ones.

A passage of the judgement is particularly relevant to the conception of sustainability. The Council of State argues that "the production of electricity from renewable sources is [...] an activity of public interest that contributes not only to the protection of environmental interests but also, albeit indirectly, to that of landscape values".[23] By taking this view, the Council of State stresses the public nature of the production of electricity from renewable energy sources, while devaluing its inherently private nature as a business activity. This implies that the balancing exercise is not one between public and private interests, as all interests involved are public in nature. Such line of reasoning is clearly influenced by the case-law of the Constitutional Court, and in particular by its principle of widest distribution.[24] The most peculiar aspect of the ruling, however, is the devaluation of the balancing activity itself. Indeed, the Council of State considers the production of energy from renewable sources as an interest encompassing environmental protection and landscape protection, which become components of the overarching public interest to a green energy transition.

The reasoning of the Council of State raises doubts about the protection granted to the constitutional interests at stake. The claim that the production of electricity from renewable energy sources also protects the landscape is clearly problematic. It involves a legal leap that is difficult to justify. It is not at all clear how the presence of power generation facilities can protect the landscape (in this specific case, agricultural landscape). And it is difficult to follow the explanation given by the Council of State when it declares that the production of electricity from renewable sources is a measure of mitigation and, as such, would be taken to protect the current state of the landscape, which is destined to be affected proportionally to the intensity of climate change.

Judgment 2983/2021, in any case, is not at all an isolated case. A few years earlier, in its ruling 1201/2016[25], for example, the Council of State held that "the production of electricity from solar energy is itself an activity

---

[23] The original wording in Italian is the following: "La produzione di energia elettrica da fonti rinnovabili è infatti un'attività di interesse pubblico che contribuisce anch'essa non solo alla salvaguardia degli interessi ambientali ma, sia pure indirettamente, anche a quella dei valori paesaggistici".

[24] The judgment expressly refers to Constitutional Court 3 December 2019, No. 286.

[25] Council of State, VI, 23 March 2016, No. 1201.

that contributes, albeit indirectly, to the preservation of landscape values (in particular, enabling the exercise of sustainable agriculture and the preservation of the ecosystem, both of which are preconditions for the preservation of the rural landscape)".

Again, the ruling points to the nature of electricity production from renewable sources, stressing that this is a distinct activity, inherently public in nature. This line of reasoning, however, is not convincing. By stating that the energy transition is capable of reconciling all the various aspects of environmental protection, the Council of State actually ends up considering energy transition as a *panacea* for any environmental problem[26] and reducing any environmental issue to decarbonization. If a project has a positive impact in terms of CO_2 emissions reduction when compared to the *status quo*, then it is assumed to be beneficial also for other aspects of the environment. These include landscape protection and ecosystems and other interests.[27] This presumption seems to be grounded on the idea that the goal of reducing CO_2 emissions – a key element in combatting climate change – implicitly serves broader environmental interests. Thus, green energy production overrides and even absorbs other environmental interests, thereby placing CO_2 reduction at the forefront of environmental initiatives. Yet, this line of reasoning lacks a clear cause-and-effect relationship between the installation of a renewable energy power plant and the protection of environment and landscape.

Most importantly for the purpose of our inquiry, the position taken by the Council of State has some implications on the understanding of sustainability in the Italian legal order. In the Council of States' view, as it has been observed, decarbonization through the establishment of renewable energy plants is inherently supposed to match all environmental protection targets. Such approach implicitly dismisses the need to balance different interests within environmental protection efforts. Administrative courts certainly recognize the economic dimension of green energy production, raised to a matter of public interest. This might seem in line with the consolidated notion of sustainable development. In this case, though, sustainable development tends to overlap with the call for decarbonization and transition to renewable energies: the understanding of sustainability that the Council of State seems to have in mind is one in which the green energy

---

[26] In the same vein, Carpentieri P., "Paesaggio, Ambiente e Transizione Ecologica", in *Giustizia Insieme*, 4 May 2021, available at https://www.giustiziainsieme.it/en/diritto-e-processo-amministrativo/1710-paesaggio-ambiente-e-transizione-ecologica?hitcount=0.

[27] Other administrative judgments have tried to argue that solar panels and wind farms would have become an element of the landscape itself; see e.g. T.A.R. Campania, Salerno, II, 28 February 2022, No. 564.

production is prioritized and sustainability tends to coincide with the policy goal of decarbonisation.

2.3. Step back? The rescue of balancing

The innovative approach taken by the Council of State has been somehow contradicted by a later judgment. Indeed, in ruling 7550/2021,[28] the Council of State has expressly denied that the principle of widest distribution of renewables can indistinctly take precedence over environmental protection.

Again, the reasoning of the ruling raises some doubts. In this judgment, the principle of widest distribution of renewables and the environment are considered as potentially conflicting interests. In particular, the Council of State argues that a balancing would be always needed and that a mere prevalence of the concept of widest distribution over a – not better specified – environmental protection cannot be endorsed. In the words of the Council of State, "the Court does not agree with the appellant's option, which goes so far as to interpret the principle as meaning that the interest in the construction of facilities should always be considered to take precedence over the interest in environmental protection". Granting absolute precedence to the principle of widest distribution of renewables over the interests related to environmental protection would unlawfully avoid the necessary balance between the various interests at stake.

Notably, the Council of State stresses that the need to balance also derives from Directive (EU) 2018/2001 and Directive 2011/92/EU, which concern respectively renewable energy generation and the environmental impact assessment.[29] Hence, the Council of State does not argue that the widest distribution of green energy sources would be in any case justified by EU law. This position has been confirmed by Council of State 8167/2022, which emphasizes the balancing of interests, recognizing that no interest can be given absolute precedence over the others and that a systemic activity of mutual integration by the administration in the proceeding is always necessary.[30]

It should be noticed that in this ruling the phrase "sustainable development" is used. More precisely, the Council of State observes that "the Administration, in re-examining the power, must this time seek not the to-

---

[28] Council of State, VI, 12 November 2021, No. 7550.

[29] Directive (EU) 2018/2001 (*ibidem,* 7); and Directive 2011/92/EU of the European Parliament and of the council of 13 December 2011 on the assessment of the effects of certain public and private projects on the environment (2011) OJ L 26.

[30] Council of State, VI, 23 September 2022, No. 8167.

tal sacrifice of the productive use of clean energy (…) according to a merely inhibitory logic, but a comparative and dialectical solution between the needs of sustainable development and those pertaining to the cultural landscape". Interestingly, the Council of State refers to sustainable development as a concept which might be in conflict with other interests pertaining to environmental protection, such as cultural landscape. In this perspective, sustainable development comprises economic, social and *some* environmental objectives. Other environmental interests, such as landscape protection, are deemed as external and even conflicting with the objective of sustainable development. This approach implicitly entails that sustainable development does not only imply a balance between the various interests at stake, but it may also require to be balanced with environmental interests which are considered to be inconsistent with it.

3. Conclusions

The analysis carried out in this Chapter has revealed an evolution in the case-law of Italian administrative courts in the field of electricity production plants from renewable energy sources. This evolution is also indicative of a changing conception of sustainability.

In a first phase, a careful activity of balancing interests, including environmental interests, was considered fundamental and indispensable, as exemplified by ruling 1768/2016 of the Council of State. This phase was then followed by a second stage, exemplified by the judgments 1201/2016 and 2983/2021, where the Council of State, through a disputable legal reasoning, has considered the principle of widest distribution of renewable energies as a prevailing interest. Some recent judgments, however, might have opened a third phase, as the Council of State has emphasized again the activity of balancing conflicting interests as the core of administrative function. By returning to distinguish between the various environmental interests at stake, the Council of State seems to avoid the risk to identify environmental concerns with the principle of widest distribution of renewables.

Such judicial evolution is certainly significant. First, it shows that most rulings are still strongly grounded on the traditional understanding of sustainability as sustainable development. At least so far, the new conceptions of sustainability emerging in the context of the European Green Deal – examined more punctually in other sections of this book – have not been absorbed and articulated by administrative jurisprudence. This is demonstrated not only by the explicit use of the sustainable development vocabulary in rulings such as 8167/2022, but also by the reasoning followed by the Council of State, which has never theorized a supremacy of the ecological aspects of sustainability over the economic ones. The economic dimension is always intrinsically part of the concept of sustainability used by Italian administrative courts. This is evident in the judgments where the production of green energy, despite being a private economic activity, is given the status of a public interest which would take precedence over other environmental concerns.

The inquiry also shows that the Council of State has applied different interpretations of sustainability over time, reflecting a fluctuation in the understanding of the very function of balancing between the involved interests. In some judgments, sustainable development is an implicit overarching objective, which overlaps with the objective of widest diffusion of renewables. In other judgments, it is referred to as an objective to be balanced with other external interests, such as landscape protection. A definitive doctrinal theorization of the new models of sustainability appears necessary. This would be fundamental both to bring some conceptual clarity and to orientate the case-law of Italian and other Member States' courts.

Chapter 6

POWERING THE SMART CITY: SUSTAINABLE ENERGY IN THE NEW SMART CITY

Georgios Christou

ABSTRACT: *Cities play a significant role in the field of climate change, not least because of their large energy consumption and massive emissions production. This Chapter examines the European Smart City strategy through the lens of different projects it has employed and funded. Specifically, it analyses the characteristics of this strategy through its various components (i.e., policy documents and voluntary initiatives) to determine the nature and intentions of the EU's commitment behind its claim of 'sustainability'.*

KEYWORDS: *Energy transition – Smart City – Sustainability.*

1. Cities and climate change

Under the lens of the European Union (EU)'s own statistics, around 325 million people or about three-quarters of the EU population live in cities, towns and suburbs, with almost 40% residing in cities alone,[1] with the estimated urban population of Europe projected to rise to over 80% by 2050.[2] This naturally makes cities the biggest consumer of energy in Europe, and in turn, the largest origin of greenhouse gas emissions.[3]

Due to their massive importance in the climate crisis the world is currently facing, the EU has in recent years shifted its attention to address the gargantuan impact that cities have on tackling climate change. The Smart City strategy is a key component of the EU's commitment to make cities

---

[1] Eurostat, *Distribution of population by degree of urbanisation, dwelling type and income group – EU-SILC survey*, 2020.

[2] Eurostat, *Urban Europe: Statistics on cities, towns and suburbs*, Publications Office of the European Union, 2016, 9.

[3] Covenant of Mayors Office, *Reducing Energy Dependence in European Cities*, 2017.

more sustainable. This strategy is comprised of many parts and pieces and includes policy directives as well as funding projects and voluntary initiatives. While not a formulation of the Green Deal, it is informed by it, and an instrumental part of it. This paper will focus on four components of the European Smart City strategy – the Energy Efficiency Directive, the Covenant of Mayors, the Horizon Project, as well as REPowerEU – to ascertain what kind of sustainability the EU brings forth through such a package via examining these separate policies and initiatives, as well as how they evolve the concept in light of the Smart City strategy.

2. Introducing the European Smart City

As discussed above, urban cities comprise of the largest population concentrations in Europe. It was for these reasons that the former Juncker Commission made energy such a vital role in the Smart City. [4] Cities as a target for sustainability have been noted important enough to be included in the UN's Agenda for 2030, [5] and later adopted as Sustainable Development Goal 11 under the Sustainable development in the European Union plan. [6]

But what exactly is a Smart City, and how does it play a part in the EU's energy policies? [7] In essence, throughout all the definitions found by either the Commission or by scholarly literature, Smart City definitions typically include a broad use of ICT and technology, are friendly towards business innovations, while also empowering its citizens by allowing active monitoring and being open to innovation, with the latter coming into fruition through various programs and other social goals. [8] While a common, agreed upon definition for the concept of a Smart City does not exist, with multiple definitions and different interpretations existing, [9] the European Com-

---

[4] COM (2015) 80 final.

[5] United Nations, *Transforming our World: The 2030 Agenda for Sustainable Development*, 2015.

[6] Eurostat, *Sustainable development in the European Union*, 2022, ISBN 978-92-76-46573-7, doi: 10.2785/313289, Cat. No: KS-09-22-019-EN-N, remaining as SDG 11.

[7] European Commission, *Smart cities: Cities using technological solutions to improve the management and efficiency of the urban environment*, 2023, available via https://commission.europa.eu/eu-regional-and-urban-development/topics/cities-and-urban-development/city-initiatives/smart-cities_en.

[8] *Ibidem*, 6.

[9] Macaluso A., Flickenschild M., Gasparotti A., Wedman H. and Panagiotidou of Ecorys Z. et al., "Social approach to the transition to smart cities", in *Panel for the Future of Science and Technology*, 2023 (STOA), 4.

mission defines it as: "a place where traditional networks and services are made more efficient with the use of digital solutions for the benefit of its inhabitants and business." For the European Commission, "a smart city goes beyond the use of digital technologies for better resource use and less emissions. It means smarter urban transport networks, upgraded water supply and waste disposal facilities and more efficient ways to light and heat buildings. It also means a more interactive and responsive city administration, safer public spaces and meeting the needs of an ageing population. According to the European Commission, "the definition of a 'smart city' goes beyond the use of digital technologies – it also includes more energy efficient buildings, integrated renewable energy sources, sustainable heating and cooling systems, smarter urban transport networks, upgraded water supply and better waste disposal facilities to tackle the city's economic, social and environmental challenges". [10]

But a key factor is the inclusion of sustainability. What that sustainability means in the context of smart cities is a topic hotly contested by scholars, [11] and the aim of this paper will be to determine what kind of sustainability can be derived from the energy portion of the EU example. This more holistic, social approach to smart cities is recognized by the European Union itself. In a study by the European Parliamentary Research Service, smart cities are defined as a 'living concept'. [12] From the study's perspective they break down the evolution of smart cities into three distinct generations. The first generation "followed a technology-driven approach promoted by large technology companies that led this movement in urban areas with the intention of selling technological solutions to cities to provide a more efficient way of managing urban challenges and activities", a generation lead initially by companies such as IBM and Cisco. [13] The second generation follows a more ambitious development that also involved city authorities and decision makers ascertaining their reign over the development of smart cities in their individual territories. Its goal was to "enhance the quality of life in urban areas by using the beneficial aspects of technolo-

[10] European Commission, *In focus: Energy and smart cities*, 2022, available at https://commission.europa.eu/news/focus-energy-and-smart-cities-2022-07-13_en.

[11] See for example, Hassan A.M. and Lee H., "The paradox of the sustainable city: Definitions and examples", in *Environ. Dev. Sustain.*, 2015, 17, 1267-1285 and Choi H.S. and Song S.K., "Direction for a Transition toward Smart Sustainable Cities Based on the Diagnosis of Smart City Plans", in *Smart cities*, 2023, 6, 160.

[12] Macaluso A., Flickenschild M., Gasparotti A., Wedman H. and Panagiotidou of Ecorys Z. et al, "Social approach to the transition to smart cities", cit., available at https://www.europarl.europa.eu/stoa/en/document/EPRS_STU(2023)737128.

[13] *Ibidem*, 5.

gies".[14] While this generation was marked by the employment of technical facilities to a great extent, it did not allow technology to expand uncontrollably, dominate urban life, or acquire decision-making authority. It also involved a more social approach to city development by addressing social challenges, enhancing citizen well-being and public services, as well as touching on other endogenous problems.[15] The third generation was marked by the increasing role of citizens in addressing their issues and assisting city managers in solving them.[16] In Smart City 3.0, all individuals shared their opinions and helped decision-makers find the most reliable and practical solutions for social, environmental, and government challenges in cities.[17] It was at this point where the social aspect of smart cities was starting to blossom, and according to the European Parliament study, on its social aspects too, with not all smart solutions being necessarily tech-driven ideas, with urban topics being addressed "without solely focusing on the technological dimension".[18]

Finally, the study moves on to describe the European study's perception of the future of the Smart City, or what they call the fourth generation. They state that this fourth transition combines the priority of matching the expected benefit of the digital transition with those of the green transition. They also observe the "need for a digital transition that is not limited to urban areas, but rather concerns any community, whatever its size. With the improvement of fixed broadband and mobile networks, thanks to national plans supported by EU funds, all communities in the EU are confronted with the challenge of accompanying the digital transition of their territories, which has led to some proposing the term smart community or smart territory as an alternative to the city-centric view".[19] They continue to express how the recent Covid-19 pandemic has exemplified how "digital resilience and the ability to continue daily life during a pandemic as an essential pillar of smart communities".

---

[14] *Ibidem.*

[15] Trencher G., "Towards the smart city 2.0: Empirical evidence of using smartness as a tool for tackling social challenges", in *Technological Forecasting and Social Change*, 2019, 142, 117-128.

[16] Hernàndez C.A., "The role of citizens in smart cities and urban infrastructures", in *Solving Urban Infrastructure Problems Using Smart City Technologies*, Elsevier, 2021, 213-234.

[17] Singh P., Lynch F. and Helfert M., "Role of Citizens in the Development of Smart Cities: Benefit of Citizen's Feedback for Improving Quality of Service", in *SMARTGREENS*, 2021, 35-44.

[18] *Ibidem*, 12, 6.

[19] *Ibidem.*

This ethos of the fourth generation of smart cities that the study describes, is also present in what they consider the EU's strategy's best practices. For example, the Irish "Digital inclusion for women" best practice is arguably a practice that is entirely socially oriented. The best practice targets female teenagers and young adolescents allowing them to enjoy two weeks work placements in STEM related companies, as well as additional courses and seminars.[20] The focus here is people, with the goal of "equal quality of life for all citizens".[21] In comparison, the other highlighted best practice from Tallin, 'Free public transport for residents', also targets people, but especially those with low-income. Spurred by the 2008 financial crisis, the project started with the intent to offer public transport to citizens with low-income who needed to spend a significant part of their budget on public transport. The project then transformed into focusing more on "promoting modal shift from private car to public transport, improving the mobility of unemployed and low-income residents, and stimulating the registration of inhabitants as residents of Tallinn to increase the municipal income tax with which the new system is paid".[22] The project was successful in reducing car usage,[23] showing that behavioural changes could lead to more sustainable outcomes, even if ecological well-being might not have been the focus.

3. Energizing the European city: four illustrations

The Union's Smart City strategy is comprised of a myriad of different parts and initiatives. Some of it is contained in directives and regulations, while other parts of it rest in fundings and other voluntary initiatives. This Chapter will choose to focus on three initiatives: the energy performance of buildings directive, the Covenant of Mayors for Climate and Energy as well as the Horizon Project. These were chosen as they illustrate firstly, the direct 'sustainable' intent of the EU through the directive, as well as other potential intrinsic or extrinsic motivations that can be derived from indirect fundings and non-legal initiatives. It is notable however that the list chosen here is far from exhaustive,[24] and analysing them

---

[20] *Ibidem*, 37.

[21] *Ibidem*.

[22] *Ibidem*, 39.

[23] Cats O., Susilo Y. O. and Reimal T., "The prospects of fare-free public transport: evidence from Tallinn", in Transportation, 2017, 44(5), 1083-1104, though the effect on emissions was not as significant as desired.

[24] A more comprehensive list of smart cities initiatives can be found scattered in the European Commission's website, such as https://smart-cities-marketplace.ec.europa.

independently is also naïve. As such, a reference to the general EU energy strategy will be made as well, particularly REPowerEU,[25] in order to better understand how the EU channels their intentions through these various initiatives and directives.

4. Energy Efficiency Directive: a tale of two goals

The first part of the strategy to look at is the Energy Efficiency Directive 2012/27/EU.[26] The directive was published in 2012, repealing the previous Energy Services Directive 2006,[27] it sought to establish a set of binding measures to help the EU reach its 20% energy efficiency target by 2020. The directive would require to improve its energy efficiency and use in multiple stages of the energy cycle, from energy generation transmission, distribution, and end-use consumption.[28] The targets set by the directive were overachieved, although the Commission states that the Covid-19 pandemic had an influence on those numbers.[29] The directive was then amended in 2018 with the amending Directive on Energy Efficiency[30] as part of the "Clean energy for all Europeans package" in order to update the policy framework of the EU for 2030 and beyond, and was later recast in 2023[31] as part of the "Fit for 55" Package, introducing stricter goals and higher ambitions to the Member States. By far the most vital element was its update to the targets it sets, with an efficiency target of 32.5% to be collectively met across the EU, a number that was built with relative model

---

eu/action-clusters-and-initiatives/other-initatives which includes a list of various Smart Cities Marketplace collaborations.

[25] COM (2022) 108.

[26] Directive 2012/27/EU of the European Parliament and of the Council of 25 October 2012 on energy efficiency, amending Directives 2009/125/EC and 2010/30/EU and repealing Directives 2004/8/EC and 2006/32/EC, OJ 2012 L 315.

[27] Directive 2006/32/EC of the European Parliament and of the Council of 5 April 2006 on energy end-use efficiency and energy services and repealing Council Directive 93/76/EEC, OJ 2006 L 114.

[28] European Commission, *Energy efficiency directive*, available at https://energy.ec.europa.eu/topics/energy-efficiency/energy-efficiency-targets-directive-and-rules/energy-efficiency-directive_en.

[29] *Ibidem.*

[30] Directive (EU) 2018/2002 of the European Parliament and of the Council of 11 December 2018 amending Directive 2012/27/EU on energy efficiency, OJ 2018 L 328.

[31] Directive (EU) 2023/1791 of the European Parliament and of the Council of 13 September 2023 on energy efficiency and amending Regulation (EU) 2023/955 (recast), ELI: http://data.europa.eu/eli/dir/2023/1791/oj.

projections from 2007. The 2023 recast would also establish an EU legally binding target to reduce the EU's final energy consumption by 11.7% by 2030 (relative to the 2020 reference scenario).[32] The technological component of the Energy Efficiency Directives comes in the form of how it tries to improve on the energy efficiency on buildings. Buildings were chosen in particular due to their consumption size, as they comprise 40% of EU energy consumption and are responsible for 36% of the energy-related greenhouse gas emissions.[33] This makes buildings the single largest energy consumer in Europe, with heating, cooling and domestic hot water account for 80% of the energy that European citizens, consume.[34] A large cause of this is that about 35% of the EU's buildings are over 50 years old and almost 75% of the building stock is energy inefficient, with only 1% of the building stock being renovated each year.[35]

Introduced initially in the Energy Efficiency Directive of 2012,[36] as well as the Energy Performance of Buildings Directive of 2010,[37] the EU wanted to promote policies that would achieve a highly energy efficient and decarbonised building stock by 2050, create stability for investors, and empower consumers and businesses to make better decisions regarding energy and financial savings.[38] The directives were later amended alongside the general Energy Efficiency Directive in 2018 and 2019 with the Directive amending the Energy Performance of Buildings Directive.[39] The Commission also published two recommendations in 2019, one for building renovation[40] and another for building modernization[41] to facilitate their applica-

[32] European Commission, *European Green Deal: Energy Efficiency Directive adopted, helping make the EU 'Fit for 55'*, D.G. For Energy, 2023.

[33] European Commission, *Energy performance of buildings directive*, available at https://energy.ec.europa.eu/topics/energy-efficiency/energy-efficient-buildings/energy-performance-buildings-directive_en.

[34] *Ibidem.*

[35] *Ibidem.*

[36] At 26.

[37] Directive 2010/31/EU of the European Parliament and of the Council of 19 May 2010 on the energy performance of buildings (recast), OJ 2010 L 153.

[38] At 31.

[39] Directive (EU) 2018/844 of the European Parliament and of the Council of 30 May 2018 amending Directive 2010/31/EU on the energy performance of buildings and Directive 2012/27/EU on energy efficiency, OJ 2018 L 156.

[40] Commission Recommendation (EU) 2019/786 of 8 May 2019 on building renovation, ELI: http://data.europa.eu/eli/reco/2019/786/oj.

[41] Commission Recommendation (EU) 2019/1019 of 7 June 2019 on building modernisation, OJ 2019 L 127.

tion. Finally, the Commission has also proposed a revision for the directive that would upgrade the existing regulatory framework to reflect higher ambitions, with a stated goal of addressing climate and social needs while taking into account the diverse building stock currently present in Europe.[42] The proposal[43] also sets out how Europe can achieve a zero-emission and fully decarbonised building stock by 2050 through an increased rate of renovation for poor building stock, set a higher standard of near-zero emission for buildings, better long-term renovation strategies, but crucially, modernisation of buildings and their systems, and better energy system integration (for heating, cooling, ventilation, charging of electric vehicles, renewable energy).[44]

In general, the Energy Efficiency Directive introduces several measures that boost energy performance of buildings and improve the existing building stock. For instance, it aims to decarbonize the national building stocks by 2050 and requires the Member States to set cost-optimal minimum energy performance requirements for new buildings, for existing buildings undergoing major renovation, and for the replacement or retrofit of building elements like heating and cooling systems, roofs and walls. New buildings are also addressed, with all constructions after 2021 being required to be nearly zero energy buildings, with an introduction of a certification system for inspection schemes for heating and air-conditioning. Notably, the 2023 recast also obliges EU Member States to prioritise vulnerable customers and social housing within the scope of their energy savings measures.[45] The technological component of the directive is, however, optional. The Commission through this directive adopts an optional scheme for rating the smart readiness of buildings.[46]

The Commission essentially wants to promote digitalisation of the energy system to smart grids and smart-ready buildings. The Commission's rationale for this certification system is to "measure the capacity of buildings to use information and communication technologies and electronic systems to adapt the operation of buildings to the needs of the occupants and the grid and to improve the energy efficiency and overall performance of buildings", as well as "raise awareness amongst building owners and occupants of the value behind building automation and electronic monitoring of technical building systems" and "give confidence to occupants about the

[42] At 31.

[43] COM (2021) 802.

[44] At 30.

[45] Under Article 22.

[46] *Ibidem*, Article 8, para. 10.

actual savings of those new enhanced-functionalities".[47] In addition to this, measures for electro-mobility are also introduced, in order to efficiently integrate new loads into the electricity system, such as electric vehicles, using smart charging and vehicle to grid technologies in buildings such as cat parks or charging homes.[48] The Commission's intention here seems to be threefold; reduce energy consumption while also making energy cheaper and improve the community's access and livelihoods in urban areas and even beyond.

5. Covenant of mayors: the three pillars of Smart Cities

One of the most unique parts of the Smart City strategy is that of the Covenant of Mayors. The project was launched by the European Commission in 2008, and its goal was to bring together local and regional authorities who voluntarily commit to implementing the EU's climate and energy objectives on their territory in a joint effort to reduce by at least 20% of their emissions by 2020, which was the same target of the EU at the time.[49] The covenant would later evolve into the Covenant of Mayors 2030 in 2015, which would increase the minimum mitigation target by 2030 by up to 40% and include two new pillars: adaptation to climate change and secure, sustainable and affordable access to energy.[50] The Covenant would evolve once more the following year, merging with the Compact of Mayors into the Global Covenant of Mayors for Energy & Climate (GCoM).[51]

The Covenant currently includes over 11,000 signatories under a joint effort to "increase resilience and prepare for the adverse impacts of climate change, and tackle energy poverty as one key action to ensure a just transition".[52] The Covenant, which is funded almost entirely through public funds, essentially supports its signatories through these three key pillars of mitigation, adaptation, and energy poverty, in their efforts to plan, implement and monitor adaptation actions – by providing methodological guid-

[47] *Ibidem.*

[48] At 35, Article 6.2.

[49] European Commission, *Energy and smart cities*, cit.

[50] Rivas S., Urraca R., Palermo V. and Bertoldi P., "Covenant of Mayors 2020: Drivers and barriers for monitoring climate action plans", in *J. Clean. Prod.*, 2022, 332, 130029, https://doi.org/10.1016/j.jclepro.2021.130029.

[51] *Ibidem.*

[52] Excerpt from the official Covenant of Mayors Commitment Document, available at https://eu-mayors.ec.europa.eu/system/files/2022-07/eumayors-commitment-2021-EN.docx.

ance, capacity building activities, knowledge resources and opportunities for collaboration.

But what exactly does the Covenant do? Each partner in the Covenant of Mayors is required to develop a Sustainable Energy Action Plan (SEAP) once they join within 2 years. That SEAP includes action plans and projects in order to operationalize the strategies for achieving the associated targets. The SEAP is a politically approved document, describing the long-term strategy and the measures planned by the local authority to reach the target. It is also a technical document and a communication tool addressing citizens and local stakeholders. The European Commission's Joint Research Centre (JRC) then evaluates the local action plans and proceeds to provide the signatory with complete feedback, highlighting both the main strengths, as well as the weaknesses and giving recommendations for improvement.[53] The signatory then adapts city structures, to make sure that all the relevant departments of the local authority are involved in the SEAP process and proceeds to mobilise its citizens and local stakeholders in order to begin and complete the SEAP development and implementation. The process then finishes with a submission by the signatory of an implementation report every second year after submission of the SEAP, for the purposes of monitoring and verification. This report has to also be accompanied by a monitoring emission inventory every fourth year.[54] The signatory is required of course, to work on all aspects of the commitment they sign, and not simply ecological ones, and are measured based on each category separately by the JRC. The three pillars mentioned above is what is most notable about the Covenant, as it shows the priority of the EU for Smart Cities, both involving emission reductions, or otherwise ecological goals, as well as reduction in energy poverty, or otherwise social goals.

6. Horizon project: an urban sustainability blueprint

Moving on, it is worth looking more into how the European Commission has used its funding towards trying to make smart cities a reality. The Horizon Europe Mission on Climate-Neutral and Smart Cities is one such initiative. The Commission launched the project in 2020 with a €360 mil-

[53] Melica G., Bertoldi P., Kona A., Iancu A., Rivas S. and Zancanella P., "Multilevel governance of sustainable energy policies: the role of regions and provinces to support the participation of small local authorities in the Covenant of Mayors", in *Sustain. Cities Soc.*, 2018, 39, 729-739, 10.1016/j.scs.2018.01.013, 731.

[54] *Ibidem*, 730.

lion funding, where they announced the so called 'Cities Mission', where 100 EU cities will participate in the EU Mission for 100 climate-neutral and smart cities by 2030.[55] In the Commission's President's Ursula von der Leyen own words, these cities are meant to "show us the way to a healthier future",[56] meaning that these cities are almost emblematic of what the Commission has in mind for the future of European Cities in terms of sustainability. Cities were invited to express their interest to become part of the Mission by the end of January 2022, with 100 cities being selected out of the interested 377. The Mission was part of five other approved initiatives within Horizon, with the other three also being environmentally oriented goals such as 'Restore our Ocean and Waters by 2030',[57] with the final one being an initiative to curing and treatment of cancer.[58]

Much like the Covenant of Mayors and the Energy Efficiency Directives discussed above, the Horizon project also considers urban action vital to achieving climate mitigation,[59] and in order to achieve the wider European climate goals such as the Green Deal, the cities have to become more 'green' and 'digital' and "offer cleaner air, safer transport and less congestion and noise to their citizens".[60] In fact, the Commission directly states that "Technology alone, will not solve any of a city's challenges".[61] According to the Commission's own words in the project's foresight, "transformation towards climate neutrality will require a coordinated approach including well-thought urban planning, a combination of largescale public

---

[55] European Commission, *Commission announces 100 cities participating in EU Mission for climate-neutral and smart cities by 2030*, Press Release, 2022, available at https://ec.europa.eu/commission/presscorner/detail/en/ip_22_2591.

[56] *Ibidem.*

[57] European Commission, *EU Missions in Horizon Europe*, 2023, available at https://research-and-innovation.ec.europa.eu/funding/funding-opportunities/funding-programmes-and-open-calls/horizon-europe/eu-missions-horizon-europe_en.

[58] For more information, European Commission, *EU Mission: Cancer*, 2023, available at https://research-and-innovation.ec.europa.eu/funding/funding-opportunities/funding-programmes-and-open-calls/horizon-europe/eu-missions-horizon-europe/eu-mission-cancer_en.

[59] European Commission, *EU Mission: Climate-Neutral and Smart Cities*, 2023, available at https://research-and-innovation.ec.europa.eu/funding/funding-opportunities/funding-programmes-and-open-calls/horizon-europe/eu-missions-horizon-europe/climate-neutral-and-smart-cities_en.

[60] *Ibidem.*

[61] European Commission, *Mission Area: Climate-Neutral and Smart Cities, Foresight on Demand Brief in Support of the Horizon Europe Mission Board*, Publications Office of the European Union, 2021, 18.

and private investments, and co-creation between city policy makers, economic actors and citizens".[62]

When it comes to energy, Horizon acknowledges that there are close interconnections between energy, transportation and building sectors. This is also reflected in their actual approach too, as it seeks to not only work on just improving energy technologies, but also address the energy crisis in an interdisciplinary way. It acknowledges that "city dwellers' lifestyles can help significantly reduce their climate footprint, such as adopting healthy diets, reducing waste, using active, shared or public mobility or choosing sustainable energy source, even producing their own energy",[63] something that improvements in technology as well as their accessibility can provide to a city. Thus, for the Commission, zero net emissions can only be achieved only if "technology development and business models emerge together and large- and small-scale energy initiatives and solutions are being integrated, including major infrastructure investments, citywide improvements in energy efficiency, and distributed energy resources".[64] The Commission continues to emphasize the role of the behavioural aspects in achieving Horizon's greenhouse gas emission reductions. The Commission believe that Behavioural changes can complement technological changes and drive more cost-effective solutions. They justify this approach after evidence that using emotion, social incentives, and the use of choice architecture can be a very potent way of influencing behaviour towards conservation goals.[65] This could include "shifting to a more healthy and balanced diet, eating less meat and dairy products, buying and using a smaller car or an electric car, teleworking, adjusting room temperature and optimising ventilation".[66]

This interdisciplinary approach to fight climate change is exemplified in Horizon's plan for transport. Horizon uses the Netherlands as an example of this in motion. After noticing a massive increase in car ownership leading to heavy traffic, a lot of Danish municipalities started to shift towards developing policies for cycling in the 1970's and 1980's, only to realize that such an act on its own was not enough to dethrone the car as the prime

[62] *Ibidem.*

[63] *Ibidem*, 24.

[64] *Ibidem.*

[65] Williamson K., Satre-Meloy A., Velasco K. and Green K., *Climate Change Needs Behavior Change: Making the Case For Behavioral Solutions to Reduce Global Warming*, Center For Behavior & The Environment, 2018: Rare is one of the studies cited for the potency of behavioural changes in greenhouse emissions.

[66] *Ibidem.*

mode of transport.[67] To do so, it had to delve deeper into the behavioural and social aspects of cycling. Other factors such as "clearly indicated safe, separate cycling lanes with route signs to major destinations, priority at crossings, optimisation of traffic lights for cyclists, provision of parking spaces (preferably guarded), optimisation of specific local and regional routes in so-called bicycle highways, and good connection to the public transport" were some other additional things that needed to be implemented before cycling had to become more popular.[68] The project also references other similar examples. Amsterdam nudged its inhabitants away from heavy car usage through the reduction of individual transport through reduced space consumption for parking cars, essentially forcing the inhabitants (albeit somewhat controversially) to give up their cars.[69] The program even seems to try and address the problem of the aging building stock of Europe like the Directives mentioned above. For instance, they identify that the retrofitted technology applied to these buildings to increase their efficiency involves a high upfront cost, which would in time result to annual cost savings, making them attractive from a purely economic point of view.[70] Thus, they propose a business model based on a new financing scheme that is built upon programs that support the overcoming of barriers related to high upfront costs. These can be also incentive schemes through taxes or giving the producer of renewable energy a direct payment per unit of energy produced, which would create additional "value of a product/service from the environmental, social, and economic point of view, in relation, for instance, to a high score in a voluntary sustainability assessment scheme".[71] It is those kinds of innovations and policies that the Horizon project seems to have a desire of adopting upon its 100 selected cities, and slowly permeate across the rest of Europe to promote sustainability and achieve its goals. Much like the previous examples mentioned, this project echoes an understanding that smart cities are neither simply ecological or about technological advancement, but something that involves both, in the interest of improving the populations of these respective cities in a holistic manner.

---

[67] *Ibidem*, 58, 25.

[68] *Ibidem*, referring to the New Town of Houten.

[69] *Ibidem*, 26.

[70] *Ibidem*, 27.

[71] *Ibidem*.

7. The general framework: REPowerEU

Finally, the last component worth examining is that of REPowerEU. While not a direct component of the Smart City initiative by itself, the REPowerEU plan introduces components and strategies that do affect cities and urban areas directly. The plan was introduced for two reasons. One is a response to the hardships and global energy market disruption caused by Russia's invasion of Ukraine, a move that sought to end fossil fuel dependence on Russia. The other is simply tackling the economic crisis further.[72] The plan therefore seeks to achieve this through multiple goals. Namely, through energy savings, diversification of energy supplies, and accelerated roll-out of renewable energy to replace fossil fuels in homes, industry and power generation.[73]

What makes the plan vital to smart cities is how it seeks to diversify the European energy supply. While securing alternative liquefied natural gas (LNG) imports and higher pipeline gas deliveries is one part of that, the plan also seeks to diversify by building long-term partnerships with suppliers of alternative technologies, including cooperation on hydrogen or other green technologies.[74] Technology plays a vital part in REPowerEU, helping to scale-up and speeding-up of renewable energy in power generation, industry, buildings and transport. Among others, the REPowerEU plan introduces a dedicated EU Solar Strategy to double solar photovoltaic capacity by 2025 and install 600GW by 2030, A Solar Rooftop Initiative with a phased-in legal obligation to install solar panels on new public and commercial buildings and new residential buildings, doubles the rate of deployment of heat pumps, and measures to integrate geothermal and solar thermal energy in modernised district and communal heating systems. These improvements are backed by a €225 billion already available in loans out of the €260 required under the RRF. REPowerEU also aims to save on energy in an urgent manner, with the Commission proposing to enhance long-term energy efficiency measures, including an increase from 9% to 13% of the binding Energy Efficiency Target under the "Fit for 55" package of European Green Deal legislation in order to prepare for a challenging winter, something that became part of the recasted Energy Efficiency Directive of 2023 examined earlier. They aim to do so through behavioural

[72] European Commission, *REPowerEU: A plan to rapidly reduce dependence on Russian fossil fuels and fast forward the green transition*, 2022, available at https://ec.europa.eu/commission/presscorner/detail/en/ip_22_3131.

[73] *Ibidem.*

[74] *Ibidem.*

changes such as campaigns targeting households and industry stakeholders, which could cut oil and gas demand significantly.[75] This could include incentives such as through the reduction of VAT rates on energy efficient heating systems.[76] Once more, much like the previous examples of the European energy policy, we see the EU Commission take an interdisciplinary approach towards tackling the climate crisis through energy, combining both social and ecological causes and behaviours into a singular approach to tackle the crisis through energy.

8. Sustainability in the Smart City

With these four examples explored, we can now attempt to extract the EU's intention for smart cities. It is difficult to declare, even from a surface understanding of the material examined in this Chapter that the EU's intentions are purely ecological or technological in nature. The energy policy discussed above very much reflects the fourth generation of the Smart City envisioned in this study. For instance, while the Energy Efficiency Directive and the Energy Performance of Buildings Directive were created with the intention of reducing greenhouse gas emissions by reducing electricity waste and inefficiency while facilitating the modernization of cities through technological integration, a deeper reading into the Commission's stated goals reveals a sustainability intention beyond the purely ecological. In fact, it seems that the goal of the Commission to improve the environment is something purely incidental that will happen once European cities become more modern and more energy efficient. The wording and goals of the directive are emblematic of such approach. The technological aspect of the directive is simply an optional certification scheme. The Directive's aim was, once again, to "create stability for investors, and empower consumers and businesses to make better decisions regarding energy and financial savings", which echoes the idea of a smart community of multiple stakeholders, trying to tackle endogenous issues beyond simply ecological, such as by improving the buildings, reducing energy costs, and overall improving the quality of life for the city's citizens, especially when noting the recast Directive's focus on prioritizing the vulnerable.

Similar sentiments can also be derived from the work of the Covenant of Mayors. The Covenant, while clearly has an intention to support its signatories in complying with the EU's targets for climate action, it is also go-

[75] COM (2022) 240 final.

[76] *Ibidem*, 69.

ing beyond that singular goal as well, by also focusing on social aspects of energy policy and aid, such as alleviating energy poverty. The Horizon Project and other similar initiatives the Commission has funded also reinforce this sentiment. The cities chosen to pave the way for the future European Smart City on one hand have to become more 'green' and 'digital' and "offer cleaner air" for its citizens, but at the same time, it actively refers as to how these citizens' lifestyles can help significantly reduce their climate footprint and incorporates many behavioural and social goals such as electric car mobility and teleworking.

The REPowerEU plan is perhaps the most telling of these components, as it directly displays the European Commission's intentions. While tackling the climate is once again stated as a direct point of grievance, as shown by the increase from 9% to 13% of the binding Energy Efficiency Target, it does not seem to take more precedent against the political agenda of tackling Russian aggression and fossil fuel dependency. The urgency for action and sustainability is not simply brought by the sole desire for a better environment, but also European sentiments that Europe should not be dependent on Russia's fossil fuels, as shown by the cited approval ratings,[77] but also by the stated plans to not just support the European energy sector, but also to "support Ukraine, Moldova, the Western Balkans and Eastern Partnership countries, as well as our most vulnerable partners".[78] With such strong ties to principle and politics, it bears a stark resemblance to the purely social-oriented programmes that the European Parliament has recognized as 'best practices' in smart cities, such as the 'Digital inclusion for women' programme. Notably, the plan also tries to leverage behavioural changes in order to drive change within the energy sector, trying to target both industry and consumer, acknowledging an intertwining between the two in this new generation of smart cities, much like other energy policy and initiatives discussed above.

9. Conclusion

In toto, it is clear that the EU strategy for smart cities is very much a reflection of the fourth generation of smart cities. The four segments examined show a combination of digital and green transition and aim at addressing the interest of the community at large. The energy characteristics of the

[77] European Commission, *Eurobarometer: Europeans approve EU's response to the war in Ukraine*, Press Release, 2022, available at https://ec.europa.eu/commission/presscorner/detail/en/ip_22_2784.

[78] *Ibidem*, 69.

Smart City strategy reveals an amalgamation of different motivations and interests, from political to private, with the 'benevolent' intent of an ecological understanding of sustainability and protection of the environment against climate change seemingly taking a backseat or even being an afterthought entirely. The energy policy resembles something akin to what can be described as a fourth generation of Smart City, a structure that looks more like that of a smart community. Here, a combination of matching the expected benefit of the digitalisation of the energy system with those of the green transition results in an amalgamation in which social and ecological sustainability becomes intertwined. But as the European Parliament research group states, smart cities are an evolving concept, and the Smart City of today looks significantly different than the Smart City of a decade ago. This means that the Smart City will likely continue evolving, and perhaps with potential shifting priorities that might arise in the future, the next Smart City will adapt, alongside its energy policy.

Part 3

THE ECOLOGICAL TRANSITION

Chapter 7

FROM NATURA TO NATURE RESTORATION. THE ECOLOGICAL OBJECTIVE OF THE GREEN DEAL AT THE LEGAL LITMUS TEST

Michela Biscosi

ABSTRACT: *This Chapter explores the ecological declination of sustainability as articulated in the Nature Directives and its further consolidation and strengthening through the new Nature Restoration Law (NRL). The NRL tackles most of the past shortcomings by setting forth a multi-layered and graduated governance that intertwines old and new legal elements. Besides the dilution of ambition due to interference from major farming lobbies in the adoption process, the achievement of the NRL's objectives is still constrained by narrow geographical boundaries and reliant on the effectiveness of its implementing mechanisms, which require coordination among European and national authorities.*

KEYWORDS: *Nature restoration law – Ecological sustainability – Natura 2000.*

SUMMARY: 1. Which sustainability in the European Green Deal? – 2. Ecological sustainability in Natura 2000. – 2.1. Tracing Natura's perimeter. – 2.2. Which room for development activities? – 2.3. Old limits and unexplored potential – 3. Nature Restoration Law, Europe's "best hope". – 3.1. The contents: mending and strengthening. – 3.2. The NRL's governance. – 4. Conclusion.

1. Which sustainability in the European Green Deal?

A host of action plans,[1] sectoral strategies[2] and an all-comprehensive legislative programme, the "Fit for 55" package,[3] made of fourteen interconnected legislative proposals, have been elaborated with the view to

---

[1] See e.g. the new circular economy action plan for a cleaner and more competitive Europe (COM (2020) 98) and the European Green Deal Investment Plan (COM (2020) 21).

[2] See e.g. the new industrial strategy for Europe (COM (2020) 102), the EU biodiversity strategy for 2030 (COM (2020) 380) and the New EU Forest Strategy for 2030 (COM (2021) 572).

[3] COM (2021) 550.

achieving the two binding targets set by the EU Climate Law:[4] climate neutrality by 2050[5] and, intermediately, the reduction of net GHGs emissions by at least 55% compared to 1990 levels by 2030.[6] Despite the clear mid- and long-term targets, the normative horizon of the European Green Deal[7] is divisive.

The Green Deal introduces itself as a "new growth strategy". At first glance, the prominence still reserved to the economic objective does not seem to betray the traditional alignment of European Union (EU) law and policy with the general tenets of sustainable development. In the Brundtland report's original formula, sustainable development designates the 'development that meets the needs of the present without compromising the ability of future generations to meet their own needs'.[8] It consists of three environmental, social, and economic heads to reconcile in a balancing exercise informed by the integration principle. Specifically in the EU legal context, sustainable development has gained the constitutional status of both an objective[9] and a legal principle.[10] In one of the few judicial cases[11] offering a definition, it is said: "not (to) mean that the interests of the environment must necessarily and systematically prevail over the interests defended in the context of the other policies pursued by the Community (...) On the contrary, it emphasises the necessary balance between various interests which sometimes clash, but which must be reconciled".[12]

However, this does not clarify the Green Deal's normative horizon: sustainable development is an "essentially contested concept",[13] contingent in

---

[4] Regulation (EU) 2021/1119 of the European Parliament and of the Council establishing the framework for achieving climate neutrality (European Climate Law) OJ 2021 L 243.

[5] *Ibidem,* Article 2(1).

[6] *Ibidem,* Article 4(1).

[7] COM (2019) 640.

[8] World Commission on Environment and Development (WCED), *Our Common Future,* OUP, 1987.

[9] Article 3(3) and (5) TEU; Article 21(2), (d) to (f) TEU; Article 11 TFEU.

[10] Article 37 EU Charter of Fundamental Rights.

[11] Scotford E., *Environmental Principles and the Evolution of Environmental Law,* Hart Publishing, 2017, 192-198.

[12] Case C-371/98 *First Corporate Shipping* [2000] ECR I-9235, Opinion of AG Philippe Léger [2000], para. 54.

[13] Gallie W.B., "Essentially Contested Concepts. In Proceedings of the Aristotelian Society", in *Aristotelian Society*, 1955, 56, 171-172, where the author lays down the four characteristics for a concept to count as "essentially contested". For a prospect on the different models of sustainable development, Hopwood B., Mellor M. and O'Brien G., "Sustainable Development: Mapping Different Approaches", in *Sustain. Dev.*, 2005, 38.

its practical implementation.[14] It has been variably implemented across the EU's legal and policy fields and has served as an umbrella of different sustainability options. Thus, the reference made to sustainable development in the Green Deal[15] is, as such, insufficient to clarify the sustainability option that the EU aims at operationalizing in the framework of the green transition. But this is not all: some of its policy objectives do not even fit harmoniously into the general sustainable development framework.

As pointed out in the Introduction of this book, the protection and restoration of the integrity of natural ecosystems – as predicated in the Biodiversity,[16] Forest[17] and Soil[18] Strategies and formalised in the Nature Restoration Law (NRL)[19] – depart from the three-head scheme of sustainable development. This objective "assumes that ecosystems' health must prevail over social and economic exigencies".[20] The very idea of ecological integrity "is not internal to the market, but external. Taken seriously, it does not shape the market, but operates as an external limitation".[21] The level playing field between environmental, social, and economic interests on which sustainable development is supposed to rest appears hierarchised to endorse an "ecological primacy".[22]

This Chapter aims at providing a legal analysis of such ecological objective. It juxtaposes the NRL with the existing EU legislation for biodiversity. The inquiry should shed light on the way in which sustainability is actually

---

[14] Not least, as environmental laws and principles at large. See Pedersen O.W., "The Contingent Foundations of Environmental Law", in *J. Env. L.*, 2018, 30, 359; Warnock C., "Environment and the Law: The Normative Force of Context and Constitutional Challenges", in *J. Env. L*, 2020, 32(3), 365-389.

[15] The Green Deal refers to the United Nation General Assembly (UNGA) Res 70/1, 'Transforming our world: the 2030 Agenda for Sustainable Development" (21 October 2015) UN Doc A/RES/70/1.

[16] COM (2020) 380.

[17] COM (2021) 572.

[18] COM (2021) 699.

[19] Regulation (EU) 2024/1991 of the European Parliament and of the Council of 24 June 2024 on nature restoration and amending Regulation (EU) 2022/869, OJ L, 2024/1991.

[20] Chiti E., "Managing the Ecological Transition of the EU: The European Green Deal as a Regulatory Process", in *CMLRev*, 2022, 35.

[21] *Ibidem.*

[22] Sbert C., *The Lens of Ecological Law: a Look at Mining*, Edward Elgar Publishing, 2020; Anker K. et al. (eds.), *From Environmental to Ecological Law,* Routledge, 2020. Alongside others, the principle of "ecological primacy" marks the passage from environmental protection law to a properly ecological legal rationale.

constructed in the newly proposed regulation. It might also clarify the extent to which such construction represents a genuine novelty, as claimed by the legal scholarship.[23]

It will be argued that an "ecological" declension of sustainability has already been consolidated in the rationale of the EU biodiversity regime and in particular in the so-called Nature Directives, that is the Habitats Directive (HD)[24] and the Birds Directive (BD)[25] (§ 2). Instead of "reconciling" the three heads of sustainable development, some of the core provisions of the HD and BD exclude socio-economic interests from consideration (§ 2.1) or impose very stringent conditions to their balancing (§ 2.2). Nonetheless, the ecological rationale informing their judicial enforcement has proven insufficient for the appropriate protection of biodiversity. While the potential of some of their provisions is yet to be fully explored, the legal design of the two Directives present some shortcomings that significantly impair their efficacy (§ 2.3). Against this background, the NRL tackles most of the Nature Directives' shortcomings (§ 3.1) by setting forth a multi-layered and multi-graduated governance attuned to the interests affected (§ 3.2). However, if its text is not revised and improved during the adoption procedure, the capability of the NRL to reach its ecological goals will ultimately depend on the effectiveness of the implementing mechanisms (§ 3.3). The Chapter will end by presenting some general conclusions (§ 4).

2. Ecological sustainability in Natura 2000

Biodiversity protection is a multilayered legal domain, crossing the international, European, and national legal orders. The EU is not only a party to most of the global and regional treaties on biodiversity protection, but it has also made a great diplomatic effort to promote their drafting and raise the bar of environmental protection.[26] Its leverage action in the Convention on Biological Diversity (CBD), which marked a turning point in the field – transitioning biodiversity protection from a sectoral and eco-centric to a holistic and humanist approach – is a case in point.[27]

---

[23] Chiti E., *supra* fn. 20.

[24] Directive 1992/43/EEC of the Council of 21 May 1992 on the conservation of natural habitats and of wild fauna and flora, OJ 1992 L 206/7.

[25] Directive 2009/147/EC of the European Parliament and of the Council of 30 November 2009 on the conservation of wild birds, OJ 2010 L 20/7.

[26] del Castillo T.F., "The EU Diplomacy for Biodiversity", in Campins Eritja M. (ed.), *The European Union and Global Environmental Protection*, Routledge, 2020, 35-49.

[27] Groen L., "Explaining European Union effectiveness (goal achievement) in the

In this wider framework, the Nature Directives are two core pieces of the large volume of EU legislation aimed at implementing at the regional level the international commitments on biodiversity protection. The HD and the BD together trace the perimeter of the largest ecological network of protected areas in the world – i.e., Natura 2000. They conform to the CBD's holistic orientation: human activities are neither excluded nor discouraged but compelled to respect the ecological standards of the species and habitats in these protected areas. In this sense, a large portion of the Natura 2000 network is destined for agriculture, farming and forestry.

Despite that, the two Directives have been the centre of much controversy for their allegedly 'rigid, rather static' approach, 'not always capable to facilitate sustainable development' and 'not fully updated with modern sustainability and climate change demand'.[28] Their 'ecological' focus has frequently come into conflict with concurring socio-economic interests in the protected areas. The EU case-law that has addressed such a conflict[29] has notably focused on two issues: the enforcement of the national duty to select and designate the Natura 2000 sites; and the implementation of the exemption clause admitting development activities therein.

2.1. Tracing Natura's perimeter

The Nature Directives have slightly different approaches to formulating the obligations to select and designate the protected sites.[30] In the 13-year lapse between the two, the legislator has refined formulas and filled the lack of definitions in the BD: whereas the BD establishes a generic obligation to designate Special Protection Areas (SPAs),[31] the HD lies down a

Convention on Biological Diversity: the importance of diplomatic engagement", in *International Environmental Agreements: Politics, Law and Economics*, 2019, 19(1), 69-87 focusing on the successful performance of the EU as a mediator and bridge builder in the CBD negotiations processes.

[28] Kistenkas F.H., "Rethinking European nature conservation legislation: towards sustainable development", in *JEEPL*, 2013, 10(1), 72-84.

[29] For a comprehensive and detailed review of the case-law in this field, see Ureta A.G., *EU Biodiversity Law: Wild Birds and Habitats Directives,* European Law Publishing, 2020.

[30] For a comprehensive and attentive overview, see Schoukens H. and Woldendorp H.E., "Site Selection and Designation under the Habitats and Birds Directives: a Sisyphean Task?", in Born C.H. et al. (eds.), *The Habitats Directive in its EU Environmental Law Context*, Routledge, 2014, 31-55.

[31] Article 4(1) BD.

three-tiered procedure for the selection and designation of Special Conservation Areas (SCAs).[32]

Specifically, Member States are first called to draft a list of Sites of Community Interest (SCIs) containing the habitats and species in Annex I and II, including those under priority protection. This list is submitted to the Commission, which scrutinises each biogeographical region in light of the Annex III criteria. Subsequently, in agreement with Member States, the Commission adopts a final list of SCIs. The final stage falls back on the Member States, which are granted six years to designate the areas scored in the final SCIs list as SACs and priority habitats and species.

The SPAs under the BD and the SACs under the HD form the Natura 2000 network, which counts for approximately 18% of the land and 8% of the marine territory in the EU.

The first case in which the EU Court of Justice (ECJ) has defined the Member States' discretion on the designation criteria for the SPAs has involved one of the Iberian Peninsula's most important wetland ecosystems, which is home to several aquatic birds – i.e., the Santoña marshes.[33] Faced with the obstinate refusal to classify this whole area as a SPA, the ECJ has held that, in the classification proceeding, preeminence has to be given to the 'ornithological criteria determined by the directive, such as the presence of birds listed in Annex I, on the one hand, and the designation of a habitat as a wetland area, on the other'.[34] Hence, Spain has not been authorised to invoke additional non-ornithological criteria of its choosing as grounds for derogation.

Shortly after, in the landmark *Lappel Bank* case,[35] the ECJ had the opportunity to highlight that the new regime introduced by the HD had not altered the stringent implementation of the designation process. Although Article 6(4) of the HD 'widened the range of grounds on which it may be justified to encroach upon SPAs already designated as such, by expressly including therein reasons of a social or economic nature, it nevertheless did not make any change regarding the initial stage of classification referred to in Article 4(1) and (2) of Directive 79/409, and therefore the classification of sites as SPAs must in all circumstances be carried out in accordance with the criteria accepted by those provisions'[36] – i.e., the sole ornithological criteria.

[32] Article 4 HD.

[33] C-355/90 *Commission v Spain*, ECR I-4221.

[34] *Ibidem,* para. 26.

[35] C-44/95 *Regina v Secretary of State for the Environment, ex parte: Royal Society for the Protection of Birds,* ECR I-3805.

[36] *Ibidem,* in the case summary.

Even the attempt from Ireland to narrow the Sandymount Strand and Tolka Estuary SPA boundaries around 'core bird habitats' has been crossed out.[37] Although the ECJ has acknowledged a national margin of discretion on choosing the 'most suitable areas' as SPAs, it has also emphasized that such a 'classification cannot be the result of an isolated study of the ornithological value of each of the areas in question but must be carried out in the light of the natural boundaries of the (...) ecosystem'.[38] In this way, the Court has intended to prevent the instrumentalisation of the available data through their isolation, namely, not considering the entire natural ecosystem in which the protected species are embedded.

Moving to the implementation of the HD, there has been an evolution in the judicial orientation on the habitats selection and designation. While apparently compromising, such evolution has kept rather strict requirements in the mapping of Natura 2000.

The first and landmark occasion for the Court to clarify its approach has arisen in the *First Corporate Shipping*[39] case concerning the development of port facilities in Bristol. The Court, in line with the jurisprudence about the SPAs designation, has dismissed the possibility to 'take account of economic and social requirements or regional and local characteristics, as mentioned in Article 2(3) of that directive, when selecting and defining the boundaries of the sites to be proposed to the Commission as eligible for identification as sites of Community importance'.[40] During the first stage of the procedure, making available to the Commission the 'exhaustive list' of national sites having 'an ecological interest which is relevant from the point of view of the directive's objective of conservation of natural habitats and wild fauna and flora'[41] has been deemed essential to the creation of a coherent European ecological network.[42] Although this position has been endorsed in its Opinion, Advocate General Léger has softened the approach, opening a narrow leeway to Member States' socio-economic interests at a later stage. As he has asserted, 'in the second stage, at the time of concertation between the Member States and the Commission on the selection of the SCIs, economic and social requirements may justify a site which hosts one of the natural habitat types in

---

[37] Case C-418/04 *Commission of the European Communities v Ireland*, ECR I-10947.

[38] *Ibidem,* para. 142.

[39] Case C-371/98 *First Corporate Shipping,* ECR I-9235.

[40] *Ibidem,* para. 25.

[41] *Ibidem,* para. 22.

[42] Article 3(1) HD.

Annex I or native species in Annex II not being selected as an SCI, and consequently not being designated as an SAC'.[43]

The justification put forward in his Opinion is telling. The reasoning has turned around the objective of sustainable development, which informs the third recital, Articles 2(3) and 6(4) of the HD. According to Advocate General Léger, the concept of sustainable development 'does not mean that the interests of the environment must necessarily and systematically prevail over the interests defended in the context of the other policies pursued by the Community (...) On the contrary, it emphasises the necessary balance between various interests which sometimes clash, but which must be reconciled'.[44]

However, this compromising stand about the procedure's second stage has not had much of a following in the case-law. In *Stant Papenburg,*[45] for instance, the Court has excluded the possibility for a 'Member State to refuse to agree on grounds other than environmental protection to the inclusion of one or more sites in the draft list of SCIs drawn up by the Commission'.[46] The argumentation has been very precautionary: the refusal would have compromised the achievement of a coherent European ecological network. Moreover, provisions opening room for socio-economic evaluations would not have justified it. Article 2(3) of the HD 'does not constitute an autonomous derogation from the general system of protection put in place by that directive',[47] whereas Article 6(3) and (4) of the HD 'provide for such interests to be taken into account at a (further) later stage'[48] rather than at the time of the selection sites as SCIs and their subsequent designation as SACs.

Given these stringent requirements and the high number of infringement proceedings, it has come as no surprise that the aspiration to complete the mapping of Natura 2000 by 2012[49] has soon eclipsed.

2.2. Which room for development activities?

A second issue of judicial contestation has been the admission of development activities in Natura 2000, once established its perimeter. Article 6 of

[43] Case C-371/98 *First Corporate Shipping,* ECR I-9235, Opinion of AG Philippe Léger (2000), para. 51.

[44] *Ibidem,* para. 54.

[45] Case C-226/08 *Stadt Papenburg v Bundesrepublik Deutschland*, ECR I-00131.

[46] *Ibidem,* para. 33.

[47] *Ibidem,* Opinion AG Sharpston (2009), para. 37.

[48] *Ibidem.*

[49] Commission, "Environment 2010: Our future, Our choice", COM (2001) 31.

the HD, applicable to both Nature Directives,[50] has often been at the centre of litigation, 'being the one which most determines the relationship between conservation and other socio-economic activities'.[51]

Article 6 contains three main provisions: a conservation duty, requiring positive and proactive measures to maintain and restore natural habitats and species population;[52] a preventive duty to avoid their deterioration and disturbances;[53] and a series of substantive and procedural safeguards governing plans and projects 'likely to have significant effect' thereon.[54]

As for the latter set of provisions, Article 6(3) of the HD establishes an 'appropriate impact assessment' (AIA) to distinguish between innocuous and harmful development activities, whereas Article 6(4) of the HD allows space for its derogation. Unsurprisingly, the two paragraphs have been the eye of the storm and animated the creativity of national authorities and private undertakings[55] aimed to carve out a bigger socio-economic room for intervention.

First of all, it is worth expanding on the very introduction of the exemption clause as telling of the contrast of interests lying behind.[56] The provision has stemmed from the Member States' discontent about the resolution in one of the first infringement procedures involving the interpretation of Article 4(4) of the BD, which establishes a duty 'to avoid pollution or deterioration of habitats or any disturbances affecting the birds' inside and outside the protected areas'. The case has dealt with the dyke reinforcement and related reduction of size of a SPA in the Leybucht.[57] On that occasion,

---

[50] Article 7 HD reads "Obligations arising under Article 6(2), (3) and (4) of this Directive shall replace any obligations arising under the first sentence of Article 4(4) of Directive 79/409/EEC in respect of areas classified pursuant to Article 4(1) or similarly recognized under Article 4(2) thereof, as from the date of implementation of this Directive or the date of classification or recognition by a Member State under Directive 79/409/EEC, where the latter date is later".

[51] Commission, "Managing Natura 2000 Sites: The Provisions of Article 6 of the "Habitats" Directive 92/43/EEC", 2000, latest version Commission notice C (2018) 7621, 7.

[52] Article 6(1) HD.

[53] Article 6(2) HD.

[54] Article 6(3) and (4) HD.

[55] Squintani L. and Zijlmans J., "Mitigation and Compensation Measures under the EU Habitats Directive in Selected Member States", in *Eur. Energy Environ. Law Rev.*, 2019, 28(1), 2; see also Ruge R., "The Reality Gap: Simplification of Environmental Law as Key for the Acceleration of Permit Procedures for Europe's Green Deal", in *Eur. Energy Environ. Law Rev.*, 2022, 31(4), 258.

[56] Schoukens H. and Woldendorp H.E. (fn. 30).

[57] C-57/89 *Commission of the European Communities v Federal Republic of Germany,* ECR I-00883.

the ECJ has affirmed that the development activities in question could have been "justified only on exceptional grounds corresponding to a general interest which is superior to the general interest represented by the ecological objective of the directive. In that context, the economic and recreational requirements referred to in Article 2 of the BD do not enter into consideration, since that provision does not constitute an autonomous derogation from the system of protection established by the directive".[58] This reading has urged the Member States to introduce the missing autonomous derogation for socio-economic stakes in Article 6(4) of the HD and to divert the obligations under Article 4(4) of the BD to this new provision.[59]

However, the interpretation of this clause has not quite satisfied the expectations accompanying its formulation. In a series of landmark judgments, the ECJ has progressively refined the scope and content of the AIA under Article 6(3) of the HD and the conditions for its derogation under Article 6(4) of the HD, echoing the same precautionary approach as for the protected sites' selection and designation. The balance between environmental, social, and economic interests has leaned decidedly toward the environmental head of sustainable development. This is evident when considering the interpretation given to each element composing the AIA and the derogation clauses.

To begin with the AIA, the first indicator is the extensive scope of its application. The procedure spans over a potentially limitless list of development activities[60] – among others, urban developments for industrial construction projects;[61] annual permits for mechanical fishing;[62] dredging works in navigable channels;[63] authorizations of open-cast coal mines;[64] up to grazing of cattle and the application of fertilizers on the land.[65] Accord-

---

[58] *Ibidem*, in the case summary. See for an overview, Wils W.P.J., "The Birds Directive 15 Years Later: A Survey of the Case Law and a Comparison with the Habitats Directive", in *J. Env. L.*, 1994, 6(2), 219-242.

[59] Article 7 HD.

[60] For an attentive and in-deepth overview de Sadeleer N., "Assessment and Authorisation of Plans and Projects Having a Significant Impact on Natura 2000 Sites", in Vanheudesen B. and Squintani L. (eds.), *EU Environmental and Planning Law Aspects of Large-Scale Projects,* Intersentia, 2016, 263, at 269-270.

[61] Case C-179/06 *Commission v Italy*, ECR I-8131.

[62] Case C-127/02 *Waddenzee*, ECR I-7405.

[63] Case C-226/08 *Stadt Papenburg v Bundesrepublik Deutschland* [2010] ECR I-131.

[64] Case C-404/09 *Commission v Spain,* ECR I-11853.

[65] Joined Cases C-293/17 and C-294/17, *Cooperatie Mobilisation for the Environment UA and Vereniging Leefmilieu v College van Gedeputeerde Staten van Limburg and College van Gedeputeerde Staten van Gelderland,* ECLI:EU:C:2018:882.

ing to the established interpretation, the definition of 'plans' and 'projects' to which the assessment applies follows an 'effect-based test':[66] any human activity, both inside and outside the Natura 2000 perimeter, falls within its scope whenever it is 'likely to have a significant effect' on the protected area. Moreover, the choice of the EU legislator to account for not only the isolated impact but also the cumulative effects of development activities is an important precautionary supplement. However, when put in practice, this guarantee may propel a less coherent 'first come, first served'[67] dynamic – i.e., the first plan/project to be subjected to the AIA may be more likely to be authorized than a subsequent one.

Once a generic assessment has established the likelihood of significant effects, national authorities must proceed to the AIA. The AIA consists in evaluating whether the development activities 'adversely affect the integrity of the site'.[68] The assessment converges a triumvirate: public decision-makers, scientific advisors, and courts.[69] Each authority modulates its decisions based on different and sometimes conflicting parameters. Needless to say, the 'integrity of the site' standpoint refers much of the decisional power to scientific expertise as best placed to interpret ecological criteria.[70] In this regard, the Court has repeatedly emphasised the necessity to rely on 'the best available knowledge in the field' and that 'no reasonable scientific doubt (shall) remain as to the absence of such effects'.[71]

A final element in the AIA procedure that has much engaged the scholarly literature is that of mitigation measures. Mitigation measures are integral parts of the plans/projects under the AIA and are devoted to avoiding or reducing the negative impacts of development activities on the protected sites. Not mentioned by the legislative provision, those measures are creative devices used by national governments and undertakings to alleviate the stringency of the AIA.[72] The ECJ has progressively refined the conditions

---

[66] Squintani L., "Balancing Nature and Economic Interests in the European Union: On the Concept of Mitigation under the Habitats Directive", in *RECIEL*, 2020, 29(1), 129-137.

[67] Lees E., "Allocation of Decision-Making Power under the Habitats Directive", in *J. Env. L.*, 2016, 28(2), 194.

[68] Article 6(3) HD.

[69] Lees E. (fn. 67).

[70] *Ibidem*, see also the recent book by Eliantonio M., Lees E. and Paloniitty T. (eds.), *EU Environmental Principles and Scientific Uncertainty before National Courts: The Case of the Habitats Directive,* Hart Publishing, 2023.

[71] C-127/02, *Waddenzee*, para. 59.

[72] Squintani L. and Senoner A., "Mitigation and Compensation Measures under the EU Habitats Directive in Selected Member States", in Ruge R., "The Reality Gap: Sim-

under which they may be accounted for and take part in the AIA. Four cumulative criteria have been singled out:[73]

i. the mitigation measure has to be "specific" – i.e., preventing the damage caused by the plan or project at issue and targeting the conservation objective likely to be undermined;[74]
ii. it has to be "preventive" in nature – i.e., it cannot merely substitute elsewhere the ecological function of the site impaired;[75]
iii. there must be a "functional link" between the plan/project and the mitigating action – i.e., management measures, as under Article 6(1) or (2) of the HD, generally and autonomously devoted to conservation and prevention of the site, are excluded;
iv. there should be a guarantee beyond "all reasonable doubts" that the plan/project, accompanied by those measures, will not adversely affect the site's integrity.

The last requirement poses a further difficulty as directly involving scientific knowledge. The case-law suggests two main paths to fulfill it: either the mitigation measures have been already carried out to prove their effectiveness or "scientific certainty" on damage prevention needs to be established.[76] The second option clearly raises a question about the burden of

---

plification of Environmental Law as Key for the Acceleration of Permit Procedures for Europe's Green Deal", in *Eur. Energy Environ. Law Rev.*, 2019, 28(1), 2-16.

[73] See Squintani L., *supra* note 66, 129-137, the author reconstructs the ECJ's reasoning as follows.

[74] Case C-258/11, *Peter Sweetman and Others v An Bord Pleanála,* ECLI:EU:C:2013:220.

[75] The replacement of an ecological function in another site is the function played by compensatory measures under Article 6(4) of the HD. In this sense, for a distinction between mitigation and compensatory measures and pointing at the "preventive" nature of mitigation, see Case C-521/12 *Briels*, ECLI:EU:C:2014:330, paras. 28-29, reads "Consequently, the application of the precautionary principle in the context of the implementation of Article 6(3) of the HD requires the competent national authority to assess the implications of the project for the Natura 2000 site concerned in view of the site's conservation objectives and taking into account the protective measures forming part of that project aimed at avoiding or reducing *any direct adverse effects for the site*, in order to ensure that it does not adversely affect the integrity of the site. However, protective measures provided for in a project which are aimed at *compensating* for the negative effects of the project on a Natura 2000 site cannot be taken into account in the assessment of the implications of the project provided for in Article 6(3)".

[76] Squintani L. (fn. 66). See also Joined Cases C-293/17 and C-294/17, *Cooperatie Mobilisation for the Environment UA and Vereniging Leefmilieu v College van Gedeputeerde Staten van Limburg and College van Gedeputeerde Staten van Gelderland* [2018] ECLI:EU:C:2018:882, para. 130.

proof to be accepted. The recent and very vocal case about the Dutch nitrogen programme may illustrate the attitude the ECJ will likely maintain in this respect. On that occasion, the judicial resolution has been to entrust the decision to the national court.[77] Given the great variety of approaches towards scientific knowledge across Member State jurisprudences, it is reasonable to assume that the ECJ would privilege this attitude towards judicial subsidiarity even in the future.[78]

To conclude, moving to the derogation clause, the Commission's Guidelines and the European jurisprudence lean towards a very narrow interpretation of its scope.[79] There are some cumulative requirements to fulfil for the plans/projects to be admitted in spite of a negative assessment under Article 6(3) of the HD:

i. plans and projects in question must serve an imperative and explicitly public interest;
ii. alternative and less-damaging solution must be proven unfeasible;
iii. Member States must take compensatory measures – i.e., a "like-for-like"[80] replacement of the ecological function of the impaired site somewhere else 'to ensure that the overall coherence of Natura 2000 is protected';[81]
iv. where priority habitats or species would be affected, the plans/projects may only be justified through health or public safety reasons, whereas socio-economic grounds are excluded from the discretionary purview of national authorities.

2.3. Old limits and unexplored potential

The ecological declension of sustainability that can be drawn from the cursory overview of the Nature Directives is in stark contrast with Europe's

---

[77] Squintani L. (fn. 66) 134.

[78] Bogojević S., "Judicial Protection of Individual Applicants Revisited: Access to Justice through the Prism of Judicial Subsidiarity", in *Yearb. Eur. Law*, 2015, 34(1), 5-25.

[79] Commission notice Assessment of plans and projects in relation to Natura 2000 sites – Methodological guidance on the provisions of Article 6(3) and (4) of the Habitats Directive 92/43/EEC 2021/C 437/01; see McGillivray D., "Compensating Biodiversity Loss: The EU Commission's Approach to Compensation under Article 6 of the Habitats Directive", in *J. Env. L.*, 2012, 24, 417.

[80] Schoukens H. and Cliquet A., "Mitigation and Compensation under EU Nature Conservation Law in the Flemish Region: Beyond the Deadlock for Development Projects?", in *Utrecht L. Rev.*, 2014, 10, 194.

[81] Article 6(4) HD.

bleak state of biodiversity,[82] including in the Natura 2000 framework.[83] This is also due to some legal design defects, which significantly impair the Directives' effectiveness. Besides their narrow geographical scope, requiring a resolute political decision to enlarge the ecological network, the lack of specific and enforceable restoration norms and the disregard for climate mitigation and adaptation deserve closer legal analysis.

To begin with restoration, both Directives imply an obligation to restore natural habitats.[84] Restoration may come under consideration in three different legal situations. The HB mentions restoration in association with conservation.[85] Article 3(1) of the HD reads 'this network (...) shall enable the natural habitat types and the species' habitats concerned to be maintained or, where appropriate, restored at a *favourable conservation status* in their natural range'. Conservation and restoration obligations are both qualified by reference to the 'favourable conservation status' (FCS). The FSC, as many other legal benchmarks in the Nature Directives, has posed interpretative problems.[86] Unsurprisingly, its content and scope have been concretised through a case-by-case approach and relying greatly on scientific knowledge and available data to acquire a somewhat concreteness. Restoration may also come under mitigation measures – where included in the plan/project subjected to the AIA and meeting the stringent criteria specified above, under Article 6(3) of the HD – or under compensatory measures – which Member States are obliged to take whenever the plan/project to carry out falls under the derogation in Article 6(4) of the HD.

In these three prospects, the Nature Directives only account tangentially for restoration. Most importantly, restoration is not a binding duty: no *spe-*

---

[82] Brondizio E.S. et al (eds.), *The Global Assessment Report on Biodiversity and Ecosystem Services*, IPBES secretariat, 2019, available at https://doi.org/10.5281/zenodo.5657041.

[83] Report from the Commission to the European Parliament, the Council and the European Economic and Social Committee, "The state of nature in the European Union Report on the status and trends in 2013 – 2018 of species and habitat types protected by the Birds and Habitats Directives", COM (2020) 635. See also the European Environmental Agency (EEA) website, available at https://www.eea.europa.eu/en/topics/at-a-glance/nature/state-of-nature-in-europe-a-health-check and https://www.eea.europa.eu/en/topics/at-a-glance/nature/state-of-nature-in-europe-a-health-check/habitats-and-species-latest-status-and-trends.

[84] In the BD, restoration is referred only in the preamble, whereas, in the HD, it recurs in several points in association with 'conservation'.

[85] Articles 2(2), 3(1), 4(4) HD.

[86] Bijlsma R.J. et al., *Defining and Applying the Concept of Favourable Reference Values for Species and Habitats Under the EU Birds and Habitats Directives*, Wageningen Environmental Research, Report 2929, 2018.

cific targets, *deadlines* or a *historical baseline* are envisaged.[87] Hence, there is no incentive for Member States to go beyond the objective of maintaining the biodiversity *status quo*.[88] Furthermore, the Directives focus solely on the habitats and species listed in their Annexes, whereas scientific studies have long recognised the need for a more holistic approach to conservation and restoration.[89]

The lack of a climate-sensitive approach in the two legislative texts is partly illustrative of their 'age'. Nonetheless, the two Directives open the way to climate mitigation and adaptation.[90] One legal avenue is offered by Article 6(2) of the HD, which obliges Member States to avoid deterioration and disturbances of the protected habitats and species. During an infringement procedure against the UK, the Court has clarified that 'in implementing Article 6(2) of the HD, it may be necessary to adopt both measures intended to avoid external man-caused impairment and disturbance and measures to prevent natural developments that may cause the conservation status of species and habitats in SACs to deteriorate'.[91] In other words, the preventive clause extends beyond damages on habitats and species *directly* caused by human action to include also the damages prompted by natural development *indirectly* caused by development activities, such as for climate change. The Commission itself has highlighted in its Guidelines that in the case 'of climate change effects, measures would need to be taken to halt or counter this process if it is deemed to be negatively impacting on the species and habitat types for which the site has been designated'.[92] Another legal avenue to tackle climate change is Article 6(3) of the HD. As mentioned above, the Court has established an 'effect-based approach' to define plans and projects under this provision. Where the causal linkage between climate change and biodiversity degradation is es-

---

[87] The year 1992 is the implied baseline for most of the habitats and species of the Nature Directives.

[88] Hoek N., "A Critical Analysis of the Proposed EU Regulation on Nature Restoration: Have the Problems Been Resolved?", in Ruge R., "The Reality Gap: Simplification of Environmental Law as Key for the Acceleration of Permit Procedures for Europe's Green Deal", in *Eur. Energy Environ. Law Rev.*, 2022, 31(5), 41-53.

[89] *Ibidem*, 52.

[90] Commission, *Guidelines on climate change and Natura 2000*, EU Publications, 2024.

[91] Case C-6/04 *Commission of the European Communities v United Kingdom of Great Britain and Northern Ireland* [2005] ECR I-09017, para. 34, and the Opinion of the Advocate-General Kokott [2005], para. 19.

[92] Commission, Managing Natura 2000 sites. The provisions of Article 6 of the "Habitats" Directive 92/43/EEC, Notice C (2018) 7621, 26.

tablished, its scope is wide enough to encompass those human activities fostering climate change.

3. Nature Restoration Law, Europe's "best hope"

The Biodiversity Strategy for 2030, with its commitment to "bringing back nature into our life", is one of the main pillars of the Green Deal. The horizontal scope of the Strategy is enlarged, its interaction with other EU policy sectors and legal regimes refined, and the alignment with the international agenda tightened when compared to the previous Biodiversity Strategies and Action Plans.[93] Most importantly, the longstanding plea to formalise the policy objectives into binding targets has been addressed. The lack of progress in the Biodiversity Strategies up to 2020 has unequivocally showed that "voluntary commitments by Member States are not enough to achieve the EU's objectives for restoring ecosystems".[94] This is the context in which the NRL – Europe's new "best hope", to recall the title of a book concerned with the HD – has been conceived and adopted. The NRL complements an extensive set of environmental regimes already in place,[95] connects with the new Forest, Soil and Circular Economy Strategies, the EU Pollinator Initiative, and embraces the Fishery and Agriculture Common Policies within its purview. The ecological concept of "ecosystem" serves as legal pivot to its whole architecture.

3.1. The contents: mending and strengthening

The NRL pursues some macro-objectives: "(a) to contribute to the long-term and sustained recovery of biodiverse and resilient nature across the Member States' land and sea areas through the restoration of degraded ecosystems; (b) achieving the Union's overarching objectives concerning climate change mitigation, climate change adaptation and land degradation neutrality; (c) enhancing food security; (d) meeting the Union's international commitments".[96] To achieve them, the EU legislator has opted for a regulation. In principle, the shared legal competence in the environmental

---

[93] For a more detailed analysis of the Biodiversity Strategy see Biscosi M., "Two Parallel Discourses and a New Path for Policy-Making. The Biodiversity Strategy for 2030", in *RQDA*, 2021, 1, 44-68.

[94] NRL proposal, COM (2022) 304, 7.

[95] *Ibidem*, 4.

[96] NRL, Article 1.

field, the sensitive interests the NRL touches upon, and the great heterogeneity between national territories would have suggested drafting a directive leaving the Member States a decisional leeway in the legal transposition. Yet, the choice is not fortuitous. The NRL does not only aim at ensuring legal consistency and uniformity across Member States but also reflects the short-term nature of the established targets and obligations, which do not withstand delays from national transpositions.

The NRL is construed around two key concepts, namely, "ecosystem" and "restoration". The legal definition of ecosystem echoes international texts. It refers to "a dynamic complex of plant, animal, and microorganism communities and their non-living environment, interacting as a functional unit, and includes habitat types, habitats of species and species populations".[97] The sister concept of 'restoration' is much more refined than the FCS benchmark in the HD. Restoration include active and passive nature recovery and encompass a range of gradations. The restoration scale ranges from "good conditions" of the ecosystem to "sufficient quality and quantity" of a habitat type.[98] However, despite this definitional refinement, the role of the Court is to remain central to concretise the content and scope of such a scale on a case-by-case basis.

Based on these two pillars, the NRL fills the Nature Directives' lacuna by establishing specific *restoration targets* accompanied by the operational elements of *environmental baselines* and *deadlines.*

The regulation introduces a multi-tiered framework of binding restoration targets and obligations spanning various ecosystem types. It addresses terrestrial, coastal and freshwater,[99] marine,[100] renewable energies,[101] urban ecosystems,[102] the restoration of the natural connectivity of watercourses and the natural functions of adjacent floodplains,[103] the restoration of pollinator populations,[104] the restoration of agricultural[105] and forest ecosystems.[106] All together, these ecosystems shall cover at least 20% of the EU's land and sea areas by 2030 and all ecosystems in need of restoration

---

[97] *Ibidem*, Article 3(1) and Article 8 CBD.

[98] NRL, Article 3(3).

[99] *Ibidem*, Article 4.

[100] *Ibidem*, Article 5.

[101] *Ibidem*, Article 6.

[102] *Ibidem*, Article 8.

[103] *Ibidem*, Article 9.

[104] *Ibidem*, Article 10.

[105] *Ibidem*, Article 11.

[106] *Ibidem*, Article 12.

by 2050.[107] The goal set for 2030 is disappointing, particularly when compared to the commitment established in the Biodiversity Strategy for 2030. The target has been downscaled from 30% to 20% of the EU territory. Such downward compromise should not be minimised. As the Natura 2000 network already covers approximately 18% of land and 8% of marine territory in the EU, the ambition for land areas has been drastically cut.

Targets and timeframes vary significantly based on the specific ecosystem being regulated, thus resulting in a framework of distinct ecosystem-specific regimes operating at different paces. The obligations laid down for terrestrial, coastal, and freshwater ecosystems and marine ecosystems are grounded on the Nature Directives' existing framework, essentially replicating the same annex-based model. Likewise, for various other ecosystems, the NLR builds upon and strengthens the legal frameworks already in place.

As for the operational elements of restoration, the so-called 'shifting baseline syndrome',[108] partly attributable to a protracted legal oversight, has finally been addressed. According to the NRL, Member States shall quantify the area to be restored taking into account a number of different factors.[109] Although such a choice may be unsatisfactory for some, the revision represents nonetheless a great step forward. Moreover, the regulation is structured along three decade-long deadlines. This legal design – including two interim timeframes in 2030 and 2040 – is welcomed as it strengthens the credibility of its more ambitious long-term horizon.

Last but not least, the text bridges ecosystem health and climate change action objectives. Member States are prescribed to "identify synergies with climate change mitigation, climate change adaptation, land degradation neutrality and disaster prevention and prioritise restoration measures accordingly".[110]

3.2. The NRL's governance

As already highlighted, the NRL supplements and intertwines various legal regimes already in place, conferring a multi-layered format to the overall framework. To consolidate and functionalise the ensemble, the NRL establishes an innovative governance bearing resemblance with

---

[107] *Ibidem*, Article 1(2).

[108] Papworth S.K. et al., "Evidence for Shifting Baseline Syndrome in Conservation", in *Conservation Letters,* 2009, 2(2), 93-100.

[109] NRL, Article 14(2).

[110] *Ibidem*, Article 14(9).

some of the characteristics of the Open Method of Coordination (OMC).[111]

It features the typical iterative traits[112] of the OMC policy cycle: setting common benchmarks; providing for statistical databases; requiring national reports; and arranging a multilateral surveillance. They are a series of measures aimed at comparing implementation progresses across Member States and, this way, disseminating and incentivising best practices while naming and shaming deflections. The OMC is conceived as an attempt to obviate the issue of competence allocation in areas intersecting shared competences and sensitive national interests, which make a more stringent legal approach impracticable.[113] The legal pervasiveness of the ecosystem restoration objectives suits it perfectly.

The implementation of this scheme unfolds in multiple stages. First, Member States shall prepare their National Restoration Plans (NRPs), describing and identifying the restoration measures to meet the targets and obligations set out in Articles 4 to 13 of the NRL. In this preliminary drafting work, national authorities are required to account for the latest scientific evidence, coordinate their action with other Member States, and accomplish a synergetic and co-beneficial intervention among biodiversity, climate change, and social objectives. Subsequently, they shall submit the draft Plans to the Commission, which, acting closely with national authorities and assisted by experts and the European Environmental Agency (EEA), evaluate their compliance with the NRL's targets and obligations. In this regard, the Commission may address some observations, which are to be duly considered by Member States for eventually adjusting and integrating the final version of their NRPs. Once this final version is published and submitted, Member States are entrusted with two other supplementary responsibilities: monitoring the development of the restoration measures to carry out and reporting findings to the Commission, which, in turn, share the reports with the EU Parliament and Council.

Overall, the governance model establishes a net of informational and

---

[111] Porte C.d.l., "Is the Open Method of Coordination Appropriate for Organising Activities at European Level in Sensitive Policy Areas?", in *Eur. L. Rev.*, 2002, 8(1), 38-58; Szyszczak E., "Experimental Governance: the Open Method of Coordination", in *Eur. L. Rev,* 2006, 12(4), 486-502; Armstrong K. and Kilpatrick C., "Law, Governance, or New Governance? The Changing Open Method of Coordination", in *Colum. J. Eur. L.*, 2006, 13, 649.

[112] Porte C.d.l. and Stiller S., "Lessons about the "Harder" Elements of OMC Governance for the EU Energy Union", in *J. Environ. Policy Plan.*, 2020, 22(6), 830-42.

[113] Not incidentally, the OMC's ideation dates back the Lisbon European Council in 2000 and targeted employment, social, and redistributive policies.

communicative exchanges between the European and national authorities. It fabricates a "soft" framework, resembling the OMC format, around a "hard" core of targets and obligations, which departs from the latter. Such a governance mix is not unfamiliar to the EU climate and environmental policy field. The EU Climate Law offers a proximate example of its deployment.[114] However, compared to it, the NRL stands out for the richer legal details and the central role played by the Commission. The executive body is endowed with powers to adopt delegated and implementing acts to: develop a uniform format for NRPs; revise annexes; specify the monitoring methods; develop a framework for setting satisfactory levels of restoration; establish the format, structure, and detailed arrangements for reporting duties.[115]

4. Conclusion

This Chapter has reconstructed the evolution of ecological sustainability in EU biodiversity law. As it has been argued, the ecological declension of sustainability that can be found in the NRL is not a novelty in itself. The prioritisation of environmental interests over socio-economic ones is already a well-established component of EU biodiversity law, as the implementation of some of the core provisions of the two Nature Directives may prove.

The original proposal for a NRL, so favourably received by NGOs and activists, also faced much opposition. A strong obstructing campaign, gathering big agriculture businesses[116] and spreading misleading information about the alleged threat that the NRL may cause to food security in the EU,[117] aimed at sinking the draft down. And it partly succeeded, as many critical obligations of the original proposal have been sacrificed by the EU legislator in the final text of the NRL.

One should not miss, however, the novelty of the NRL. The regulation proposal intervenes on the legal framing of the Natura 2000 regime by filling some of the main gaps compromising its effectiveness. First, it shifts

[114] Lionello L., "Il Green Deal europeo. Inquadramento giuridico e prospettive di attuazione", in *Jus*, 2020, 2, 105-142.

[115] Articles 22 to 24 NRL set out the conditions for the Commission to adopt the delegated and implementing acts.

[116] Taylore K., *EU's Nature Restoration Law hangs in the balance ahead of decisive July vote*, Euractiv, 28 June 2023, available at https://www.euractiv.com/section/climate-environment/news/eus-nature-restoration-law-in-the-balance-ahead-of-decisive-july-vote/.

[117] Conversely, see the NRL proposal, 1, referring to Commission, Safeguarding food security and reinforcing the resilience of food systems, COM (2022) 133 about the need to preserve biodiversity for a long-term food security.

from habitats and species to "ecosystems", thus widening the scientific perspectives of the regulation. Second, the NRL interweaves the many and disparate legal regimes on biodiversity protection under a unique regulatory framework, aimed at reaching a number of restoration macro-targets. Third, the NRL operationalises the obligation to restore natural environment by introducing clear targets, time baselines and deadlines to restoration duties. At the same time, contrary to more enthusiastic predictions, it is difficult to assume that these innovations will have any influence beyond the biodiversity legal regimes and contribute to the establishment of a fully accomplished ecological sustainability.

The model of ecological sustainability, already enshrined in the legal regime of biodiversity, has been decisively consolidated and strengthened by the NRL. But it is still to be read as an ideal whose actual realisation remains tied to this area of application within well-defined, and still too narrow, geographical boundaries.

Chapter 8

NATURE RESTORATION LAW: RESHAPING SUSTAINABLE DEVELOPMENT?

Licinia Pascucci

ABSTRACT: *This Chapter analyses the main features of the Nature Restoration Law. In particular, it examines whether such Law represents a shift towards a genuine ecological understanding of sustainability. Additionally, it explores how the objective of ecosystems restoration is implemented and operationalized within the Member States, discussing the regulatory choices made by the EU legislator.*

KEYWORDS: *Nature restoration – Ecological sustainability – Ecosystem integrity – Biodiversity protection.*

SUMMARY: 1. Introduction. – 2. Situating the Nature Restoration Law. – 3. The legal construction of sustainability in the Nature Restoration Law. – 4. Conclusions.

1. Introduction

The Nature Restoration Law (NRL) is the most important European Union (EU) ecological law stemming from the European Green Deal. [1] It is part of the EU Biodiversity Strategy for 2030, which calls for binding targets to restore degraded ecosystems, in particular those with the most potential to capture and store carbon and to prevent and reduce the impact of natural disasters. It aims to protect and restore ecosystems, habitats, and species across the EU's land and sea areas, to enable a long-term and sustained re-

[1] Regulation (EU) 2024/1991 of the European Parliament and of the Council of 24 June 2024 on nature restoration and amending Regulation (EU) 2022/869, OJ L, 2024/1991. It should be noted that the final draft, entered into force on the 18th of August 2024, is quite different from and less ambitious than the original version proposed by the EU Commission. In particular, it contains some exemptions like the one that derogates from restoration obligations for lands dedicated to renewable energy generation and areas used for activities the sole purpose of which is national defence if measures are deemed incompatible with the continued military use of the areas in question. Moreover, it pauses restoration affecting agricultural lands in case the agricultural production for the EU food consumption is threatened and postpones the goals in case of exceptional socioeconomic circumstances.

covery of biodiverse and resilient nature, combining an overarching restoration objective for the long-term recovery of nature in the EU's land and sea areas with binding restoration targets for specific habitats and species. Meeting these targets will also contribute to achieving the EU's climate mitigation and adaptation objectives, and fulfil other international commitments contained in the Kunming-Montreal Global Biodiversity Framework signed in December 2022. The measures envisaged by the NRL should cover at least 20% of the EU's land and sea areas by 2030, and ultimately all ecosystems needing restoration by 2050.

The NRL frequently refers to sustainable development. However, one may wonder in which way sustainable development is actually constructed in this legislation. Is it based on the usual and more common idea of balancing economic, social and environmental interests? Or does it entail a different rationale? In order to address such questions, this Chapter will first recall the background of NRL and its main features (§ 2); it will then discuss whether a new idea of ecological sustainability is in the process of emerging and the instruments through which the NRL intends to achieve it (§ 3). Some final thoughts will be presented in the conclusions of the Chapter (§ 4).

2. Situating the Nature Restoration Law

Although biodiversity protection is one of the Green Deal's main goals, the EU action for saving biodiversity dates back to the last two decades of the 1990s when some essential legislations were delivered, the so-called cornerstone of Europe's nature conservation policy. This is the case, in particular, of the Birds and the Habitat Directives.

The Birds Directive,[2] released in 1979 and amended in 2009, aims at providing long-term protection and conservation of all bird species naturally living in the wild within the European territory of the Member States. For all wild bird species, Member States have an overarching objective of preserving, maintaining, and re-establishing bird habitats to ensure sufficient diversity and extent of habitat, while for threatened species they have an additional duty. They are required to establish a Special Protection Areas (SPAs) network for the 197 species and sub-species listed in Annex I of the Birds Directive, along with other migratory birds, including all the most suitable territories for these species. To help Member States fulfill their obligation to restore and maintain bird populations to good conservation sta-

[2] Directive 2009/147/EC of the European Parliament and of the Council of 30 November 2009 on the conservation of wild birds, OJ 2009 L 20.

tus, since 1993, the EU has funded the development of European Bird Species Action Plans for over 60 of the most threatened species listed in Annex I of the Birds Directive.

The Habitats Directive,[3] dating back to 1992, aims to protect over a thousand species, including mammals, reptiles, amphibians, fish invertebrates, and plants, and 230 characteristic habitat types (Articles 3 and 4). In addition to halting the further decline or disappearance of these species and habitats, the Directive aims to facilitate their long-term recovery and thriving. Member States are required to designate, protect, and manage core areas for habitat types listed in Annex I (natural habitat types of community interest whose conservation requires the designation of special areas of conservation) and species listed in Annex II of the Directive (animal and plant species of community interest whose conservation requires the designation of special areas of conservation). These designated areas are known as Special Areas of Conservation (SACs) and are crucial to ensure the favourable conservation status of each habitat type and species across the EU. Every six years, Member States must report to the Commission on the conservation status of protected species and habitat types within their territories as outlined in the Habitats Directive. The results are published, together with the reporting on bird species under the Birds Directive, in a "State of Nature in the European Union" report. In 1994, the Habitats Directive established Natura 2000, a network of sites selected to ensure the long-term survival of Europe's most valuable and threatened species and habitats. This network includes both SPAs and SACs. Natura 2000 is not solely comprised of strict nature reserves from which all human activities are excluded; instead, it encompasses various types of sites, including privately owned lands. For the latter sites, Member States must ensure that they are managed sustainably, both ecologically and economically.

Building on these two foundational directives, the Commission then clarified the EU mission to preserve nature by adopting an EU Biodiversity Strategy for 2020 (2011-2020). Such Strategy aimed to halt the loss of biodiversity and ecosystem services in the EU by 2020 and to restore them to the greatest extent possible while also contributing to curbing global biodiversity loss.[4]

At the end of the 2010s, a number of critical assessments of the EU policy and law for nature conservation were provided. In its Report No 10/2020, entitled "State of Nature in the EU, Results from reporting under

---

[3] Council Directive 92/43/EEC of 21 May 1992 on the conservation of natural habitats and of wild fauna and flora, OJ 1992 L 206.

[4] COM (2011) 244.

the Nature Directives 2013-2018", the European Environment Agency (EEA) pointed to the need to increase efforts to restore ecosystems.[5] A number of scientific studies focused on the reasons for the failure of ecosystem restoration, specifically highlighting the non-binding nature of targets.[6] The lack of commitment and political priority for restoration activities was a key barrier, leading to a lack of financing and resources being allocated to restoration. Moreover, many aspects of the existing legislative framework were considered not sufficiently specific, time-bound, or measurable to achieve restoration objectives. The absence of a comprehensive approach, resulting in a lack of coordination in the implementation process, was another major issue. A further study carried out as part of the evaluation of the EU Biodiversity Strategy for 2020 stressed the EU's failure to halt biodiversity loss between 2011 and 2020 and the shortcomings of the approach to biodiversity protection taken so far.[7]

It is in this context that the ecological move of the Green Deal is to be positioned. To solve the critical issues highlighted by the policy evaluation process, the EU Commission has renewed and strengthened its commitment to preserving and restoring biodiversity. It has done so by adopting a new EU Biodiversity Strategy for 2030[8], which aims to address these gaps and to ensure that ecosystems are healthy, resilient to climate change, rich in biodiversity, and deliver the range of services essential for citizens' prosperity and well-being. Unlike the previous Strategy, the new one focuses on restoring ecosystems rather than merely averting degradation and biodiversity loss and responds to key gaps and pressures identified in the State of Nature assessment. To this end, the current EU Biodiversity Strategy for 2030 sets out ambitious targets to enhance the protection of nature within the EU and to address the main

---

[5] The full report is available at https://www.eea.europa.eu/publications/state-of-nature-in-the-eu-2020 (last access 30 April 2024).

[6] See, in particular, Tucker G. et al., *Study on identifying the drivers of successful implementation of the Birds and Habitats Directives, Report to the European Commission, DG Environment on Contract ENV.F.1/FRA/2014/0063*, Institute for European Environmental Policy, 2019; Langhout W., *The EU Biodiversity Strategy. Progress report 2011-2018*, BirdLife International, 2019; Röschel L. et al., *State of nature in the EU—Methodological paper. Methodologies under the Nature Directives reporting 2013-2018 and analysis for the State of Nature 2020*, ETC/BD Technical paper 2/2020, 2020, https://www.eionet.europa.eu/etcs/etc-bd/products/etc-bd-reports/etc-bd-technical-paper-2-2020-state-of-nature-in-the-eu-methodological-paper-methodologies-under-the-nature-directives-reporting-2013-2018-and-analysis-for-the-state-of-nature-2000.

[7] Trinomics B.V., *Support to the evaluation of the EU Biodiversity Strategy to 2020 e follow up: Final study report*, EU Publication Office, 2021.

[8] COM (2020) 380.

drivers of biodiversity loss. Such targets aim to reduce the main pressures on nature and ecosystem services in the EU.

The new Biodiversity Strategy differs in many regards from the previous one. Whereas the Biodiversity Strategy for 2020 was structured around six objectives, the new strategy appears to be organized around two main goals: the expansion of a connected network of protected areas and the establishment of a nature restoration plan. The new Strategy considers both as key nature-based solutions to climate change mitigation and adaptation. However, it underlines that protection alone would not be enough: to reverse biodiversity loss, more significant efforts are needed to bring nature back to good health across the EU, in protected areas and beyond. In this respect, the most relevant innovation is the greater focus on the enabling framework, i.e. the instruments and channels for implementing the program.[9]

The new NRL stems from this policy framework. Its main novelty is the attempt to keep together an overarching goal with a number of legally binding objectives specific to each ecosystem, such as farmlands, pollinators, free-flowing rivers, and marine ecosystems. The overarching goal is to restore degraded ecosystems across the EU to good condition by 2050 and put them on the path to recovery by 2030. More precisely, the restoration measures should cover, by 2030, at least 20% of the Union's land and sea areas and, by 2050, all ecosystems in need of restoration, especially those with the most potential to remove and store carbon and prevent and reduce the impact of natural disasters. Ecosystem restoration includes measures for the improvement of the condition of an ecosystem but also the re-creation of an ecosystem where lost, as well as measures to improve the connectivity of natural and semi-natural ecosystems and to enhance species populations, also across national borders. The Impact Assessment accompanying the original proposal for a NRL includes both active and passive restoration actions. The first kind of measures aim to eliminate the source of degradation and disturbance of an ecosystem, implement measures to accelerate its recovery, and overcome obstacles to that recovery. Passive restoration, instead, eliminates the factors of degradation and disturbance and permits natural regeneration of the ecosystem.[10]

---

[9] For further comments on the new Strategy: European Environmental Bureau (EEB), *EEB Assessment of the EU Biodiversity Strategy for 2030*, 2021, https://eeb.org/publications/54/nature/101581/eeb-assessment-of-the-biodiversity-strategy.pdf; ClientEarth, *Lawyers react to new EU strategies: ambition welcome but policy clashes must be resolved*, May 2020, https://www.clientearth.org/latest/pressoffice/press/lawyers-react-to-new-eu-strategies-ambition-welcome-but-policy-clashes-must-beresolved/; Biscosi M., "Two Parallel Discourses and a New Path for Policy-Making: The Biodiversity Strategy for 2030", in *RQDA,* 1-2021.

[10] Commission staff working document Impact assessment accompanying the pro-

As for the ecosystem-specific targets, the NRL lays down an implementation framework to translate those targets into concrete actions, which include requirements for monitoring, assessment, planning, reporting, enforcement, financing, capacity building, and when necessary, remedial or corrective action. As previously said, it establishes legally binding duties and targets to restore and maintain ecosystems to good condition, starting from the restoration of habitats and species protected under the regime of the previous EU nature legislation. However, to meet the NRL's targets, Member States can designate additional areas as "protected areas" or "strictly protected areas" and promote private land conservation measures outside the sites provided by the previous legal regime.

The activity of protecting and restoring biodiversity is made measurable and monitorable by requiring Member States to assess ecosystems status and set up National Restoration Plans (NRPs) for reporting and review purposes. The Commission evaluates these plans before their adoption and monitors progress on a periodic basis, leveraging data gathered and analyzed by the European Environment Agency. Based on Member States' mandatory reporting, the Commission also assesses progress toward achieving good ecosystem conditions.

A further relevant point is the strict connection between the contents and objectives of the NRL and those of the EU Climate Law.[11] Ensuring healthy ecosystems and tackling climate change are intrinsically linked. In fact, global warming directly impacts ecosystems; the extinction of species is an irreversible impact of climate change, the risk of which increases steeply as global temperature rises. Indeed, species are the fundamental units of ecosystems, and increased threat to species enhances the risk to ecosystem integrity and resilience. As species become rare, their role in the functioning of the ecosystem diminishes. The loss of species reduces the ability of an ecosystem to provide services, lowers its resilience, and diminishes its capacity to counter climate change. The duty to recover ecosystems' health, as provided by the NRL, is functional in increasing the ability of ecosystems to act as natural sinks by absorbing climate-altering emissions. This is required by the overall strategy towards climate neutrality devised by the EU Climate Law, which is grounded in the synergy between mitigation and absorption measures.

Biodiverse and healthy ecosystems are more resilient to climate change

---

posal for a regulation of the European Parliament and of the Council on Nature Restoration (SWD (2022) 167).

[11] Regulation (EU) 2021/1119 of the European Parliament and of the Council of 30 June 2021 establishing the framework for achieving climate neutrality and amending Regulations (EC) 401/2009 and (EU) 2018/1999 (European Climate Law), OJ 2021 L 243.

and are also effective in preventing disasters and reducing their risks. In particular, degradation and loss of ecosystems are important causes of greenhouse gas emissions and are at risk of being exacerbated by climate change impacts, including droughts and wildfires. These threats can however be reduced or aggravated, depending on how land, sea, and freshwater are managed or protected. Thus, investing in protecting nature and rebuilding ecosystems reduces a range of climate change risks, with multiple co-benefits for people and biodiversity. An increasing body of evidence demonstrates that climate risks can be lowered by strengthening nature and focusing on effective Ecosystem-based Adaptation (EbA). As the second working group of the IPCC's latest assessment suggests: "Flood risk along rivers, for instance, can be reduced by restoring wetlands and other natural habitats in flood plains, by restoring natural courses of rivers, and by using trees to create shade. Again, cities can be cooled by parks and ponds and by greening streets and buildings' rooftops and walls". [12] Nature-based Solutions (NbS), including protecting and restoring mangroves, forests, and peatlands, also play an important part in reducing greenhouse gas emissions and taking carbon dioxide out of the atmosphere. [13]

Recent analyses, drawing on various lines of evidence, suggest that maintaining the resilience of biodiversity and ecosystem services on a global scale depends on effective and equitable conservation of approximately 30% to 50% of Earth's land, freshwater, and ocean areas, including currently near-natural ecosystems. [14] The connection with the objectives of the EU Climate Law and, more generally, with the rationale of the European Green Deal is also underlined by Article 1 of the NRL, which lays down the goals: "to contribute a) to the long-term and sustained recovery of biodiverse and resilient nature across the Member States' land and sea areas through the restoration of degraded ecosystems; b) achieving the Union's

---

[12] Intergovernmental Panel on Climate Change (IPCC), Working group II, Sixth Assessment Report, *FAQ 5: What strategies could increase the climate resilience of people and nature?*, 2022, https://www.ipcc.ch/report/ar6/wg2/about/frequently-asked-questions/keyfaq5/.

[13] For further insights: de los Santos C.B. et al., "Recent trend reversal for declining European seagrass meadows", in *Nat. Commun.,* 10(1), 3356, 2019; Duarte C.M. et al., "Rebuilding marine life", in *Nature,* 580(7801), 2020, 39-51; Scheffer M. et al., "Catastrophic shifts in ecosystems", *Nature,* 413(6856), 2001, 591-596; Folke C. et al., "Regime shifts, resilience, and biodiversity in ecosystem management", in *Annu. Rev. Ecol. Evol. Syst.,* 35, 2005, 557-581; Luther D. et al., "Global assessment of critical forest and landscape restoration needs for threatened terrestrial vertebrate species", in *Glob. Ecol. Conserv.,* 24, 2020.

[14] Intergovernmental Panel on Climate Change (IPCC), Working Group II, Sixth Assessment Report, Ch. 2, 6, 2022.

overarching objectives concerning climate change mitigation, climate change adaptation and land degradation neutrality".

The analysis so far suggests that the EU legislator has taken a more holistic approach to biodiversity restoration, trying to overcome the failures of the previous legislations. [15] It is now appropriate to verify whether the NRL, with its renewed interest in ecological and natural issues, is operationalizing the traditional rationale of sustainable development or shaping a more ecological type of sustainability.

3. The legal construction of sustainability in the Nature Restoration Law

In the EU order, the sustainability issue was introduced in 1992, when the Maastricht Treaty referred to the rationale of sustainable development in Article 2: "The Community has the task of promoting [...] a harmonious and balanced development of economic activities throughout the Community, sustainable, non-inflationary and environmentally friendly growth". The current Treaty is consistent with that approach. The preamble to the Treaty on European Union (TEU) refers to Member States' determination "to promote economic and social progress for their peoples, taking into account the principle of sustainable development and within the context of the accomplishment of the internal market and of reinforced cohesion and environmental protection". This orientation is confirmed by Article 3, which states that the establishment of an internal market, considered to be the core of the European Union, must work for the sustainable development of Europe based on balanced economic growth and price stability, a highly competitive social market economy, aiming at full employment and social progress, and a high level of protection and improvement of the quality of the environment. Article 21 also provides for sustainable development to play a guiding role in the Union's external action, committing the EU to promote this objective in developing countries across economic, social, and environmental dimensions, with the primary goal of eradicating poverty. Sustainable development is also referred to in the preamble and Article 37 of the Charter of Fundamental Rights, which echoes the principle of integration (Article 11 TFEU) by stating that "A high level of environmental protection and the improvement of the quality of the environment must be integrated into

[15] Hoek N., "A critical analysis of the Proposed EU Regulation on Nature Restoration: Have the problems been resolved?", in *Eur. Energy Environ. Law Rev.*, 31, 2022, 5, 320-333.

the policies of the Union and ensured by the principle of sustainable development".

Over the years, sustainable development has become a common reference and a leading objective of a wide range of EU policies and legislation. However, despite many efforts to clarify the concept, sustainable development has remained relatively open-ended, providing "a space for dissension and socio-political struggle where competing discourses of the economic and environmental paradigms are joined". [16] There are still some grey areas where it is difficult to reconcile the promises of economic growth, social justice, and ecological sustainability through the balancing exercise envisaged by sustainable development. This is the case, for example, with biodiversity protection issues, where ecological concerns for ecosystem restoration may clash with the need to strengthen human livelihoods and the economic development of societies themselves.

It is then appropriate to discuss the choices made by the EU legislator in the NRL. One should begin by observing that the primary objective of the NRL is, as observed by the Commission in the original proposal, "an ecological one (i.e. to improve the condition of ecosystems). However, improved ecosystem condition also goes hand in hand with the delivery of a range of ecosystem services that result from the improved condition". [17] This was re-stated with reference to the expected results and impacts: "Society, as a whole, benefits from nature restoration through enhanced climate change mitigation and adaptation and disaster risk management. Nature restoration furthermore provides job and income opportunities. It has positive effects on citizens' health, enhanced natural and cultural heritage, and identity, as well as enhanced quality and security of food and water. A wide range of economic sectors will also benefit, particularly those highly dependent on ecosystem services, such as agri-food, fisheries, forestry, water companies, tourism, and the financial sector". [18]

Admittedly, the NRL also promotes a clearly Anthropocentric perspective, as sustainability is strictly related to human beings. There is no reference to the capacity of an ecosystem to ensure and sustain its own life and

---

[16] Hajer M.A., *The Politics of Environmental Discourse: Ecological Modernisation and the Policy Process*, Oxford University Press, 1995. See also Pozzo B., "Sustainable Development", in Baldin S. and De Vido S. (eds.), *Environmental Sustainability in the European Union: Socio-Legal Perspectives,* Edizioni Università di Trieste, 2020, 11-38.

[17] Commission staff working document Impact assessment, accompanying the proposal for a regulation of the European Parliament and of the Council on Nature Restoration (SWD (2022) 167, para. 4.2.).

[18] COM (2022) 304, Legislative financial statement, 1.4.2 Expected result(s) and impact.

health, but instead the idea of serving citizens and societies: an ecosystem is considered to be in good condition when it may operate as a tool for social incomes and economic benefits. Protecting the basic necessities of human life – clean air, drinkable water, fertile soil, healthy oceans – is a win-win situation for securing livelihoods and thriving economies. This aspect of the legal construction of sustainability in the NRL reflects the rationale of EU environmental law, developed under the aegis of the sustainable development philosophy, whereby the issue of development pushed the regulators to prevent future adversity, rather than to deal with past mistakes, on the assumption that nature has the capacity to passively restore itself through its own processes.[19]

Yet, NRL also promotes a more ecological understanding of sustainability, inspired by the ecology's ideology and principles, including ecological primacy.[20] Ecological sustainability is usually defined as the maintenance or restoration of the composition, structure, and processes of ecosystems, to remain diverse and productive over time.[21] Ecological restoration, the overarching objective of NRL, encapsulates such rationale. It also represents a radical departure from the "enclave theory of conservation", which assumes that designating small sanctuaries and parks would suffice to meet all conservation objectives, leaving the remaining, much larger areas for economic development and human settlement.[22] While NRL contains several references to sustainable development,[23] it implies the prioritization of ecosystem protection over socio-economic concerns. Admittedly, healthy ecosystems may bring many benefits to human beings, ranging from human health and resilience to preventing future diseases. Yet, the NRL recognizes that the good status of ecosystems represents the *condicio sine qua non* for enabling human life itself. This might be the most innovative aspect of NRL. In fact, it relies on the assumption that, without the precondition of life, there would be no point in discussing social justice or economic growth issues. The prioritization of environmental protection is an original

---

[19] Akhtar-Khavari A. and Richardson B.J. (eds.), *Ecological restoration law concepts and case studies*, Routledge, 2019.

[20] Sbert C., *The lens of ecological law*, Elgar, 2020, 77-98.

[21] Bram G. and Aarts W., "Ecological sustainability and biodiversity", in *Int. J. Sustain. Dev. World Ecol.*, 1999, 89-102.

[22] Richardson B.J., "The Emerging Age of Ecological Restoration Law", in *RECIEL*, 2016, 25, 3, 273-401.

[23] See e.g. Article 14, linking ecosystem restoration to sustainable growth, and Recital 65, providing that the restoration targets potentially contribute to the sustainable development of regions and communites, given the productivity potential of a healthy environment.

regulatory option, aiming at giving prominence to ecological concerns while at the same time implying that the three pillars of sustainable development are not mutually exclusive but can reinforce each other through the integration mechanism.

Such prioritized link between a healthy and resilient nature, on the one hand, and human well-being, on the other, is reiterated in the NRL in Article 22, where reference is made to the One Health Approach. As well known, this is "an integrated approach that aims to sustainably balance and optimize the health of people, animals, and ecosystems. It recognizes the health of humans, domestic and wild animals, plants, and the wider environment (including ecosystems) are closely linked and interdependent".[24] In its current conceptualisation, One Health combines the integration approach with the protection of ecosystem health, in line with the general meaning that the concept of sustainability has in the NRL framework.

4. Conclusions

The NRL may represent an important step in the juridification process of the ecological dimension of sustainability, in line with the overall rationale of the European Green Deal.[25] The targets envisaged by the EU legislator should ensure the health and resilience of European nature. Moreover, the sustainability and functional resilience of ecosystems are now objectives of a legislative act, mandatory and directly applicable to the Member State in all its elements when approved. They might also play a vital role in operationalizing the ecological dimension of sustainability at the national level, as the NRL commits public authorities at the national, regional and local levels to map and assess ecosystems and their services and to plan, fund, implement and monitor restoration programs.

Nevertheless, the NRL leaves the Member States a door open to postponing restoration targets in case of exceptional socioeconomic consequences. Although in exceptional situations, this amendment reverses the priority given by to the protection of the quality of the environment over socio-economic concerns. Moreover, targets might become non-binding and voluntary, opening the way to a serious risk of non-compliance by Member States.

---

[24] One Health High-Level Expert Panel, "One Health: A new definition for a sustainable and healthy future", in *PLoS Pathog.* 2022, 23, 18(6).

[25] Chiti E., "Oltre la disciplina dei mercati: la sostenibilità degli ecosistemi e la sua rilevanza nel Green Deal europeo", in *Riv. Reg. Mer.*, 2022, 468.

In any case, the NRL remains an innovative and potentially important contribution to the ecological transition of the EU. The core of the innovation lies in the attempt to strengthen ecological concerns in EU policy and law, as well as, at the conceptual level, in the redefinition of the relationship between ecological, economic and social concerns, beyond the consolidated construction of sustainable development.

Chapter 9

SERVING SUSTAINABILITY THROUGH CRIMINAL LAW: THE ITALIAN CASE

Antonio Taurelli

ABSTRACT: *The Chapter aims to investigates the relationship between Criminal Law and the regulatory goal of sustainability, focusing specifically on Environmental Criminal Law. It examines Italian legislation, European directives, and in particular the recent directive on environmental crimes, which is part of the broader framework of the Green Deal. After recalling the main conceptualizations of sustainability, historically developed in contexts unrelated to punitive law, the contribution seeks to ascertain whether and to what extent the concept of sustainability has been integrated into the field of Criminal Law and its implications for the legal system. Having established the penetration of sustainability into Criminal Law, the work addresses two conceptual challenges posed by sustainability within the criminal justice system: the first concerns temporality, while the second pertains to the type of relevant facts and the nature of offenses.*

KEYWORDS: *Sustainability – Sustainable development – Criminal law – Future generations – Intergenerational justice.*

SUMMARY: 1. Introduction. – 2. Penetrating Criminal Law. – 3. Environment and sustainability: two different approaches. – 4. Legislative choices. – 5. The EU criminal framework: a paradigm shift? – 6. Structural tensions.

1. Introduction

This Chapter presents some reflections on the role and relevance of sustainability in the context of Environmental Criminal Law. It asks whether the legal concept of sustainability, as currently formalized in the European Union (EU) order, is gradually becoming a regulatory objective of Domestic Environmental Criminal Law and, if so, how it has been shaped and formulated so far. In line with the overall perspective of this book, we register an ongoing transformation of the legal objective of sustainability at the EU level and we discuss whether a parallel evolution of sustainability is taking place in Domestic Criminal Law, paying particular attention to the Criminal Law of one EU Member State, namely Italy. This might shed some light on the evolution of contemporary Criminal Law and the role played by the changing features of sustainability.

The inquiry is organized as follows. It opens with a discussion of the ways in which Italian Criminal Law has incorporated sustainability among its objectives and the effects that this has produced on its contents and structure (§ 2). It is then argued that the actual meaning of sustainability in Italian Criminal Law depends on the way in which environmental protection is represented: while an ecocentric idea of environmental protection may be associated with ecosystem sustainability, an anthropocentric perspective of the environment corresponds to the more traditional objective of sustainable development (§ 3). Using this interpretive framework, it is then discussed which concept of environment and sustainability dominates Italian Criminal Law (§ 4). Subsequently, attention is paid to the new EU directive on the protection of the environment through Criminal Law made by the Commission within the context of the Green Deal, with a view to understanding whether the evolution of sustainability triggered by the Green Deal is also affecting EU criminal policy (§ 5). The Chapter ends by highlighting the deep structural tension between the objective of sustainability and the fundamental rationale of Criminal Law (§ 6).

2. Penetrating Criminal Law

In its 2019 Communication on the Green Deal, the Commission stated to be ready to «promote actions through the EU, its Member States and the international community to step up efforts against environmental crime».[1] Such reference to environmental crime leaves no doubt that Criminal Law is included in the set of legal instruments for the ecological transition and its sustainability concerns. The relationship between Criminal Law and sustainability, though, deserves some clarification: in which ways Criminal Law is actually incorporating sustainability among its objectives? And with what effects?

Our starting point may be Claus Roxin's well-known distinction between «criminal policy» and the «system of criminal law»:[2] while the former refers to the social content and purposes of Criminal Law, the latter focuses on the conceptual analysis of the current legal system.[3] For the purposes of our inquiry, we may refer both to criminal policy and law, on the assumption that Criminal Law pursues the social purposes set down

---

[1] COM (2019) 640.

[2] Roxin C., *Kriminalpolitik und Strafrechtssystem*, Walter de Gruyter, 1973; Roxin C., *Politica criminale e sistema del diritto penale*, Edizioni Scientifiche Italiane, 2009, 37.

[3] *Ibidem*, 43.

over time by policy-making. In this broad perspective, sustainability is certainly part of the scope of Criminal Law and policy, as it emerges from the mentioned Communication on the Green Deal. Its precise relevance in the criminal legal system, however, remains unclear.

Admittedly, in Italian Criminal Law sustainability does not operate as a limit or guarantee for the offender. Nor it can be easily reconstructed as a principle or as a legal good. For some authors, sustainability cannot be operationalized into a specific legal discipline because it concerns the entire body of environmental law and its overall purposes.[4] Moreover, sustainability is rarely invoked in judicial litigation: it is difficult to find cases in which courts asked to evaluate the sustainability of conduct. Sustainability is mainly addressed to legislator and public administrations, provided that it requires to make discretionary choices and to balance the economic, social and environmental interests at stake. Criminal courts are mainly called to assess the correspondence between a specific conduct and an administrative decision, without the need to reconsider the way in which the sustainability objective has been operationalized by the public authority.

Nevertheless, Italian Criminal Law is certainly influenced by sustainability, which exerts a transformative force on the system and shapes its contents and structure. Examples of this transformation include the proliferation of clauses of special unlawfulness,[5] the so-called «protection of administrative function», and the spread of abstract endangerment offenses.[6] These examples suggest that sustainability is becoming relevant in the realm of Criminal Law as a «legal good».[7] This determines a peculiar twist

---

[4] Fimiani P., "Il Diritto Penale di fronte alla Sostenibilità e ai Principi Ambientali", in *Lexambiente*, 2023, 1, 20.

[5] According to Italian Criminal Law, special unlawfulness refers to the circumstance that the constitutive elements of a typical fact include elements inherently implying a qualification in terms of unlawfulness according to a norm different from the one directly incriminating a cerain conduct; see Padovani T., *Diritto Penale*, 13, Giuffrè, 2023, 192. For the application of this clause to environmental crimes, see Ruga Riva C., *Diritto penale dell'ambiente*, 4, Giappichelli, 2021, 257.

[6] Abstract danger offenses refer to those behaviours for which the legislator has presumed that a danger is posed to one or more legal interests. In these cases, the judge must merely ascertain the existence of the relevant behavior. In case of crimes of concrete danger, instead, no presumption is established by the legislator and the court is called to ascertain whether the legal interest has been actually exposed to danger. See A.A.V.V. Marinucci G. and Dolcini E. and Gatta G.L., *Manuale di Diritto Penale*, 12, Giuffrè, 2023, 287.

[7] Clauses of special unlawfulness reveal how the protected interest in Environmental Criminal Law tends to coincide or at least to align with the administrative function. Indeed, the public administration determines what is (and what is not) sustainable in relation to the balancing of interests inherent in political and administrative discretion.

in Criminal Law. Criminal offense seems to respond not so much to an idea of primary selection of wrongdoing but rather to the question of the extent to which a specific conduct is tolerable.[8] Polluting conducts, as archetypal expressions of environmental damage, represent a «tolerable evil»[9] if they remain within certain formal limits of acceptability. In the words of the Italian Criminal Lawyer Filippo Sgubbi, such relativism leads not so much to preventing evil, but rather to proposing a «methodology of evil»[10] and a methodology of environmental harm. Between lawfulness and unlawfulness, conditional lawfulness has been conceptualized as a tertium genus,[11] one which conceives criminal offensiveness in a gradable way. Nature preservation does not operate in the criminal legal system as a tendentially insurmountable limit, as it is normally the case for individual rights. This should not be seen as a failure to update the legal system to new sensibilities or a conservative resistance to legal change. Should we understand any environmentally impacting activity as criminally relevant, we would reach the paradoxical conclusion that human life itself is inherently criminally relevant. Our era is one in which the human imprint has become systemic, as suggested by the concept of «anthropocene» elaborated by Paul Crutzen to refer to a geological era in which human beings are capable of modifying not only the environment in the traditional sense, but even the structural elements of the planet, such as climate, geology and the biology of the Earth system. It is an era in which the human imprint has become systemic and human beings have become a geomorphic force. And it is within this intricate landscape that Criminal Law is asked to establish limits.

Sustainability is thus a «stone guest» of Italian contemporary Criminal Law. On the one hand, it is not a principle and is almost absent from nor-

---

From this perspective, adherence to a criminal model aimed at protecting functions implies a reference to sustainability, which is substantiated in the balancing of interests by public administrations. We can observe a connection between the technique of criminalization and the logic of sustainability. Abstract danger offenses distinctly reflect the preventive and often precautionary nature of sustainability. Moreover, they are more suitable for protecting interests that are not empirically tangible, such as sustainability. For a comprehensive reconstruction of the theory of legal interests and the transition from the protection of interests to the protection of functions, see Manes V., *Il principio di offensività nel diritto penale. Canone di politica criminale, criterio ermeneutico, parametro di ragionevolezza*, Giappichelli, 2005.

[8] Porciello A., *Filosofia dell'ambiente. Ontologia, etica, diritto*, Carrocci, 2022, 159.

[9] Sgubbi F., "Il diritto penale incerto ed efficace", in *Riv. It. Dir. Proc. Pen.*, 2011, 4, 1193.

[10] *Ibidem*, 1197.

[11] Bernasconi C., *Il reato ambientale. Tipicità, offensività, antigiuridicità, colpevolezza*, Edizioni ETS, 2008, 124.

mative texts. On the other hand, it looms over the legal system as an objective of criminal policy, exerting a transformative force capable of altering some fundamental structures of Criminal Law, such as the typification of legal offenses and the configuration of the protected legal interest. These effects suggest that sustainability, although barely visible, is penetrating Criminal Law.

3. Environment and sustainability: two different approaches

As argued by an authoritative Italian scholar, environment, as an object of legal protection, tends to overlap with sustainability.[12] In this perspective, environmental protection represents a condition for development and environmental law is essentially a law of sustainability, in line with the provisions of Articles 191 and 193 of the Treaty on the Functioning of the European Union (TFEU). Moreover, Environmental Criminal Law is ultimately oriented to safeguard human interests.

Following this overall approach, it should be first of all highlighted that the notion of environment in Italian Criminal Law does not refer to an objective and clearly identifiable empirical object. Rather, it is a concept shaped in a specific cultural context and requiring agreement on its conventional definition.[13] Moreover, it points to a relationship between humans and the space surrounding them,[14] which needs to be defined and unveiled in order to be protected.

It is also appropriate to stress that there are two main approaches to construct environment as an object of legal protection in Criminal Law, corresponding to two different models of sustainability.[15] According to the first approach, that may be labelled as «anthropocentric», the environment is functional to the human well-being and is framed as a resource to be ex-

---

[12] See Fracchia F., "Sviluppo sostenibile e diritti delle future generazioni", in *RQDA*, 2010, 0, 13.

[13] See Giunta F., "Tutela dell'ambiente", in *Enc. Dir.*, 2008, 1551, where it is clarified that the environment is a «conventional entity», it is not a natural element, and precisely for this reason, it carries a clear and unavoidable political significance.

[14] The term «environment» is derived from the present participle of the Latin word «ambire» which means to go around. Similarly, the English term «environment» and the French term «environnement» are composed of the prefix «en» (around) plus the verb «virer» (to turn). The German term «Umwelt» also follows this pattern, composed of the prefix «um» before the noun «Welt» (world). The environment is what surrounds human beings, and it is in this relationship that language tends to frame it.

[15] For a more comprehensive understanding see Pisanò A., *Diritti Deumanizzati. Animali, ambiente, generazioni future, specie umana*, Giuffrè, 2012.

ploited for the benefit of civilization. In such axiological perspective, environmental protection is instrumentally aimed at ensuring the protection of other legal goods or interests pertaining to human beings: the environment thus represents a sentinel-indicator capable of acting as an alarm before other legal goods, such as life and health, are offended. According to a second, «ecocentric» view, the environment has an inherent value, regardless of its usefulness for human purposes: it is a legal good, axiologically self-sufficient and requiring protection through Criminal Law. Such a view reflects a specific ethics, based on the moral premise identified in 1949 by Aldo Leopold: «all ethics so far evolved rest upon a single premise: that the individual is a member of a community of interdependent parts (...) The land ethic simply enlarges the boundaries of the community to include soils, waters, plants, and animals, or collectively: the land». [16]

These two political-interpretative approaches broadly correspond to the two main declinations of sustainability in the EU. As argued in the opening Chapter of this volume, sustainable development, historically the exclusive form of sustainability in the EU order, is now accompanied by a new and more ecological understanding of sustainability, elaborated in the legislation stemming from the Green Deal. Sustainable development and ecological sustainability represent the double engine of the Green Deal, although their co-existence is far from being harmonious. The two models in principle identifiable in domestic Criminal Law mirror the distinction between sustailable development and ecological sustainability emerging at the EU level. The ecocentric approach encapsulates the preference for ecological primacy, the «do no harm» imperative and the prioritization of ecosystem health over social and economic concerns, while the anthropocentric view clearly reflects the wider rationale of sustainable development.

4. Legislative choices

We may now ask how the Italian legislator has actually declined sustainability, whether in the vest of sustainable development, ecological sustainability or other kinds of sustainability.

While several provisions of the Italian Criminal Code have been used for environmental protection purposes in the past, [17] the field has been re-

---

[16] Leopold A., *A Sand County Almanac, and Sketches Here and There*, Oxford University Press, 1949, 203.

[17] Bernasconi clarifies that although the term «environmental criminal law» is a relatively recent formulation, it can be observed that many provisions of the Italian penal code have been used for environmental protection purposes.; see Bermasconi C., *Il*

shaped only in 2006, with the adoption of the so called Environmental Code,[18] a legal text encompassing both administrative offenses and criminal offenses. Subsequently, in 2015, environmental crimes have been outlined in a separate section of the Criminal Code, namely Title VI bis. This reform was certainly prompted by EU Directive 99/2008/EC, which requires Member States to take the necessary measures to ensure that a number of environmental offences are punishable by effective, proportionate and dissuasive criminal penalties. In 2021, the Commission has then presented a proposal for a new directive, amending the 2008 one and expanding the list of environmental offences, in line with the objectives of the Green Deal.[19]

Identifying the object of protection under Italian Environmental Criminal Law may help to detect the specific type of sustainability to which Criminal Law refers. Since positive law does not provide a definition of environment, it is appropriate to analyze the typification of the offense. In the Environmental Code, the object of protection is not conceived in its empirical dimension and the crime of abstract danger represents the predominant scheme of offence:[20] the object of protection is not conceived as a super-individual legal interest[21] and the relevant criminal conduct involves either exceeding predefined threshold values or engaging in an activity without valid permits. Accordingly, Criminal Law depends on administrative law: the balancing made by the relevant administration defines the object of legal protection and plays a pivotal role in delineating the boundary between legality and illegality.[22] Indeed, concentration thresholds of polluting substances are the result of a political balance made by the legislator or administrative authority, which identifies the criminally relevant activities.

Such a criminal model inherently implies a choice about sustainability.

---

reato ambientale. Tipicità, offensività, antigiuridicità, colpevolezza, cit. By way of example, the Author cites offenses such as arson (Article 423 of the Italian Criminal Code), contamination of water or food substances (Article 439), spreading diseases among plants or animals (Article 500), damage (Article 635), non-compliance with Authority's orders (Article 650), dangerous throwing of things (Article 674), and destruction or defacement of natural beauty (Article 734).

[18] Legislative Decree 152/2006.

[19] COM (2021) 851.

[20] Bernasconi C., cit., 199; Giunta F., "Il diritto penale dell'ambiente in Italia: tutela di beni o tutela di funzioni?", in *Riv. It. Dir. Proc. Pen.*, 1997, 1097.

[21] Grasso G., "L'anticipazione della tutela: i reati di pericolo e i reati di attentato", in *Riv. It. Dir. Proc. Pen.*, 1986, 711.

[22] Giunta F., "Tutela dell'ambiente", in *Enc. Dir.*, 2008, 2, 1152.

In essence, it relies on an understanding of the environment aligned with the notion of sustainable development, as environmental protection is instrumental to the protection of other legal goods or interests pertaining to human beings. Yet, it is also appropriate to consider legislation No 68 of 2015, which has introduced to the Italian Criminal Code a new title dedicated to the environment. Such reform has brought about a significant shift in the typification of offenses, from abstract danger offenses to concrete danger and harm offenses.[23] The new crimes have been legally constructed in such a way to consider the actual damage caused to the ecosystem and biodiversity, as exemplified by the two paradigmatic offenses of «environmental pollution»[24] and «environmental disaster».[25] One may wonder whether the Italian legislator has opted for an ecological understanding of sustainability, going beyond sustainable development and the connection between Criminal Law and administrative law. Admittedly, ecosystems now emerge as the possible object of harm. However, the typicality of the act is still conditioned by an additional administrative unlawfulness, proving that, even in the most serious offenses, harm to the environment, considered in naturalistic terms,[26] is not sufficient on its own to allocate criminal disvalue. A balancing exercise is envisaged by the legislator, the so-called anthropization margin. The model is one defined as «partially punitive» because it is not entirely autonomous in the primary selection of the offense, although the protected value is partly concretized in terms of the ecosystem and biodiversity.

In the aftermath of this reform, some scholars have argued that it has brought about an ecocentric shift,[27] while others have contended that the anthropocentric approach is still firmly rooted in Italian Criminal Law.[28] It

---

[23] Telesca M., *La tutela penale dell'ambiente. I profili problematici della Legge n. 68/2015*, 2, Giappichelli, 2021, 34.

[24] Article 452-bis of the Italian Criminal Code.

[25] Article 452-quater of the Italian Criminal Code.

[26] See Gargani A., "Ius in latenti. Profili di incertezza del diritto penale dell'ambiente", in *Discrimen*, 2020, 22, where the Author shows how the special unlawfulness clause corresponds to the deontic-evaluative nature that the legal interest assumes in environmental offenses. In these crimes, the harm cannot be evaluated in naturalistic terms because the environment does not lend itself to being considered as a direct and immediate material referent, as a «self-contained, self-sufficient, phenomenally accessible reality in itself». The notion of environmental integrity, instead, emerges as the result of a different judgment. What matters is that the alteration of the balance of an ecosystem has occurred without a legitimate authorization or beyond the limits set by it.

[27] Severino P., "Il nuovo diritto penale dell'ambiente. Problemi di teoria del reato e profili sanzionatori", in *Dir. Pen. Cont. Riv. Trim.*, 2018, 190.

[28] Ruga Riva C., *I nuovi ecoreati. Commento alla legge 22 maggio 2015 n. 68*, Giappi-

has also been argued that the new legislation places human beings and the environment on an equal footing, as it establishes comprehensive protection against certain behaviors[29] without making specific reference to anthropocentric interests. In this perspective, the environment has become an object of protection regardless of specific connection with other social and human interest. A further and most common view is that an intermediate choice between an anthropocentric and ecocentric perspective has been made by the 2015 reform.[30] While it refers to biodiversity and ecosystems as such, it also allows humans to engage in activities under the shield of administrative lawfulness.

5. The EU criminal framework: a paradigm shift?

As already observed, the 2015 reform of the Italian Criminal Code was prompted by EU Directive 99/2008/EC, requiring Member States to take the necessary measures to ensure that a number of environmental offences are punishable by effective, proportionate and dissuasive criminal penalties.[31] The offenses envisaged by Directive 99/2008/EC mainly relate to the risk of death or serious harm to individuals. The Directive requires Member States to make activities listed in Article 3 criminally relevant, when unlawful and committed intentionally or with at least serious negligence: the situation is thus one of additional unlawfulness. As for the protected legal interest, Alberto Gargani has observed that the emerging EU Criminal Law should be framed «neither [as] the protection of administrative functions nor [as] a pure penal model, but rather [as] an intermediate, partially punitive paradigm of European origin: it is required that actions affecting environmental values be committed in violation of European or national regula-

---

chelli, 2015; Caterini M., *Effettività e tecniche di tutela nel diritto penale dell'ambiente. Contributo ad una lettura costituzionalmente orientata*, Edizioni Scientifiche Italiane, 2017, 32; Lo Monte E., *Diritto penale e tutela penale dell'ambiente*, Giuffrè, 2004, 324.

[29] Scarcella A., "Tutela dell'ambiente, verso una concezione ecocentrica", in *Ecoscienza*, 2019, 68.

[30] Telesca M., *La tutela penale dell'ambiente. I profili problematici della Legge n. 68/2015*, 2, Giappichelli, 2021, 39.

[31] Directive 2008/99/EC, along with Directive 2009/123/EC, were transposed into Italian legal system through Law 96/2010, which delegated the authority to the Government to adopt a legislative decree. However, Article 2 of the delegation law prevented a full alignment with the directives, leading to the postponement of the actual transposition to a subsequent intervention. Subsequently, with Legislative Decree 121/2011, parts of the 2009 directive were partially transposed. However, overall, the legislature did not fully comply with the European obligations, continuing to maintain an administrative offense system based on abstract danger and offenses consisting of formal violations.

tions, or the corresponding implementing administrative measures».[32] Unsurprisingly, Directive 99/2008/EC was implemented through a legislation referring to additional unlawfulness by using the adverb «abusively», a choice which has created a number of uneasy interpretive issues.

After the launch of the Green Deal project, a new EU directive on the protection of the environment through Criminal Law has been put forward by the Commission.[33] Such new EU directive aims at replacing the previous Directive, given the shortcomings ascertained in its implementation and enforcement. As Criminal Law is expressly presented as a tool for the achievement of the Green Deal's objectives, it is appropriate to ask whether the new Eu directive encapsulates the new policy objective of ecological sustainability, for example by referring to ecosystem integrity and ecological primacy, or it is rather aligned with the traditional rationale of sustainable development.

The answer to this question is nuanced. To begin with, the new directive[34] revises the list of environmental criminal offences which were set out in Directive 2008/99/EC, by adding additional categories of offences based on the most serious breaches of EU environmental law. In doing so, it confirms the additional unlawfulness option, as Member States are required to ensure that the listed conducts constitute criminal offences when they are unlawful and committed intentionally. As in the past, the duty to criminalize only applies to conducts that are deemed «unlawful», leaving Member States a wide margin of administrative discretion. Furthermore, in continuity with the previous, the new Directive refers to offences capable of leading to significant negative consequences to the environment, although no express reference is made to the «do no significant harm»[35] ob-

---

[32] Gargani A., "Ius in latenti. Profili di incertezza del diritto penale dell'ambiente", cit., our translation.

[33] COM (2021) 851 final.

[34] Directive (EU) 2024/1203 of the European Parliament and of the Council of 11 April 2024 on the protection of the environment through Criminal Law and replacing Directives 2008/99/EC and 2009/123/EC, ELI: http://data.europa.eu/eli/dir/2024/1203/oj.

[35] The objective 'do not significant harm' is formulated in Regulation 852 of 2020, known as the Taxonomy Regulation, in line with the approach of the previous Regulation 2088 of 2019 on sustainability disclosure in the financial services sector. The criterion of 'not causing significant harm' has subsequently been employed in other disciplines, including Regulation 241 of 2021, which establishes the framework for recovery and resilience and binds it to compliance with this criterion, qualified as a "horizontal principle" of the discipline. Let's consider that the objective under scrutiny was initially put forth in the Green Deal Communication (28 COM 2019 640, p. 21) in terms of 'do not harm'. Such a shift is not without implications: for an overall framework see Chiti

jective. Thirdly, the criminalization of certain specific conducts indirectly promotes biodiversity protection: this is the case, for example, of conducts causing the deterioration of a habitat within a protected site, as well as of introduction or spread of invasive alien species of Union concern. A specifically ecological concern may be found also in the provision which requires Member States to consider a criminal offence the abstraction of surface water or groundwater which causes or is likely to cause substantial damage to the ecological status or potential of surface water bodies or to the quantitative status of groundwater bodies. In any case, the new Directive does not seem to convey a fully accomplished understanding of ecological protection, based on ecosystem integrity and ecological primacy. This is far from surprising, considering not only the specific features of Criminal Law (*extrema ratio*) and its limited regulatory potential, but also that the new EU directive aims at establishing only a common framework that Member States will articulate and further develop.

6. Structural tensions

In the previous pages it has been argued that sustainability is gradually penetrating into the realm of Criminal Law. By referring to the specific case of the Italian order, we have showed that Criminal Law can be used as a tool to support sustainability and that such use is indirectly promoted by the EU legislator. At the end of this short analysis, it is appropriate to highlight the structural tension inherent in the process described so far.

Criminal law and sustainability operate within largely different timeframes.[36] Sustainability is primarily an expression of intergenerational justice[37]:

E., "Verso una sostenibilità plurale? La forza trasformatrice del Green Deal e la direzione del cambiamento giuridico", in *RQDA*, 2021, 3, 140.

[36] As international literature is progressively demonstrating, the conception of temporality is integral to the identity of a legal system: see eg. Mawani R., "Law as Temporality: Colonial Politics and Indian Settlers", in *U.C Irvine L.*, 2014, 4, 65; Cusato E, "Progress and Linear Time: How to Rethink International Law to Account for Ecologically Precarious Presents?", in Völkerrechtsblog, 2023, available at https://voelkerrechtsblog.org/progress-and-linear-time-how-to-rethink-international-law-to-account-for-ecologically-precarious-presents/; Hunfeld K., "The coloniality of time in the global justice debate: de-centring Western linear temporality", in *Journal of Global Ethics*, 2022, 100; Mcneilly K. and Warwick B., *The times and temporalities of international human rights law*, Bloomsbury Publishing, 2022; Grear A., "Anthropocene 'Time'? – A reflection on temporalities in the "New Age of the Human", in *Routledge Handbook of Law and Theory*, 2019, 297.

[37] For a comprehensive discussion of the philosophical issues raised by intergenerational justice, refer to Pontara G., *Etica e generazioni future*, Mincione Editore, 2021.

it makes full sense when viewed in the context of the relationship between generations. Criminal law, instead, may be seen as a law of contemporaneity, based on an ethics of proximity: as observed by Sgubbi, «the criminal responsibility and obligations towards others are based [...] on the social contract, but always on the assumption of temporal and spatial proximity».[38] Differently from civil law, whose provisions are often oriented to the future, as in the paradigmatic case of successions, Criminal Law has historically regulated relationships between human beings living in the same time and space. Legal institutes such as prescription and the principle of offensiveness illustrate that the temporal horizon of Criminal Law is closely related to the time of the offense itself. This timeframe never exceeds the duration of an individual's life, as the offender's lifespan, according to a well established tradition that can be traced back to the Enlightenment, is the measure of the penalty. Seen in this perspective, sustainability represents a direct challenge to the temporal rationale of Criminal Law. An environmentally or ecologically unsustainable behavior is not necessarily harmful or dangerous in the short term. Typically, its consequences will become apparent in the medium or even long term. If this is case, can Criminal Law hold together multiple generations without fundamentally changing the rationale of penalties and punishment?

A further dimension of the structural tension between sustainability and Criminal Law concerns events and their measurement scale. Sustainability encapsulates an idea of global responsibility that deals with general behaviours and widespread effects, whereas Criminal Law is based on a closely personal concept of responsibility, associated to individual behaviors and specific events linked by a clear causal nexus. Ferrajoli has appropriately warned about the difficulties that Criminal Law may have in dealing with «systemic crimes», characterized by «the indefinite and indeterminable nature of both action and usually catastrophic event, and the indefinite and multi-subjective nature of both their authors and their victims, who are usually entire populations and sometimes the entire humanity».[39] According to Ferrajoli, authors «are not identifiable as individual persons but rather as mechanisms of the economic and political system».[40] This is precisely the empirical situation of an unsustainable offensive behaviour. It is difficult for Criminal Law, as currently designed in Italy and most EU countries, to deal with this type of empirical situations: there are tensions between the principle of offensiveness, causal nexus,

---

[38] Sgubbi F., *Il diritto penale totale*, Il Mulino, 2019, 33, our translation.

[39] Ferrajoli L., *Per una Costituzione della Terra*, Feltrinelli, 2022, 45, our translation.

[40] *Ibidem*, 41, our translation.

the principle of personal responsibility, on the hand, and phenomena like climate change, environmental harms and unsustainable behaviours, on the other.

Criminal law can be used as a tool to support sustainability, as suggested by the ongoing developments in the Italian order. Yet, sustainability is a concept potentially capable of shaking the very foundations and rationale of Criminal Law. Whether Criminal Law will be reshaped by sustainability, it remains to be seen.

Part 4

THE DIGITAL TRANSITION

Chapter 10

DATA-DRIVEN ECOSYSTEMS: COMPETITION LAW AS A WAY TO LINK SUSTAINABILITY AND DIGITALISATION

Emanuele Fazio

ABSTRACT: *The European Green Deal and the Digital Decade Policy Programme 2030 identify digitalisation as the key enabler for steering the EU's economy and society towards sustainability. This involves increased use of data to address economic, social, climate, and environmental challenges. Concurrently, digitalisation and data-related practices must prioritize sustainability. This Chapter explores how the liaison between sustainability and digitalisation within data-driven ecosystems influences competition law. It advocates for a shift from monocentric to polycentric competition law, engaging multiple actors in achieving the objective of climate neutrality.*

KEYWORDS: *Data-driven ecosystems – Sustainability – Digitalisation – Competition – Analytical shortcuts.*

1. The liaison between sustainability and digitalisation in data-driven ecosystems

In this Chapter, the concept of *data-driven ecosystems* refers to data resources that enable a network of actors (both supply- and demand-side) to rely on each other's activities in order to create value from online and/or offline interactions.[1] They are generally characterised by the co-evolution of the collaborating actors under an aligned vision, modularity, interdependencies and non-generic technological complementarities that bind together data-driven ecosystem participants.[2] However, similar to the numerous conceptualisa-

[1] Compare with the ecosystem definition provided by Jacobides M., Cennamo C., and Gawer A., "Towards a theory of ecosystems", in *SMJ*, 2018, 39, 2256.

[2] *Modularity* refers to the ability to divide different stages of production and consump-

tions of *ecosystems* in management literature, data-driven ecosystems are a governance model that diverges from both full integration and the use of arm's-length contracts.[3] For example, personal and non-personal data can be used to carefully track consumer preferences and product supply chains, providing reliable information to make sustainable and informed consumer choices, without unified governance. Thus, as long as the capabilities to integrate technologies and exploit data exist, participants can leverage their data-driven ecosystems and drive significant technological, economic, social and environmental changes beyond any single ecosystem.[4] Accordingly, data-driven ecosystems must be considered a key enabler for addressing the European Union's green and digital transformation.

With the *twin* transitions, green and digital, the European Union has defined two priority initiatives, focusing on sustainability and digitalisation respectively, each following its own agenda while also impacting upon the other.[5] The green transition seeks for the EU to achieve climate neutrality by 2050[6] setting out the pathway for sustainability in the EU's society and economy. The digital transition, instead, lays down a set of regulatory initiatives to harness digital technologies for the benefit of citizens, businesses and public administrations,[7] and to achieve the EU's digital targets.[8]

---

tion chains. *Interdependencies* identify structural relationships between actors in terms of the connection of their offers for the value to be created. *Non-generic complementarities* require specific arrangements and investments to make ecosystem participants' activities complementary to the others. *Ibidem*; Jacobides M., Cennamo C. and Gawer A., "Distinguishing between Platforms and Ecosystems: Complementarities, Value Creation, and Coordination Mechanisms", in *Working Paper, London Business School*, 2020; Moore J., "Business ecosystems and the view from the firm", in *The Antitrust Bulletin*, 2006, 51, 34.

[3] *Ibidem*, 13; Kapoor R., "Ecosystems: broadening the locus of value creation", in *Journal of Organization Design*, 2018, 7; Adner R., "Ecosystem as Structure: An Actionable Construct for Strategy", in *Journal of Management*, 2016, 43, 39.

[4] Iansiti M. and Levien R., *The Keystone Advantage: What the New Dynamics of Business Ecosystems Mean for Strategy, Innovation, and Sustainability*, Harvard Business Review Press, 2004, 211-224.

[5] Ursula von der Leyen, "A Union that strives for more: My agenda for Europe. Political guidelines for the next European Commission 2019–2024", 2019, available at https://commission.europa.eu/system/files/2020-04/political-guidelines-next-commission_en_0.pdf.

[6] Regulation (EU) 2021/1119 of the European Parliament and of the Council of 30 June 2021 establishing the framework for achieving climate neutrality and amending Regulations (EC) 401/2009 and (EU) 2018/1999 [2021], OJ L 243/1 (European Climate Law), Article 1.

[7] To follow the digital transition initiatives see the webpage dedicated to "A Europe fit for the digital age", available at https://commission.europa.eu/strategy-and-policy/priorities-2019-2024/europe-fit-digital-age_en.

[8] Decision (EU) 2022/2481 of the European Parliament and of the Council of 14

By outlining the *finalité* of the transitions,[9] the European Green Deal (EGD) and the Digital Decade Policy Programme 2030 point to the Union's collective ability to put its competitive economy and society on a more sustainable path through digital technologies.[10] To track the progress towards sustainability through digitalisation, the Commission uses the indicator on Information Communication Technology (ICT) for environmental sustainability, part of its Digital Economy and Society Index, to measure the share of enterprises having medium/high intensity of green action through ICT.[11] The level of intensity is based on the number of environmental actions (*e.g.*, the development of energy-saving, climate-neutral, high-efficiency and interconnected services as well as the use of fewer materials, equipment or consumables) that have been facilitated by the adoption of ICTs.

Highlighting the importance of the interplay between the twin transitions, the digitalisation of the EU's economy and society in itself is a significant factor in the green transition while also acting as a *key enabler* for the changes necessary in pushing towards the sustainability goals.[12] More precisely, the free flow of data, as well as the extended use of ICT, such as data management systems, artificial intelligence,[13] internet of things[14] and others, can further the impact of policies dealing with climate change

---

December 2022 establishing the Digital Decade Policy Programme 2030 [2022] L 323/4, (Digital Decade Policy Programme 2030), Article 4.

[9] Chiti E., "Managing the ecological transition of the EU: the European Green Deal as a regulatory process", in *CMLRev*, 2022, 59, 40.

[10] Commission, "Communication from the Commission to the European Parliament, the European Council, the Council, the European Economic and Social Committee and the Committee of the Regions – The European Green Deal", COM (2020) 640 final, (The European Green Deal), 4; Digital Decade Policy Programme 2030 (fn. 8), Article 3(c)(e)(h); Commission, "Implementation of the Digital Decade objectives and the Digital Rights and Principles", SWD (2023) 570 final, 49-58.

[11] Commission, Digital Economy and Society Index (DESI 2022), 47-48.

[12] The European Green Deal (fn. 10), 4, 7 and 9; Digital Decade Policy Programme 2030 (fn. 8), Recital 6; Commission, "Communication from the Commission to the European Parliament, the Council, the European Economic and Social Committee and the Committee of the Regions – Shaping Europe's digital future", COM (2020) 67 final, (Shaping Europe's digital future), 11.

[13] European Parliament and Council Regulation (EU) 2024/1689 of 13 June 2024 laying down harmonised rules on artificial intelligence and amending Regulations (EC) 300/2008, (EU) 167/2013, (EU) 168/2013, (EU) 2018/858, (EU) 2018/1139 and (EU) 2019/2144 and Directives 2014/90/EU, (EU) 2016/797 and (EU) 2020/1828 (2024) OJ L (Artificial Intelligence Act), Article 3(1).

[14] European Parliament and Council Regulation (EU) 2023/2854 of 13 December 2023 on harmonised rules on fair access to and use of data and amending Regulation (EU) 2017/2394 and Directive (EU) 2020/1828 (2023) OJ L 2023/2854 (Data Act), Recital 14.

and environmental issues, including sustainable lifecycles.[15] At the same time, in pursuing both the digital and green transitions, digitalisation *must put sustainability at its heart.*[16] The extended use of digital technologies, especially data management systems, risks an increase in greenhouse gas emissions and energy use.[17] Therefore, digital and data-related practices should promote a circular and climate-neutral economy while concurrently ensuring inherent sustainability within themselves. As a result, this liaison between sustainability and digitalisation is functionalised to bring about the achievement of the climate neutrality target.

To pursue sustainable and digital transformation, the EGD and the Digital Decade Policy Programme 2030 require the contribution of all EU policies, including competition policy.[18] Consequently, competition policy and the associated rules are undergoing an unprecedented revision process to complement[19] the Union's transition initiatives through their implemen-

---

[15] The European Green Deal (fn. 10) 9; Digital Decade Policy Programme 2030 (fn. 8) Recital 6.

[16] *Ibidem*; Shaping Europe's digital future (fn. 12) 12.

[17] The ICT sector is responsible for 5 to 9% of the world's total electricity consumption and more than 2% of global emissions. In 2018, data centres accounted for 2,7% of the electricity demand in the 28 Member States. Despite the high demand for data centre services, data centres' emissions and energy use (excluding crypto mining) have grown only moderately. This result can be attributed to the replacement of coal and other fossil fuels with less emissive energy sources. In addition to this, it is partly due to efficient and innovative solutions in IT hardware and cooling systems, as well as a shift towards more efficient cloud and hyperscale data centres. Hyperscale data centres are often associated with large companies that require vast data processing and storage requirements, such as Alphabet, Amazon, Meta, Apple and Microsoft. For a thorough analysis of the ICT's footprint and energy demand, along with the associated progressing solutions, see Commission, "Implementation of the Digital Decade objectives and the Digital Rights and Principles", SWD (2023) 570 final, 50-55; Rozite V., Bertoli E. and Reidenbach B., "Data Centres and Data Transmission Networks", in *IEA*, 2023, available at https://www.iea.org/reports/data-centres-and-data-transmission-networks; Rifkin J., *Green New Deal – Il crollo della civiltà dei combustibili fossili entro il 2028 e l'audace piano economico per salvare la Terra*, Mondadori, 2021, 57-67; Jones N., "The Information Factories", in *Nature*, 2018, 163, available at https://www.nature.com/articles/d41586-018-06610-y.pdf?pdf=button%20sticky.

[18] The European Green Deal (fn. 10) 3; Digital Decade Policy Programme 2030 (fn. 8) Recital 3.

[19] The boundaries between competition law and regulation have long been debated. A shared conclusion in the European Union is that competition rules have a complementary role to *ex ante* regulations under certain conditions. See Case C-252/21 *Meta Platforms Inc and Others v Bundeskartellamt* [2023] ECLI:EU:C:2023:537. For the evolution of the complementary role of competition law, see Drexl J. and Di Porto F., *Competition Law as Regulation*, Edward Elgar, 2015, 153-162.

tation and enforcement.[20] In practice the Commission has broadened the contents of pro-competitive disciplines to increase the weight of environmental and social goals, seeking to boost sustainability and strengthen privacy protection. For instance, the Commission reviewed the vertical and horizontal agreements guidelines to stress the necessity of pro-competitive agreements, under which any harm to competition is outweighed by counterbalancing sustainability and/or digital benefits. Even on the State Aid front, the Commission reviewed the State Aid Guidelines and Block Exemption Regulations to channel private and public investments towards sustainable and digital infrastructures.[21]

The purpose of this Chapter is to discuss the aforementioned liaison within data-driven ecosystems, and its effects on the direction of competition law in data-related practices. The methodology of the research is doctrinal in analysing the EU Data Strategy, the new data regulatory framework, and the complementary enforcement of competition law in data-related challenges. The Chapter will investigate the effects of the liaison in reorientating competition law (§ 2). The Commission recently published the Revised Notice on the Definition of Relevant Market, providing a clear example of boosting environmental and social goals in competition assessments. This environmental and social consideration in competition law is readily apparent nowadays, although it still raises doubts on the conceptualisation of *sustainability* and needs to be operationalised. To fulfill the operationalisation need, the Chapter will then examine analytical shortcuts that can be explored by companies and competition authorities (§ 3). The last section will present some final considerations (§ 4).

2. Facing the challenges of sustainable data-driven ecosystems: a shift towards polycentric competition law

The European Data Strategy and associated regulations consider data an essential resource not only for economic development but also for tack-

---

[20] Commission, "Communication from the Commission to the European Parliament, the Council, the European Economic and Social Committee and the Committee of the Regions – A competition policy fit for new challenges", COM (2021) 713 final, (A competition policy fit for new challenges).

[21] For insight into the current revision process of competition policy and rules see Majcher K. and Robertson V., "The Twin Transition to a Green and Digital Economy: The Role for EU Competition Law", in *Graz Law Working Paper No 05-2022*, 2022; Fazio E., "Adapting Competition Law to the Digital Transition. Two Challenges", in *European Papers*, 2022, 7, 981.

ling social, climate and environmental challenges.[22] It is the lifeblood for training artificial intelligence systems and other ICT, as well as the basis for personalised and monitored productions.[23] Increasing data sharing can further the ability of data recipients to innovate, reduce production costs, enter new markets, and personalise goods and services. In addition, it can advance the EU towards its climate neutrality target by encouraging the reuse of data, improving the quality of goods and services, reducing CO_2 emissions, and enhancing supply chain controls, among other things.[24]

Despite the sustainability-related and digital benefits of access to data, only a limited number of companies *share* or *pool* their data with others. This phenomenon is referred to as the *data-sharing paradox*: on the one hand, data is increasing in value for the EU's economy and society; on the other hand, companies are reluctant to share the collected data.[25] The data-sharing paradox affects business-to-business (B2B), government-to-business (G2B) and business-to-government (B2G) transactions.[26] Following the EU data regulatory framework, data should be available to any private and public entity to foster innovation and competition within the EU Single Market, and realise the environmental and social benefits of

---

[22] Commission, "Communication from the Commission to the European Parliament, the Council, the European Economic and Social Committee and the Committee of the Regions – A European Strategy for data", COM (2020) 66 final, (European Data Strategy), 2-3; European Parliament and Council Regulation (EU) 2023/2854 of 13 December 2023 on harmonised rules on fair access to and use of data and amending Regulation (EU) 2017/2394 and Directive (EU) 2020/1828 (2023) OJ L 2023/2854 (Data Act), Recital 1; Regulation (EU) 2022/868 of the European Parliament and of the Council of 30 May 2022 on European data governance and amending Regulation (EU) 2018/1724 [2022] OJ L 152/1, (Data Governance Act), Recital 2; Regulation (EU) 2022/1925 of the European Parliament and of the Council of 14 September 2022 on contestable and fair markets in the digital sector and amending Directives (EU) 2019/1937 and (EU) 2020/1828 [2022] OJ L 265/1, (Digital Markets Act), Recital 3.

[23] European Data Strategy (fn. 22) 2-3; Shaping Europe's digital future (fn. 12), 11; DESI 2022 (fn. 11) 51; Ezrachi A. and Stucke M., "Digitalisation and its impact on innovation", *R&I Paper Series Working Paper 2020/07*, 2020, 5; Yu P., "Data Producer's Right and the Protection of Machine-Generated Data", in *TulLRev.*, 2019, 93, 860; Finck M., "Digital Regulation: Designing a Supranational Legal Framework for the Platform Economy", in *LSE Law, Society and Economy Working Papers 15/2017*, 2017, 2.

[24] See Botta M., "Shall we share? The principle of FRAND in B2B data sharing", in *RSC 2023/30 Working Paper*, 2023, 18-19; JRC Technical Reports, *Competitiveness and Sustainable Development Goals*, 2016, 13.

[25] Botta (fn. 24) 8.

[26] *Ibidem.*

data-driven ecosystems.[27] The European approach to creating a single European data space, including several common EU data spaces,[28] shifted from an individualistic human-centred perspective to a broader societal one.

To realise the potential of the extended use of data without distorting competition,[29] competition purposes must consider the broader perspectives of data regulations in balancing access and restrictions to data. Competition is a dynamic process that is not defined in legislative sources. The lack of a definition is the result of a historical legacy which leads us to consider self-evident the idea of competition as a natural state of the market.[30] Many scholars have long debated the controversial scope of competition law by adopting textual, teleological and historical methods.[31] To identify the goals of competition law, and verify whether sustainability and privacy protection might be considered, this Chapter follows the recent empirical analysis of Konstantinos Stylianou and Marios Iacovides.[32]

Their quantitative analysis suggests that the academic debate is characterised by a great variety of opinions and wide disagreements on the objectives of competition, especially with regard to sustainability and privacy protection.[33] This reflects EU competition law's pursuit of multiple goals with fluctuating significance. Indeed, coherent with EU institutional practice, competition law does not pursue only one main goal at the expense of

---

[27] European Data Strategy (fn. 22) 1; Drexl J., "Designing Competitive Markets for Industrial Data Between Propertisation and Access", in *JIPITEC*, 2017, 262.

[28] Commission, "Staff Working Document on Common European Data Spaces", SWD (2022) 45 final.

[29] Consolidated version of the Treaty on European Union – Protocol (No 27) on the internal market and competition [2008], OJ C 115.

[30] Libertini M., "Concorrenza", in *Enc. Dir.*, *Annali*, III, 2010.

[31] The scientific discussion on the goals of competition law is vast and there is no way to refer to it exhaustively. See, however, Holmes S., "Climate change, sustainability, and competition law", in *J Antitrust Enforc*, 2020, 8, 354; Dunne N., "Public Interest and EU Competition Law", in *The Antitrust Bulletin*, 2020, 65, 256; Ezrachi A., "EU Competition Law Goals and The Digital Economy", in *Oxford Legal Studies Research Paper No 17/2018*, 2018, available at https://papers.ssrn.com/sol3/papers.cfm?abstract_id=3191766; Khan L., "Amazon's Antitrust Paradox", in *YaleLJ*, 2017, 126, 710; Amato G., *Antitrust and the Bounds of Power: The Dilemma of Liberal Democracy in the History of the Market*, Oxford Hart Publishing, 1997, 95-129; Bork R., *The Antitrust Paradox: A Policy at War with Itself*, Basic Books, 1978.

[32] Stylianou K., Iacovides M., "The goals of EU competition law: a comprehensive empirical investigation", in *Legal Studies*, 2022, 42, 620.

[33] *Ibidem*, 624-631.

others but rather includes a variety of objectives without rejecting the relevance of others.[34]

The authors grouped the traditional competition law goals into seven broad families that feed into their methodology: efficiency, welfare, freedom to compete, market structure, fairness, European integration, and competitive process. All goals are considered in competition practice, even though the related objectives of protecting a market structure based on an effective competitive process are mentioned more frequently.[35] In addition to the traditional objectives, the contemporary goals upheld by the new competition policy,[36] *id est* sustainability and privacy protection, are already part of the academic debate and institutional practice. Ultimately, these contemporary aims are becoming part of EU competition law in their own right.[37]

Seeking to meet multiple objectives, scholars have used a variety of terms to identify a multifaceted and versatile manner to promote competition, such as *experimentalist* competition law,[38] *responsive* competition law,[39] *participatory* competition law,[40] and *polycentric* competition law.[41] Notably, the idea of polycentric competition law is emerging in the academic and institutional debate to face the challenges of sustainable data-driven ecosystems.[42] So far, competition law has been developed around a

---

[34] *Ibidem*, 636-639.

[35] *Ibidem,* 639 and 641. The related objectives of competition process and market structure appear more frequently in the Court of Justice and General Court' decisions ("hard law" sources), as well as Advocate Generals' opinions.

[36] A competition policy fit for new challenges (fn. 20).

[37] Stylianou, Iacovides (fn. 32) 647.

[38] Svetiev Y., *Experimentalist Competition Law and the Regulation of Markets*, Hart Publishing, 2020; Fazio E., "Experimentalist Competition Law Enforcement as a Complementary Data Sharing Toolkit: Learning from *AGCM v. Google – Ostacoli alla Portabilità dei Dati*", in *Yearbook of Antitrust and Regulatory Studies*, 2024, 17.

[39] Makris S., "EU Competition Law as Responsive Law", in *Cambridge Yearbook of European Legal Studies*, 2021, 23; Ioannidou M., "Responsive Remodelling of Competition Law Enforcement", in *Oxf. J. Leg. Stud.*, 2020, 40, 846.

[40] Kathuria V., "The Rise of Participative Regulation in Digital Markets", in *JECLP*, 2022, 13, 537. The term *participative competition law* is attributed to the Nobel Prize-winning economist Jean Tirole, available at: http://qz.com/1310266/nobelwinning-economistjean-tirole-on-to-regulate-tech-monopolies.

[41] Lianos I., "Polycentric Competition Law", in *Curr Leg Probl*, 2018, 71.

[42] The term *polycentric competition law* refers to a system of many decision-making centres having autonomous and limited prerogatives and operating under an overarching set of rules. It has three main characteristics: the multiplicity of decision centres, the overarching set of rules defining the polycentric system, and the spontaneous order aris-

monocentric problem, namely the price and output costs of market power, and relied on a de-socialised conception of individuals.[43] Arguably, this approach is not adequate for data-driven ecosystems, where actors rely on each other's activities. Indeed, to fully take into account the liaison between sustainability and digitalisation, individuals' interactions, as well as the broader environmental and social effects of their conduct, must be considered in competition assessments. Thus, polycentric theory suggests considering many centres of decision-making that are formally independent of each other yet take each other into account in competitive relationships.[44] In other terms, competition in sustainable data-driven ecosystems should be seen as a polycentric system including a network of diverse actors that adjust their behaviour to the decisions made by others and share the climate neutrality target recalled by the liaison.

Contrary to the monocentric perspective, a polycentric problem/solution does not solely affect the relationship between the parties of the specific transaction but also expands beyond the strict confines of bilateral exchanges.[45] One example from within data-driven ecosystems, occurs when companies seek to exchange data. Rather than providing access to data in exchange for monetary compensation, they usually establish *data platforms*.[46] Data platform participants are remunerated by having access to a common and larger data pool. For instance, the data platform Skywise was

---

ing from dynamic competition between the several decision centres' ideas, methods, and operations. See Lianos I., "Value extraction and institutions in digital capitalism: Towards a law and political economy synthesis for competition law", in *European Law Open*, 2022, 1, 887-888; Libertini M., "Digital markets and competition policy. Some remarks on the suitability of the antitrust toolkit", in *Orizzonti del Diritto Commerciale*, 2021, 351-352; Lianos (fn. 41); Ezrachi (fn. 31). For the evolutionary theory of polycentricity see Polanyi M., *The Logic of Liberty: Reflections and Rejoinders*, University of Chicago Press, 1951; Fuller L., "The Forms and Limits of Adjudication", in *HarvLRev*, 1978, 92, 353; Ostrom V., "Polycentricity" in McGinnis M. (ed.), *Polycentric governance and development: readings from the Workshop in Political Theory and Policy Analysis*, University of Michigan Press, 1999; Ostrom E., *Governing the Commons: The Evolution of Institutions for Collective Action*, CUP, 1990; Aligiga P. and Tarko V., "Polycentricity: From Polanyi to Ostrom, and Beyond", *Governance*, 2012, 25, 237.

[43] Lianos (fn. 41) 9-10.

[44] Lianos (fn. 41) 7-8.

[45] Lianos (fn. 41) 6.

[46] Access to data can take place in accordance with a multitude of data-sharing models. However, the most common categories of data-sharing are currently data platforms, data marketplaces, technical enablers, data philanthropy, data prizes, and data partnerships. Botta (fn. 24); Commission, 'Staff Working Document on Guidance on sharing private sector data in the European data economy', SWD (2018) 125 final, Sections 3 and 4.

set up by Airbus and airlines that purchased Airbus airplanes to freely provide the company with real-time diagnostic data about their airplanes.[47] The data pool allows Airbus to improve the quality and maintenance of its airplanes in the long term; simultaneously, it accelerates decarbonisation by offering data insights on CO_2 emissions. Thus, the data-sharing practice serves not only the interests of the parties but has broader environmental and social effects.

Data platforms are a clear example of the type of vertical or horizontal cooperation agreements which might be subject to competition law scrutiny under Article 101 TFEU.[48] The monocentric perspective on the one hand would only consider the fact that by restricting competition in a specific relevant market these practices can increase prices and output costs, concentrating market power. The polycentric perspective, instead, also takes factors, such as the liaison between sustainability and digitalisation into account, thus also considering the possible benefits to the sustainability of goods and services in the same or different markets.

2.1. Revised relevant market definition

The definition of the relevant market is an analytical tool used to identify and define the boundaries of competition between undertakings. It is strictly related to the market power issue at the heart of competition policy and law,[49] with market power defined as the measure of the ability of an undertaking to profitably raise prices, limit output, suppress innovation, reduce the variety or quality of goods and services, and restrict consumer choice in relevant markets.[50]

EU competition law has a two-stage procedure to determine whether one or multiple companies have or would have market power. Firstly, it is important to identify the relevant market in which market power might ex-

---

[47] See https://aircraft.airbus.com/en/services/enhance/skywise.

[48] The Commission has recently published new Guidelines which set out principles for the assessment of vertical and horizontal cooperation agreements, decisions and concerted practices between undertakings ("agreements") under Article 101 TFEU. Commission, "Guidelines on vertical restraints", C(2022) 248/01 [2022] OJ C 248 (Guidelines on vertical restraints); Commission, "Guidelines on the applicability of Article 101 of the Treaty on the Functioning of the European Union to horizontal cooperation agreements", (2023) OJ C 259 (Guidelines on horizontal cooperation agreements).

[49] Whish R. and Bailey D., *Competition Law*, 10th ed., OUP, 2021, 22-25.

[50] Whish and Bailey (fn. 49); Vickers J., "Market Power in Competition Cases" in *European Competition Journal*, 2006, 2, 3; Posner R. and Landes W., "Market Power in Antitrust Cases", in *HarvLRev*, 1981, 94, 937.

ist: this first stage requires a definition of both the relevant product and the relevant geographical market.[51] Secondly, it must be determined whether market power exists in the relevant market.[52] From this process, it becomes clear that market definition is an important tool that supports the assessment of the critical question of whether a company or companies have market power. Defining the relevant market becomes necessary, for instance, when considering whether an agreement has the effect of restricting competition under Article 101 TFEU[53] or whether an undertaking has a dominant position according to Article 102 TFEU.[54]

Useful guidance on the relevant product and the relevant geographical market definition is provided by the Commission's Notice on the Definition of Relevant Market.[55] By disclosing the criteria and procedures adopted in the definition of relevant markets, the Commission expects to increase the transparency of its competition policy and decision-making. Concurrently, undertakings can consider the Notice in their own internal decision-making when contemplating their competitive conduct, such as concluding certain agreements or engaging in certain behaviour unilaterally.[56]

So far, the 1997 Notice on Market Definition has adopted the so-called *hypothetical monopolist* test (*i.e.*, the SSNIP test) to determine whether particular products are within the same market.[57] The 1997 Notice relies on a

---

[51] The *relevant product market* refers to all those goods or services (products) that customers consider interchangeable or substitutable to the product(s) of the undertaking(s) involved, based on the products' features, their prices and their intended use; on the other hand, the *relevant geographic market* identifies the area in which the relevant products are supplied or demanded by the undertaking(s) involved, namely the area in which the conditions of competition are sufficiently homogeneous and can be distinguished from neighbouring ones. Commission, "Notice on the definition of the relevant market for the purposes of Community competition law" [1997] OJ C 372 (1997 Notice on Market Definition), paras. 7-8.

[52] Whish and Bailey (fn. 49) 26-48.

[53] See e.g. Case C-234/89 *Delimitis v Henninger Bräu* [1991] ECLI:EU:C:1991:91, para. 16.

[54] See e.g. Case 6-72 *Continental Can v Commission* [1973] ECLI:EU:C:1973:22, para. 32.

[55] 1997 Notice on Market Definition (fn. 51).

[56] *Ibidem*, paras. 4-5.

[57] The SSNIP test requires verifying whether a Small but Significant Non-transitory Increase in Price (in the range 5% to 10%) could be raised profitably by the economic operator. If an undertaking can raise its price significantly and retain its customers, this means that the market is worth monopolising. On the contrary, if customers switch their purchases to other products, this suggests that the market is at least as wide as the other products and includes those products as well. 1997 Notice on Market Definition (fn. 51), paras. 15-17.

conceptual framework based on price parameter within which to reflect on market definition and thus determine the boundaries of competition. However, the 1997 Notice on Market Definition too is part of the current revision process of competition rules to favour sustainable and digital transformation. Indeed, the first evidence of the shift towards polycentric competition law can be traced to the revised Market Definition Notice.

On 8 February 2024, the Commission published the Revised Relevant Market Definition Notice to align the market definition with the Commission's practice, the EU courts' case law, and new market realities, in particular sustainability and digitalisation.[58] It is interesting to note that the 2024 Revised Notice on Market Definition highlights the importance of going beyond the price parameter to define the relevant markets. In particular, it puts emphasis on the level of *innovation* and the *quality* of goods and services in various aspects, such as their sustainability and privacy protection.[59] This is the first time that sustainability and privacy protection are explicitly named in the *quality* parameter.[60]

When the competition assessment is based on the level of innovation or quality rather than the price parameter, the SSNIP test is difficult to apply; in particular, the SSNIP test does not work in data-related disputes which are highly innovative contexts of zero monetary price products. To face data-driven challenges, the 2024 Revised Notice on Market Definition suggests applying the so-called Small but Significant Non-transitory Decrease of Quality assessment (SSNDQ test).[61]

Even though the SSNDQ qualitative test poses the risk of subjective assessments, the General Court has recently stated that a precise quantitative measure of degradation of the quality of goods or services is not a compulsory prerequisite.[62] Indeed, it is not possible to require a precise standard of quality degradation to apply the SSNDQ test, as this would render it impracticable: "All that matters is that the quality degradation remains small, albeit significant and non-transitory".[63] On the other hand, even the

---

[58] Commission, "Notice on the definition of the relevant market for the purposes of Union competition law" [2024] OJ C/2024/1645 (2024 Revised Notice on Market Definition).

[59] *Ibidem*, paras. 15, 27, 50 and 90.

[60] For the debate on the difficulty of *quality* assessment see Colangelo G. and Maggiolino M., "Data Protection in Attention Markets: Protecting Privacy through Competition?", in *JECLP*, 2017, 8, 363; Ezrachi A. and Stucke M., "The Curious Case of Competition and Quality", in *J Antitrust Enforc*, 2015, 3, 227.

[61] 2024 Revised Notice on Market Definition (fn. 58) para. 30.

[62] Case T-604/18 *Google LLC and Alphabet, Inc. v European Commission* [2022] ECLI:EU:T:2022:541, paras. 177-180.

[63] *Ibidem*, para. 180.

SSNIP test requires subjective assessments of the relevant market in certain sectors, particularly in cases where price information about substitutability is unavailable (*e.g.*, data-related cases).[64] Thus, it stands to reason that sustainability degradation or improvement stemming from data-related practices can indeed be considered in competition assessments.

2.2. The concepts of sustainability evolving from data-driven ecosystems

It appears the Commission is embracing a market-based policy approach by incorporating sustainability considerations into its competition rules.[65] Similar to the emerging industrial policy,[66] this EU approach to competition seeks to embed the green and digital transformations into economic development. The result being the integration of sustainability into the paradigm of the (digital) social market economy.[67] However, neither the EGD nor the Digital Decade Policy Programme 2030 clearly define the concept of sustainability and how it is affected by the liaison with digitalisation. This section suggests a possible conceptualisation of sustainability evolving from data-driven ecosystems.

Many scholars have already noted that the conceptualisation of sustainability has not been stationary but rather complex and progressive.[68] In ecology, *sustainability* identifies a state that can be preserved indefinitely, but this definition has taken on distinct connotations over time.[69] Since the 1980s, it has been associated with the *sustainable development* model that involves a balance between economic growth, environmental protection and social well-being.[70] The digital strategy, the legislative and non-

---

[64] Whish and Bailey (fn. 49) 35.

[65] Arguably, like any other EU institution, the Commission has a duty to integrate environmental protection into its policies, including competition policy, according to Article 11 TFEU.

[66] Monti G., "The European climate law: Making the social market economy fit for 55?", in *CMLRev*, 2021, 58, 1321.

[67] Article 3(3) and Article 11 TEU.

[68] For a historical overview of the various conceptualisation see Du Pisani J., "Sustainable development – historical roots of the concept", in *Environ. Sci.*, 2007, 3, 83.

[69] *Ibidem*.

[70] Commission, "Communication from the Commission A Sustainable Europe for a Better World: A European Union Strategy for Sustainable Development", COM (2001) 264 final, 2. In the Brundtland Report, *sustainable development* is defined as "development that meets the needs of the present without compromising the ability of future generations to meet their own needs". Gro Harlem Brundtland, Report of the World

legislative acts laid out in this Chapter make general reference to the sustainable development model. Nonetheless, the EU's comprehensive approach to data potential differentiates between concepts of *sustainability* in relation to the benefits provided and the internal functioning of data-driven ecosystems.

As for the benefits that can be derived for the European society and economy from data-driven ecosystems, the concept of sustainability seems to still revolve around sustainable development.[71] Data-driven ecosystems should indeed drive the creation of well-balanced opportunities for economic growth and jobs, and ensure competitive, secure and sustainable digital technologies.[72] In the context of data-driven ecosystems, and despite the Commission's reference to economic growth – which is a controversial issue in the sustainable development discourse[73] – the sustainable development model is shifting to a focus on *qualitative* rather than quantitative parameters. Data is a non-rival resource, which means that its consumption does not decrease its availability to others and that the same data can support the life-cycle monitoring of heterogeneous products and services.[74] Hence, data-driven ecosystems allow the replacement of consumable resources with non-rival ones (data) while supporting the monitoring of resource consumption. Indeed, the deployment of data-driven ecosystems often incurs increases in returns to scale and scope where the consumption of rival material resources is partially replaced by the exploitation of non-rival data. The non-rivalrous nature of data may therefore circumvent the need to balance the three economic, social and environmental pillars, as they are no longer necessarily in conflict with each other. This implies a reconceptualisation of *sustainable development* from and beyond data-driven ecosystems: a sustainable development model that is not simply a quantitative environmental tempering of economic *growth*, but rather an economic *development* geared towards prioritising qualitative parameters.[75]

Commission on Environment and Development: Our Common Future (1987), United Nations General Assembly A/42/427.

[71] The European Green Deal (fn. 10), 3; Digital Decade Policy Programme 2030 (fn. 8), Recital 6.

[72] Digital Decade Policy Programme 2030 (fn. 8), Article 3(e).

[73] Worster D., *The Wealth of Nature: Environmental History and the Ecological Imagination*, OUP, 1993, 218-219.

[74] Micheletti G., IDC Italia, *Report for the European Commission: The European Data Market Monitoring Tool*, 2020, European Commission, available at https://op.europa.eu/en/publication-detail/-/publication/9fb0599f-c18f-11ea-b3a4-01aa75ed71a1/language-en, 55-56.

[75] Chiti E., "Verso una sostenibilità plurale? La forza trasformatrice del Green Deal e la direzione del cambiamento giuridico", in *Riv. Quad. Dir. Amb.*, 2021, 3, 145.

Looking at the internal functioning of data-driven ecosystems, the conceptualisation of sustainability is closely related to the consumption of data centres.[76] Digital infrastructure and technologies should become increasingly energy- and resource-efficient, thereby minimising their negative environmental and social impact.[77] The latest Energy Efficiency Directive introduces a reporting scheme of energy performance and water footprint in large data centres, giving the *energy efficiency first principle* substantial legal standing for the first time.[78] By 15 May 2025, the Commission shall assess the available information on the energy efficiency of data centres and propose additional measures to improve energy efficiency, including an assessment concerning the feasibility of transitioning towards a net-zero emission data centre sector.[79] In this regard, it is not economic growth or the market that should be sustainable, but data-driven ecosystems themselves.[80] Thus, the sustainability model emerging from the internal functioning of data-driven ecosystems can be identified as *ecosystem sustainability* rather than sustainable development.

The different paradigms evolving from data-driven ecosystems, namely the reconceptualised sustainable development model and ecosystem sustainability can be simultaneously realised by stimulating data sharing and pooling initiatives. To be effective in these data-related initiatives, it is necessary firstly to operationalise pro-competitive collaboration between stakeholders and then incentivise competition on quality parameters.

---

[76] A data centre is "a structure or a group of structures used to house, connect and operate computer systems/servers and associated equipment for data storage, processing and/or distribution, as well as related activities". Regulation (EC) 1099/2008 of the European Parliament and of the Council of 22 October 2008 on energy statistics [2008], OJ L 304, Annex A, point 2.6.3.1.16; see fn. 17.

[77] Digital Decade Policy Programme 2030 (fn. 8) Article 3(h).

[78] The *energy efficiency first principle* refers to "taking utmost account in energy planning, and in policy and investment decisions, of alternative cost-efficient energy efficiency measures to make energy demand and energy supply more efficient, in particular by means of cost-effective end-use energy savings, demand response initiatives and more efficient conversion, transmission and distribution of energy, whilst still achieving the objectives of those decisions". Directive (EU) 2023/1791 of the European Parliament and of the Council of 13 September 2023 on energy efficiency and amending Regulation (EU) 2023/955 (recast), Article 2(2).

[79] *Ibidem*, Article 12.

[80] Compare with the analysis provided by Chiti (fn. 9) 35.

3. The direction of digital analytical shortcuts

To avoid any possible conflict between the sustainability paradigms, the operationalisation need must be taken seriously. The relevant market definition is certainly an important analytical tool to identify market power, but it is not an end in itself.[81] To realise the benefits of the liaison between sustainability and digitalisation, and thus the twin transitions of the EU's society and economy, competition law has to deal with the issue of *spontaneity*.[82] Spontaneity describes a state where individuals have adequate incentives to institute appropriate patterns of economic relationships.[83] To solve the challenges arising from spontaneous order, other analytical shortcuts are available to guide individuals and authorities in their decision-making. These analytical toolkits need to be examined to determine whether the liaison between sustainability and digitalisation is being adequately operationalised.

Analytical shortcuts can be defined as an accelerated way of achieving targets by orientating the spontaneous order.[84] They include a vast array of tools and procedures that have the common capacity to simplify and rationalise competition enforcement.[85] Some examples included in the broad definition are safe harbours, guidelines, statements of objections, interim measures, and commitment procedures. These tools and procedures affect the reasoning characterising the enforcement of competition law, in their simplified forms of *premises*, *proxies* and *presumptions*.[86] This third section

---

[81] Whish and Bailey (fn. 49) 46-48.

[82] See fn. 43.

[83] Aligiga and Tarko (fn. 42) 246-247.

[84] Kalintiri A., "Analytical Shortcuts in EU Competition Enforcement: Proxies, Premises, and Presumptions", in *J Compet Law Econ*, 2020, 16, 392-393.

[85] *Ibidem*.

[86] *Premises* refer to normative and positive assertions or propositions, which form the basis for a choice or a theory. They shape competition enforcement in many ways. For instance, the dominant premises steer administrative action and lead authorities to develop policy priorities. *Proxies* may be defined as metrics adopted to provide indirect and imperfect approximations of the investigated issues. They have two important roles in competition enforcement: adjudicators use them to draw inferences from the available evidence and to develop filters and screens with a view to demarcating lawful from unlawful conduct. Finally, *presumptions* allow for an unknown fact to be deemed as demonstrated based on proof of another fact. They enable the actor with the burden of persuasion concerning an issue to provisionally discharge it by providing proof of another issue to the standard of proof. Although premises, proxies, and presumptions are distinct, they are used in combination as well as in parallel. Moreover, they may well be replaced over time in line with developments in knowledge and shifts in the contextual

seeks to determine whether the liaison between sustainability and digitalisation within data-driven ecosystems is being adequately operationalised in analytical shortcuts.

As for the new safe harbours and guidelines concerning cooperation agreements, it is worth noting that the EU approach consists of an extended relaxation of competition rules to strengthen the liaison.[87] For instance, in certain cases of dual distribution vertical agreements are exempted from the prohibition usually imposed in competition law (*i.e.,* safe harbour). Dual distribution refers to suppliers that sell goods or services both upstream and downstream, thereby competing with their independent distributors.[88] In this scenario, the potential negative effects of the vertical agreement on the competitive relationship between the supplier and buyer at the downstream level are less relevant than the potential positive impact on competition in general.[89] Similarly, data-sharing between a supplier and buyer can increase the pro-competitive effects of vertical agreements, especially the optimisation of production and distribution systems. The sharing of certain information, however, may raise horizontal concerns.[90] Therefore, data-sharing between a supplier and a buyer in a dual distribution scenario is exempted exclusively when the information exchange is both directly related to the implementation of the vertical agreement and necessary to advance the quality of the production or distribution of goods and services (*e.g.*, the data-sharing case of Skywise).[91]

The revision of State aid controls resembles the new direction of antitrust rules.[92] The Commission suggests channelling private and public in-

---

environment within which competition is enforced, such as sustainable and digital contexts. See Kalintiri (fn. 84), 396-398.

[87] Guidelines on vertical restraints (fn. 48); Guidelines on horizontal cooperation agreements (fn. 48); Commission Regulation (EU) 2022/720 of 10 May 2022 on the application of Article 101(3) of the Treaty on the Functioning of the European Union to categories of vertical agreements and concerted practices [2022] OJ L 134/4, (VBER). To monitor the revision of Horizontal Block Exemption Regulations (HBERs) see the following webpage: https://ec.europa.eu/info/law/better-regulation/have-your-say/initiatives/13058-Horizontal-agreements-between-companies-revision-of-EU-competition-rules_en.

[88] VBER (fn. 87) Recital 12.

[89] *Ibidem*; Guidelines on vertical restraints (fn. 48) paras. 8, 144 and 316.

[90] Guidelines on horizontal cooperation agreements (fn. 48) Section 6.

[91] VBER (fn. 87) Recital 13.

[92] See e.g. Commission, "Sixth Amendment to the Temporary Framework for State aid measures to support the economy in the current Covid-19 outbreak and amendment to the Annex to the Communication on the application of Articles 107 and 108 TFEU to short-term export-credit insurance" COM (2021) 8442 final; Commission Regulation (EU) 2021/1237 of 23 July 2021 amending Regulation 651/

vestments towards sustainable and digital infrastructures with the goal of enabling breakthrough innovations and the necessary large-scale investments to deliver on the twin transitions.[93] Similarly to the previously mentioned initiatives on cooperation agreements, the revision of State aid frameworks equates to an extended relaxation of the prohibitions.[94] For instance, based on Article 107(3) TFEU, the Commission may approve public investments funding multi-purpose data infrastructures to support the liaison between sustainability and digitalisation.[95] From the new safe harbours and guidelines, it is clear that the liaison is going to play a significant role in competition assessments.

Although the aforementioned tools and procedures are going to epitomise the liaison between sustainability and digitalisation within data-driven ecosystems, the reasoning affected by the initiatives also must evolve accordingly. Normative and economic premises of competition enforcement can thus consolidate the liaison. This Chapter has already provided evidence that the normative statements on competition goals will consider innovation, sustainability and privacy protection in their own right. At the same time, economic statements about the pro-competitive and anti-competitive effects of conduct need to elaborate on the liaison too. In the author's opinion, competition law and its economic analysis are not free of normative influence.[96] Consequently, economic theories must take into account the multiple goals of EU competition law, in particular the contemporary goals of sustainability and data protection that stand out currently in competition policy, regulations, and related measures.

Together with normative and economic premises, proxies that consider sustainability degradation or improvement in data-related practices also need to be explored. Competition enforcement uses many general concepts such as *restriction*, *abuse*, *indispensability*, and others, that are difficult to establish directly.[97] For instance, the *indispensability* criterion of anti-competitive agreements requires a proxy for defining those situations

---

2014 declaring certain categories of aid compatible with the internal market in application of Articles 107 and 108 of the Treaty [2021] OJ L 270/39; Regulation (EU) 2021/1153 of the European Parliament and of the Council of 7 July 2021 establishing the Connecting Europe Facility and repealing Regulations (EU) No 1316/2013 and (EU) No 283/2014 [2021] OJ L 249.

[93] A competition policy fit for new challenges (fn. 20), 17-18.

[94] *Ibidem.*

[95] Commission Regulation (EU) 2021/1237 (fn. 92); Regulation (EU) 2021/1153 (fn. 92), Recitals 1 and 43, as well as Articles 8 and 9.

[96] Ezrachi (fn. 31) 15-16 and 22-23.

[97] Kalintiri (fn. 84) 401.

where companies' incentives to innovate may be undermined.[98] In data-related disputes, it might be possible to interpret that requirement with a view to sustainable and digital considerations, following the liaison between the transitions.

Finally, rebuttable presumptions imply that conducts are presumed to be anti-competitive, unless the undertakings challenge this conclusion "on the basis of supporting evidence".[99] Obstacles to data-sharing practices that negatively affect sustainability should be considered unlawful unless an explicit and specific defence is provided by the company. In addition to this, in cases where the effect of a data-related practice is uncertain, statements of objections, interim measures and commitment procedures can be explored to investigate and monitor ongoing solutions with the involvement of stakeholders.[100]

4. Final considerations

The European Green Deal and the Digital Decade Policy Programme 2030 identify digital technologies as the *key enabler* to put the EU's economy and society on a more sustainable path. In data-driven ecosystems, this will lead to increased use of data that provides solutions for economic development as well as social, climate and environmental challenges. At the same time, in alignment with the links between the digital and green transitions, digitalisation and data-related practices *must put sustainability at their heart* to reduce the risk of increasing greenhouse gas emissions and energy use. This liaison between sustainability and digitalisation is functionalised to achieve the climate neutrality target by 2050.

This Chapter has reflected on the effects of the liaison between sustainability and digitalisation within sustainable data-driven ecosystems. It has been argued that such liaison demands competition law shift from a monocentric to a polycentric perspective. Polycentric competition law in this case implies a network of diverse actors that adjust their behaviour to the

[98] *Ibidem*, 402; Whish and Bailey (fn. 49) 162-173.

[99] See e.g., Case C-413/14 P *Intel v. Commission* [2017] ECLI:EU:C:2017:632, para. 138; see also Case 62/86 *AKZO v. Commission* [1991] ECLI:EU:C:1991:286, para. 60.

[100] With regard to the procedures for the adoption of interim measures and the acceptance of commitments, see Council Regulation (EC) 1/2003 of 16 December 2002 on the implementation of the rules on competition laid down in Articles 81 and 82 of the Treaty [2003], OJ L 1, Recitals 11 and 13, as well as Articles 5, 8 and 9. For an example of implementation at national level, see the Italian Law of 10 October 1990, n. 287 – Norme per la tutela della concorrenza e del mercato, Articles 14-bis and 14-ter; Fazio (fn. 38); Makris (fn. 39).

decisions made by others and share the EU's climate neutrality ambitions. Contrary to the monocentric perspective, polycentric competition law does not limit its assessment to the strict confines of bilateral exchanges but also takes the environmental and social effects of data-related practices into account. In practice, the Commission has broadened the contents of pro-competitive disciplines to increase the weight of environmental and social goals, seeking to boost sustainability and strengthen privacy protections.

Under the ongoing revision process of competition law, sustainability and privacy protection are becoming part of EU competition law in their own right. This is particularly apparent in the 2024 Revised Relevant Market Definition that considers sustainability and privacy protection as part of the *quality* of goods and services in competition assessment. This emphasis on the quality parameter appears to be related to the reconceptualisation of *sustainable development* evolving from data-driven ecosystems together with the paradigm of *ecosystem sustainability*. To pursue simultaneously the different paradigms of sustainability, it is necessary to stimulate data sharing and pooling initiatives in a wider context of pro-competitive collaboration between stakeholders.

Beyond the relevant market definition, other analytical shortcuts have also been revised to integrate sustainability and digital considerations. For example, to solve the challenges arising from spontaneous order, analytical tools, such as safe harbours and guidelines, are available to guide individuals and authorities in their decision-making. Through this revision of analytical tools, the liaison between sustainability and digitalisation is already being operationalised in competition law. In the same vein, the reasoning affected by the analytical shortcuts must take into account the liaison between sustainability and digitalisation within data-driven ecosystems. It is essential that economic premises, proxies, and rebuttable presumptions must evolve accordingly to consider sustainability and digital benefits.

Chapter 11
SUSTAINABLE SMART CITIES

Beatrice Baldini

ABSTRACT: *The Chapter aims to understand whether smart cities align with the traditional notion of sustainable development or leave room for ecological sustainability and ecosystem health. To this end, it explores the gradual shift from a technology-driven approach to a human rights-based and ecological conception of urban areas, by presenting and discussing recent documents adopted by the EU Commission.*

KEYWORDS: *Smart cities – Twin transitions – Sustainability – Sustainable development – Technology – Nature-based solution – Green urban areas.*

1. Smart City and sustainability

The European Union (EU) institutions support the development of smart cities,[1] usually meant as a type of city characterized by continuous innovation, attention to the social and economic needs of local citizens and capability of addressing complex issues. In the perspective of sustainability, smart cities are called to manage a variety of sectors, ranging from transportation and buildings to waste and noise, by making use of information and communication technology (ICT) and the Internet of Things (IoT). The connection between the social and economic needs of citizens and the use of technology suggests that sustainability is essentially declined, in the Smart City model, in the traditional sense of sustainable development.

---

[1] The relevance of smart cities is recognized in programmes such as the Multiannual Financial Framework (MFF) for 2021-27, the NextGenerationEU (NGEU) and the Recovery and Resilience Facility, as well as in plans such as "REPowerEU" and "Save Gas for a Safe Winter". Investments from private stakeholders are also important: see the Commission's initiatives for a "Smart Cities Marketplace" (SCM) and the "Local Green Deals" Bluprint for action. For an overall account, see Grea G. and Misitano R., "Città del futuro e fondi d'investimento europei", in Ferrari G.F. (ed.), *Le* smart cities *al tempo della resilienza*, Mimesis, 2021, 127-133.

One might reasonably wonder whether and how smart cities can effectively promote also a different and more ecological understanding of sustainability, namely ecosystem health, which has been identified as a policy objective in the main ecological strategies adopted in the context of the Green Deal. This is what the present Chapter aims at discussing. In line with the overall perspective of this book, its main purpose is to explore the sustainability idea underlying the digital urban model and ask if this entirely aligns with the traditional notion of sustainable development or rather leaves some room to ecosystem health as an autonomous policy objective.

The Chapter opens with a short discussion of the origins of smart cities in Western institutional thinking and illustrates, with particular consideration for the European experience, the gradual departure from a technology-driven approach. It then examines the European Mission 100 Climate-Neutral Smart Cities[2] and the Opinion adopted by the Committee of the Regions (CoR) in 2020, which outlines some recommendations for designing this urban model.[3] The selection of those documents is justified by the functionalization of smart cities to the goal of climate neutrality set by the EGD. Finally, the paper determines the role of the environmental dimension in the evolutionary process of rethinking urban areas and verifies whether the sustainability concept promoted by smart cities is in line with the Green Deal's ecological vision.

2. A gradual move away from the technology-driven approach

While a plurality of views have been expressed on the origins of smart cities in Western countries,[4] the rationale behind their spread has been mostly associated to the desire to stimulate a strategic design for economic growth, in the sense of attracting investment in technological infrastructures and boost the development of the urban area. The technology-driven approach led to the belief that ICT, as a source of the triple-down effect, would sim-

[2] European Commission, *EU Mission: Climate-Neutral and Smart Cities*, Publications Office of the European Union, 2021.

[3] Opinion of the European Committee of the Regions, Smart cities: new challenges for a just transition toward climate neutrality – how to implement the SDGs in real life? (2020/C39/17). See Nicolosi S.F. and Mustert L., "The European Committee of the Regions as a watchdog of the principle of subsidiarity", in *Maast. J. Eur. & Comp. L.*, 2022, 3, 284-301.

[4] See the overall accounts provided by Bibri S.E. et al., "Smart Sustainable cities of the Future: An Extensive Interdisciplinary Literature Review", in *SCS*, 2017, 31, 191; and Huovila A. et al., "What are the differences between sustainable and smart cities?", in *Cities*, 2017, 60, 234-245.

ultaneously ensure economic competitiveness, greater social inclusion, and a healthy environment, capable of guaranteeing the well-being of citizens[5]. In this framework, environmental concerns were considered only incidentally, as functional to the economic development of Big-Tech:[6] in some cases, they were balanced with other interests relevant to urban development, in others, they were simply ignored.[7]

Over time, especially on the European continent, two parallel developments led to reconsidering the initial beliefs and developing a new understanding of the Smart City.

First, institutions and scholars pointed out the weaknesses of a type of urbanization mainly based on the need to disseminate technological tools, highlighting how an uncontrolled use of technology, far from spreading general well-being, facilitates surveillance, is detrimental to privacy and individual freedoms, and gives rise to phenomena such as social exclusion, discrimination and the digital divide. Instead, a "human rights-based" or "people-center" approach would be required to ensure private actors' participation in decision-making process before local authorities, promote public-private co-operation and enhance transparency and accountability. Such position, which is now widely spread, stands on the assumption that technological solutions must be functional to greater efficiency in the provision of services to citizens, instead of being a goal of the city's development.[8]

The shift from a technology-driven to a people-center approach is inherent to the EU notion of smart cities, considered as «the place where traditional networks and services are made more efficient with the use of digital solutions for the benefit of its inhabitants and business».[9] The gradual

---

[5] Chiappini L. and Vicari Haddock S., "*Smart city* in Europa: a che punto siamo? Sperimentare e co-creare, il laboratorio urbano di Amsterdam", in Nuvolati G. (ed.), *Sviluppo Urbano e politiche per la qualità della vita*, Firenze University Press, 2018, 31-32; see also Caragliu A. et al., "Smart Cities in Europe", in *J. Urban. Technol.*, 2011, 18, 65-82.

[6] Simon D., "Green cities: from Tokenism to incrementalism and transformation", in Simon D. (ed.), *Rethinking sustainable cities*, Bristol University Press, 2016, 61-105, 80.

[7] Yigitcanlar T. et al., "Can cities become smart without being sustainable? A systematic review of the literature", in *SCS*, 2019, 45, 348-365; see also Joss S. et al., "The Smart City as Global Discourse: Storylines and Critical Junctures across 27 Cities", in *J. Urban Technol..*, 2019, 26, 20 where it is emphasized that the «environment is afforded a rather more marginal role in the smart city than one would expect from comparable sustainable city concepts and initiatives».

[8] European Parliament, *Social approach to the transition to smart cities. Panel for the Future of Science and Technology*, 2023, 5-6. See also Wernick A. et al., "Future-proofing the city: A human rights-based approach to governing algorithmic, biometric and smart city technologies", in *IPR*, 2023, 1, 2-26.

[9] This definition is given in the "Smart city" section of the EU official website on EU

move away from a purely technological approach clearly results also from a recent administrative proposal on data interoperability, aiming to shape the digital future of the EU, [10] where technology is presented as a key enabler of innovation rather than as an objective as such. [11]

Second, the absolute urgency of finding climate solutions put new emphasis on environmental concerns and led to conceive smart cities as fundamental actors in the fight against CO_2 emissions. [12] Indeed, smart cities are supposed to provide «smarter urban transport, upgraded water supply, waste disposal facilities and more efficient ways to light and heat buildings». [13] This development, which preceded the launch of the Green Deal, characterized smart cities as "sustainable cities", that is as local areas aimed to «maintain natural resource supplies while achieving economic, physical, and social development, ensuring protection from environmental risks». [14] In this approach, a city is sustainable if it operationalizes sustainable development in the urban context, by balancing economic, social and environmental interests. [15] Digital solutions thus become the new glue between the different components of sustainable urban development, a powerful instrument [16] to create smart sustainable cities. [17]

Such evolution reflects, at the level of urban areas, the interplay between the twin transitions, namely the digital and ecological transitions, [18]

---

regional and urban development available at https://commission.europa.eu/eu-regional-and-urban-development/topics/cities-and-urban-development/city-initiatives/smart-cities_en (last access 24 May 2024).

[10] Commission Staff Working Document – European Interoperability Framework for Smart Cities and Communities, COM (2022) 710.

[11] Christou G., "*Powering the Smart City: Sustainable Energy in the New Smart City*", in this book.

[12] Chiappini L. and Vicari Haddock S., "*Smart city* in Europa: a che punto siamo?", cit., 32.

[13] See https://commission.europa.eu/eu-regional-and-urban-development/topics/cities-and-urban-development/city-initiatives/smart-cities_en (last access 24 May 2024).

[14] Choi H.S. and Song S.K., "Direction for a transition toward Smart Sustainable Cities Based on the Diagnosis of Smart City Plans", in *Smart cities*, 2023, 6, 156-178, 158.

[15] Ahvenniemi H. et al., "What are the differences between sustainable and smart cities?", in *Cities*, 2017, 60, 239.

[16] Hassan A.M. and Lee H., "The paradox of the sustainable city: Definitions and examples", in *Environ. Dev. Sustain.*, 2015, 17, 1267-1285.

[17] Choi H.S. and Song S.K., "Direction for a Transition", cit., 160. See also Bibri S.E. and Krogstie J., "Smart Sustainable cities of the Future", cit., 200; Bibri S.E. and Krogstie J., "The core enabling technologies of big data analytics and context-aware computing for smart sustainable cities: a review and synthesis", in *J. Big Data*, 2017, 2.

[18] Fazio E., "Data-Driven Ecosystems: Competition Law as a Way to Link Sustainability and Digitalisation", in this book.

which characterizes part of the Green Deal project. However, to fully align with the Green Deal, smart cities must place the legal construction of ecological sustainability at the core of their institutional project. This goes beyond merely merging the concepts of smart and sustainable cities, as it is not limited to incorporating the environmental component within economic and social aspects. Instead, it requires giving prominent relevance to ecosystem restoration, if necessary even in the form of its prioritization over economic and social concerns, while still relying on technological tools. Full alignment with the Green Deal, in other terms, implies a dual leap for smart cities: one towards creating smart sustainable cities,[19] and another towards articulating a new concept of sustainability within the urban realm, that is ecosystem sustainability.

Is that ambitious process achievable in practice? The are no reasons to be particularly optimistic. As a legal study carried out before the launch of the Green Deal has demonstrated, smart cities tend to under-represent environmental concerns.[20] Moreover, the integration of technology into urban areas does not effectively tackle these concerns.[21] However, the discussion on the importance of environmental and ecological issues in the legal construction of sustainability in smart cities has gained relevance in the last years. This is illustrated by the increasing number of EU initiatives that associate smart cities with the macro-objective of the Green Deal, that is climate neutrality.

3. Orienting Smart Cities towards climate neutrality

It is appropriate to refer first of all to the "Climate-Neutral and Smart Cities" Mission, launched in 2021 as part of the Horizon Europe research and innovation programs 2020. Aiming «to enhance cities' role as accelerators of Europe's green transition by acting as laboratories for experimentation and innovation»,[22] this action firmly links the Smart City architecture to the functional center of Green Deal. The final purpose is to create 100 decarbonized smart cities by 2030 that serve as a model for climate-neutral

---

[19] Fernández C.G. and Peek D., "Smart and Sustainable? Positioning Adaptation to Climate Change in the European Smart City", in *Smart Cities*, 2020, 3, 511-526.

[20] Ahvenniemi H. et al., "What are the differences between sustainable and smart cities?", cit., 239 explains that environmental factors are undersized by economic issues.

[21] Hojer, M. and Wangel J., "Smart Sustainable Cities: Definition and Challenges", in Hilty L.M. and Aebischer B. (eds.), *ICT Innovations for Sustainability*, Springer, 2015, 1-17.

[22] Abdullah H., "Introduction", in Abdullah H. (ed.), *Towards a European Green Deal with cities. The urban dimension of the EU's sustainable growth strategy*, CIDOB edicions, 2021, 14.

urban development in all Member States by 2050. Cities with over 50.000 inhabitants should act to reduce greenhouse gas emissions by 55% «across all sectors such as energy, buildings, waste management, and transport»,[23] stimulating the attraction of additional investment, especially from qualified companies in digital innovation. The Mission also favors a sustainable model of inclusive growth, based on new ways of producing and consuming, such as the circular economy approach.

The instrumentality of smart cities to carbon neutrality is not new. As early as 2009, the SET Plan – Investing in the development of low-carbon technologies[24] advocated for the advancement of energy-efficient practices within the proliferation of the Smart City model, even if the term "Smart City" was not yet widely utilized in Europe. To fulfill the Plan's objective of producing clean technologies, participating cities and regions were asked to demonstrate whether and how they could ensure a 40% reduction in greenhouse gas emissions by 2020.[25]

Although not new, the Climate-Neutral and Smart Cities Mission is of some relevance. In the Commission's view, its added value is that it recognizes the individual needs of each city, while raising the bar of greenhouse gas emission reduction. This is made possible through to the use of innovative governance models, such as co-creation, which engages citizens, local governments, and other relevant stakeholders. Another relevant element, built upon co-creation and the urban-integrated planning model, is the application and implementation of climate city contracts (CCC). They are conceived as a sort of Memorandum signed by the cities themselves and, therefore, serve as a non-binding instrument indicating a political commitment taken by the local community.[26] The CCC's specificity is to «put cities in the driver's seat», since they follow «a cross-sector, demand-based and bottom-up approach»,[27] fully respecting the principle of subsidiarity. To favor this project, the Commission plans various supporting silo-breaking tools, such as: 1) a specific platform; 2) a wide array of funding and financing instruments of investments, both public and private; 3) a supportive regulatory framework based on recommendations; 4) a dedicated national network of contacts. The idea of mutual dialogue through a bottom-up approach, based on the co-

---

[23] European Commission, *EU Mission: Climate-Neutral and Smart Cities*, cit., 7.

[24] COM (2009) 519,

[25] As indicated by Bolognini S., "La politica di coesione *2021-2027* e le città", in Ferrari G.F. (ed.), *Le* smart cities *al tempo della resilienza*, cit., 108.

[26] European Commission, *100 Climate-neutral Smart Cities by 2030. Implementation Plan*, available at https://research-and-innovation.ec.europa.eu/system/files/2021-09/cities_mission_implementation_plan.pdf (last access 24 May 2024), 19.

[27] *Ibidem*, 20.

creation methodology, is now considered one of the main drivers of innovation in the management of various urban intervention sectors. While the increase in participatory instruments is certainly admirable for its focus on a democratic understanding of local needs, the procedural mechanisms that facilitate the mutual dialogue between citizens, institutions and other actors are not specified. The entire Mission relies on the elaboration of a simple, accountable, and robust monitoring system to measure and evaluate progress in reducing greenhouse gas emissions in cities, but also on an unspecified responsibility of the Commission in managing the implementation phase.[28] Therefore, the success of this project depends on the capacity of each city to not only adopt new governance approaches but also adhere to high standards largely set by non-binding legal instruments. In a somewhat indeterminate framework, cities will be free to shape the roads to achieve the EU target, potentially leading to heterogeneity of choices.

Considering the governance aspect, it is useful to underline that a bottom-up approach seems to be more in line with the necessity of finding a balance between different interests, belonging to actors both public and private.

Focusing on the sustainability construction, the overall rationale is certainly that of balancing economic, social and environmental interests, according to the sustainable development model. Such rationale is connected to climate neutrality. This is done by paying attention to "real energy efficiency",[29] committing the cities not to exceed a maximum limit percentage of offsetting emissions established by the Commission. Digital transformation is instrumental to such purpose, since it offers «opportunities to plan, implement and monitor reductions in emissions across a range of sectors, such as urban mobility, energy efficiency in buildings, monitoring of air pollution, water and waste management».[30] The room left to environmental concerns is rather limited. As argued by Nitoslawski and others, «most of the funding from the EU and associated partners for smart-city projects» has been limited to energy, transit, and mobility, with «little mention of green infrastructure and natural asset management».[31]

A slightly different approach has been taken by the Committee of the Regions (CoR) in the policy recommendations adopted in 2020, entitled "Smart cities: new challenges for a just transition toward climate neutrality

---

[28] As anticipated in European Commission, *Proposed Mission: 100 Climate-neutral Smart Cities by 2030 – by and for the Citizens*, Publications Office of the European Union, 2020, 23 and 39.

[29] *Ibidem*, 22.

[30] *Ibidem*, 7.

[31] Nitoslawski S.A. et al., "Smarter ecosystems for smarter cities? A review of trends, technologies, and turning points for smart urban forestry", in *SCS*, 2019, 51, 2.

– how to implement the SDGs in real life?". This Opinion reaffirms the link between smart cities and climate neutrality and provides various indications for climate neutral smart cities. These indications are in line with the ones laid down by the previously mentioned Mission for what concerns the centrality of citizens' engagement and the need for a multi-level governance approach. They take a further step, however, in relation to sustainability. On the one hand, the Opinion confirms the anthropocentric, pluri-dimensional, and digital-based notion of the Smart City widely used by the European Commission. In doing this, it refers to the traditional concept of sustainable development and its balancing exercise. On the other hand, smart cities are presented as an institutional model that can go beyond the goals and rationale of sustainable development. This is due to the correlation which is made between the smart institutional architecture and the various transitions associated to climate neutrality, including the ecological transition. For example, the CoR's Opinion refers to the protection of biodiversity in the urban ecosystem, while the above-mentioned Mission focuses mainly on the energy and mobility sectors. In particular, the Opinion calls local authorities to consider «nature-based solutions and green infrastructure as essential complementary policies to ensure the conservation of ecosystem services and biodiversity and to promote their sustainable use and limit land take».[32] In this way, in spite of the prominence of sustainable development, which obviously represents the key rationale of smart cities, the need for ecosystem protection through different types of solutions,[33] including nature-based solutions, is considered desirable.

4. Green areas and infrastructures for the restoration of urban ecosystems

Admittedly, the relevance given in the mentioned EU documents to ecosystem restoration is very limited and does not at all imply any prioritization of ecological concerns over economic and social interests. Yet, one should not under-estimate the new attention paid to biodiversity and ecosystem health.

Some possible applications are mentioned in the Biodiversity Strategy, where the importance of the urban context and the need to rely on nature-

[32] Opinion of the European Committee of the regions, *Smart cities*, cit., 39-40.

[33] Pineda-Pinto M. et al., "The potential of nature-based solutions to deliver ecologically just cities: Lessons for research and urban planning from a systematic literature review", in *Ambio*, 2021, 167-168.

based solutions and land-sparing interventions have been stressed.[34] In the same vein, the establishment of additional protected areas and ecological corridors has been envisaged and a specific action called "Greening urban and peri-urban areas" has been launched. The latter is an action that calls cities with at least 20,000 inhabitants to introduce Urban Greening Plans by 2030. Its first step has been the development of a comprehensive technical guide to mobilize funds and promote the capacity of buildings to increase green urban areas.[35] Indeed, green urban areas are recognized as pivotal for adapting to climate change, while also being praised for their aesthetic value. By reducing various forms of pollution through the filtration of airborne particles, purification of water, and reduction of noise, green spaces facilitate the connection between artificial areas and natural or semi-natural spaces; by promoting the integration of nature-based solutions and buildings, green infrastructures (such as green walls in the design of buildings, or semi-natural spaces such as parks, private gardens, hedges, or agricultural fields to cover built artificial features) aim to ensure the provision of ecosystem services.[36] Beyond that, understanding the various components of urban ecosystems implies additional forms of mapping and measurement. This is where the use of technology can be relevant to collect data and support the green transition.[37]

Furthermore, urban green areas planning should incorporate the target set by the Nature Restoration Law and integrate the nature and biodiversity criteria outlined in the Green City Accord into urban ecosystems. Given that the urban ecosystem represents about 22% of the territory of the Union, the Nature Restoration Law gives a crucial role to the diffusion of greenery in cities for «natural disaster risk reduction and control (e.g.,

---

[34] World Economic Forum BiodiverCities by 2030: Transforming Cities' Relationship with Nature, Insight report, 2022, 25.

[35] See the Urban Nature Platform, available at https://environment.ec.europa.eu/topics/urban-environment/urban-nature-platform_en (last access 24 May 2024).

[36] In the Commission Staff Working Document, EU guidance on integrating ecosystems and their services into decision-making, SWD (2019) 305, green infrastructures are defined as «a strategically planned network of natural and semi-natural areas, designed and managed to deliver a wide range of ecosystem service» (p. 7). For an assessment of the specific experience of a Member State, see *New research explores how "green infrastructure" policy is applied in Sweden*, 2023, available at https://environment.ec.europa.eu/news/new-research-explores-how-green-infrastructure-policy-applied-sweden-2023-06-27 (last access 24 May 2024).

[37] The link between smart growth and green solutions is discussed by Artmann M. et al., "How smart growth and green infrastructure can mutually support each other – A conceptual framework for compact and green cities", in *Ecol. Ind.*, 2019, 96, 10-22, who introduce a framework of city by combining smart growth with green infrastructures.

floods, heat island effects)», but also to favor «cooling, recreation, water and air filtration, as well as climate change mitigation and adaptation».[38] The innovative element of the law lies in the establishment of regulatory parameters addressed to local authorities to ensure the preservation of urban green spaces. In particular, Article 8 of the regulation calls for «an increasing trend of urban green areas» and of «urban tree canopy», until the achievement of a «satisfactory level» «in the total national area».[39] In this regard, the Commission requires Member States to conduct preliminary monitoring of the areas to be restored, and then prepare and implement National Plans, as stipulated in Article 14.

One should also mention the Green City Accord, a movement of mayors promoted in 2021 by the European Commission to influence the future of cities by 2030. The Accord is something more than a Memorandum for signer. It is not based on a loose commitment to environmental protection, but it specifically identifies five environmental management areas, namely air and water quality, natural biodiversity, waste, circular economy, and noise. For each of these areas, a number of specific actions and measures have been identified.[40] In addition, a set of mandatory indicators serves as a baseline for the signatory cities' monitoring and reporting processes.[41]

As for the existing projects, the BiodiverCities project deserves to be mentioned.[42] It has been set up in 2020 at the request of the European Parliament and it encourages ten cities to experiment with innovative approaches to biodiversity in urban areas. It promotes participatory democracy, which identifies educating citizens and public institutions as the primary means of ensuring their well-being and that of the environment where they live. To this end, the concept of co-creation is emphasized to promote

[38] Regulation of the European Parliament and of the Council on Nature Restoration of 24 June 2024 (Reg. UE 2024/1991), entered into force on 18 August 2024.

[39] The original text submitted by the European Commission to Parliament is COM (2022) 304. It required an increase of urban green space in cities, towns and suburbs of at least 3% by 2040, and of 5% by 2050. The amended text of the Nature Restoration Law defines more general objectives.

[40] In relation to the protection of biodiversity, such actions include the increase in the extension and quality of infrastructure, the expansion of nature-based solutions and new urban infrastructures.

[41] European Commission, Green City Accord. GCA Mandatory Indicators Guidebook, available at https://environment.ec.europa.eu/document/download/7801980d-3b0a-4bd6-927c-a458369a5387_en?filename=Green%20City%20Accord%20Indicators%20Guidebook.pdf (last access 24 May 2024). In literature see Bevilacqua D., *Il Green New Deal*, Giuffrè, 2024, 124.

[42] See the information provided at https://knowledge4policy.ec.europa.eu/projects-activities/biodivercities-project_en (last access 24 May 2024).

the participation of civil society in urban planning and decision-making processes of public institutions, reflecting the desire to achieve a shared vision of the green city. Strengthening biodiversity protection and stimulating citizens' interest in the urban issue relies on mapping ecosystem services and introducing green infrastructure.

This reflects an awareness of the need to transform the anthropic space par excellence, guaranteeing the integration of nature concerns within a smart paradigm rather than the simple diffusion of technology. However, given the limited available evidence, it is still difficult to understand how these solutions and instruments can make a real and long-term contribution to both the protection and restoration of biodiversity. [43] Moreover, the non-binding European tools – often totally left up to individual city initiatives – present the risk that the growing attention to the environment may merely result in political commitment that lacks consistent enactment across Member States. In addition, Member States are called to adopt various plans (such as Urban Greening Plans and National Restoration Plan), which may not only face challenges in their concrete implementation (due to the huge flexibility of EU indications) but also encounter coordination issues.

5. Urban sustainability after the Green Deal

The analysis carried out in the previous pages suggests that the evolution of smart cities in the EU context is still linked to the well-established objective of sustainable development. [44] Technology is promoted to improve the efficiency of services that can impact on energy consumption and to increase the well-being of citizens, while environmental concerns are part of a holistic vision that includes other interests, starting with the social and economic ones. Even if Smart City projects are often justified by the desire to reduce greenhouse gas emissions, in line with the goal of climate neutrality, the objective of ecosystem integrity is not explicitly formulated. Thus, referring to "Climate Neutral Smart Cities" is a way to highlight the need to ensure a high degree of environmental protection in the urban context, but it remains limited to sectoral interventions, dependent on technological solutions and focused on the efficient management of energy, mobility, lighting or waste. Also, even when there is a clearer emphasis on biodiversity

[43] Kabish N. et al., "Nature-based solutions to climate change mitigation and adaptation in urban areas: perspectives on indicators, knowledge gaps, barriers, and opportunities for action", in *Ecol. Soc.*, 2021, 2, 39.

[44] See § 3.

protection, as in the opinion adopted by the CoR, EU institutions make a step back to sustainable development.

The challenges of prioritizing ecological concerns arise due to the multidimensional nature of the urban context: its main components – economic, social, environmental – are closely interconnected to meet the needs of citizens. This dynamic is particularly clear in smart cities, where the widespread use of technology makes it essential not to lose sight of the social component. Failure to do so could result in an exclusionary city that is inaccessible due to technological and economic barriers,[45] potentially leading to issues like gentrification, digital divide, and discrimination.[46]

However, the urban discourse is still evolving. Despite the complexities of integrating ecosystem health into smart cities, its importance within the EGD prompts ongoing deliberations on how to effectively emebed ecological considerations into urban environments. This is achieved by promoting nature-based solutions, expanding green spaces, and integrating blue and green infrastructure. The focus is on developing green cities, leveraging new mapping and monitoring tools, and stimulating bottom-up initiatives to ensure shared decisions between local authorities and citizens. These efforts aim not only to protect biodiversity but also to enhance the well-being of inhabitants. In this regard, while technology can play an important role, it is not necessarily fundamental. Rather, it raises the challenge of how to coordinate and synchronize the Smart City model with natural regeneration. This governance approach also acknowledges that regardless of the formal designation of the city (e.g. Smart City, green city, sustainable city), every urban area faces the same imperative: accommodating human needs. This task makes it complex to impose top-down solutions and completely depart from the paradigm of sustainable development and its underlying rationale.

---

[45] Palmer H. and Simon D., "Conclusions, «Implications and Practical Guidelines»", in S. Simon (ed.), *Rethinking Sustainable Cities. Accessible, green and fair*, cit., 145-165.

[46] Various Authors underline the mentioned risks. Morozov E. and Bria F., *Rethinking the smart city. Democratizing Urban Technology*, the Rosa Luxemburg Stiftung, 2018, 14; Fracchia F., "Smart City: condividere per innovare (e con il rischio di escludere?)", in *federalismi.it*, 2015, 22, 1-27; Giannelli M. and Pagnanelli V. (eds.), *Smart cities. Diritti, libertà e governance*, Giappichelli, 2023, *passim*. Caragliu A. and Del Bo C. F., "Smart cities and urban inequality", in *Regulation Stud.*, 2022, 56, 1098; Lee N. and Pose A.R., "Innovation and spatial inequality in Europe and USA", in *J. Econ. Geo.*, 2013, 13, 1-22.

Part 5

THE ECONOMIC TRANSITION

Chapter 12

TOWARDS A GREEN DEAL-ORIENTED INTELLECTUAL PROPERTY LAW? TACKLING REMEDIES AGAINST ABUSES

Camilla Signoretta

ABSTRACT: *This Chapter advances a Green Deal-oriented approach to IP law, specifically focusing on remedies. After illustrating the international IP law provisions which may be helpful to foster the dissemination of green technologies, the Chapter continues with an overview of their implementation from a comparative perspective between US and EU. Convergences in the remedies deployed to condemn abuses in the enforcement of IPRs are highlighted. The Chapter concludes with three case studies about green technologies.*

KEYWORDS: *Green Deal – Intellectual property – Competition – Abuse – Essential facilities doctrine – Misuse – Regulation – Enforcement.*

1. Introduction

This Chapter tries to shed light on the interface between the European Green Deal and intellectual property (IP) law, with the aim of understanding how IP rules can be reinterpreted for the purpose of climate neutrality, in line with the macro-objective of the Green Deal.

To begin with, we will concentrate on the provisions of the Agreement on Trade-Related Aspects of Intellectual Property Rights (TRIPS) and IP law remedies on which it is possible to rely on in order to align IP law with the latest trends in EU environmental policy, with a view to guaranteeing a higher level of dissemination of climate neutral technologies (§§ 2-3). Remedies inspired by Article 8(2) of the TRIPS Agreement will be then investigated from a comparative perspective, by taking into account the Unites States (US) and European Union (EU) experiences (§ 4). Thereafter, the focus will shift to the essential facilities doctrine, thanks to which EU and US judges resorted to a compulsory licensing regime following the logic of Article 31(k) of the TRIPS Agreement (§ 5). Once noted the divergences and convergences between the US and the EU approaches, we will evaluate whether and how to apply these remedies to three types of green technologies selected as examples (§ 6).

2. A Green Deal-oriented IP policy

"Adaptation" is identified as "a key component of the long-term global response to climate change" in Recital 31 of the European Climate Law.[1] The same Recital emphasizes the necessity of coherence and consistency among EU legislations and policies. In this light and within the broader context of the Green Deal, the Union aims at building "a favorable regulatory environment" with a view to achieving climate neutrality by 2050.[2] Member States are also encouraged to enact measures and national policies to "adapt to climate change."

The process of "adaptation and change" mentioned above implies both a technological and legal shift. In fact, the deployment of technologies that favor the ecologic transition can be facilitated and incentivized thanks to tailormade rules and policies at the EU level. This is necessary in order to meet the challenge of decarbonization and reach climate neutrality by 2050. In this sense, the Green Deal supports the transition towards electric cars and renewable energy, as well as of a broad array of technologies, including clean hydrogen and low-carbon technologies. In order to accomplish such an ambitious project, the legal framework should be functionally reinterpreted.[3] Competition law can be held as example of how EU rules can be

---

[1] Council Regulation (EU) 2021/1119 of the European Parliament of 30 June 2021 establishing the framework for achieving climate neutrality and amending Regulations (EC) 401/2009 and (EU) 2018/1999 ("European Climate Law"), OJ 2021 L 243, Recital 31. See also EU Commission Communication, *The European Green Deal*, COM (2019) 640, 23.

[2] COM (2021) 550.

[3] Chiti E., "Managing the Ecological Transition of the EU: The European Green Deal as a Regulatory Process", in *CMLRev*, 2022, 59, 19-48. See also Id., "Oltre la disciplina dei mercati: la sostenibilità degli ecosistemi e la sua rilevanza nel *Green Deal* europeo", in *Riv. Reg. Mer.*, 2022, 2, 468-477; Liberati E.B., "Politiche di decarbonizzazione, costituzione economica europea e assetti di governance", in *Dir. Pubbl.*, 2021, 2, 415-442; Moliterni A., "La sfida ambientale e il ruolo dei pubblici poteri in campo eco-

reshaped in line with the goals of the Green Deal, moving towards an integration of different EU policies. The Horizontal Guidelines expand the application of Article 101(3) TFEU in order to exempt, under specific conditions, cartels from competition scrutiny, with the aim of bolstering trade and dissemination of green technologies. Accordingly, Article 101(3) TFEU can be reinterpreted in order to cope with the lack of incentives to innovation in the field of climate neutrality-enhancing technologies. Also thanks to a flexible interpretation of Article 101(3) TFEU, companies can be pushed to develop technologies useful to achieve climate neutrality.[4]

Following the same rationale, it is worth considering that also IP law can contribute to the objectives of the Green Deal, curtailing those exercises of exclusionary prerogatives that may ultimately hamper development and trade of technologies that help the Union with moving towards the ecologic transition.[5] IP rules can be fundamental to enhance environment-sensitive innovation *ex-ante*, as well as to increase dissemination of green technologies *ex-post*. Yet, limits to IP exclusivity must be enacted in line with the TRIPS Agreement, as these limits can never reach the point of encroaching on the minimum protection requirements set therein.[6] The

nomico", in *RQDA*, 2020, 2, 32-71; Id., "Transizione ecologica, ordine economico e sistema amministrativo", in *Riv. Dir. Comp.*, 2022, 2, 395-452.

[4] EU Commission, *Communication from the Commission – Approval of the content of a draft for a Communication from the Commission – Guidelines on the applicability of Article 101 of the Treaty on the Functioning of the European Union to horizontal co-operation agreements* (2022) O.J. L 164/1; see *Commission Staff Working Document Evaluation of the Horizontal Block Exemption Regulations'* (2021) SWD (2021) 103 final, 19; see on the matter Inderst R. and Thomas S., "Sustainability Agreements in the European Commission's Draft Horizontal Guidelines", in *JIPLP*, 2022, 13(8), 571-578; Malinauskaite J., "Competition Law and Sustainability: EU and National Perspectives", in *JIPLP*, 2022, 13(5), 336-348; see also Holmes S., "Climate Change, Sustainability, and Competition Law", in *J Antirust Enforc*, 2020, 8(2), 354; Gerbrandy A., "Solving a Sustainability-Deficit in European Competition Law", in *World Comp*, 2017, 40(4), 539; Wouters D., "Which Sustainability Agreements are Not Caught by Article 101(1) TFEU?", in *JECLP*, 2021, 12(3) 257.

[5] In the literature about the role of IP in the green sector, see in particular Zhuang W., *Intellectual Property Rights and Climate Change*, Cambridge University Press, 2017, 1-369; Howe H.R. and Griffiths J., "Property, Sustainability and Patent Law – Could the Stewardship Model Facilitate the Promotion of Green Technology?", in Howe H.R. (ed.), *Concepts of Property in Intellectual Property Law*, Cambridge University Press, 2013, 282-305; Lane E.L., "Building the Global Green Patent Highway: A Proposal for International Harmonization of Green Technology Fast Tracks Programs", in *BTLJ*, 2012, 27(3), 1120-1170; Fair R., "Does Climate Change Justify Compulsory Licensing of Green Technology", in *Int'l L & Mgmt Rev*, 2009, 6, 21-42; Taylor S., "Where are the Green Machines: Using the Patent System to Encourage Green Invention and Technology Transfer", in *Geo Int'l Envtl L Rev*, 2011, 23, 577-607.

[6] See also Walker S., "The TRIPS Agreement, Sustainable Development and the

TRIPS Agreement allows signatory countries to introduce delimiting rules also against the abusive and anti-competitive exercise of intellectual property rights (IPRs). A Green Deal-oriented view of its provisions might foster EU trade policy in the field of climate neutral technologies. [7]

3. IP delimiting clauses within the TRIPS Agreement

The TRIPS Agreement includes three provisions endowing signatory countries with the prerogative of condemning anti-competitive exercises of IPRs: Article 8(2) allows measures against the unduly restriction of trade or technology transfer; Article 40 allows remedies against anti-competitive behaviors within the field of licensing malpractice; Article 31(k) allows to deploy compulsory licenses against unjustified refusals to deal of a dominant IP-holder. [8]

Article 8(2) is referred to as an IP law articulation of the equitable principle of the abuse of right. A right is exercised abusively when in contrast with the rationale for what the same was originally conferred, the general or the individual interest of third parties. [9] The public policy behind IP is generally identified with the pro-competitive stance of promoting innovation and technology transfer. [10] For this reason, the concept of abuse of IPRs

Public Interest", Discussion Paper, IUCN, Gland, p. x; Ruse-Khan H.G., "The Concept of Sustainable Development in International IP Law – New Approaches from EU Economic Partnership Agreements?" Max Planck Institute for Intellectual Property, Competition & Tax Law Research Paper, 2010, 10(4), 1-30.

[7] TRIPS Agreement, Article 1(1) and, in general, Parts II (especially Sections 5 and 7) and III. See in this regard Cottier T. and Véron P., *Concise International and European IP Law: TRIPS, Paris Convention, European Enforcement and Transfer of Technology*, 2nd ed., Kluwer Law International, 2011, 10; Kur A., "International Norm-Making in the Field of Intellectual Property: A Shift towards Maximum Rules?", in *The WIPO Journal*, 2009, 1, 27. See also Zhuang W. (fn. 5) 311 et seq.

[8] Article 8(2) states what follows: "Appropriate measures, provided that they are consistent with the provisions of this Agreement, may be needed to prevent the abuse of intellectual property rights by right holders or the resort to practices which unreasonably restrain trade or adversely affect the international transfer of technology." See, in particular, Appellate Body Report, US – Shrimp, para. 158; Cottier T. and Véron P. (fn. 7) 35.

[9] Article 8(2) states what follows: "Appropriate measures, provided that they are consistent with the provisions of this Agreement, may be needed to prevent the abuse of intellectual property rights by right holders or the resort to practices which unreasonably restrain trade or adversely affect the international transfer of technology." See, in particular, Appellate Body Report, US – Shrimp, para. 158; Cottier T. and Véron P. (fn. 7) 35.

[10] Zhuang W. (fn. 5) 317.

tends to be coincide with encroachment of competition policy both at the international and EU level. [11]

However, Article 8(2) can also be read as a more flexible instrument, useful to articulate a set of remedies on IP policy grounds without relevance for competition law. A list of behaviors including unfair licensing, refusal to license, price discrimination, excessive royalties, mandatory package licensing, tying, unfair conduct before IP public authorities and frivolous litigation can be put under the umbrella of this provision. [12] As its text does not expressly refer to an anti-competitive exercise of IPRs, the concept of abuse can lead to also condemn a misconduct irrelevant under competition law. [13]

Article 40 is fashioned as a competition-like rule. It allows to enact remedies against licensing practices "which restrain competition" and "may have adverse effects on trade and may impede the transfer and dissemination of technology". [14] It allows to devise competition law remedies tailor-made for IP sector, in account of the fact that an abuse of IPRs can "in particular cases" lead to an unfair free trade restraint or negatively affect competition within the relevant market. [15] The same rationale underlies Article

---

[11] In the EU competition law literature, see e.g. Anderman S. and Ezrachi A., *Intellectual Property and Competition Law*, Oxford University Press, 2011, 3-487; Maggiolino M., *Intellectual Property and Antitrust: A Comparative Economic Analysis of US and EU Law*, Edward Elgar Publishing, 2011, 147; for an analysis of the international context see Yamane H., "Competition Analysis of Licensing Agreements: Considerations for Developing Countries under TRIPS", Discussion Paper, 2014, ICTSD Innovation, Technology and Intellectual Property, 39; Park J.H., *Patents and Industry Standards*, Edward Elgar Publishing, 2010, 169.

[12] Gervais D., *The TRIPS Agreement: Drafting History and Analysis*, Thomson Reuters, 2012, 240; Correa C.M., *Trade Related Aspects of Intellectual Property Rights: A Commentary on the TRIPS Agreement*, Oxford University Press, 2007, 112; Zhuang W. (fn. 5) 321.

[13] On the concept of "abuse" as an equitable concept, see e.g. Paulsson J., *The Unruly Notion of Abuse of Rights*, Cambridge University Press, 2020, 1-144; De Morree P., *Rights and Wrongs under the ECHR: The Prohibition of Abuse of Rights in Article 17 of the European Convention on Human Rights*, Intersentia, 2016, 1-304; Byers M., "Abuse of Rights, An Old Principle, A New Age", in *McGill L J*, 2002, 47, 389-431; Snell J., "The notion of and a general test for abuse of rights: some normative reflections", in De La Feria R., Vogenauer S. (eds.), *Prohibition of Abuse of Law: A New General Principle of EU Law?*, Hart Publishing, 2011, 220; Katz L., "Spite and Extortion: A Jurisdictional Principle of Abuse of Property Right", in *Yale L J*, 2013, 122(6), 1372-1669.

[14] TRIPS, Article 7. See also Zhuang, W. (fn. 5) 343.

[15] Anderson R.D., Wager H., "Human Rights, Development and the WTO: The Case of Intellectual Property Rights and Competition Policy", in *J Int'l Econ L*, 2006, 9(3), 742; of the same author, "Competition Policy and Intellectual Property in the WTO: More Guidance Needed?", in Drexl J. (ed.), *Research Handbook on Intellectual*

31(k), which allows to resort to compulsory licensing when refusal to deal has anti-competitive relevance.[16] While Article 8(2) has been mostly implemented through the US doctrines of misuse and inequitable conduct, Article 31(k) rests on the application of the essential facilities doctrine in both EU and US.[17]

As Article 40 TRIPS is purely competition law oriented, its implementation runs out the scope of this Chapter, which only addresses the way Articles 8(2) and 31(k) have been operationalized in remedies against the abusive enforcement of IPRs in EU and US. Unlike Article 40 TRIPs, these remedies converge in their rationale and might be more useful to curtail the overenforcement of exclusive rights insisting on technologies whose dissemination is crucial to achieve the goals behind the Green Deal.

4. Implementing Article 8(2)

4.1. US: misuse and inequitable conduct

In the US, two IP law doctrines tailormade for unfair behaviors before private parties and public authorities emerged. These remedies can be seen as implementing Article 8(2) of the TRIPS Agreement. Both misuse[18] and inequitable conduct[19] stem from equitable principles and are ultimately root-

---

Property and Competition Law, Edward Elgar Publishing, 2010, 452; Taubman A., Wager H., Watal J., *A Handbook on the WTO TRIPS Agreement*, Cambridge University Press, 2012, 133.

[16] UNCTAD-ICTSD, *Resource Book on TRIPS and Development*, Cambridge University Press, Cambridge, 2005, 476. See Ford S.M., "Compulsory Licensing Provisions under the TRIPs Agreement: Balancing Pills and Patents", in *Am U Int'l L Rev*, 2000, 15, 941-974.

[17] WIPO, *Refusals to License IP Rights – A Comparative Note on Possible Approaches*, 2013, prepared by the Secretariat. See Zhuang W. (fn. 5) 339 et seq. It is stated that "a patent holder's right to refuse to license is not absolute. Under exceptional circumstances, refusal to license may constitute anti-competitive practices to the extent that such a license constitutes "an attempt to monopolize or to maintain a monopoly in the relevant market or, in broader terms, it constitutes an abusive expression of a market dominant position".

[18] See "Is the Patent Misuse Doctrine Obsolete?", in *Harv L Rev*, 1997, 110, 1922; Golden J.M. and Scot F., *Principles of Patent Law: Cases and Materials*, 7th ed, Foundation Press, 2018, 892 et seq.; Lim D., "Misconduct in Standard Setting: The Case for Patent Misuse", in *IDEA*, 2011, 51, 559; Feldman R.C., "The Insufficiency of Antitrust Analysis for Patent Misuse", in *Hastings LJ*, 2003, 55 399, 403; "Exclusive Use Contract Is Patent Misuse", in *Stan Intramural L Rev*, 1948, 1, 154.

[19] Golden J.M. amd Scot F., cit., 868 et seq.

ed in the principle of "unclean hands".[20] Accordingly, an IP-holder cannot exercise his exclusive rights before a court if the same has "unclean hands", i.e., being in bad faith. For this reason, in US case-law, courts have progressively elaborated the principle under which, until the "purge", the IPR is unenforceable on a temporary (misuse) or permanent (inequitable conduct) basis.

Misuse has been inaugurated in *Motion Picture*.[21] Thereby, an IP-holder devised some post-sale restrictions, going beyond the scope of the IPR. A line was drawn between exercises of IPRs that are coherent with their scope and those exceeding it. Exercising IPRs in a way that overcomes the monopoly granted under IP policy is unenforceable for being in contrast with the purpose for which such right was conferred in the first instance. In this sense, IP policy is internally balanced through a remedy reflecting an equitable abuse of right-like rationale. This goes in parallel with a purely "equitable" reading of Article 8(2), under which the possibility of protecting the monopoly acquired through IPRs is only granted to a limited extent. In fact, misuse was originally intended as an IP law remedy, susceptible of being read broadly by courts in order to encompass all IP-driven unfair behaviors that can materialize in case law.

As unenforceable exercises of IPRs are necessarily to be determined on a case-by-case basis, the open-ended character of misuse had the ultimate effect of hampering its effectiveness. In particular, this led to associate an unfair exercise of IPRs with an anti-competitive one. Although in *Morton Salt* the Supreme Court affirmed the autonomy of misuse as an IP law internal balancing instrument,[22] since 1944, in two landmark cases, *Mercoid I* and *II*,[23] misuse began to be linked to competition law and policy. In this way, the Supreme Court inaugurated a trend under which, in order to prevent the over-application of misuse, it was necessary to assess whether the IP-holder acted against competition law.[24] This increased the threshold to

---

[20] See, e.g., Anderson R.D., "Antitrust Law Violations Possible from Application of the Doctrine of Unclean Hands to Conduct during the Procurement of a Patent", in *J Pat Off Soc'y*, 1967, 49, 117-129; Anenson T.L., "Limiting Legal Remedies: An Analysis of Unclean Hands", in *Ky LJ*, 2010, 99, 63-118.

[21] *Motion Picture Patents Co. v. Universal Film Mfg.*, 243 US 502, 517 (1917), 892.

[22] *Morton Salt Co. v. G. S. Suppiger Co.*, 314 US 488-492 (1942).

[23] *Mercoid Corp. v Mid-Continent Investment Co.*, 320 US 661 (1944) [*Mercoid I*]; *Mercoid Corp. V Minneapolis-Honeywell Regulator Co.*, 320 US 680 (1944) [*Mercoid II*].

[24] See, e.g., Mueller M., "Patent Misuse through the Capture of Industry Standards", in *BTLJ*, 2002, 17, 623; Hoerner R.J., "Patent Misuse", in *Antitrust LJ*, 1984, 53 641-662; Nicoson, W.J., "Misuse of the Misuse Doctrine in Infringement Suits", in *UCLA L Rev*, 1962, 9, 76-110; Bilicki, B.A., "Standard Antitrust Analysis and the Doctrine of

apply the doctrine and underpinned its role as a balancing mechanism within IP law.

Moreover, courts have been skeptical about setting the basis for a federal cause of action (antitrust violation) on the grounds of an IP law affirmative defense (misuse), susceptible of a broad application. They have been much more eager to delimit the scope of misuse to genuinely anti-competitive exercises of IPRs. In *Windsurfing*,[25] the Supreme Court held that in no way a behavior that is the fruit of "business prudence" can produce the unenforceability of an IPR, provided that every license has a collateral foreclosure effect in the market of the licensed good or service.[26]

In the Bill modifying the Patent Act in 1988,[27] it was held that proof of evidence of market power was required to find misuse in the case of tying. In a post-sale restriction case, *Mallinckrodt*,[28] the Federal Circuit held that post-sale restrictions are not *per se* illegal.[29] By way of contrast, freedom of contract is to be intended as a prerogative of IP-holders, who are free of imposing restrictive licensing terms and suing licensees for infringement under contract rather than patent law. Applying misuse to encroach the possibility for rightsholders to sue alleged infringers would put IP-holders in a worse position than other contractors for the sole fact of holding an exclusive right.

Although misuse became an ancillary instrument in the interface between competition and IP law, the revitalization of the autonomous relevance of IP policy in constraining the over-enforcement of IPRs can be found in *Kimble*.[30] In this case, the Supreme Court avoided evaluating anti-competitive effects, addressing the misconduct under patent law policy.[31]

Patent Misuse: A Unification under the Rule of Reason", in *U Pitt L Rev*, 1984, 46, 209-239; Potenza J., Bennett P. and Roth C., "Patent Misuse – The Critical Balance, a Patent Lawyer's View", in *Fed Cir BJ*, 2005, 15, 69-100; Leaffer M., "Patent Misuse and Innovation", in *J High Tech L*, 2010, 10, 142-167; Cotter T.F., "Four Questions Rationales for the Patent Misuse Doctrine", in *Minn JL Sci & Tech*, 2011, 12, 457.

[25] *Windsurfing Int'l, Inc. v AMF, Inc.*, 782 F.2d 995, 1001 (Fed. Cir. 1986).

[26] *Ibidem*, para. 1002.

[27] Patent Misuse Reform Act of 1988, 35 USC. § 271 (1988) (amended in 2003).

[28] *Mallinckrodt, Inc. v Medipart, Inc.* 976 F.2d 700 (Fed. Cir. 1992).

[29] *Ibidem*, paras. 703-705.

[30] *Kimble v. Marvel Entertainment, LLC*, 576 US (2015). See also Lim D., "Patent Misuse and Antitrust: Rebirth or False Dawn", in *Mich Telecomm & Tech L Rev*, 2014, 20, 299-389.

[31] *Ibidem*, 2. See Shelbourne S., "Balancing Acts: Using a Mixed Test to Ensure Better Results in Rule of Reason Patent Misuse Analysis within Section 337", in *Marq Intell Prop L Rev*, 2011, 15, 485-501.

In this judgement, concerning post-expiration royalties, the Court held that IP policy itself prescribes that the protected item shall be freely available.[32]

The second equitable defense elaborated in US case law to deal with unfair IP-driven behaviors is inequitable conduct.[33] Still stemming from the "unclean hands" doctrine, this remedy produces the permanent unenforceability of an IPR.

The most refined test to find inequitable conduct has been delineated in *Therasense*.[34] The judgement moves from allegedly false declarations made by the patent applicant before the Patent and Trademark Office (PTO). Once that the case was brought before the Federal Circuit, the court noted that inequitable conduct mostly rests on finding of two elements: a subjective ("intention to harm") and an objective ("material") one. Both elements are evaluated under a "sliding scale", thus broader evidence of the former lessens the requirement to find the other.[35] In this case, materiality was so blatantly evident that there was no need to prove "intention to harm" as well.

Yet, the "sliding scale", held by the Federal Circuit as the most commonly applied test, could become an excuse not to require proof of the subjective element.[36] Due to this, more objective benchmarks have been elaborated, such as the "but for materiality rule".[37] According to this test, inequitable conduct can be found when the IPR would not be granted but for the "material conduct", e.g., the omission/non-disclosure or false declarations. In *Therasense*, the Federal Circuit privileged an intermediate solution, under which, while materiality should not be considered indefectible, the subjective element can also be assumed under specific circumstances.[38] The criteria elaborated for inequitable conduct reflect the efforts to guarantee legal certainty, while, at the same time, preserving the equitable nature of IP delimiting doctrines.

4.2. EU: stretching boundaries of good faith

In the EU, the efforts to implement the rationale of Article 8(2) of the

---

[32] *Kimble* (fn. 30) 15.

[33] Golden J.M. and Scot F. (fn. 18) 868 et seq.

[34] *Therasense Inc. v Becton, Dickinson & Co.* 649 F.3d 1276 (2011) (en banc).

[35] *Ibidem*, para. 1288.

[36] *Ibidem*, para. 1287.

[37] *Ibidem*, para. 1291.

[38] Dissenting Circuit Judge O'Malley (*ibidem*), para. 1320.

TRIPS Agreement have been much weaker and fragmented than in the US. Only few judgments reflect the attempt to condemn abuse of infringement proceedings under general principles of private law. These principles firstly appeared in antitrust judiciary,[39] so that scholars criticized how competition law remedies have been distorted to preserve IP policy.[40]

The first case where the procedural good faith of the IP-holder gained relevance is *Huawei.*[41] Following a reasoning opposed to *Mallinckrodt*, the holder of an industry standard within the telecommunication market, Huawei, has allegedly been found infringing Article 102 TFEU by a standard implementer with whom negotiations failed. At the same time, Huawei brought an infringement action against the implementer, accusing the same of using the standard without a license.

Remarkably, the European Court of Justice (CJEU) laid down a list of procedural steps that both parties in a specific situation, i.e., licensing of a patented industry standard, should follow in order, respectively, not to be held as infringers of competition law (prospective licensors) and/or infringers of IP law (prospective licensees). In the former situation, the implementer is granted a defense in an infringement suit, whilst, in the latter, the IP-holder is granted a defense in the antitrust suit. Thus, "presumptions" of unfair behavior have been identified within the context of pre-licensing negotiations. Accordingly, the lack of offers/counteroffers in a timely manner can lead to a rebuttable presumption of infringement of IP law/Article 102 TFEU.[42]

---

[39] See, e.g., Case T-321/05 *AstraZeneca v Commission* [2010] ECR II-0000GC, commented on by Pitruzzella G. and Muscolo G. (eds.), *Competition and patent law in the pharmaceutical sector: an international perspective*, Wolters Kluwer, 2016, 78; Maggiolino M. and Montagnani Lillà M., "AstraZeneca's Abuse of IPR-Related Procedures: A Hypothesis of Anti-Trust Offence, Abuse of Rights, and IPR Misuse", in *World Comp*, 2011, 34(2), 245; Bakhoum M., "Abuse Without Dominance in Competition Law: Abuse of Economic Dependence and its Interface with Abuse of Dominance", Max Planck Institute for Innovation and Competition Research Paper 15-15, 2015, 1-31.

[40] See, e.g., Drexl J., "*AstraZeneca* and the EU Sector Inquiry: When Do Patent Filings Violate Competition Law?", Max Planck Institute for Intellectual Property & Competition Law Research Paper, 2012, 12-02; Kjølbye L., "Article 82 EC as Remedy to Patent System Imperfections: Fighting Fire with Fire?", in *World Comp*, 2009, 32(2), 163-188.

[41] Case C-170/13 *Huawei v ZTE* [2015] ECR II-0000.

[42] Comments on the judgement are numerous: see, e.g., Tsilikas H., "*Huawei v. ZTE* in Context – EU Competition Policy and Collaborative Standardization in Wireless Telecommunications", in *IIC*, 2017, 151, 169; Batista P. and Mazutti G., "Comment on "*Huawei Technologies*" (C-170/13): Standard Essential Patents and Competition Law – How Far Does the CJEU Go?", in *IIC*, 2016, 244; Mciver T., Pomana A. and Schmidt J., "Between patent protection and abuse of dominance: highest EU court issues land-

This judgement has caused a turmoil especially because the relationship between the infringement of competition law and "unwillingness to license" under contract law has not been clarified and mostly left to judicial discretion. As a result, various approaches emerged in case law.[43] However, similar to what occurred with the evolution of misuse, domestic courts[44] tend to resize the relevance of *Huawei* in order not to ground a "shortcut"[45] to antitrust liability on indetermined principles.

A different kind of IP remedies against the enforcement of IPRs beyond their scope can be found in isolated attempts to combat abuses of procedural IP law embraced by EU courts. An emblematic decision in this respect is *Bayer*,[46] which deals with the abuse of patent infringement proceedings.[47]

---

mark decision on standard-essential patents", in *ECLR*, 2015, 36(12), 533; Jakobs, M. and Hüberner F., "SEP or no SEP? Open questions after *Huawei/ZTE*", in *ECLR*, 2016, 37(1), 33-34; Wilson D., Moir A., Euesinkbrown N. and Fountoukakos K., "CJEU permits standard essential patent (SEP) injunctions against infringers who engage in delaying tactics or do not respond diligently with a good faith counteroffer", in *EIPR*, 2015, 37(11), 741, 742; Angwenyi V., "Hold-up, Hold-out and F/RAND: The quest for balance", in *JIPLP*, 2017, 12(12), 1012-1023.

[43] Leistner M., "FRAND Patents in Europe in the Post-*Huawei* Era: A Recent Report from Germany", in Hilty R.M., Liu K.C. (eds.), *SEPs, SSOs and FRAND – Asian and Global Perspectives on Fostering Innovation in Interconnectivity*, Springer, Heidelberg, 2018, 1-23; see also Slowinski P.R, "Licensing Standard Essential Patents and the German Federal Supreme Court Decisions *FRAND Defence I* and *FRAND Defence II*", in *IIC*, 2021, 1490-1497; Heitto J., "The lost tribe: SEP licensing practices in German post-*Huawei* jurisprudence", in *JIPLP*, 2021, 16(1), 56-65.

[44] See e.g. the approach of British courts in *Unwired Planet v Huawei* [2017] EWHC 711 (Pat), commented on by, *inter alia*, Treacy P. and Hunt M., "Litigating a 'FRAND' patent license: the *Unwired Planet v Huawei* judgement", in *JIPLP*, 2018, 13(2), 124-131; Semenov V., "Between exclusivity: proportionality and permanent injunctions in German, English and US patent disputes", in *JIPLP*, 2019, 14(2), 942-948; Picht P., "*Unwired Planet v Huawei*: A Seminal SEP/FRAND decision from the UK", in *JIPLP*, 2017, 12(10), 867-880.

[45] Kalintiri A., "Analytical Shortcuts in EU Competition Enforcement: Proxies, Premises, and Presumptions", in *J Compet Law Econ*, 2020, 16(3), 392-433.

[46] Case C-688/17 *Bayer/Richter, Exeltis* [2019] ECR II-722. See, e.g., Tilmann W., "Consequences of the CJEU's *Bayer v Richter decision*", in *JIPLP*, 2022, 17(6), 526-532; Strowel A. and Léonard A., "The Risks of Patent Litigation Within the EU Enforcement Framework – How to Address Abusive Practices", CRIDES Working Paper Series, 2020, 2, 1-30.

[47] Case C-597/19, *Mircom International Content Management & Consulting (M.I.C.M.) Limited v Telenet BVBA* [2021] II-492. See Léonard A., "Excessive or abusive reliance on measures, procedures and remedies under Directive 2004/48/EC-the issue of 'trolls' in the IP enforcement framework in light of Case C-597/19 *Mircom*", in *JIPLP*, 2022, 17(4), 387-396.

In *Bayer*, the legal quandary consists of whether Article 9(7) of the Intellectual Property Rights Enforcement Directive (IPRED) should be intended as giving Member States room for providing compensation for provisional measures issued on the grounds of an invalid patent. The CJEU highlighted that, although Member States are not compelled to prescribe compensation in the case of "unjustified application of provisional measures", national courts are free to determine whether IPRED provisions have been distorted from their purpose and/or the IP litigation system has been "abused".[48] Hence, whether to introduce a rule compensating for the losses suffered by the alleged infringer from the application of provisional measures subsequently revoked is a free choice that belongs to Member States, on condition that whether an abuse of the infringement process took place is also evaluated. The Court also hinged on the concept of "appropriate compensation". Accordingly, compensation becomes appropriate when enforcement remedies are applied beyond their scope or groundlessly.

The patchwork of legal solutions akin to Article 8(2) tackled above reflects the attempt to transfuse the concept of "abuse" within EU procedural IP law.[49] In spite of the silence of the CJEU, national courts are slowly moving towards the delineation of a notion of abuse of the IP litigation system, which may also be helpful to discourage the over-enforcement of IPRs over green technologies.

5. Implementing Article 31(k)

While Article 8(2) of the TRIPS Agreement led to fragmented legal responses, Article 31(k) has mostly been implemented both in EU and US through the essential facilities doctrine. This doctrine is a peculiar approach to antitrust that serves to prevent the exploitation of monopolies when a "dominant firm owns or controls a facility that is indispensable to its competitors and refuses to grant access to it".[50] It can be applied to a

---

[48] *Bayer* (fn. 46), para. 60.

[49] See, e.g., Léonard A., "Abuse of Rights' in Belgian and French Patent Law – A Case Law Analysis", in *JIPITEC*, 2016, 7(30), para. 1, 38; Scharen W., "The practice of claiming injunctive relief for patent infringement in Germany", in *JIPLP*, 2019, 14(2), 112-126; Strowel A., Léonard A., "Cutting Back Patent Over-Enforcement–How to Address Abusive Practices Within the EU Enforcement Framework", in *JIPITEC*, 2020, 11, 3, para. 1; Blok P., "A harmonized approach to prohibitory injunctions: reconsidering Article 12 of the Enforcement Directive", in *JIPLP*, 2016, 11(1), 56-60.

[50] Commission Notice on the Application of the Competition Rules to Access

heterogenous array of items, including, e.g., railway facilities, telecommunication networks and IPRs.[51] Within the field of IP law, it can be considered the most remarkable effort to set limits to IPR over-enforcement on pro-competitive grounds. Despite the critics,[52] this remedy has tenaciously resisted throughout the years.

5.1. US: the evolution of the essential facilities doctrine

In the US, the essential facilities doctrine firstly emerged in *Terminal Railroad*.[53] The dispute arose because a company controlling bridges and terminals was denied access to one of the main rail hubs of the Midwest. Because such denial would lead to an inefficient solution, the Supreme Court imposed to grant access on "just and non-discriminatory terms".[54] In *Associated Press*,[55] the Court affirmed that the wire reports held by the firm were essential facilities as well, and should therefore be accessible to nonmember newspapers, who were unduly banned from access through bylaws.

Agreements in the Telecommunications Sector, OJ 1998 C 265, defining an "essential facility" as a "facility or infrastructure which is essential for reaching customers and/or enabling competitors to carry on their business, and which cannot be replicated by any reasonable means." See Gitter D., "The Conflict in the European Community Between Competition Law and Intellectual Property Rights: A Call for Legislative Clarification of the Essential Facilities Doctrine", in *ABLJ*, 2003, 40, 218-300, 229.

[51] See, e.g., Waller S.W., Frischmann B., "Revitalizing Essential Facilities", in *Antitrust LJ*, 2008, 75(1), 7 et seq, also mentioning the expansive reading of the doctrine early embraced by US courts.

[52] See, e.g., in US antitrust law, Pitofski R., "Challenges of the New Economy: Issues at the Intersection of Antitrust and Intellectual Property", in *Georgetown Law Faculty and Other Works*, 2001, 314(68), 913-924; Pitofski R., Patterson D. and Hooks J., "The Essential Facilities Doctrine under United States Law", in *Georgetown Law Faculty Publications and Other Works*, 2002, 70, 443-462; Marquardt P.D. and Leddy M., "The Essential Facilities Doctrine and Intellectual Property Rights: A Response to Pitofski, Patterson and Hooks", in *Antitrust LJ*, 2003, 70(3), 847-873; Sidak J.G. and Lipski A.B., "Essential Facilities", in *SLR*, 1999, 51(5), 1187-1249; Areeda P., "Essential Facilities: An Epithet in Need of Limiting Principles", in *Antitrust LJ*, 1989, 58(3), 841-853; Gundlach G.T. and Bloom P.N., "The 'Essential' Facilities Doctrine: Legal Limits and Antitrust Considerations", in *JPP&M*, 1993, 12(2), 156-169; Frischmann B., Waller S.W., "Revitalizing Essential Facilities", in *Antitrust LJ*, 2008, 75(1), 1-65; Gerber D.J., "Rethinking the Monopolist's Duty to Deal: A Legal and Economic Critique of the Doctrine of "Essential Facilities", in *Va L Rev*, 1988, 74(6), 1069-1113.

[53] *United States v. Terminal Railroad Association* 224 US 383 (1912). See Reiffen D. and Kleit A.N., "Terminal Railroad Revisited: Foreclosure of an Essential Facility or Simple Horizontal Monopoly?", in *JL & Econ*, 1990, 33, 419.

[54] *Ibidem*, paras. 410-411.

[55] *United States v. Associated Press* 326 US 1, 4 (1945), paras. 9-10, 13, 21.

In *Otter Tail*,[56] the doctrine was applied to ensure competition in the downstream market. Otter Tail held a natural monopoly over a widespread electric transmission service, also providing customer cities with retail and distribution facilities. At some point, several customer towns decided to develop their own retail service. In response, Otter Tail denied access to the transmission service. In the opinion of the Supreme Court, Otter Tail exploited its natural monopoly over electric transmission services in order to prevent the emergence of a downstream market of retail services.[57] In addition to that, the Court recognized the link among the finding of essential facility, the imposition of a duty to deal and lawful basis for an antitrust claim.[58]

In *MCI* a "five-factor" test has been developed.[59] Accordingly, a facility can be deemed essential if there is "(1) control of an essential facility by a monopolist; (2) the competitor's inability practically or reasonably to duplicate the essential facility; (3) the denial of the use of the facility to a competitor; (4) the feasibility of providing the facility; and (5) the essential facility is a necessary input in a distinct, vertically related market". It is clear that the main constraint comes from factor (5).[60] It follows that the doctrine can be applied only if the facility owned by the monopolist is indispensable for the competitor in order to enter in a different or new market.[61]

However, the most expansive interpretation of the doctrine has been set out in the Tenth Circuit's decision in *Aspen Skiing*.[62] Commentators highlighted that, in this case, both factors (2) and (5) of the *MCI* test were hardly satisfied.[63] The defendant controlled four ski mountains in Aspen, while the plaintiff held control over the fourth. The two offered a popular multi-day joint ticket for all the mountains, but, at a certain point, the defendant unexpectedly withdrew, without providing any business justification. Under the *MCI* test, the Tenth Circuit applied the essential facilities doctrine. Yet, to

---

[56] *Otter Tail Power Co. v. United States*, 410 US 366 (1973).

[57] Ibid, paras. 378-379.

[58] Vaheesan S., "Reviving an Epithet: A New Way Forward for the Essential Facilities Doctrine", in *Utah L Rev*, 2010, 920.

[59] *MCI Commc'ns Corp. v. AT&T*, 708 F.2d 1081, 1132-33 (7th Cir. 1982), paras. 1132-33.

[60] Vaheesan S. (fn. 58) 921-22.

[61] Marquardt P.D. and Leddy M. (fn. 52) 855-59.

[62] *Aspen Skiing Co. v. Aspen Highlands Skiing Corp.*, 738 F.2d 1509, 1519-22 (10th Cir. 1984), affd on other grounds, 472 US 585, 611 (1985).

[63] Lao M., "Networks, Access, and Essential Facilities: From *Terminal Railroad* to *Microsoft*", in *Smu L Rev*, 2009, 62, 571-72.

which extent it is "socially wasteful" not to provide customers with a specific ticket format can be argued.[64] Moreover, in *Aspen*, it is hard to give evidence of the fact that the competitor desperately needed the facility at stake (the ticket or the mountains?)[65] as an input to penetrate a different market.

In *Trinko*, the Supreme Court made several steps back.[66] The Telecommunications Act of 1996 imposed to local telephone monopolies to provide competitors with access to portions of their networks. An association of customers filed an antitrust claim due to failure to obtain access to some portions. Striking enough, the Supreme Court sided for the defendant, holding that noncompliance with the Telecommunications Act cannot in itself constitute a valid ground for an antitrust claim, especially as in the specific case parties have no previous relationship.[67] Going further, the Tenth Circuit seemed to question the soundness of the doctrine itself, or, at least, its usefulness for the case at issue, as there is no need for a court to impose a duty to deal when the same has already been mandated by law. Crucially, the Tenth Circuit also set a two-step benchmark to deregulate the interplay between antitrust liability and duty to deal under the *MCI* test. Accordingly, a duty to deal can lead to antitrust liability under two exceptional circumstances: "(1) the monopolist and the competitor were in previous course of dealing; (2) the monopolist is willing to sacrifice short-term profits through refusal to deal in order to achieve an anti-competitive end."[68]

Hence, the Tenth Circuit recognized a link between a presumption of anti-competitive intent, stemming from the fact that refusal to deal represents a loss of short-term profits for the monopolist, and antitrust liability. This produces the effect of strait jacking the criteria to apply the doctrine to a significant extent, yet, at the same time, creating a presumption of antitrust liability in specific refusal-to-deal cases.

In the US, the essential facilities doctrine has been hardly applied to IPRs.[69] In *Data General*,[70] although its applicability was not outright ruled

---

[64] *Ibidem*, 567.

[65] *Ibidem*, 570.

[66] *Verizon Commc'ns, Inc. v. Law Offices of Curtis V. Trinko, LLP*, 540 US 398, 410-11 (2004). For the impact in the EU, see, e.g., Geradin D., "Limiting the Scope of Article 82 EC: What Can the EU Learn from the US Supreme Court's Judgment in *Trinko* in the Wake of *Microsoft, IMS* and *Deutsche Telekom*?", in *CMLRev*, 2004, 1519-1553.

[67] *Ibidem*, paras. 415-416.

[68] *Ibidem*, para. 409.

[69] Lao M. (fn. 62) 572.

[70] *Data General Corp. v. Grumman Sys. Support Corp.*, 761 F. Supp. 185 (D. Mass. 1991), affd in part and remanded, 36 F.3d 1147 (1st Cir. 1994).

out, the district court held that the same could not work for the case. In *Intergraph*,[71] the dispute arose from the refusal to license patented chips to computer manufacturers. The court applied the essential facilities doctrine because the patented chips could not be found elsewhere and were hardly duplicable, in spite of being crucial to preserve a competition in the micro-processor market. In *Kodak*,[72] the Supreme Court asserted, upon remand, that an IP-holder abuses his dominant position when the market power conferred by IPRs is misused to prevent access in the downstream market. In *Xerox*, the Federal Circuit deviated from *Kodak* and held that the only exceptions to the absolute exclusionary power of patent holders are "sham litigation, fraud … and illegal tying".[73]

5.2. EU: the pathway of the essential facilities doctrine from a pro-competitive to a regulatory tool

In the EU, the essential facilities doctrine emerged in *Commercial Solvents*,[74] where refusal to supply raw materials to a competitor in the same market was condemned in view of the fact that such materials were held "essential facilities". Two years later, in *United Brands*,[75] the doctrine was applied to a situation where the prospective licensee was not (yet) a competitor of the dominant firm. Whilst in the former case the "essential character" of the facility was not crucial, as the parties were in a "competitive relationship", in the latter, this circumstance was paramount, increasing the threshold in an unpredictable way.

While not expressly mentioned, the doctrine became progressively identified with a duty to deal when there is no "objective justification" for doing otherwise, but for infringing Article 102 TFEU.[76] As a result, it begun being applied overbroadly until the leading case *Oscar Bronner*, where the CJEU held that refusal to deal might trigger the application of the doctrine

---

[71] *Intergraph Corp. v. Intel Corp.*, 3 F. Supp. 2d 1255 (N.D. Ala. 1998), vacated, 195 F.3d 1346, 1367 (Fed. Cir. 1999).

[72] *Image Technical Servs. v. Eastman Kodak Co.*, 125 F.3d 1195 (9th Cir. 1997).

[73] *In re Indep. Serv. Orgs. Antitrust Litig.*, 203 F.3d 1322 (Fed. Cir. 2000), para. 158.

[74] Joined Cases 6 and 7/73, *Istituto Chemioterapico Italiano and Commercial Solvents v Commission* [1974], ECR I-0223, para. 250-251.

[75] Case 27/76, *United Brands*, [1978] ECR I-0207, para. 217.

[76] Opi S.B., "The Application of the Essential Facilities Doctrine to Intellectual Property Licensing in the European Union and the United States: Are Intellectual Property Still Sacrosanct?", in *Fordham Intell. Prop. Media & Ent. L.J.*, 2001, 11, 429. See also Treacy P., "Essential Facilities-Is the Tide Turning", in *ECLR*, 1988, 8, 501-04.

only when the facility is "indispensable" for the business in question and denial of supply is likely to eliminate all competition in the relevant market.[77] In particular, "indispensability" should be intended as "economic impracticability".[78] In fact, competition law is not entitled to serve the interests of "particular competitors".[79]

In *Magill* the CJEU dealt with the conflict between the exclusionary power conferred to IP holders and the pro-competitive instances underlying the essential facilities doctrine.[80] In fact, although IPRs constitute an exception to free trade under Article 36 TFEU, the CJEU settled the concept of "exercise-existence dichotomy",[81] carrying with it the corollaries of the "specific subject matter"[82] and "essential function"[83] in order to shed light on the thorny interface between competition law and IP law. Accordingly, the objective scope of the exception to free trade, which "immunizes" exclusive rights from competition scrutiny, is not to be extended in order to cover those exercises of IPRs, which, similar to the rationale of misuse, go beyond the scope and the *raison d'être* of IPRs,[84] i.e., their specific subject matter, in turn reflecting their essential function.

Therefore, in order to apply the essential facilities doctrine to IP cases,

---

[77] Case C-7/97, *Oscar Bronner GmbH & Co KG v. Mediaprint Zeitungs-und Zeitschriftenverlag GmbH & Co. KG* [1998] ECR I-7791, para. 41.

[78] *Ibidem*, I-7832, para. 46.

[79] *Ibidem*, I-7811, para. 58.

[80] Joined Cases C-241/91 P and C-242/91 *P RTE and ITP v Commission* [1995] ECR 1-743.

[81] The doctrine was inaugurated in Joined Cases 56 and 58/64 *Etablissements Consten SARL and Grundig-Case Verkaufs-GmbH v Commission* [1966], ECR I-0429. See also Kallaugher J., "Existence, Exercise, and Exceptional Circumstances: the limited scope for a more economic approach to IP issues under Article 102 TFEU", in Anderman S. and Ezrachi A. (eds.), *Intellectual Property and Competition Law, New Frontiers*, Oxford University Press, 2011, 73-92; Keeling D.T., "The existence of the right and its exercise", in *Intellectual Property Rights in EU Law Volume I: Free Movement and Competition Law*, Oxford University Press, 2004, 52.

[82] Case 78/70 *Deutsche Grammophon Gesellschaft mbH v Metro-SB-Großmärkte GmbH & Co. KG* [1978], ECR I-0487, para. 8.

[83] [1995] ECR I-756, para. 28 of the Opinion of Advocate General Gulmann in *Magill* (fn. 95). See also MacFarlane N., Wardle C. and Wilkinson J., "The Tension between National Intellectual Property Rights and Certain Provisions of EC Law", in *EIPR*, 1994, 16, 12, 525-530; Marenco G. and Banks K., "Intellectual Property and the Community Rules on Free Movement: Discrimination Unearthed", in *Eur. L. Rev.*, 1990, 224, 232.

[84] Keeling D.T., "The specific subject-matter of the right", in *Intellectual Property Rights in EU Law Volume I: Free Movement and Competition Law*, Oxford University Press, 2004, 63.

it is crucial to understand whether IPRs are exercised in accordance with their essential function.[85] In fact, by establishing the conditions under which a refusal to license a protected item amounts to an infringement of competition law, the CJEU also inevitably contributes to delineating the contours of the essential function of IPRs. Through the essential facilities/essential function doctrine, exclusivity comes in conflict with the overarching interest in promoting free competition, which shapes and triggers the application of anti-abuse remedies. In this light, the essential function can be held as a key benchmark to evaluate the existence of an abuse of IPRs.

In subsequent case-law, the essential facilities and the essential function doctrines were refined and adjusted.[86] For the purposes of our analysis, it is appropriate to stress that the essential asset is an IPR, the essential facilities and the essential function doctrines can be held as two sides of the same coin, despite leading to different sets of consequences. Under IP law, deviation from the essential function doctrine may lead to the unenforceability of the exclusive right, endowing alleged infringers with a defense in infringement, such as in *Huawei*. In competition law, the anti-competitive exercise of an IPR leads to impose a duty to deal on the dominant firm, whose violation can trigger antitrust liability.

As the essential facilities doctrine must be seen as a preventive measure that should be applied before competition law, one should also recognize its strong regulatory trait. As the CJEU held in *Lithuanian Railways*,[87] its application should be aligned with sector-specific regulatory choices made at the EU level, going beyond competition policy as such. In this sense, from being a proxy of an antitrust violation, the essential facilities doctrine evolves into a pure regulatory instrument. Thanks to its open texture character and high flexibility, it can be used to foster specific EU policy issues, possibly being tailored to the needs of EU environmental policy as well.

The interplay between the essential function and the essential facilities

---

[85] See, e.g., Korah V., "Dividing the Common Market Through National Industry Property Rights", in *MLR*, 1972, 634, 636; Joliet R., "Patented Articles and the Free Movement of Goods within the EEC", in *Curr Leg Probl*, 1975, 28, 15-23.

[86] See e.g. case T-201/04, *Microsoft v. Commission*, [2007] ECR II-3601, commented. by Hou, L., "The Essential Facilities Doctrine – What was Wrong in *Microsoft*?", in *IIC*, 2012, 43(4), 251-271; Angelov M., "The "Exceptional Circumstances" Test: Implications for Frand Commitments from the Essential Facilities Doctrine Under Article 102 TFEU", in *Eur Compet J*, 2014, 10(1), 37-67; Tudor J., "Compulsory Licensing in the European Union", in *Geo Mason J Int'l Com L*, 2013, 4, 222-258.

[87] Case C-42/21, *Lietuvos geležinkeliai AB v European Commission*, ECLI:EU:C:2023:12.

doctrines raises the question of what legal status should be conferred to the scattered anti-abuse remedies deployed to curb over-exclusivity by EU courts. Looking at *Magill*, scholars pointed out that the essential facilities doctrine was used to compensate for the lax protection requirements provided by IP law, conferring copyright protection to listings of TV programs.[88] In fact, while an expansive application of this doctrine is hardly justifiable from the perspective of competition law, its value as an IP law inner balancing tool is undisputable. In this sense, the application of the essential facilities doctrine to IPRs helps with clarifying the boundaries of their essential function. In this vein, the rationale of the two doctrines, disentangled from the realm of competition law, can converge on a unitary set of legal tools which can be used to balance IP against conflicting interests, such as those dictated by climate policy.

6. How to apply IP delimiting rules within a Green Deal-oriented framework: three examples

As observed in the previous paragraphs, doctrines and legal tools have been adopted by both EU and US courts in order to delimit IPRs and prevent their abusive (and anti-competitive) exercise. In spite of their shortcomings, such doctrines and legal tools can become an effective barrier against IP monopolies and contribute to integrate IP law within EU environmental policies. In the EU, the essential facilities doctrine and abuse of right-like remedies can be selectively deployed to curtail the abuse of IPRs over those types of technologies which are considered crucial to sustain the Green Deal project.

In order to reinterpret these judicial instruments with a view to maximizing the purpose of the Green Deal, it ought to come up with the thorny question of what a "green technology" is.[89] A selection of "sensitive" technologies

---

[88] Dunne N., "Dispensing with Indispensability", in *J Compet Econ*, 2020, 16(1), 74-115., 115 et seq; cf. the US perspective in Bauer J.P., "Refusals to Deal with Competitors by Owners of Patents and Copyrights: Reflections on the *Image Technical* and *Xerox* Decisions", in *DePaul L Rev*, 2005-2006, 55, 1211 et seq.; Lim D., "Copyright under Siege: An Economic Analysis of the Essential Facilities Doctrine and the Compulsory Licensing of Copyrighted Works", in *Alb LJ Sci & Tech*, 2007, 17, 532; Turney J., "Defining the Limits of the EU Essential Facilities Doctrine on Intellectual Property Rights: The Primacy of Securing Optimal Innovation", in *Nw J Tech & Intell Prop*, 2005, 3, 179, 194.

[89] Agenda 21 UN Conference on Environment and Development, Rio de Janeiro, 3-15 June 1992, 23 April 1992, Un Doc. A.CONF/151/26 (Vol. III); see also Borthakur B., "Who owns what? The patent landscape of environmentally sound technologies", in

under the label of EU environmental policy is necessary to recalibrate incentives to innovate in a way purposive to the Green Deal's objectives. If EU competition law starts being interpreted in a more relaxed way with the aim of enhancing green innovation, monopolies are likely to emerge. This can in turn produce the risk of diminishing, rather than increasing, the number of climate neutral technologies in the EU. Against this backdrop, an alternative and less exclusionary approach to IPR limits can operate as an effective counterweight to the one endorsed in EU competition law, going hand in hand with the rationale of the essential facilities doctrine as well as of the other anti-abuse remedies extensively illustrated above.

In view of the findings of a study prepared for the EU Commission, we can refer to three examples,[90] representing "green technologies" key for the Green Deal. In relation to these examples, we will try to substantiate and highlight the importance of adopting anti-abuse remedies to balance incentives to innovate against those to commercialize green technologies protected by IPRs.

6.1. Clean hydrogen

Clean hydrogen technologies are crucial to achieve climate neutrality because they allow to extract renewable energy from wind or solar energy. The best-case scenario would be the one where energy is produced without emissions, the so called "green hydrogen". Yet, an intermediate solution can be to capture and store the emissions created throughout the process of energy production ("blue hydrogen").[91]

As hydrogen can be useful to decarbonize the EU economy, several initiatives have already been taken at the EU level, such as the Fuel Cell and Hydrogen Undertaking.[92] None of these initiatives explicitly tackles the

JIPLP, 2023, 18, 18, 566-586; Pugatch M.P., "Global Challenges WIPO Report", *Intellectual Property & the Transfer of Environmentally Sound Technologies*, June 2011, 1-23.

[90] EU Commission Joint Research Center (JRC), Vysoká L., Dörr R., Sarris S. and Gáthy G., *Technology Transfer and Commercialization for the European Green Deal*, Final Report, January 2021, 34 et seq. On the lack of incentives to innovate in the green sector see Lybecker K.M., "Innovation and Technology Dissemination in Clean Technology Markets and the Developing World: The Role of Trade, Intellectual Property Rights, and Uncertainty", in *JEMI*, 2014, 10(2), 7-38.

[91] *Ibidem*, 35.

[92] *Ibidem*, 36. Extensively, e.g., Fuel Cells and Hydrogen 2 Joint Undertaking, (2019). *Hydrogen Roadmap Europe*. The full text of the study can be found and is available at the following link: https://www.fch.europa.eu/sites/default/files/Hydrogen%20Roadmap%20EuropeReport.pdf.

barrier effect that IPRs may have over hydrogen technologies. Only the HyLAW project was launched for the purpose of giving an overview of the legal and regulatory barriers to green hydrogen production and utilization. At the current date, though, the possibility of introducing new tailormade remedies against the abuse of IPRs over hydrogen technologies has not been considered yet.[93] Also considering the cost gap, that constitutes a consistent obstacle to the development of clean hydrogen technologies, limits to the enforcement of IPRs will be of great value. Instead of *ex-ante* measures such as fast-track mechanisms enacted with the aim of accelerating patent conferrals,[94] *ex-post* anti-abuse remedies can also be of high importance in order to balance the necessity of attracting both public and private investments against the risk of low dissemination of these technologies due to unaffordable royalty rates. In this respect, the applicability of misuse-like remedies coupled with a compulsory license regime by holding green hydrogen technologies as "essential facilities" might be taken into account in order to achieve the Green Deal's objectives in a more effective manner. Moreover, as the essential facilities doctrine and abuse of right-like remedies in IP stem from the same rationale, it might be feasible to introduce regulatory instruments to prohibit the deployment of IPRED remedies when IP-holders refuse to license clean hydrogen technologies or decide to license them at unaffordable royalty rates.

6.2. Lithium-ion batteries

A second relevant example mentioned by the report for the EU Commission is the one of Lithium-ion batteries ("Li-ion").[95] These batteries can be useful to accelerate the shift towards electric vehicles, moving forward carbon-neutral automotive sector. The EU market is quite slim, because most of these batteries are produced outside Europe. An EU-driven IP policy that aims at increasing the commercialization and dissemination of these technologies at affordable prices can be paramount in expanding the relat-

[93] Hydrogen Europe HyLAW Online Database, (2018), more info available here: https://www.hylaw.eu/about-hylaw.

[94] Dechezleprêtre A. and Lane E.L, *Fast-tracking green patent applications. WIPO Magazine.* 2013: https://www.wipo.int/wipo_magazine/en/2013/03/article_0002.html. See also extensively Kim H-E., *The Role of the Patent System in Stimulating Innovation and Technology Transfer for climate Change, Including Aspects of Licensing and Competition Law*, MIPLC Studies September 2010, 13, Nomos, 33 et seq. See also Lane E.L., "Building The Global Green Patent Highway: A Proposal for International Harmonization of Green Technology Fast Track Programs", in *BTLJ*, 2012, 13, 1119-1170.

[95] EU Commission JRC (fn. 89) 42.

ed EU market. Europe can smoothen its dependence on importers and move towards decarbonization. In order to achieve this aim, not only the production but also the utilization, dissemination and recycling of these batteries should be incentivized.

In this regard, limits to the exercise of IPRs can play a key role, especially in a scenario, like the European one, where the (principally publicly funded) research focuses on the optimization of the manufacturing process rather than on reuse.[96] If, for example, parts of these batteries need to be reused for recycling, an IP law-based harmonized remedy to curb the abusive enforcement of IPRs might be useful to crack the walls of IP over-exclusivity. While academic reflections mostly underlined the lack of obstacles posed *ex-ante* by IP to technology transfers and the commercialization of batteries, leaving these matters to the private ordering and industry practices can undermine the policy purposes advocated under the label of the Green Deal, increasing the inhomogeneity in the approaches endorsed by each Member State.

An obstacle stems from the absence of appropriate giga factories and infrastructures. Once the prohibitive costs to develop such infrastructures are met through public funding, an additional problem arises due to risk of natural monopolies, which might hamper commercialization and dissemination of these batteries across EU. The essential facilities doctrine might be useful to avoid that developing a battery manufacturing infrastructure leads to unattackable monopolies and to ensure a level playing field. This doctrine has been firstly applied to infrastructures, thus considering battery manufacturing infrastructures as essential facilities can be the starting point in order to conceptualize new uniform remedies both under competition law and IP law.

6.3. Carbon capture, utilization and storage

Carbon capture, utilization and storage (CCUS) is a process through which CO_2 is disentangled from gases coming from industrial processes in order to reutilize it. This is highly purposive to reducing the emissions as devised within the context of the Green Deal.[97] In line with it, CCUS and CCS should become the key source for energy production in various market sectors, such as pharmaceuticals, dry ice, construction, as well as to produce the clean hydrogen discussed above. This is a green technology where legal,

---

[96] *Ibidem*, 43-45.

[97] Ibid, 56 et seq. See COM (2019) 640, p. 6-8.

regulatory, financial and technical obstacles play a big role. It is particularly difficult to guarantee a higher level of dissemination and use CCUS in order to mitigate the environmental impact of CO_2 emissions.[98] To achieve these goals, a plethora of regulatory instruments and cooperation mechanisms such as the European Strategic Energy Technology Plan, the CCS Directive, the Taxonomy Regulation and the Emission Trading System (ETS) have been enacted.[99]

One main challenge is to develop a network of infrastructures to transport CO_2 once separated. However, it is the lack of economic incentives to capture CO_2 that should be considered the highest barrier to technological development, transfer and commercialization of CCUS. As highlighted by the study for the EU Commission, the ETS system is not workable in order to move forward CCUS, because carbon prices are set too low and therefore greener alternatives are not sufficiently incentivized. Furthermore, the lack of competitiveness and business cases to be presented to investors further discourages the development and financing of CCUS projects.[100]

A regulatory barrier to which IPRs can be related consists of ensuring that CO_2 is transported without legal obstacles across EU.[101] In fact, CCUS project may be covered by IPRs which might make it difficult for some Member States to develop their own infrastructure and thus reach the sufficient number of pipelines across EU. In fact, the risk is that the technological improvement of CCUS projects and further advancement of carbon storage techniques become a prerogative of very few Member States, outright preventing others from developing the same infrastructures, capacity and expertise.

The essential facilities doctrine and anti-abuse remedies can be crucial to incentivize Member States to invest in their own infrastructures and combat the emergence of natural monopolies, also enhancing the commercialization of CCUS.

---

[98] *Ibidem*, 58-60.

[99] EU Commission Communication, *A European strategic energy technology plan (SET Plan) – Towards low carbon future* COM (2007) 723; Council Directive 2009/31/EC of the European Parliament of 23 April 2009 on the geological storage of carbon dioxide and amending Council Directive 85/337/EEC, European Parliament and Council Directives 2000/60/EC, 2001/80/EC, 2004/35/EC, 2006/12/EC, 2008/1/EC and Regulation (EC) 1013/2006 [2009] OJ L 140/114. See also Council Regulation (EU) 2020/852 of the European Parliament of 18 June 2020 on the establishment of a framework to facilitate sustainable investment and amending Regulation (EU) 2019/2088 [2020] OJ L 198/13.

[100] EU Commission JRC (fn. 89) 58.

[101] *Ibidem*, 60.

7. Conclusion

This Chapter has discussed the potential role of remedies and doctrines delimiting the scope and enforcement of IPRs within the context of the Green Deal.

We have first of all outlined that the Green Deal implies the adjustment and re-interpretation of the EU legal framework in order to maximize its objectives. Then, it has been argued that IP law, as well as it occurred with competition law, can be reshaped in accordance with the objective of increasing the number of climate neutral technologies in the EU. Thereafter, we have searched for the provisions of the TRIPS Agreement that can be of help in this regard, focusing on those favoring the introduction of remedies which can be useful to curtail the abusive and anti-competitive misuse of IPRs. In particular, we have analyzed how Articles 8(2), 40 and 31(k) have been implemented in the US and EU, being held as the basis for the deployment of scattered judicial doctrines whose aim is to redefine the scope of IPRs and settle limits to their (abusive) enforcement.

It was highlighted how the external limits to IPRs and the essential facilities doctrine are bounded in rationale, as the possibility of applying the doctrine to impose a duty to deal on the side of the IP-holder ultimately rests on ascertaining the existence of an external limit to IPR scope. It was concluded that both remedies – one on the side of competition law and regulatory law, and the other on the side of IP law – can be weaponized in tandem in a way that conflicting and overarching EU policy instances prevail over IP exclusivity. Following this line of reasoning, it has been suggested the applicability of the essential facilities doctrine to a number of prototypes of "green technologies" deemed essential to accomplish the objectives of the Green Deal and considered key to achieve climate neutrality. The introduction of remedies against the abusive and anti-competitive enforcement of IPRs over such technologies can be held beneficial in order to enhance their dissemination across EU and avoid monopolies.

Chapter 13

SUSTAINABLE FINANCE AND BIODIVERSITY PROTECTION

Luisa Nenci

ABSTRACT: *This Chapter examines the role of the financial sector in promoting investments in sustainable economic activities and supporting projects consistent with the Green Deal objectives. After tracing the emergence of sustainable finance as an EU policy objective, the Chapter introduces the different yet related concept of climate finance and discusses its transformative potential. The aim is to assess whether and to what extent climate-related and ecological concerns are taken into account by the regulatory measures implementing the EU sustainable finance framework, beginning with its primary component: the EU Taxonomy.*

KEYWORDS: *Sustainable finance – Climate finance – Biodiversity protection – EU taxonomy.*

SUMMARY: 1. Introduction. – 2. Sustainable Finance as a Policy Objective. – 3. Climate Finance: Reshaping the Field? – 4. Regulatory Tools: the EU Taxonomy. – 5. Strategic Goals: The Sustainable Finance Agenda. – 6. An Evolving Approach?

1. Introduction

«Sustainable finance» is one of the key components of the European Green Deal. Since 2018, the Commission has developed a «sustainable finance agenda», made up of an interlinked series of strategies, action plans and regulatory proposals directly impacting the economic and financial sector and aiming at encouraging private funding of projects and technologies coherent with the Green Deal objectives.[1] In the Commission's view, the finance sector should play a vital role in encouraging industries to go green through promoting eco-friendly financing schemes and incentives to those that foster sustainable practices.[2] By developing appropriate activities of

---

[1] An excellent account of the rise and features of the EU framework of sustainable finance is provided by Busch D., Ferrarini G. and Grünewald S. (eds.), *Sustainable Finance in Europe. Corporate Governance, Financial Stability and Financial Markets*, 2nd ed., Palgrave McMillan, 2024.

[2] See e.g. COM (2020) 21, § 4.1.

green banking to actively involve customers, suppliers and employees within their sustainability values, the financial sector should facilitate the treatment of business risks by anticipation, attain new markets, attract new customers and talents, and increase the retention of the internal ones. On a more general level, investments in the green transitions, including clean energy sources and energy efficiency, are considered to be essential to move in the direction of climate neutrality.[3]

This Chapter aims at discussing a specific dimension of the framework for sustainable finance laid down by the Green Deal. In particular, it asks whether sustainable finance, as formalized by the European Union (EU) institutions, may be said to refer also to ecological concerns, and, if so, how such ecological concerns are actually taken into account. The Chapter opens by recalling the way in which sustainable finance is presented by the Commission as an EU policy objective (§ 2). It then introduces the different concept of «climate finance», elaborated in global governance and now part of the European Green Deal project (§ 3). It is argued that little attention has been paid so far to biodiversity protection in the sustainable finance framework: this is illustrated by the implementation of its main regulatory instrument, the so-called EU Taxonomy (§ 4), as well as by the overall rationale of the sustainable finance agenda (§ 5). The new package of regulatory measures presented by the Commission in 2023, however, suggests that ecological concerns are gaining a new relevance (§ 6).

2. Sustainable finance as a policy objective

Although sustainable finance has not a univocal definition,[4] the European Commission describes it as «the process of taking due account of environmental and social considerations in investment decision-making, leading to increased investments in longer-term and sustainable activities».[5] Environmental considerations are broadly understood as referring not only to environmental protection but also to climate change mitigation and adaptation, while social concerns include issues such as inequality, inclusiveness and labour relations.

Such representation implicitly recalls both the notion provided in the global governance by the United Nations Environment Programme (UNEP)

---

[3] COM (2023) 317.

[4] Siri M. and Shu S., *Will the EU Commission Successfully Integrate Sustainability Risks and Factors in the Investor Protection Regime? A research Agenda*, 2019, 11 (22) 4.

[5] COM (2018) 97, § 1.

and the concept articulated in the EU context by the High-Level Expert Group on Sustainable Finance (HLEG).

As for the first, one may refer to the Background Note prepared in the context of the Inquiry into the Design of a Sustainable Financial System initiated by UNEP. Such Note emphasizes how the components of sustainable development – environmental, social, economic and governance factors – have created nested concepts intersected both within themselves and with their related financing.[6] The environmental component integrated climate mitigation and adaptation actions, while the related green finance flows encompassed the previous dimension of low carbon and climate finance. Subsequently, the incorporation of the social, economic and governance components of sustainable development resulted in sustainable finance becoming the sum total of climate, green and sustainable development financial flows, positioning climate finance as a subset of sustainable finance.

The UNEP definition is at the basis of the approach taken in the EU order by the HLEG, appointed by the Commission at the end of 2016. According to its Final Report, released on 31 January 2018,[7] sustainable finance has two main designations. In its most narrow meaning, sustainable finance aims at integrating the Environmental Social and Governance (ESG) criteria into financial investment decisions, thus strengthening financial stability. In a broader sense, it refers to the financial system and it points to its capability of improving the contribution of finance to sustainable and inclusive growth by funding society's long-term needs: in the words of the 2017 Interim Report, sustainable finance refers to «promoting sustainable economic development rather than boom and bust; sustainable social development rather than inequality and exclusion; and sustainable environmental development rather than damaging the endowments of nature».[8] Both definitions – integrating ESG criteria into financial investment decisions and contributing to sustainable and inclusive growth – are presented as urgent «imperatives» to be implemented through the recommendations, actions and specific instruments included in the HLEG Final Report. Climate change mitigation appears as a solution for economic, social and environmental issues, while climate change adaptation is not expressly considered.

---

[6] United Nations Environment Programme, "Definitions and Concepts. Background Note", in *Inquiry Working Papers,* 13/2016.

[7] EU High-Level Expert Group on Sustainable Finance, "Financing a sustainable European economy", *Final Report,* 2018.

[8] EU High-Level Expert Group on Sustainable Finance, "Financing a sustainable European economy", *Interim Report,* 2017, 16.

The Commission's representation of sustainable finance is coherent both with the notion provided by UNEP and with that articulated by HLEG. One should not miss, however, the specific priority inherent in the Commission's approach, which clearly assumes that sustainable finance will give support to economic growth, while considering the ESG concerns. The financial system, in other terms, is not requested neither to make the effort to tackle or to integrate ESG in financial decisions, as in the definitions given by UNEP and HLEG. The relevant objective is the economic one – that is, economic growth support and stable financial markets – to which ESG or other sustainable development interests – environmental, social and governance issues – are instrumental. Furthermore, this objective is not fully aligned with climate neutrality actions, because climate change issues, where explicitly addressed, only comprise mitigation actions.

3. Climate finance: reshaping the field?

In the global governance institutional discourse, «climate finance» refers to flow of funds toward activities specifically oriented to reduce greenhouse gas emissions or help society adapt to climate change's impacts. More precisely, climate finance has emerged as a policy and legal objective in the context of the implementing process of the United Nations Framework Convention on Climate Change (UNFCCC).[9] It engages a variety of actors in the national and international arena, both public and private, comprising the financial sector, and it is concerned both with mitigation and adaptation.

Climate finance has a strong transformative potential: for example, in the implementation of the Cancun Agreements, the Conference of the Parties requested developed country Parties «to provide developing country Parties, taking into account the needs of those that are particularly vulnerable, with long-term, scaled-up, predictable, new and additional finance».[10] The transformative potential of climate finance, in any case, is also made clear by the Paris Agreement, whose Article 2.1 (c) provides that the global response to the threat of climate change should be strengthened also by «making financial flows consistent with a pathway towards low greenhouse gas emissions and climate-resilient development». Consistency of financial flows requires engagement by governments and non-state actors[11] in trans-

---

[9] UNFCCC, Introduction to Climate Finance available at https://unfccc.int/topics/introduction-to-climate-finance.

[10] See Decision 1/CP.16, § 18.

[11] Zamarioli L.H., Pauw P. König M. and Chenet H., "The climate consistency goal

forming the global financial sector. By signing the Paris Agreement, the EU and its Member States agreed to make all financial flows, related to both internal and assistance markets, devoted to climate finance.

This overall commitment to climate finance is certainly part of the European Green Deal. Although the main policy documents and legal texts of the sustainable finance framework do not use the label of «climate finance», the target of climate neutrality, identified by the Commission as the macro-objective of the Green Deal, may be achieved by relying on a wide set of diverse instruments, one of which is the economic and financial sector. Climate finance flows are inevitably part of the EU strategy for climate neutrality.

What is more problematic is the relationship between climate and sustainable finance. In principle, one might consider the two concepts as qualitatively different, as they refer to different objectives and imply potentially different balancing between the interests at stake. When taking this perspective, the relevance gained by climate finance both at the global level and in the EU order might suggest that such new policy objective is reshaping the field. In particular, climate finance might lead to expand the set of relevant interests taken into consideration in the balancing exercise, by adding ecosystem protection to economic, social and environmental concerns, provided that ecological sustainability is a fundamental component of the Green Deal strategy. Moreover, the objective of climate finance might lead to re-discuss the priority given to economic growth over social and environmental concerns in the traditional understanding of sustainable finance in the EU.

It is far from clear, however, that this is actually the case. While the Green Deal relies on finance to achieve its climate neutrality objectives, the way in which it aims at doing so largely coincides with the sustainable finance pattern. This point may be illustrated by considering one of the main legal instruments of the sustainable finance agenda, the so called «EU taxonomy». [12]

---

and the transformation of global finance", in *Nat Cli Ch*, 2021, 578-583; Whitley S., Thwaites J. Wright H. and Ott C., *Making finance consistent with climate goals insights for operationalising Article 2.1c of the UNFCCC Paris Agreement*, Overseas Development Institute, 2018.

[12] Regulation (EU) 2020/852 of the European Parliament and of the Council of 18 June 2020 on the establishment of a framework to facilitate sustainable investment, and amending Regulation (EU) 2019/2088, in OJ 2020 L 198. For an excellent account of the rationale of the EU Taxonomy and its implementing issues, see Gortsos C. and Kyriazis D. "The Taxonomy Regulation and its Implementation" in *EBI Working Paper Series,* 2023 n. 136.

4. Regulatory tools: the EU taxonomy

The EU Taxonomy is a market transparency tool, a classification system which details the criteria that qualify an economic activity as environmentally sustainable and aligned with the concerns of the transition to a safe, climate-neutral, climate-resilient, more resource-efficient and circular economy.[13] In particular, the establishing Regulation sets out the requirements which allow to qualify an economic activity as environmentally sustainable. To begin with, an economic activity has to contribute substantially to one or more of the environmental objectives laid down in the Regulation itself. Second, it should not significantly harm any of those environmental objectives. Third, it must be carried out in compliance with certain «minimum safeguards», that is through procedures aimed at ensuring the alignment with a number of international or global requirements, such as the OECD Guidelines for Multinational Enterprises and the UN Guiding Principles on Business and Human Rights. Finally, the relevant economic activity has to comply with the technical screening criteria established by the Commission.[14] Revenues, Capital Expenditures (CAPEXs) and Operational Expenditures (OPEXs) of a company are Taxonomy aligned only if the activity is eligible by making a substantial contribution to at least one of the climate and environmental objectives, does no significant harm to the remaining objectives, and meets minimum standards on human rights and labour standards.

By laying down clear criteria for environmentally sustainable economic activities, the Taxonomy aims at creating a common language and, most importantly, an EU legal concept of green economic activities to become a reference for investors and companies.[15] It also aims at mitigating market fragmentation, protecting against greenwashing and accelerating financing towards the Green Deal objectives. In fact, references to the Taxonomy have been also inserted in the Sustainability Finance Disclosure Regulation (SFDR),[16] which imposes disclosures to financial market participants and their financial products, especially when promoting environmental charac-

---

[13] Regulation (EU) 2020/852, cit., Whereas 4.

[14] Busch D. "Sustainable Finance Disclosure in the EU Financial Sector", in *EBI Working Paper* Series 2020 n.70 par 8.3, p. 12.

[15] Commission, "FAQ: What is the EU Taxonomy and how it will work in practice?", 2, available at https://finance.ec.europa.eu/system/files/2021-04/sustainable-finance-taxonomy-faq_en.pdf.

[16] Regulation (EU) 2019/2088 of the European Parliament and of the Council of 27 November 2019 on sustainability-related disclosures in the financial services sector, in OJ 2019 L317.

teristics or having sustainable investment as their objective. The SFDR reference to the Taxonomy aims to ensure that financial products' sustainability-related contributions rely on science-based criteria.[17] Admittedly, the interaction between the criteria laid down by the EU Taxonomy and the SFDR, which provides its own definitions of sustainable investment, risks and factors,[18] can result in complexity and intricacy of actions. Such complexity may be solved, though, by prioritizing the substantial contribution and alignment to the Taxonomy, as instrumental to the Green Deal macro-objective of climate neutrality.[19]

Undoubtedly, the role of the EU Taxonomy has been important to steer projects toward climate neutrality. Through its descriptive function of describing regularities and standardizing choices people are disposed to make, the Taxonomy has shifted from the application of an excludability list to the identification of clear criteria for environmental sustainability, reinforcing the applicability of green bonds, green loans and sustainable bonds as financial instruments for sustainability.[20]

For the purposes of this Chapter, what is important to stress is the wide-range nature of the objectives that an economic activity must pursue to be considered as environmentally sustainable under the Taxonomy Regulation. While such objectives are qualified by Article 9 as «environmental», some of them go beyond the traditional legal understanding of environmental protection in the EU and include climate-related concerns, such as climate change mitigation and adaptation, as well as ecological issues, namely the protection and restoration of biodiversity and ecosystems. With the adoption of the Taxonomy Regulation, the objectives of sustainable finance have been broadened in such a way to include ecological concerns, coherently with the climate neutrality rationale of the Green Deal.

Nonetheless, the actual relevance of biodiversity and ecosystem protec-

---

[17] Commission, "Enhancing the usability of the EU Taxonomy and the overall EU sustainable finance framework" in SWD (2023) 209.

[18] For example, sustainable investment is defined as « an investment in an economic activity that contributes to an environmental objective [...] or an investment in an economic activity that contributes to a social objective [...] or an investment in human capital or economically or socially disadvantaged communities, provided that such investments do not significantly harm any of those objectives and that the investee companies follow good governance practices» (Article 2, No. 17).

[19] See Commission, "FAQ: What is the EU Taxonomy and how will it work in practice?", cit.

[20] European Parliamentary Research Service "Green and sustainable finance" Briefing available at https://www.europarl.europa.eu/thinktank/fr/document/EPRS_BRI(2021)679081.

tion has been rather limited. In the first four years of application of the Taxonomy Regulation, a prominent issue has been the restricted number of sectors covered by the so called Taxonomy Delegated Acts, namely the «Climate Delegated Act»[21] and the «Environmental Delegated Act».[22] For example, the immediate priority of the Climate Delegated Act has been to finalise climate change mitigation and adaptation, creating flows of climate finance contributing to sustainable growth and not sustainable finance flows. However, significant industries, such as agriculture, have been excluded and some green harmful sectors have been included on a transitional basis.[23] For example, the forestry sector has been labelled sustainable, without excluding industrial logging and other inadequate existing forestry practices.[24] Also the limited number of listed activities[25] – only 71 climate change mitigation activities and 69 climate change adaptation activities – has reduced the opportunities for organisations already green, or with limited environmental impact, to be labelled accordingly. And it has offered little motivation for transition to organisations, whose activities are not covered by the Taxonomy.[26]

---

[21] Commission Delegated Regulation (EU) 2021/2139 of 4 June 2021 supplementing Regulation 2020/852/EU by establishing the technical screening criteria for determining the conditions under which an economic activity qualifies as contributing substantially to climate change mitigation or climate change adaptation and for determining whether that economic activity causes no significant harm to any of the other environmental objectives, OJ 2021 L 442.

[22] Commission Delegated Regulation (EU) 2021/2178 of 6 July 2021 supplementing Regulation (EU) 2020/852 of the European Parliament and of the Council by specifying the content and presentation of information to be disclosed by undertakings subject to Articles 19a or 29a of Directive 2013/34/EU concerning environmentally sustainable economic activities, and specifying the methodology to comply with that disclosure obligation, OJ 2021 L 443.

[23] For example, hydrogen and fossil gas blends to be phased out by 2035.

[24] Crêpy M. "EU climate taxonomy: the good, the bad, and the ugly", in *Ecos,* 5 May 2021, available at https://ecostandard.org/news_events/good-bad-ugly-taxonomy/.

[25] Taxonomy-aligned investments have risen in 2024 to €249 billion compared to the €191 billion in 2023 capital investment reported by approximately 600 European companies. In 2024, 20% of companies' capital investments are Taxonomy aligned, with the utilities sector leading the way, particularly electricity providers: see https://finance.ec.europa.eu/sustainable-finance/tools-and-standards/eu-taxonomy-sustainable-activities/eu-taxonomys-uptake-ground_en, accessed 2 September 24.

[26] Pettingale H., de Maupeou S. and Reilly P. "EU Taxonomy and the Future of Reporting", in *Harvard Law School Forum on Corporate Governance,* available at https://corpgov.law.harvard.edu/2022/04/04/eu-taxonomy-and-the-future-of-reporting/.

5. Strategic goals: the sustainable finance agenda

The limited recognition given to ecological concerns by the EU Taxonomy reflects the overall approach of the sustainable finance agenda. Two of the key goals of such agenda, whose basic foundations have been defined in the Action Plan on Financing Sustainable Growth[27] and the Strategy for Financing the Transition to a Sustainable Economy,[28] are those of enabling sustainable investment and of managing and integrating climate and environmental risks into the financial system to contribute to sustainability and ensure its integrity. Those goals, however, are not designed in such a way to take into account ecological issues: while ecosystem protection and restoration is a fundamental component of the EU strategy for climate neutrality, the EU political institutions do not openly recognize its role and potential in the sustainable finance framework.

Regarding the financial sector contribution to sustainability, such contribution spans from reinforced science-based targets, transparency commitments and fiduciary duties to Green Deal targets and supervisors' assessment in addressing greenwashing. These forms of contribution differ from what was initially defined by the sustainable finance agenda, essentially pointing to the increased amount of environmentally sustainable projects, identified according to the Taxonomy framework, to be financed by the private sector. While the role of the financial sector has gradually become more proactive, though, the lack of common legal definitions and principles results in a piecemeal approach[29] within which the elaboration of an integrated sustainable finance framework is becoming difficult. Moreover, no attention is paid to the specific objective of contrasting biodiversity loss and restoring ecosystem health. The overall strategy is devoted to strengthening and concentrating the financial sector contribution because instrumental to the transition to sustainability. While this is coherent with the wider goal of climate neutrality, the sustainable finance agenda, in its current version, does not envisage any specific measure to take into account ecological concerns.

As for the risks posed by climate change and environmental degradation to the stability of the financial sector itself, the sustainable finance agenda does

---

[27] COM (2018) 97.

[28] COM (2021) 390.

[29] Colaert V. "MiFID II in Relation to Other Investor Protection Regulation: Picking Up the Crumbs of a Piece-meal Approach", in Busch D. and Ferrarini G. (eds.), *Regulation of the EU Financial Markets – MiFID II and MiFIR*, Oxford University Press, 2017.

not clearly define such risks. As a result, most of institutions are currently mapping ESG risks, instead of climate change and environmental risks. As an example, ESG risks become cross cutting priority for the European Bank Authority (EBA), which aims at ensuring *that stakeholders are fully informed about institutions' ESG risks, in order to take informed decisions.*[30] The European Central Bank (ECB), instead, has absorbed the definition of investment climate-related financial risks, which have been further specified in the two components of transition and physical risks.[31] Physical risks relate to the effects of global warming on physical capital, human health, productivity and agriculture,[32] while transition risks concern the actions taken to reach net-zero greenhouse gas emissions.[33] Such variety of approaches makes the possibility of enhancing the resilience of the financial sector complicated, as different risks are identified and only few instruments are clearly related to a specific risk mitigation action to achieve climate neutrality.

Most importantly for the purpose of our analysis, no specific relevance seems to be given to ecological risks, except for the loose Commission's statement that «financial institutions are increasingly exposed to the accelerating degradation of ecosystems and loss of biodiversity, the depletion of natural resources and the levels of pollution in our water, air and soils».[34]

6. An evolving approach?

Interest in green and sustainable finance is rising very fast among investors worldwide, and the agreed classification framework of the taxonomy being made by objective and scientific assessment allows an enhanced perception and understanding of green credentials. The financial system itself is increasingly treating climate and environment-related risks as financial risks, and not just as reputational ones, because of the awareness that these risks

---

[30] See e.g. EBA/ITS/2022/01, Final draft implementing technical standards on prudential disclosures on ESG risks in accordance with Article 449a CCR.

[31] ECB/ESRB Project Team on climate risk monitoring, The macroprudential challenge of climate change, July 2022. See Gourdel R., Monasterolo I., Dunz N. Mazzocchetti A. and Parisi L. "The double materiality of climate physical and transition risks in the euro area", in *EBI Working Paper Series* 2665, May 2022.

[32] Definition from the Network of Central Banks and Supervisors for Greening the Financial System NGFS at https://www.ngfs.net/en.

[33] Definition from the Network of Central Banks and Supervisors for Greening the Financial System NGFS at https://www.ngfs.net/en.

[34] COM (2021) 390, 13.

can become financially material and affect society as a whole (citizens, consumers, employees, business partners).[35]

At the EU level, the Commission has provided a positive assessment of the consolidation of the sustainable finance framework in the last years. In particular, it has stressed the role played, next to the Taxonomy Regulation, by the Sustainable Finance Disclosure Regulation (SFDR),[36] the Benchmark Regulation,[37] the European Green Bond Regulation[38] and the Corporate Sustainability Reporting Directive (CSRD).[39] In the Commission's view, all these instruments have ensured the integration of sustainability factors in the financial sector, facilitating private finance for green and transition investments through transparency.[40] At the same time, the Commission has acknowledged the need to further develop the sustainable finance framework. For this reason, in 2023 it has presented a new package of regulatory measures, including the proposal for a regulation on transparency and integrity of ESG rating activities, aiming at increasing transparency on the market for sustainable investments.

We can certainly share the Commission's point of view. Sustainability preferences are becoming fundamental to lead to sustainability implementation by leveraging on existing instruments and making individuals to really choosing green investments to support low carbon economy transition. However, as observed by the Commission itself, small and medium-sized enterprises face a number of significant challenges in their transition to a climate neutral economy, ranging from the articulation of sustainability objectives and actions as part of business strategies to the identification of so-

[35] Commission Communication, Guidelines on non-financial reporting: Supplement on reporting climate-related information, 17 June 2019, C(2019) 4490 final, p. 7.

[36] Regulation (EU) 2019/2088 of the European Parliament and of the Council of 27 November 2019 on sustainability-related disclosures in the financial services sector, in OJ 2019 L 317.

[37] Regulation (EU) 2019/2089 of the European Parliament and of the Council of 27 November 2019 amending Regulation (EU) 2016/1011 as regards EU Climate Transition Benchmarks, EU Paris-aligned Benchmarks and sustainability-related disclosures for benchmarks, in OJ 2019 L 317.

[38] Regulation (EU) 2023/2631 of the European Parliament and of the Council of 22 November 2023 on European Green Bonds and optional disclosures for bonds marketed as environmentally sustainable and for sustainability-linked bonds, in OJ 2023.

[39] Directive (EU) 2022/2464 of the European Parliament and of the Council of 14 December 2022 amending Regulation (EU) No 537/2014, Directive 2004/109/EC, Directive 2006/43/EC and Directive 2013/34/EU, as regards corporate sustainability reporting, OJ L 322, 16.12.2022.

[40] COM (2023) 317, 2-3.

lutions where green technologies are not yet available.[41] For this reason, one should welcome the new package of regulatory measures, which is a concrete demonstration of the Commission's effort to provide practical guidance to companies, financial intermediaries and investors in the transition to climate neutrality.

In the perspective of this volume, it is appropriate to stress that ecological concerns seem to gain a new relevance in the sustainable finance framework. In particular, the Commission has adopted amendments both to the Environmental Delegated Act[42] and to the Climate Delegated Act,[43] establishing, among the other things, new technical screening criteria for economic activities that contribute substantially to the protection and restoration of biodiversity and ecosystems. In determining the conditions under which a specific economic activity qualifies as contributing substantially to the protection and restoration of biodiversity and ecosystems, those criteria not only refer to thresholds that the economic activity should achieve, but also specify the minimum requirements that the economic activity should meet to qualify as environmentally sustainable. Although taking place at the level of a delegated regulation, the recognition of ecological concerns in the establishment of technical screening criteria is a potentially relevant novelty. The revised Environmental Delegated Act is based on the assumption that the new criteria, fully in line with the rationale of ecological sustainability, «should reflect the need to protect, conserve or restore biodiversity to achieve the good condition of ecosystems or to protect ecosystems that are already in good condition».[44] Admittedly, the criteria laid down in

---

[41] *Ibidem*, 3.

[42] Commission Delegated Regulation (EU) 2023/2486 of 27 June 2023 supplementing Regulation (EU) 2020/852 of the European Parliament and of the Council by establishing the technical screening criteria for determining the conditions under which an economic activity qualifies as contributing substantially to the sustainable use and protection of water and marine resources, to the transition to a circular economy, to pollution prevention and control, or to the protection and restoration of biodiversity and ecosystems and for determining whether that economic activity causes no significant harm to any of the other environmental objectives and amending Commission Delegated Regulation (EU) 2021/2178 as regards specific public disclosures for those economic activities, ELI: http://data.europa.eu/eli/reg_del/2023/2486/oj.

[43] Commission Delegated Regulation (EU) 2023/2485 of 27 June 2023 amending Delegated Regulation (EU) 2021/2139 establishing additional technical screening criteria for determining the conditions under which certain economic activities qualify as contributing substantially to climate change mitigation or climate change adaptation and for determining whether those activities cause no significant harm to any of the other environmental objectives.

[44] Commission Delegated Regulation (EU) 2023/2486, cit., Recital 23.

Annex IV to the Commission Delegated Regulation (EU) 2023/2486 have a rather narrow focus on conservation and accommodation activities. The former include restoration activities, aimed at maintaining or improving the status of a number of ecosystems, while the latter refer to hotels, camping grounds and the like. This is not a particularly encouraging framework. At the same time, it is a legal development that might trigger a wider process.

The direction of such process is perhaps indicated by the Commission's Study for a methodological framework and assessment of potential financial risks associated with biodiversity loss and ecosystem degradation, published in March 2024.[45] This report aims to provide financial institutions with a methodological framework for detecting and measuring the risks deriving from ecosystem degradation and biodiversity loss. Flexible and scalable instruments are necessary to allow the financial sector «to integrate nature and biodiversity considerations into risk assessments and advance their strategies towards sustainable and resilient practices».[46] Reconnecting financial activities with ecological concerns is now recognized as a policy and regulatory goal. How to reach it, it remains to be seen.

[45] European Commission (Directorate-General for Financial Stability, Financial Services and Capital Markets Union), Study for a methodological framework and assessment of potential financial risks associated with biodiversity loss and ecosystem degradation (Publications Office of the European Union, 2024).

[46] *Ibidem*, at 14.

Chapter 14
CORPORATE GOVERNANCE AND SUSTAINABILITY: SOMETHING NEW UNDER THE SUN?

Federica Montanaro

ABSTRACT: *This Chapter examines the implications of the European Green Deal for corporate governance and sustainability. It focuses on the Corporate Sustainability Reporting Directive (CSRD) as a key regulatory tool designed to enhance corporate transparency and accountability regarding environmental and social impacts. The Chapter explores the evolution from the Non-Financial Reporting Directive to the CSRD, emphasizing the shift from voluntary to mandatory sustainability reporting. Additionally, it discusses the intersection of CSRD with the Corporate Sustainability Due Diligence Directive, comparing the different mechanisms of the two regulatory initiatives.*

KEYWORDS: *Economic transition – Corporate governance – Disclosure – Sustainability reporting – Information tool.*

1. The European Green Deal and the economic transition

Pursuing an economic transition is one of the declared objectives of the European Green Deal. Making the entire economic arena of the European Union (EU) a neutral one in terms of emission by 2050[1] implies, according to the European Commission, "nothing less than a new economic model".[2] This commitment is made clear in many policy documents and

[1] See "The European Green Deal", COM (2019) 640.

[2] Commission, Competition policy brief, September 2021, Competition Policy in Support of Europe's Green Ambition, available at: https://op.europa.eu/en/publication

legislations stemming from the Green Deal, including the Corporate Sustainability Reporting Directive (CSRD), whose preamble enounces the aim to "decouple economic growth from resource use, and ensure that all regions and Union citizens participate in a socially just transition to a sustainable economic system".[3]

This Chapter focuses on the CSRD and the related measures,[4] which are an important component of the regulatory process through which the economic transition is supposed to be managed. In particular, it discusses the reporting mechanism as an instrument for implementing corporate sustainability and asks which conception of sustainability the various legislative initiatives convey: whether they respond to the traditional rationale of sustainable development, as consolidated in the EU legal order; or whether they sustain a different and more ecological understanding of sustainability, namely the objective of ecosystems' sustainability which the Green Deal is promoting next to sustainable development. Since the CSRD is not the only initiative aimed at pursuing the goal of realigning the EU common market and institutions with a sustainable paradigm, it is also appropriate to consider the Corporate Sustainability Due Diligence Directive. Such Directive will not be analysed in detail, but only in relation to the link between sustainability and corporate governance.

There are at least two reasons why corporations deserve attention in an inquiry about the kind of sustainability that the regulation of the economic transition is promoting. Firstly, corporations are significant contributors to emissions. Secondly, they are key actors within the current economic system, the ones generating profits and goods. These two profiles are strictly interconnected, making a redefinition about the corporations' role essential. It is not possible to reshape or even modify the long-term equilibrium between economic and ecological concerns without tak-

-detail/-/publication/63c4944f-1698-11ec-b4fe01aa75ed71a1/language-en/format-PDF, 1 (last access 229 May 2024).

[3] Directive (EU) 2022/2464 of the European Parliament and of the Council of 14 December 2022 amending Regulation (EU) 537/2014, Directive 2004/109/EC, Directive (EC) 2006/43 and Directive (EU) 2013/34, as regards corporate sustainability reporting (Corporate Sustainability Reporting Directive: CSRD), Recital 1.

[4] Regulation (EU) 2020/852 of the European Parliament and of the Council of 18 June 2020 on the establishment of a framework to facilitate sustainable investment and amending Regulation (EU) 2019/2088. Regulation (EU) 2019/2089 of the European Parliament and of the Council of 27 November 2019 (complemented by Commission Delegated Regulations (EU) 2020/1816, (EU) 2020/1817, and (EU) 2020/1818) introduces environmental, social, and governance ('ESG') disclosure requirements for benchmark administrators and minimum standards for the construction of EU Climate Transition Benchmarks and EU Paris-aligned Benchmarks.

ing into consideration the structure of productive activities and money flows.

The inquiry opens with a brief discussion on why corporations and finance play such a fundamental role in building a more sustainable system (§ 2). It then focuses on the CSRD to show how EU institutions plan to use this legal tool to fulfil the 2019 Communication objective of the mobilisation of industry for a clean and circular economy.[5] The following sections investigate the CSRD as an important example of information tool (§ 3), the evolution of reporting mechanisms from a pure financial instrument to their current use as sustainability tool and the possible interactions with the Due Diligence Proposal, the other major initiative in the economic transition (§ 4). Finally, the relationship between sustainability and corporate governance is discussed and some conclusions are provided (§ 5).

2. The Finance Package and the role of corporations

Due to the size of the internal market, the number of actors and interests involved, and the complexity of the EU machinery, the economic transition is one of the most serious test points for the success of the Green Deal. The EU institutions responded to this challenge with a multi-step intervention consisting of numerous pieces of legislations.[6]

The general objective of this set of norms is the creation of a better functioning internal market, contributing to the implementation of sustainability goals. In fact, using the words of the preamble of the CSRD, the Green Deal "aims to protect [...] the Union's natural capital, and protect the health and well-being of Union citizens from environment-related risks and impacts".[7] A few lines later, the same Recital refers to stability, suggesting that EU institutions are trying to adapt the current market to the future consequences of the climate crisis.[8]

---

[5] See Communication from the Commission to the European Parliament, the European Council, the Council, the European Economic and Social Committee and the Committee of the Regions, The European Green Deal, 2019, 8, where it is explicitly stated that "Reliable, comparable and verifiable information also plays an important part in enabling buyers to make more sustainable decisions and reduces the risk of 'green washing'. Companies making 'green claims' should substantiate these against a standard methodology to assess their impact on the environment".

[6] See fn. 4.

[7] CSRD, Recital 1.

[8] *Ibidem*: the Green Deal "will contribute to the objective of building an economy that works for the people, strengthening the Union's social market economy, helping to ensure that it is ready for the future and that it delivers stability, jobs, growth and sustainable investment".

There are two key, interlinked strategies that the EU institutions appear to be promoting: shifting funding towards greener activities and implementing a series of mechanisms at the EU level to make corporations more accountable. This is the comprehensive logic that offers a unitarian interpretative key to and a *trait d'union* between norms regarding reporting, due diligence, investments, insurance duties. Most of these initiatives are part of the so-called Sustainable Finance Package,[9] embodying the aim to improve the flow of money towards sustainable activities across Europe. Besides it, the EU institutions have addressed the supply chains' theme, providing a set of norms that testify to the increasing attention to the interlink between trade, industry, and environment.[10]

Concerning corporations, there is a necessity to formulate an extensive sustainability framework that enables them to adjust their business models accordingly. Additionally, to facilitate the shift in finance and counteract greenwashing, every component of the Sustainable Finance Package will bolster the dependability and comparability of sustainability information.

Considering this rationale, the CSRD, together with the Regulation concerning sustainability and environmental disclosure requirements,[11] is probably the most significant intervention. In fact, this Directive provides a

---

[9] The Finance Package is a group of interrelated measures to build an EU sustainable finance framework. Its aim is to ensure that the EU sustainable finance framework continues to support companies and the financial sector, while encouraging the private funding of transition projects and technologies.

[10] This interlink has been deeply analysed in environmental sociology, and later in green criminology and a proper overview of the theme goes behind the purpose of this Chapter. However, the foundational theory is known as "the treadmill of production" theory, elaborated by Allan Schnailberg in the now-classic Schnaiberg A., *The Environment: From Surplus to Scarcity*, Oxford University Press, 1980. According to the author, powerful social actors (political and economic elites) benefit when the 'treadmill of production' (increased production and economic growth) is sped up, despite generating environmental and social problems. Since "environment" means resources, the logic of the political-economic system is in conflict with environmental protection and preservation. For further lectures, see Acosta A., "Extractivism and Neoextractivism: Two Sides of the Same Curse.", in Land M. and Mokrani D. (eds.), *Beyond Development: Alternative Visions from Latin America*, Permanent Working Group on Alternatives to Development/Transnational Institute, 2013, 61-86; Buttel F.H., "The Treadmill of Production: An Appreciation, Assessment, and Agenda for Research.", in *Organ Environ.*, 2004, 17, 3, 323-336; Gould K.A., Pellow D.N. and Schnaiberg A., *The Treadmill of Production: Injustice and Unsustainability in the Global Economy*, Paradigm Publishers, 2008. For a more criminological analysis, see Lynch M.J., Stretesky P.B. and Long M.A., "The Treadmill of Production and the Treadmill of Law: Propositions for Analyzing Law, Ecological Disorganization and Crime", in *CNS*, 2020, 31, 1, 107-122.

[11] See fn. 4.

common mandatory standard to refer to, which can serve as a basis for new sustainable corporate governance across the EU market.

Such legislations are primarily aimed at modifying the existing legal framework, proceeding with progressive and time-schedule adjustments. [12] This cautious approach, which can be criticized in the face of today's emergency, could however prove capable of promoting an overall rearrangement of a macro-sector long dominated by the logic of profit without causing collateral damages [13] but, on the contrary, fostering a just and equitable transition.

3. The Corporate Sustainability Reporting Directive as an information tool

The CSRD provides a new framework of rules for major corporations based or that operate consistently within the European market. It revises a number of previous legislations: the Non-Financial Reporting Directive of 2014, [14] the Regulation n. 537/2014 on specific requirements regarding statutory audit of public-interest entities [15] and the Directive 2004/109/EC on the harmonisation of transparency requirements. [16] The new directive modernises and strengthens the rules concerning the social and environmental information that companies must report. Indeed, it may be considered an information tool, implemented together with other kind of instruments (for example, procedural ones, such as ex-ante impact assessments

---

[12] Limiting the gaze to the Reporting Directive, it will come fully into force in several years, leaving time for recipients to adapt to it without affecting market stability. In this sense see Opinion of the European Central Bank of 6 June 2023 on the proposal for a Directive on corporate sustainability due diligence (CON/2023/15), 1.8.

[13] Social damages, for examples, induced by the companies' hurry to be compliant with new environmental standards, which could lead to reduce worker's security or salary.

[14] Directive 2014/95/EU of the European Parliament and of the Council of 22 October 2014 amending Directive 2013/34/EU as regards disclosure of non-financial and diversity information by certain large undertakings and groups Text with EEA relevance.

[15] Regulation (EU) 537/2014 of the European Parliament and of the council of 16 April 2014 on specific requirements regarding statutory audit of public-interest entities and repealing Commission Decision 2005/909/EC.

[16] Directive (EC) 2004/109 of the European Parliament and of the Council of 15 December 2004 on the harmonisation of transparency requirements in relation to information about issuers whose securities are admitted to trading on a regulated market and amending Directive (EC) 2001/34.

and ex-post evaluation and review).[17] Quite interestingly, the success of an informational instrument to intervene in corporate governance matter reflects the historical caution and difficulties of the EU in this field.[18] While in other areas EU institutions have promoted substantive legislation,[19] here the first step consists in making disclosure obligations mandatory and homogeneous across the internal market.

There is a form of continuity among EU institutions in the use of this type of instrument. Given the complexity of the sector from various perspectives, the institutions' use of legal tools imposing disclosure obligations for information and processes, thereby promoting indirect mechanisms of adaptation to standards, can be considered more suitable. This ongoing approach presents potential advantages over the direct imposition of new duties, particularly in terms of its acceptance by the recipients.

For this reason, this regulation is incorporated into an existing legal framework and indeed builds upon a direct precedent such as the Non-Financial Reporting Directive (NFRD). Focusing on this Directive as an informational tool and on how it has been used in the context of the Green Deal illustrates the European strategy to steer the market towards a more sustainable dimension, simultaneously revealing how such a strategy requires longer timelines and is not without risks.

3.1. An already existing mechanism: the Non-financial Reporting Directive

Probably the most significant among the legislations revised by CSRD, the Non-Financial Reporting Directive (NFRD) already contained provisions on the sharing of information not strictly related to the financial aspects of a company's structure and organization. This obligation applied only to a restricted number of companies, based on their size and market share.[20]

---

[17] Oberthür S. and von Homeyer I., "From emissions trading to the European Green Deal: the evolution of the climate policy mix and climate policy integration in the EU", in *J. Eur. Public Policy*, 2023, 30, 3, 445.

[18] Conac P-H., "Sustainable Corporate Governance in the EU: Reasonable Global Ambitions?", in *Revue Europèenne du droit*, 2022, 4, 111.

[19] The choice between substantive or informational dispositions is revealing of the different political approach. Informational tool, as the Reporting Directive, sets what kind of information the actors have to disclose. It's a "softer" way to intervene, and it can be read as a preliminary step. Substantive tools pose direct modification, prescribing what kind of duty the actors must satisfy. For example, in the banking sector, see the Green Paper on the EU Corporate Governance Framework, COM (2011) 164.

[20] Specifically, the NFR Directive of 1995 stated that large undertakings which are public-interest entities exceeding on their balance sheet dates the criterion of the aver-

This limited the application of the NFRD to approximately 11600 companies within the EU market.[21] Other characteristics of the NFRD reduced its incisiveness: in fact, its provisions were not mandatory and were left to the "voluntarism" of the companies.[22]

Furthermore, NFRD allowed Member States to impose state-specific requirements on companies regarding the three key aspects of reporting: reporting framework, disclosure format, and reporting content. This means that companies retained significant flexibility to disclose non-financial information in the way they considered most useful. In this scenario, companies were free to choose, according to their characteristics,[23] to either draft a separate report or embed it within the management one. Another critical point was the lack of clarity about what constituted 'non-financial information': while 'financial' information refers to a well-defined set, the term 'non-financial', which can be derived by difference, could consist of very different data in practice, making rigorous comparison difficult.

The final picture was consequently blurred: this mechanism, albeit reasonable in terms of company cost, was nevertheless incapable of guaranteeing effective disclosure and even providing enough information to stakeholders.

3.2. Reporting now: the key role of the CSRD

Since the entry into force of Reporting Directive on 5th January 2023, major and strategic companies are gradually required to disclose information on the environmental and social impact of their activity. The preamble of the

---

age number of 500 employees during the financial year shall include in the management report a nonfinancial statement containing information to the extent necessary for an understanding of the undertaking's development, performance, position and impact of its activity, relating to, as a minimum, environmental, social and employee matters, respect for human rights, anti-corruption and bribery matters. See NFRD, Article 1 "Amendments to Directive 2013/34/EU", inserts Article 19a, n. 1.

[21] NFRD, Article 1 "Amendments to Directive 2013/34/EU", inserts Article 19a, No. 1.

[22] The debate about "voluntarism" and vice versa mandatory obligations posed by States or organizations is quite old. The two are reflections of different points of view about the role of public power in economic matter and the relations between it and the economic and industrial actors. Another debate, strictly linked with this more theoretic one is about the effects of the two approaches. See for example Lagasio V. and Cucari N., "Corporate governance and environmental social governance disclosure: A meta-analytical review.", in *Corp Soc Resp. Env Ma.*, 2019, 26, 4, 701.

[23] For example, they could choose to adopt international, European, or national guidelines according to their characteristics or business.

CSRD, while underlining that the Reporting Directive is an "amendment" directive that intervenes on provisions already in force, provides a useful overview of the disclosure duties now mandated by EU law and their growing importance in the field of sustainability.[24]

The "reporting issue" is one of the major themes when it comes to evaluating corporate performances, and sustainability reporting has become widespread in recent years, as corporations start to measure and communicate their sustainability impact to stakeholders.[25] The discourse is closely intertwined with the macro-theme of corporate social responsibility.[26] However, several elements suggest that Reporting Directive can be a first step in a different direction, contributing to reshaping the equilibrium of the market.

First of all, this key mechanism passed from being optional to being qualified as "mandatory reporting".[27] Several recitals stress the necessity of policy action to bridge the information gap between users' information needs and the sustainability information provided, warning that this gap will tend to grow in the absence of such action.[28] Moreover, according to the Directive itself, the elaboration of a common mandatory framework is "an essential step to give sustainability reporting a status comparable to the

---

[24] See for example Recital No. 11, where the demand for sustainability information is described as significant increasing.

[25] Paridhi S. and Arora A., "Sustainability reporting: Current state and challenges", *Business Strategy & Development*, 2023, 6, 3, 1-20.

[26] Multiple perspectives have been explored to understand corporate responsibility towards society and environment, its role and contribution towards sustainable practices. Corporate social responsibility has been defined by the Commission "a concept whereby companies integrate social and environmental concerns in their business operations and in their interaction with their stakeholders on a voluntary basis": see European Commission, Green Paper, Promoting a European framework for Corporate Social Responsibility, Brussels, 18.7.2001 COM (2001) 366 final. However, CSR has been shaped in different ways depending on the historical period, and it is changing still today. See Dahlsrud A., "How Corporate Social Responsibility is Defined: an Analysis of 37 Definitions", in *Corp Soc Resp. Env Ma.*, 2008, 15, 1-13.

[27] CSRD, Recital No. 37: "The development of mandatory common sustainability reporting standards is necessary to reach a situation in which sustainability information has a status comparable to that of financial information.". According to Chapter 6a, Article 29b, "Sustainability reporting standards": "1. The Commission shall adopt delegated acts in accordance with Article 49 supplementing this Directive to provide for sustainability reporting standards. Those sustainability reporting standards shall specify the information that undertakings are to report in accordance with Articles 19a and 29a and, where relevant, shall specify the structure to be used to present that information".

[28] See CSRD, Recitals No. 9, 11, 14.

financial one".[29] This not only indicates its increased significance in the eyes of the European legislator but also reflects its willingness to intervene more decisively to ensure that sustainability-related information is taken seriously and reported by a much broader range of businesses. Furthermore, by establishing a common duty of disclosure, relevant information is no longer left to the discretion of economic entities but is rather defined by the public decision-maker. Therefore, it is possible to presume that with the application of Reporting Directive provisions to corporations, a general standardization will be progressively achieved. This Directive has two interconnected goals: to promote the disclosure of companies' strategies and models and to help investors choose genuinely "green" activities.

Interestingly, companies are required to report information necessary to understand both the impact the company has on sustainability matters (an "inside-out" perspective) and how sustainability matters affect a company's business development, performance, and position (an "outside-in" perspective).[30] This constitutes a broader inquiry than a mere disclosure of the types of activities that may exert an environmental or social impact. The matter is approached from both perspectives, urging businesses to engage in a form of self-reflection concerning their organizational modules and strategies. More generally, the reporting mechanism is often linked to an ongoing modification of the role of corporations in society: according to these reconstructions, companies are adjusting their objectives and placing increased emphasis on the relationship between business and society.[31]

To conclude, the Reporting Directive sets a new minimum standard regarding the transparency and propriety of practices. The explicit inclusion of the socio-environmental dimension of the company in these practices is a worthwhile innovation, particularly considering the influence that Europe-

---

[29] See CSRD, Recital No. 37.

[30] Adams C.A., Alhamood, A., He, X., Tian, J., Wang, L. and Wang, Y., "The Double-Materiality Concept: Application and Issues", in *Global Reporting Initiative*2021, 5; Förster P., "The Double Materiality Principle (Article 19a NFRD) as Proposed by the Corporate Sustainability Reporting Directive: An Effective Concept to Tackle Green Washing?", in Bäumler J. et al. (eds.), *European Yearbook of International Economic Law*, Springer, 2022, 13.

[31] Serafeim G., "The Role of the Corporation in Society: An Alternative View and Opportunities for Future Research", in *HBS Working Paper*, 2014, 14.

Admittedly, this new trend could favour corporate profitability. Although not immediately intuitive, the evidence seems to suggest a positive relationship between sustainability and future financial performance ("sustainability pays"): see Ioannis I. and Serafeim G., "The Impact of Corporate Social Responsibility on Investment Recommendations: Analysts' Perceptions and Shifting Institutional Logics", in *SMJ*, 2015, 36, 1053.

an regulation exerts on transactions beyond its borders. Concerning this passage, moreover, another consideration arises spontaneously: the EU is trying to "push beyond" the concept of sustainability and to influence global standards, extending these new duties (of reporting, if not of due diligence) even outside EU territory.[32]

This is explicitly stated in various recitals and in the 2019 Communication itself, where the Commission acknowledges that "the environmental ambition of the Green Deal will not be achieved by Europe acting alone",[33] and even if other global actors are unwilling to act, the "EU can use its influence, expertise and financial resources to mobilise its neighbours and partners to join it on a sustainable path".[34] Since corporations must disclose information to operate in the EU market, the final result will hopefully be increased transparency throughout the entire value chain where the involved corporations operate.

3.3. Sustainability reporting: indicators and standardization

In short, disclosure mechanisms have a long history, primarily focusing on financial matters due to their origin as a means to control correct corporate governance and ensure fair competition.[35]

The reporting mechanism envisaged by the CSRD, expressly extended to include "sustainable elements", fits into a problematic framework. Indeed, despite reporting being in use for some time, several questions remain unsolved. The challenges are even more evident when the focus shifts from "measurable" factors such as financial data to information about social and environmental performances.

A particularly significant issue concerns sustainability measurements: the specific type or structure of reporting that must be chosen, and the lack of standardization in measurement practices.[36] Without a harmonization,

---

[32] Both the Reporting Directive and the Due Diligence Proposal establish rules even for companies with subsidiaries outside EU territory and for companies not based in Europe but operating consistently in EU market. See CSRD, Chapter 9a, Reporting concerning third-country undertakings, Article 40a and Proposal, Article 27.

[33] *Supra*, fn. 1, 2.

[34] *Ibidem.* They address the matter again on page 5, briefly explaining the carbon leakage mechanism.

[35] And to avoid a financial crisis like in 2008. See Conac P.H., "Sustainable Corporate Governance in the EU: Reasonable Global Ambitions?", in *Revue Européenne du droit*, 2022, 4, 111-112.

[36] Paridhi S., Arora A., "Sustainability reporting: Current state and challenges", *Business Strategy & Development*, 2023, 14-15.

the framework is unlikely to provide security to investors or generate trust among shareholders.

Regarding the type of reporting, the issue lies in determining the data that should be disclosed for sustainability practices: due to the existence of different guidelines, there is significant variation in reporting among companies. This was a critical point in the previous NFRD, and a recital in the recent Reporting Directive acknowledges that some investors distrust non-financial reporting precisely because of its vagueness.[37] In fact, this often results in a mismatch between what the intended users want to know, on the one hand, and the disclosure made by corporations, on the other.

Numerous provisions are dedicated to modifying previous legislation and introducing new reporting duties, outlining the structure and the information that must be provided. While accurate and concretely applicable guidelines are awaited, pending the release of the European Financial Reporting Advisory Group (EFRAG)[38] indices[39] by June 2024, the Reporting Directive represents a decisive step towards the construction of a common information network. Its implementation will require several years, as explicitly stated, but this timeline will allow for the reorganization of the whole system. Moreover, this uniformity will serve as a solid foundation for other, more directly impactful provisions in terms of sustainable due diligence, supply chain re-design and sustainable responsibility.

Implementing this operation will require a considerable amount of time, primarily because the proposed standards will surpass the currently predominant ones. While the Commission recommends incorporating existing global standards whenever feasible, the necessity to comply with the GD requirements dictates the development of new standards.[40]

Regarding the concrete development of these new standards, in addition to their "centralized" development, other aspects are directly stressed by the Reporting Directive as prominent. In particular, the need for general coherence with the regulatory standards of other authorities is underlined.[41] As for the content, the Directive emphasizes disclosure in relation

[37] CSRD, Recital No. 8.

[38] Efrag is a private association established in 2001, encouraged by the European Commission to serve the public interest. For further information see www.efrag.org.

[39] Appendix II – Final CSRD requirements for the European Sustainability Reporting Standards (ESRS).

[40] *Ibidem*, Recital No. 38 and following.

[41] *Ibidem*, Recital No. 39 – The European Securities and Markets Authority (ESMA), the European Banking Authority (EBA) and the European Insurance and Occupational Pensions Authority (EIOPA) play a role in drafting regulatory technical stand-

to energy,[42] social factors (including working conditions)[43] and governance,[44] thus providing a holistic view of the sustainability-related aspects of the company.

Following this logic, all information should be listed in a separate section of the financial report already in use, so that the report may provide a complete picture of the activities.[45]

4. The connection with the Corporate Sustainability Due Diligence Directive (CS3D)

Disclosure has traditionally been the main tool of the EU legislator to promote sustainable corporate governance. However, the Commission is also striving to develop substantive requirements for companies in Europe. Admittedly, the CSRD is not the sole legislation addressing the role of companies in the green transition. Another significant legal text is the Corporate Sustainability Due Diligence Directive (UE) 2024/1760, amending Directive (EU) 2019/1937[46] and Regulation (EU) 2023/2859.[47]

Remarkably, the latter seems to take on board recent trends in due diligence[48] with a view to providing a European-wide regulatory framework. Such regulatory framework primarily seeks to prevent fragmentation detrimental to the internal market. It also places centrality on the value chain. The Due Diligence Directive aims to enhance corporate governance practices by integrating sustainability into corporate strategies and preventing

---

ards pursuant to Regulation (EU) 2019/2088 and there needs to be coherence between those regulatory technical standards and sustainability reporting standards.

[42] *Ibidem*, Recital No. 48.

[43] *Ibidem*, Recital No. 49.

[44] *Ibidem*, Recital No. 50.

[45] *Ibidem*, Recital No. 57: it states that a separate report could give the impression of sustainability matter as less important.

[46] Directive (EU) 2019/1937 of the European Parliament and of the Council of 23 October 2019 on the protection of persons who report breaches of Union law.

[47] Regulation (EU) 2023/2859 of the European Parliament and of the Council of 13 December 2023 establishing a European single access point providing centralised access to publicly available information of relevance to financial services, capital markets and sustainability.

[48] Rajavuori M., Savaresi A. and van Asselt H., "Mandatory due diligence laws and climate change litigation: Bridging the corporate climate accountability gap?", in *Regul. Gov*, 2023; Schilling-Vacaflor A. and Lenschow A., "Hardening foreign corporate accountability through mandatory due diligence in the European Union? New trends and persisting challenges", in *Regul. Gov*, 2021.

fragmentation of due diligence practices in the EU market. In essence, the overarching goal is to hold corporations more accountable for their negative environmental impacts.

CS3D Directive has undergone a complicated elaboration process and was approved only in May 2024, following a protracted and contentious procedure lasting months. The complexity of this process stems from the nature of the obligations it imposes. While the CSRD mandates disclosure, the CS3D establishes a corporate due diligence standard on sustainability issues for businesses operating in the EU. The new due diligence requirements apply to the company's direct actions and create legal liability for companies concerning environmental and human rights violations within their supply chain.

Under the new obligations, companies will be required to identify actual or potential adverse human rights and environmental impacts and take measures to prevent and mitigate them, resulting in a significantly more invasive intervention. However, the underlying premises of this initiative remain largely the same, i.e. the key role of corporate sustainability in transitioning to a climate-neutral and green economy and in achieving the UN Sustainable Development Goals. In this light, this proposal would ideally complement the CSRD and other initiatives stemming from the GD:[49] the goal remains unchanged, but the tools vary.

5. Sustainability and corporate governance

It is not easy to provide a definitive conclusion about the current interactions between sustainability and corporate governance.

Looking at how the CSRD affects the previous regulatory framework, it can be said that there is indeed a change of direction. Although a more precise balance sheet is not yet possible, since the concrete sustainability indicators have yet to be developed and their application will take several more years, the mandatory nature of this disclosure obligation and the size of the market share involved represent a rather important development.

The Reporting Directive, on its own, lacks decisiveness at this juncture. Nonetheless, it has the potential to represent a fundamental stride towards

[49] E.g. Regulation (EU) 2017/821 of the European Parliament and of the council 17 May 2017 laying down supply chain due diligence obligations for Union importers of tin, tantalum and tungsten, their ores, and gold originating from conflict-affected and high-risk areas, Regulation (EU) 2023/1115 of the European Parliament and of the Council of 31 May 2023 on the making available on the Union market and the export from the Union of certain commodities and products associated with deforestation and forest degradation and repealing Regulation (EU) 995/2010.

change. Positive effects can include the rise of a more responsible internal decision-making mechanism. In fact, to meet these new standards, a more proactive responsibility role will be required by management and supervisory bodies in charge of sustainability aspects.[50]

However, although the Reporting Directive primarily uses the term sustainability and references sustainable development only a few times in relation to the 2030 Agenda,[51] a direct incorporation of ecosystem sustainability into norms will likely require more effort and time. Despite its name, the CSRD embodies a conception of sustainability that is closer to the "economic nuance" of sustainable development rather than the emerging objective of ecological sustainability.

It is undeniably true that demands for increased and genuine sustainability from businesses have exponentially grown in recent years. Equally indisputable is the evolving legislative framework aligning with these changes. However, embracing a shift in corporate legitimacy towards social sustainability within the global context of the current transnational governance system, primarily rooted in capitalism, liberalism, and free trade, is inherently a long-term endeavour. The ecological dimension is a relatively recent consideration in corporate governance. Faced with this, the cautious approach and the compromising nature of the regulatory choices made in this field are no longer surprising, whereby ecological sustainability has, to date, struggled to emerge.

---

[50] Iozzelli L., "Boosting transparency or drowning in disclosure? Challenges and opportunities of the EU Corporate Sustainability Reporting Directive", 2 *GreenDeal-Net*, Policy brief, 2023.

[51] CSRD, Recitals No. 6 and 45.

Chapter 15

'SUSTAINABLE PROFIT'? THE GREEN DEAL ECONOMIC TRANSITION BETWEEN CRIMINAL LAW AND CORPORATE SOCIAL RESPONSIBILITY

Stefano Porfido

ABSTRACT: *This Chapter explores the economic transition towards sustainable corporate governance within the Green Deal. It focuses on two distinct yet interconnected directives: the new Directive on environmental crimes (ECD) and the Directive on corporate sustainable due diligence (CSDDD), highlighting their complementary relationship in tackling corporate environmental harm and their underlying notions of sustainability. The analysis suggests that the CSDDD embodies a proactive approach to due diligence obligations, potentially offering a more effective means to support the transition towards sustainable profit than traditional criminalisation approaches.*

KEYWORDS: *Environmental harm – Corporate governance – Sustainability due diligence.*

1. Introduction

In the view of the Commission, the transition towards climate-neutrality can only occur alongside a private economy transition. This entails a shift towards sustainable corporate governance models, i.e. towards 'sustainable businesses', as business plays a pivotal role "to succeed in the Union's transition to a climate-neutral and green economy and in delivering on the UN Sustainable Development Goals".[1] This is a challenging undertaking, as the move towards climate neutrality involves traditional, environmentally

[1] Proposal for a Directive on Corporate Sustainability Due Diligence, COM (2022) 71, 1.

harmful extractive practices to meet the growing demand of raw materials necessary for new technologies and energy forms.[2]

This Chapter explores two distinct, yet related directives adopted under the Green Deal and dedicated to preventing, minimising and bringing to an end corporate environmental harm: the recently adopted Directive on the Protection of the Environment through Criminal law (ECD),[3] and the long-negotiated Directive on Corporate Sustainability Due Diligence (CSDDD).[4] As better discussed later, these directives differ in nature: the former lays down criminal law measures, while the latter introduces due diligence obligations backed by administrative penalties. Despite this difference, both tackle corporate environmental harm through top-down command-and-control mechanisms of coercion to ensure corporate compliance with their obligations. This chapter delves into how these directives contribute to the shift towards sustainable businesses. Specifically, do they promote different understandings of the interplay between sustainability and business? If so, what role do their apparently similar sanctioning regimes play in supporting this interplay?

This chapter argues that these directives are complementary tools of environmental protection, revealing (at least partially) divergent understandings of sustainability. While the ECD appears to perpetuate the well-established rationale of environmental harm minimisation, the CSDDD seems to endorse a more ambitious objective. More precisely, it arguably aims to shape a novel relationship between businesses and sustainability, grounded on a convergence of private and public interests.

2. The complementary system of environmental protection: unlawful and lawful 'systemic' corporate harm

Article 3(3) of the Treaty on European Union (TEU) and Article 191 of the Treaty on the Functioning of the European Union (TFEU) set the objective of ensuring a high level of protection and improvement of the quality of the

[2] See Remme D. and Jackson J., "Green Mission Creep: The Unintended Consequences of Circular Economy Strategies for Electric Vehicles", in *J. Clean. Prod.*, 2023, 394.

[3] Directive (EU) 2024/1203 of the European Parliament and of the Council of 11 April 2024 on the protection of the environment through criminal law and replacing Directives 2008/99/EC and 2009/123/EC, OJ 2024 L 2024/1203, 30.4.2024.

[4] Directive (EU) 2024/1760 of the European Parliament and of the Council of 13 June 2024 on corporate sustainability due diligence and amending Directive (EU) 2019/1937 and Regulation (EU) 2023/2859, OJ L 2024/1760, 5.7.2024.

environment.[5] The ECD and the CSDDD constitute two complementary approaches to achieve this goal coherently with the overall Green Deal architecture. As stated in the Commission's Proposal on the Protection of the Environment through Criminal law (ECP), "criminal law is one part of a comprehensive EU strategy to protect and improve the status of the environment, a priority for the European Commission"[6] and "the envisaged new Environmental Crime Directive will help achieving the goals set by Article 191 of the TFEU, the Green Deal and the Biodiversity Strategy".[7] Grounded on the belief that "the introduction by all Member States of criminal sanctions is [...] essential to ensure the effective implementation of Union policy on environmental protection",[8] it introduces several measures to enhance the effectiveness of the ECD's regulatory regime based on a traditional command-and-control enforcement system.[9]

In a similar vein, in its Proposal for a Directive on Corporate Sustainability Due Diligence (CSDDP), the Commission emphasises the importance of promoting sustainable and responsible corporate behaviours throughout global value chains.[10] In this respect, the obligations set forth under the CSDDD are part of a broader framework of initiatives adopted pursuant to the Green Deal,[11] including the Biodiversity Strategy for 2030, the Action Plan on a Circular Economy,[12] the Farm to Fork strategy,[13] and the Chemicals strategy.[14] The CSDDD is innovative because it lays down substantive rules on sustainable corporate governance, utilizing a mix of self-regulatory

---

[5] On European Environmental Law, see Jans J.H. and Vedder H.H.B. *European Environmental Law. Treaty Based Law* (Europa Law Publishing 2023).

[6] COM (2021) 851, 2.

[7] *Ibidem*, 47 'General objectives'.

[8] COM (2021) 851, Explanatory Memorandum, §2, 7.

[9] These measures pursue key goals, namely improve harmonisation, effectiveness of investigation and prosecution, deterrence, collection and dissemination of statistical data. These goals are stated in COM (2021) 851 (fn. 6), 1-2. In this sense, the ECD pursues the harmonisation of qualified environmental offences (Article 3), and of the content of sanctions for both individuals and corporations (Articles 5 and 7); the adoption of common frame of limitation periods (Article 11), and of measure to enhance coordination and cooperation at strategic and operational levels between all competent authorities within a Member State and between Member States and EU bodies (Articles 19 and 20).

[10] COM (2022) 71 (fn. 1). See also Press Release, 23 February 2023, available at https://ec.europa.eu/commission/presscorner/detail/en/ip_22_1145.

[11] COM (2022) 71, Recital 11.

[12] COM (2020) 98.

[13] COM (2020) 381.

[14] COM (2020) 667.

instruments and coercive measures [15] primarily oriented towards ensuring compliance with corporate social responsibility (CSR) commitments. [16] As such, it goes beyond the typical procedural duties of disclosure established within the EU 'disclosure agenda'. [17] The adoption of this directive has been backed by political pressure coming from civil society, [18] the European Parliament [19] and the private sector. Specifically, companies have emphasised the need for greater harmonization in the area of due diligence to improve legal certainty and ensure a level playing field, [20] considering the growing fragmented body of national laws on human rights and environmental due diligence, such as the French 2017 *Loi relative au devoir de vigilance*, the 2019 *Loi Pacte*, and the German 2021 *Sorgfaltspflichtengesetz*. [21]

The ECD and the CSDDD converge around three environmental macro-objectives: safeguarding biodiversity, management of waste, and curbing pollution, particularly pollution caused by chemical substances. This convergence highlights where the Commission is focusing its efforts to strengthen the 'environmental rule of law' [22] and facilitate the achievement

---

[15] See *infra* at § 4 of this Chapter.

[16] See COM (2022) 71, 21. Recital 6 of the CSDDD refers to the OECD's notion of due diligence as defined in its 'Guidelines for Multinational Enterprises' 2011 as the "the process through which enterprises can identify, prevent, mitigate and account for how they address their actual and potential adverse impacts as an integral part of business decision-making and risk management systems" 24 §14. However, more recently the OECD has refined this concept as "an on-going, proactive and reactive process (emph. added)" in OECD Due Diligence Guidance for Responsible Mineral Supply Chains for Upstream Actors" 1, at https://mneguidelines.oecd.org/An-introduction-to-the-OECD-Due-Diligence-Guidance-for-upstream-actors.pdf.

[17] The legal initiatives constituting the EU disclosure agenda are listed in COM (2022) 71, Recital 11 and in CSDDD, Recital 62.

[18] See for instance the civil society organisations and trade unions joint statement 'Civil Society Statement', 2022, available at https://corporatejustice.org/wp-content/uploads/2022/05/CSO_statement_CSDDDD_EN.pdf. At the academic level, see joint Statement from Johnston A. et al, "Corporate Governance for Sustainability Statement" in The Harvard Law School Forum on Corporate Governance, 2020, at https://corpgov.law.harvard.edu/2020/01/07/corporate-governance-for-sustainability-statement/.

[19] Resolution of 17 December 2020 on Sustainable Corporate Governance 2020/2137(INI).

[20] COM (2022) 71, 11 and 18 'Stakeholder consultations'.

[21] *Ibidem*, 1, fn. 3, and CSDDD Recital 31. For a comprehensive analysis of the CSDDP and of its legal antecedents, see Pietrancosta A., "Codification in Company Law of General CSR Requirements: Pioneering Recent French Reforms and EU Perspectives" in European Corporate Governance Institute – Law Working Paper No. 639/2022, 2022, available at https://papers.ssrn.com/sol3/papers.cfm?abstract_id=4083398.

[22] The environmental rule of law is a concept firstly established within the UNEP

of the overall goals of the Green Deal. More in detail, the ECD and the CSDDD determine the material scope of their environmental obligations through a sectorial approach. The ECD outlines 20 basic criminal offences, targeting the worst types of environmental criminality,[23] as clarified in several reports from international law enforcement agencies.[24] Unlike the 2008 ECD, the new Directive on environmental crimes directly sets out the criminalized offences to improve legal certainty and harmonization when transposed at the national level. As detailed under ECD Article 3, the offences defined therein require qualified unlawful conducts, considering not only conduct breaching EU and domestic laws[25] but also those carried out under authorisations that are either illegally obtained or 'in manifest breach of relevant substantive legal requirements'.[26] Furthermore, Article 3(3) makes

Governing Council Dec. 27/9, Advancing Justice, Governance and Law for Environmental Sustainability, U.N. Doc. UNEP/GC.27/17 (Mar. 12, 2013). The UNEP (2019) 'Environmental Rule of Law: First Global Report', 8, defines this notion drawing from broader rule of law principles, as characterised by three related components, namely law should be consistent with fundamental rights; law should be inclusively developed and fairly effectuated; and law should bring forth accountability not just on paper, but in practice—such that the law becomes operative through observance of, or compliance with, the law. The environmental rule of law incorporates these components and applies them in the environmental context, governing "the vital link between humans and the environment that support human life and society, as well as life on the planet". On the environmental rule of law, see Kreilhuber A. and Kariuki A., "Environmental Rule of Law in the Context of Sustainable Development", in *Geo Envtl. L Rev*, 2020, 32, 591. See also the notion of the 'rule of ecological law' elaborated by Garver to capture a normative idea of law that is founded not only in legal principles but also in planetary boundaries and ecological limits. In his words: "the 'rule of law' means that global regulatory limits required to meet ecological limits and ensure fair sharing of the earth's bounty must be respected": see Garver G., "The Rule of Ecological Law: The Legal Complement to Degrowth Economics", in *Sustainability*, 2013, 5, 316, 319.

[23] See the offences listed under Article 3 ECD, which include qualified penal statues sanctioning serious breaches of EU legislation on chemicals (c)(d); waste disposal and shipments (f)(g); ship recycling (h); ship-source discharges of polluting substances (i); water abstraction (m); wildlife and habitat protections (n)(o)(q)(r); harvesting and trade in timber (p); handling of fluorinated greenhouses gases causing ozone depletion (s)(t).

[24] E.g. UNEP-Interpol Rapid Response Assessment: 'The Rise of Environmental Crime: A Growing Threat to Natural Resources Peace, Development and Security' June 2016. See further the Commission's Communication on stepping up the fight against environmental crime, COM (2021) 814, 1.

[25] Article 3 § 1. Specifically, a conduct is unlawful when either (1) constitutes a breach of Union law contributing to the pursuit of at least one of the objectives of the Union's policy on the environment or (2) a law, regulation or administrative provision of a Member State or a decision taken by a competent authority of a Member State that gives effect to such Union law.

[26] *Ibidem.* Article 3 § 1 reaffirms the illegal nature of the authorisation when it is ob-

clear that in addition to the 'unlawfulness clause',[27] offences must be qualified by causing severe environmental damage.[28] Such high thresholds of severity, typically associated with corporate harm,[29] make the offences under the ECD comparable to Ecocide.[30] The scope of the CSDDD is limited to obligations for European and non-European companies regarding actual and potential human rights adverse impacts and environmental adverse impacts, with respect to their own operations, the operations of their subsidiaries, and the operations carried out by their business partners in the chains of activities of those companies.[31] Such impacts are relevant under the CSDDD if they constitute a breach of human rights and environmental obligations set forth by several international instruments listed in the Annex to the CSDDD, part I and II. The international environmental obligations listed therein mainly parallel the sectors covered by the provisions under the ECD, including the protection of wildlife, management of waste and chemical pollution.[32]

---

tained fraudulently or by corruption, extortion or coercion. The latter requirement -'in manifest breach of relevant substantive legal requirements' – is a novelty compared to 2008 ECD, and according to Recital 10 ECD, it should be interpreted as referring to an obvious and substantial breach of relevant substantive legal requirements, and is not intended to include breaches of procedural requirements or minor elements of the authorization. This requirement seems expanding the unlawfulness of the conducts beyond the traditional purview of administrative law, as to encompass a systemic scope. On the traditional use of the 'unlawfulness clause' see the following fn. 27.

[27] On the 'unlawfulness clause' as traditionally understood as a coordination clause between administrative and criminal law, see Di Landro A., "Models of Environmental Criminal Law, Between Dependence on Administrative Law and Autonomy", in *Eur. Energy Environ. Law Rev*, 2022, 31, 272; Faure M., "The Revolution in Environmental Criminal Law in Europe", in *VELJ*, 2017, 35, 321.

[28] Specifically, Article 3 § 3 requires that penalties "consisting of (a) the destruction of, or widespread and systematic damage, which is either irreversible or long-lasting to, an ecosystem of considerable size or environmental value or a habitat within a protected site, or (b) widespread and substantial damage which is either irreversible or long lasting to the quality of air, soil, or water".

[29] These include criteria such as 'non-negligible quantity' in Article 3 § 1, lett. (e)(i); (f); (l); (m); (n); (o); 'substantial damage' in Article 3 § 1, lett (d); (e)(ii); (i); (j); § 3; or the exclusion of individual behaviours relevance, such as in Article 3, § 1 let. (h) "(...) shall not apply to individual cases". See also § 5, which sets the criteria to discern between negligible and non-negligible quantity of harm.

[30] As stated in Recital 21 ECD.

[31] As set out in Article 1 § 1 of the CSDDD.

[32] Annex I to the CSDDD, part I, points 15 and 16 and Part II, list environmental numerous conventions, including those on protection of wildlife, e.g. the 1973 Convention on International Trade in Endangered Species of Wild CITES and the 1992 Convention on Biological Diversity; on waste disposal, e.g. the 1989 Basel Convention on

As stated earlier, the two directives enforce a complementary system of environmental protection. Complementarity here derives from the qualification of corporate environmental harm. From a social perspective, corporate environmental harm *ex crimine* represents a narrow and legally qualified set of broader and often qualitatively and quantitatively more disruptive exploitation of nature for economic purposes.[33] This exploitation is 'systemic' insofar as built into the fabric of everyday, ordinary life, through ideological strategies of sterilisation of the public perception of the harm and of its consequent social acceptance.[34] Significantly, James McCarthy and Scott Prudham connect environmental harm with neoliberalism, contending that neoliberalism is necessarily a project of environmental destruction, for it is rooted in classical liberal understanding on social relations to nature.[35]

One could better grasp the sense of this complementarity by framing corporate environmental harm within two dimensions of corporate activity, namely the pathological and physiological one. The claimed complementarity refers to a continuum of environmental protection that extends from the pathological sphere, encompassing harmful corporate activities labelled as criminal, to the broader dimension of the 'adverse impacts' stemming from the physiological corporate life.[36]

While the ECD *ex post* criminal liability system is limited to defining and addressing corporates' pathological, i.e. criminal activities, the CSDDD pursues a wider goal, namely, to promote corporate responsibility for the "environmental adverse impacts generated throughout the life cycle of production and use and disposal of product or provision of services, at the level of own operations, subsidiaries and in value chains".[37] In short, through *ex*

---

the Control of Transboundary Movements of Hazardous Wastes and their Disposal; on curbing pollution due to chemical pollutants, e.g. the 2013 Minamata Convention on Mercury, the 2001 Stockholm Convention Persistent Organic Pollutants.

[33] See e.g. Hall M., *Exploring Green Crime: Introducing the Legal, Social and Criminological Contexts of Environmental Harm*, Bloomsbury, 2017.

[34] White R., *Crimes Against Nature: Environmental Criminology and Ecological Justice*, Routledge, 2013, 148.

[35] McCarthy J. and Prudham S., "Neoliberal Nature and the Nature of Neoliberalism", in *Geoforum*, 2004, 35, 275.

[36] The distinction between pathological and physiological activities echoes the legal-illegal continuum classificatory approach to 'power crimes', developed within sociological scholarship. See Ruggiero V., *The Crimes of the Economy: A Criminological Analysis of Economic Thought*, Routledge, 2013.

[37] COM (2022) 71, see for instance Recitals 17 and 27. See also, for instance, the provisions in CSDDD Article 1 referring to the operations of the company and of its

ante social responsibility-tailored tools, it attempts to redefine physiological yet harmful operations, i.e. the "lawful but awful" activities.[38]

Such qualitative complementarity also has implications for the scope of application of the measures. The ECD operates within the legal frameworks of Member States' criminal law and thus primarily falls within their territorial jurisdiction. Differently, the CSDDD envisions a system of extraterritorial, global due diligence obligations. Precisely, Article 1 extends such obligations to EU companies' own operations, those of their subsidiaries and the value chain operations carried out by entities with which the company has an established business relationship. In essence, it covers the whole global value chain of EU companies. Given the potential economic impact of such obligations, Article 2 of the CSDDD limits its personal scope to certain companies only, those which meet specific quantitative thresholds.[39]

3. A paradigmatic example of 'sustainability law': the criminalisation duties of the ECD

The ECD introduces a novel approach to penalties that represents a significant improvement compared to the previous punitive regime under the 2008 ECD. While this latter directive only referred to the generic 'effective, proportionate and dissuasive' formula,[40] the new ECD determines the typology and the quantum of sanctions, traditionally considered an exclusive prerogative of national legislatures.[41] In addition to dictating specific terms

subsidiaries and partners in the value chains, to be understood as the routinely operations of all businesses throughout their global value chains, as clarified in its Recitals, e.g. No. 5, 7, and 29.

[38] Passas N., "Lawful but Awful: Legal Corporate Crimes", in *J. Socio Econ.*, 2005, 34, 771.

[39] CSDDD Article 2, § 1 and § 2. These thresholds are based on two concurring criteria, namely the number of employees and the net generated either globally (for the EU company) or within the EU (for the non-EU company). The final agreed text has amended the reference to high-risk sector that was established under the original text proposed by the Commission. Precisely, previous COM (2022) 71, Article 2, § 1, (b) and §2, (b) limited the scope of the CSDDD to high-risk sectors only, such as textiles, agriculture, forestry, fisheries, and mining, for which OECD's guidelines existed.

[40] See Vagliansindi G.M. "The EU Environmental Crime Directive", in Farmer A., Faure M. and Vagliasindi G.M. (eds.), *Environmental Crime in Europe*, Bloomsbury Publishing, 2017, 31, 50, for whom lack of harmonisation in this sector constituted one of the major shortcomings of the 2008 ECD.

[41] See di Martino A., "Inter-legality and Criminal law", in Klabbers J. and Palombella G. (eds.), *The challenge of inter-legality*, CUP, 2019, 250, 362. The legislative compe-

of imprisonment for individuals and fines for legal persons,[42] the ECD mandates that Member States adopt a toolbox approach to sanctioning.[43] This approach includes reparation duties for both legal and individual persons, recognizing that effective environmental protection requires both *ex ante* deterrent measures and *ex post* remediation in accordance with the polluter pays principle.[44]

Despite this innovative approach, the ECD justifies the criminalisation of legal persons on utilitarian grounds, with deterrence as the core rationale for both the 2008 ECD and the new Directive.[45] More precisely, criminal law in the environmental sector has evolved in line with patterns of economic rationalisation of punishment.[46] The underlying assumption

---

tency of the EU in this sector is based on Article 83 §2 of the Treaty on the Functioning of the European Union (TFEU), which was introduced in 2012 with the Lisbon Treaty, and thus after the adoption of the 2008 ECD. This Article provides the EU institutions with the competency to adopt harmonisation rules with regard to the definition of criminal offences and sanctions in the area concerned.

[42] Articles 5 and 7 of the ECD. Respectively: Article 5 §2 stipulates that sanctions for individual must include maximum terms of imprisonment of at least ten, eight, five, or three years depending on the specific offense; Article 7 §3 stipulates that Member States are to ensure that the maximum level of fines is, depending on the specific type of offending, not less than 5% of the worldwide turnover or €40 million; or 3% of the worldwide turnover or €24 million.

[43] For an early discussion on toolbox approaches for environmental crimes, see Faure M. and Svatikova K., "Criminal or Administrative Law to Protect the Environment? Evidence from Western Europe", in *J. Env. L.*, 2012, 24, 253. For a more recent discussion on the synergies between behavioural instruments and standard regulatory tools in environmental law and policy, see Shen Y. and Faure M., "Behavioural Instruments in Environmental Law and Policy: Potential and Challenges", in *RECIEL*, 33, 2024, 3.

[44] Faure M., "Effective, Proportional and Dissuasive Penalties in the Implementation of the Environmental Crime and Ship-Source Pollution Directives: Questions and Challenges", in *Eur. Energy Environ. Law Rev*, 2010, 256.

[45] See the Commission Proposal of 9 February 2007, COM (2007) 51, 2007/0022 (COD), particularly § 1: "only criminal penalties will have a sufficiently dissuasive effect for several reasons". Almost 15 years later, the ECD shows that the Commission's position on the matter has not changed. The underlying assumption is that the threat of harsh punishment, including prison, would achieve better compliance with environmental law provisions than any other sanctions. In this regard, see for instance Seerden R., Heldeweg M.A. and Deketelaere K.R. (eds.), *Public Environmental Law in the European Union and the United States. A Comparative Analysis*, Kluwer Law International, 2002. For early critics to the Commission's position in this sector, see Öberg J., "Criminal Sanctions in the Field of EU Environmental Law", in *New J. Eur. Crim. Law*, 2011, 2, 402, who points out that this assumption is often not supported by empirical evidence.

[46] Prittwitz C., "Teoria e prassi del diritto penale dell'ambiente", in *Riv. Trim. dir. pen. Econ.*, 2010, 3, 487, who claims that environmental criminal law should be considered as economic criminal law, for it pursues the enforcement of economic rationalisation of ecological policies.

is that perpetrators are 'rational actors' who conduct costs-benefit analyses when deciding whether to comply with environmental regulations.[47] In this respect, criminal punishment is meant to represent a 'cost' that should outweigh the potential economic gains from the crime.[48] The public stigma attached to it, along with the more pervasive investigative powers afforded to law enforcement agencies in criminal law procedures, represent additional costs improving the overall deterrent effects of criminalisation.[49]

From this economic behavioural perspective, criminal environmental harm stemming from licit economic activities constitutes a market failure, i.e., an adverse externality. Externalities are here understood as 'costs' not accounted for in dyadic market exchanges mediated by price, which spill over to affect third parties.[50] The imposition of top-down coercive legal measures, such as criminal sanctions, aims to correct these failures through non-market costs. Coherently with this approach, the ECD intertwines the concept of 'effectiveness' with the general theory of deterrence.[51] Through the standard formula of 'effective, dissuasive and proportionate' sanctions, the Union intends to enforce a system of measures that are functional in enhancing dissuasiveness, i.e. effective in influencing (allegedly) rational economic actors to internalise such costs.[52]

---

[47] In a seminal paper developing an economic analysis of criminal law, Becker G.S., "Crime and punishment: An Economic Approach" in Journal of Political Economy, 1968, 76, 169, 171, argues that firms and individuals are rational economic actors who are motivated by wealth or utility-maximising intentions. See however Baldwin R., "The New Punitive Regulation", in *Mod. L. Rev.*, 2004, 67, 351, who claims that companies (even top ones) deal with punitive regulatory risks in a confused manner and that even when they do act rationally, this may not lead to compliance.

[48] Economic scholarship has attempted to calculate the exact threshold of severity for a sanction to be effectively deterrent. In this regard, see Faure M. and Partain R.A., *Environmental Law and Economics: Theory and Practice*, CUP, 2019, 222-225.

[49] Particularly, when the offender belongs to those social groups that are sensitive to status deprivation and censure, such as corporate officials. On the expressive function of criminal law for environmental crimes see Hedman S., "Expressive Functions of Criminal Sanctions in Environmental Law", in *Geo Wash L Rev*, 1990, 59, 889.

[50] See William D., "The Politics of Externalities: Neo-liberalism, Rising Powers and Property Rights", in *ESCR Rising Powers Programme*, 2010, available at https://www.compas.ox.ac.uk/wp-content/uploads/WP-2010-OS Davies_Social_Externalities_Neo-Liberalism.pdf.

[51] Effectiveness is a relational concept. It presupposes a functionalist nexus between particular goals set by the policy maker and the instruments used to reach such goals. See Faure, "Effective, Proportional and Dissuasive Penalties in the Implementation of the Environmental Crime and Ship source Pollution Directives: Questions and Challenges", cit., 259, supra fn. 44.

[52] COM (2021) 851, 7 reaffirms the necessity of criminal law sanctions for achieving

The unlawfulness clause set under Article 3 of the ECD serves this behavioural perspective, by providing these actors with a pre-assessed and certainty-oriented legal guidance on the lawfulness perimeter. In essence, the ECD aims to influence the behaviour of economic operators, i.e. corporations, by mandating the internalisation of costs associated with environmental compliance consistently with economic efficiency concerns.

For the purposes of this Chapter, such unlawfulness clause is indicative of a logic, where the goal of enhancing environmental protection must be balanced with other economic and social goals.[53] These include ensuring a level playing field within the EU internal market by protecting economic actors from unfair competition due to illegal business activities.[54]

This balancing rationale characterises the ECD and mirrors the traditional understanding of sustainable development, bringing together economic, environmental and social concerns. Notably, this understanding has been subjected to criticism, including the view that it reflects an artificial anthropocentric perspective, thereby neglecting direct obligations towards an overarching conceptualisation of the ecological dimension.[55]

Beside these criticisms, the ECD appears to promote a model of sustainable business that lacks transformative ethos, for it sets out environmental obligations within a broader discourse of economic efficiency. In this sense, the ECD's deterrence rationale aligns with the traditional goal of environmental law, which is to set external constraints on both public and private activities. As Viñuales argues, this goal fails to challenge the conceptual foundations of

---

deterrence. For a critical reading, see Öberg, "Criminal Sanctions in the Field of EU Environmental Law", cit., 406, supra fn. 45.

[53] Such negotiations are reflected in the different and often conflicting EU institutions' positions emerging during legislative processes, as one could see by examining the internal documents available at https://eur-lex.europa.eu/legal-content/EN/HIS/?uri=celex:52021PC0851#2022-04-29_DIS_byCONSIL. The underlying complexity of the negotiations between different political spheres and clusters of interests characterising the negotiations that leaded to the adoption of the ECD could be appreciated by consulting the Commission Staff Working Document Impact Assessment Report Accompanying the document Proposal for a Directive of the European Parliament and of the Council on the Protection of the Environment through Criminal Law and replacing Directive 2008/99/EC – SWD/2021/465 final, particularly Annex 7 Public Consultation Report, available at https://eur-lex.europa.eu/legal-content/EN/TXT/?uri=celex%3A52021SC0465.

[54] COM (2021) 851, 15.

[55] See, e.g., Bosselmann K., "Strong and Weak Sustainable Development: Making Differences in the Design of Law", in *SAJELP*, 2006, 13, 39. On this point, see *infra* fn. 59. On the meaning and evolution of sustainable development in the EU, see Barral V., "The Principle of Sustainable Development" in Krämer L. and Orlando E. (eds.), *Principles of Environmental Law,* Elgar, 2017, 103.

such activities, including the notion of linear economic growth and the legal category of property.[56] Thus, in his view, classical environmental law and related enforcement measures, such as environmental criminal law, function as "external shocks or exogenous disturbances to normal economic processes",[57] i.e. they remain external to and at the core of economic transactions. Therefore, they do not possess transformative force.

For these reasons, one could infer that the criminalisation duties under the ECD belong to a model of law that could be broadly understood in terms of 'sustainability law', i.e. the law that implements the compromise logic informing sustainable development. In other words, the ECD's criminal law constrains corporate freedom to operate in an environmentally detrimental manner, as long as the detrimental impacts remains within legal thresholds of non-criminal harms.[58] Thus understood, the ECD could not be associated with a thicker notion of 'sustainable law', which entails an idea of law that shapes its legal categories by triggering the structural prioritisation of positive obligations towards nature over profit-oriented corporate ends.[59] Therefore,

---

[56] Viñuales J., *The Organisation of the Anthropocene: In Our Hands?*, Brill, 2018.

[57] *Ibidem*, 17.

[58] One could object that the consistency of the operator's conduct with the authorisation legally issued by the public authorities prevents labelling the consequences of such conduct as environmentally detrimental. This thesis should be rejected under two considerations. To begin with, it contrasts with the new Article 3 §1 that, as earlier stated (see supra fn. 25-27), requires the authorisation not to be 'in manifest breach of relevant substantive legal requirements'. As such, the legitimacy of the operator's conduct should be assessed systemically, being its consistency with the authorisation a relevant yet not decisive indicator of a legitimate behaviour. In the second place, such an objection misleadingly confuses the legal qualification of a certain behaviour as criminally or administratively licit, with the empirical reality underlying this qualification. In plain words, the qualification of a conduct as criminally licit does not excluded the environmentally detrimental nature of such conduct, as acknowledged by the European Parliament that in its 'Resolution of 24 November 2021 on a European strategy for critical raw materials' 2021/2011(INI), let. (w) states: "whereas in its report entitled 'Growth without economic growth', the European Environment Agency says that economic growth is closely linked to increased production, consumption and use of resources, with negative effects on nature, climate and human health *and that current research suggests that it is unlikely economic growth can be completely divorced from its environmental impact* (emph. added)", available at https://www.europarl.europa.eu/doceo/document/TA-9-2021-0468_EN.html.

[59] In this sense, the notion of sustainable law recalls that of 'ecological law' as developed by Garver (fn. 22). For a comprehensive analysis on ecological law, see Sbert C., *The Lens of Ecological Law. A look at Mining*, Edward Elgar, 2020; Anker K., Burton P.D., Garver G., Maloney M. and Sbert C., *From Environmental Law to Ecological Law*, Routledge, 2021. For a discussion on the relationships, as well on the differences, between international environmental law and ecological restoration, see Cliquet A., *Eco-*

despite its relevance in ensuring corporate compliance with environmental regulations, the ECD seems lacking that transformative force needed to achieve the Green Deal's goal of managing the transition that "will lead to significant structural changes in business models".[60]

4. The CSDDD and corporate governance

In line with the aforementioned complementarity, the CSDDD addresses corporate environmental harm through the CSR rationale.[61] Despite its growing popularity, CSR remains a complex and elusive notion that has evolved over time, intersecting with social themes, such as ethics, environment, poverty, and sustainable development.[62] Traditionally, CSR could be broadly defined as a voluntary approach adopted by corporations beyond regulatory compliance by incorporating social and environmental concerns in decision-making processes.[63]

---

logical Restoration and International Law (Routledge 2016). On the normative and transformative dimension of sustainable law, as shaping legal categories such as property rights, see the contributions collected in Taylor P. and Grinlinton D. (eds.), *Property Rights and Sustainability: Toward A New Vision of Property Rights to Meet Ecological Challenges*, Nijhoff Publishers, 2011, particularly the contribution of Bosselmann K., "Property Rights and Sustainability: Can They Be Reconciled", therein at 23.

[60] COM (2019) 640, § 2.2.1. If criminal law could be used for such a purpose is a topic that entails both regulatory and enforcement-related issues and falls outside the scope of this analysis.

[61] See, e.g., Bueno N., Bernaz N., Holly G., and Martin-Ortega O., "The EU Directive on Corporate Sustainability Due Diligence (CSDDD): The Final Political Compromise" in *BHRJ*, 2024. The scholarship on business and human rights is massive. Among the Italian literature, see Bonfanti A., *Business and Human Rights in Europe. International Law Challenges*, Routledge, 2019; Macchi C., *Business, Human Rights and the Environment: The Evolving Agenda*, Springer, 2022; Fasciglione M., *Impresa e diritti umani nel diritto internazionale. Teoria e prassi*, Giappichelli, 2024.

[62] Kolk A., "The Social Responsibility of International Business: From Ethics and the Environment to CSR and Sustainable Development", in *J. World Bus.*, 2016, 51, 23. On CSR, see also, e.g., Ramasatry A., "Corporate Social Responsibility versus Business and Human Rights: Bridging the Gap between Responsibility and Accountability", in *Journal of Human Rights*, 14, 2015, 237; Bijlmakers S., *Corporate Social Responsibility, Human Rights and the Law*, Routledge, 2018; McWilliams A.,, Waldman D.A., Rupp D.E., Siegel D.S, and Stahl G.K., *The Oxford Handbook of Corporate Social Responsibility. Psycological and Organizational Perspectives*, OUP, 2019.

[63] See Mazurkiewicz P., "Corporate Environmental Responsibility: Is a Common CSR Framework Possible?", in *World Bank Group*, 2004, available at https://documents.worldbank.org/en/publication/documents-reports/documentdetail/577051468339093024/corporate-environmental-responsibility-is-a-common-csr-framework-possible; Scherer A.G., Palazzo G., "Toward a political conception of corporate responsibility: Business and society seen from a Habermasian perspective", in *Academy of Management Review,*

The CSDDD innovates this understanding. It marks the shift from a voluntary approach to CSR to a mandatory due diligence (MDD) regime. [64] This evolution has been gradual. The EU's initial approach to CSR in 2001 defined it as "a concept whereby companies integrate social and environmental concerns in their business operations and in their interaction with their stakeholders on a voluntary basis". [65] Post the 2008 global financial crisis, the EU's CSR approach changed. The 2011 Communication 'A renewed EU strategy 2011/2014 for Corporate Social Responsibility' redefined CSR as "the responsibility of enterprises for their impact on society", linking it to international legal instruments such as the UN Global Compact and the OECD Guidelines for Multinational Enterprises. [66] The removal of the "voluntary basis" formula, coupled with the preference for "impact" over "concerns", suggests a shift towards a mandatory connotation in this new EU approach to CSR. [67]

The EU's 'disclosure agenda' has further promoted a concept of responsibility based on obligations rather than solely voluntary commitments. The recent Corporate Sustainability Reporting Directive (CSRD) is illustrative of this. [68] It mandates an audit certification for sustainability information, thereby enhancing the reliability of duties to disclose relevant non-financial information, such as environmental performance. In Faure's words, "CSR is no longer only seen as voluntary, but increasingly replaced by an institutional framework for corporate accountability,"[69] encompassing rights and duties for companies along global value chains. Tort lawyers expect CSR playing a novel role in corporate (climate) litigation, particular-

2007, 1096. For a critique on CSR, see Pillay G., "The Limits to self-regulation and voluntarism: from corporate social responsibility to corporate accountability" in *Amicus Curiae,* 99, 2014, 10.

[64] This regime is based on civil liability. See Jędrzejowska-Schiffauer I., Szoszkiewicz L., Wilde-Ramsing J., Booth K., Barraud de Lagerie P. and Faracik B., "Towards EU-wide mandatory human rights and environmental due diligence for business: a breakthrough in Europe and beyond?", in *Polish YBInt'l Law*, 2023, XLII, 245.

[65] Commission 'Green Paper on Promoting a European Framework for Corporate Social Responsibility' COM (2001) 366.

[66] COM (2011) 681.

[67] In this sense, see Greco R., "Corporate Human Rights Due Diligence and Civil Liability: Steps Forward Towards Effective Protection?", in *Diritti umani e diritto internazionale*, 1, 2023, 5.

[68] Directive 2022/2464/EU L 322/15, 14.12.2022, amending Directive 2014/95/EU L 330/1, 15.11.2014.

[69] Faure M., "Environmental liability of companies" in European Parliament's Policy Department for Citizens' Rights and Constitutional Affairs, 2020, 89, available at https://www.europarl.europa.eu/thinktank/en/document/IPOL_STU(2020)651698.

ly in North-South relationships.[70] Arguably, the CSDDD represents the culmination of this shift towards MDD regimes,[71] establishing a robust enforcement apparatus based on "national supervisory authorities"[72] with powers including ensuring remediation of actual adverse impacts,[73] imposing administrative penalties,[74] assessing the effectiveness of voluntary remedial actions,[75] and enforcing civil liability for damage caused to natural or legal persons entailing a right to full compensation.[76]

Does this new coercive approach to CSR imply a different understanding of sustainability compared to the ECD, aligning with a vision of sustainable law? The answer seems to be negative.

The CSDDD does not pursue transformative goals regarding the profit-oriented essence of business. It leaves the private property structure of corporations and, consequently, their profit-centred ends are unchanged. This point relates to Beate Sjåfjell's work on the shareholder primacy norm in corporate law.[77] Such norm reflects the core duty of corporate boards to promote the company's interests. However, as Sjåfjell argues, shareholder primacy is not a legal requirement, since legal systems allow some margin to the board, and by extension to the management, to shape business activities in a sustainable manner.[78] It is rather a 'social norm', rooted in legal-economic theories and manifested as a "legal myths […] dictating that the

[70] See, e.g., Van Dam C., "Tort Law and Human Rights: Brothers in Arms on the Role of Tort Law in the Area of Business and Human Rights", in *JETL*, 2011, 2, 221; Enneking L., Foreign *Direct Liability and beyond. Exploring the Role of Tort Law in Promoting International Corporate Social Responsibility and Accountability*, Eleven International Publishing, 2012, 758.

[71] See Rajavuori M., Savaresi A. and Van Asselt H., "Mandatory Due Diligence Laws and Climate Change Litigation: Bridging the Corporate Climate Accountability Gap?", in *Regul. Gov*, 2023, available at https://onlinelibrary.wiley.com/doi/10.1111/rego.12518.

[72] CSDDD Articles 24, 25 and 28.

[73] *Ibidem*, Article 12. Ex Article 3 let. (t) 'remediation' means restoration of the affected person or persons, communities or environment to a situation equivalent or as close as possible to the situation they would have been in had an actual adverse impact not occurred, in proportion to the company's implication in the adverse impact, including by financial or non-financial compensation provided by the company to a person or persons affected by the actual adverse impact and, where applicable, reimbursement of the costs incurred by public authorities for any necessary remedial measures.

[74] *Ibidem*, Article 27.

[75] *Ibidem*, Article 25 § 4 and 27 § 2, let. (f).

[76] *Ibidem*, Article 29.

[77] Sjåfjell B., *Reforming EU Company Law to Secure the Future of European Business*, University of Oslo Faculty of Law Research Paper 2021-05, 2021, 191.

[78] *Ibidem*, 205.

board and senior managers are the 'agents' of the shareholders and must maximise returns to shareholders".[79] Thus, the corporate shareholders primacy paradigm constitutes "a systemically entrenched barrier to the contribution of business to sustainability".[80]

The CSDDD does not displace shareholders' primacy in favour of sustainable value creation. In June 2023, the European Parliament voted to open inter-institutional negotiations based on the proposed Article 25 of the CSDDD, which would have required directors to consider the consequences of their decisions for sustainability, including human rights, climate change and environmental impacts, in the short, medium, and long terms.[81] However, the final text of the CSDDD does not contain this provision. While these duties aimed to bridge social and environmental concerns with company interests,[82] they likely held more symbolic value than practical relevance. Specifically, former Article 25 of the Proposal did not seem to transform the company's defining objective, i.e. profit.[83] As Sheldon Leader notes, from a corporate law perspective, the Board of Directors, the Managerial Board and/or the CEOs are (or perhaps should be) accountable to those holding sovereign interests, usually the shareholders, whose interests determine the corporation's purposes.[84] Thus, to radically challenge the Friedmannian prioritisation of profitability over equitable goals,[85] the Commission's Proposal and the current CSDDD should have targeted the cluster of sovereign interests, i.e. the

[79] *Ibidem*, 206. The difference between shareholder primacy and the legal notion of shareholder value is stressed by Millon D., "Radical Shareholder Primacy", in *University of St. Thomas Law Journal*, 2013, 10(4), 1013.

[80] Sjåfjell (fn. 77), 205. On this topic, see also Sjåfjell B., Johnston A., Anker-Sørensen L. and D. Millon, "Shareholder Primacy: The Main Barrier to Sustainable Companies", in Sjåfjell B. and Richardson B.J. (eds.), *Company Law and Sustainability: Legal Barriers and Opportunities*, CUP, 2015, 79.

[81] However, it deleted Article 26 that related to setting up and oversight of due diligence by giving due considerations to inputs from stakeholders and civil society organisations.

[82] COM (2022) 71, Recitals 63-64.

[83] This provision sparked criticisms. See, Krüger A.P. and. Hansen J.L, *Response to the Proposal for a Directive on Corporate Sustainability Due Diligence by Nordic and Baltic Company Law Scholars*, Nordic & European Company Law Working Paper, 2022, 22(01), 20-21, available at https://papers.ssrn.com/sol3/papers.cfm?abstract_id=4139249.

[84] Sheldon L., "Accountable Corporate Governance", in Bovens M., Goodin R. and Schillemans T. (eds.), *The Oxford Handbook of Public Accountability*, OUP, 2014, 354, 360-363.

[85] Friedman M., "The Social Responsibility of Business Is to Increase Its Profits", in *New York Times Magazine*, 13 September 1970, https://www.nytimes.com/1970/09/13/archives/a-friedman-doctrine-the-social-responsibility-of-business-is-to.html.

property, rather than those subordinated to it. Despite the CSDDD's emphatic wording serving social interests and aligning with original ethical conceptions of CSR,[86] under this directive's regime, profit still defines the corporation's end.

Nothing new under then sun, then? In other words, does the CSDDD merely perpetuate the balancing logic among intersecting spheres that characterise the traditional understanding of sustainable development?

While the foregoing considerations might suggest so, there are also reasons to conclude otherwise. For one, a more nuanced understanding of sustainability seems to emerge from the CSDDD compared to the ECD. This understanding goes beyond the simple dichotomy of business versus environment by presenting sustainability not only as an external limitation to economic activities, but also as a prerequisite, possibly the *conditio sine qua non*, for EU businesses to thrive. In short, the CSDDD conflates the idea of limitation to and of necessity for businesses within the concept of sustainability, following a double materiality approach.[87] In Recital 4, the CSDDD makes this double materiality perspective clear, by stating that "The behaviour of companies across all sectors of the economy is key to success with regard to the Union's sustainability objectives as Union companies, especially large ones, rely on global value chains. It is also in the interest of companies to protect human rights and the environment, in particular given the rising concern of consumers and investors regarding these topics".[88] This perspective informs the subject matter of the CSDDD which, as detailed in its Article 1, concerns rules for corporations on actual and potential human rights and environmental adverse impacts throughout business global value chains, a civil liability regime for such impacts, and the obligations to put in place a transition plan to a sustainable economy within the limits of global warming to 1.5 °C in line with the Paris Agreement.

The original text of Article 15 of the Commission's Proposal, devoted to "Combating Climate Change", now CSDDD Article 22, exemplified this perspective. Its first paragraph referred to the obligations upon companies to adopt a transition plan in compliance with the limit of global warming to 1.5 C in line with the Paris Agreement of 2015.[89] Its second paragraph

[86] On these conceptions, and their geopolitical roots, see e.g. David D., "Business responsibilities in an uncertain world", in *Harvard Business Review*, 1949, 27(3), and Spector B., "Business Responsibilities in a Divided World": The Cold War Roots of the Corporate Social Responsibility Movement", in *Enterprise & Society*, 2008, 9(2), 314.

[87] The double materiality requirement obliges firms to disclose information when social and environmental harms impact on the company value.

[88] As also stated in previous COM (2022) 71, Recital 4.

[89] Current CSDDD Article 22 § 1 largely reproduces the previous text, albeit some dif-

stated that: "The company should identify whether climate change is a *risk for*, or *an impact of*, the company operation and if so it should include emission reduction objectives in its plan. (emph. added)." Besides the clear reference to the Green Deal's overarching goal, this provision considered climate change in terms of the "impact of", but also a "risk for" companies. This dual perspective emphasised the shift from one meaning of sustainability to another. The "impact of" refers to the adverse effects of businesses' activities, and thus enshrines the traditional idea of establishing limits to reduce such impacts. However, this provision also justified emission reduction obligations by framing global warming as a "risk for" business, particularly concerning "company operation" rather than simply its economic value. As such, the Proposal clarified that the unsustainability posed by global warming could jeopardise the pursuit of economic activities, and thus the possibility of business to thrive.

The text of the CSDDD no longer contains this provision. Nevertheless, this dual perspective still informs the obligations set forth under this directive. In addition to the recalled Recital 4, both its Articles 22(2) and 16(2) "Communicating" include indirect reference to the double materiality perspective. These Articles require that their provisions be read in conjunction with, and in accordance with, the sustainability reporting obligations set out under the repealed Directive 2013/34/EU.[90] For instance, Article 19a(1) "Sustainability reporting" sets out the obligation for large undertaking to "report information necessary to understand the undertaking's impacts on sustainability matters, and information necessary to understand how sustainability matters affect the undertaking's development, performance and position". The same applies to parent undertakings under Article 29a(1) "Consolidated Sustainability reporting". Therefore, despite the CSDDD not directly mentioning the "impact for" dimension, it still demonstrates an awareness of the importance of considering the impact that unsustainability has on corporate activities.

This awareness points to the need to move beyond the business/susta-

ferences, ruling that Member States shall ensure that companies referred to in Article 2 §1, points (a), (b) and (c), and Article 2 § 2, points (a), (b) and (c), adopt and put into effect a transition plan for climate change mitigation which aims to ensure, through best efforts, that the business model and strategy of the company are compatible with the transition to a sustainable economy and with the limiting of global warming to 1.5 °C in line with the Paris Agreement and the objective of achieving climate neutrality as established in Regulation (...). Differently from previous Article 15, the CSDDD Article 22 is more detailed, setting in lett. (a)-(d) criteria to be met when drafting the transition plan under para. 1.

[90] Specifically, under Articles 19a, 29a or 40a, of Directive 2013/31/EU, which has been lastly amended by Directive 2022/2464/EU L 322/15, 14.12.2022 on corporate sustainability reporting.

inability dichotomy towards an integrated vision of sustainable business. Utilitarian economic reasons underpin this shift. Beate Sjåfjell grasps this aspect when elucidating the connections between business and scenarios of global unsustainability.[91] She posits that ongoing unsustainability triggers multiple, entangled orders of risks affecting market stability and, consequently, global trade. For example, 'physical risks' of unmitigated environmental degradation could take "the lives of a significant portion of the human population and may leave survivors at enhanced risk by undermining global resilience".[92] These risks intertwine with 'societal risks' associated with social inequality, human rights violations and the weakening of states' welfare systems. Likely consequences include social unrest, increased authoritarianism and societal collapse, all of which can hinder global economic governance over the medium to long term.[93] Therefore, whether business cares about sustainability or not, "(un)sustainability will sooner or later, in one way of another, affect most businesses".[94]

The global scope of the CSDDD's due diligence obligations responds to these concerns, aiming to preserve social stability across supply chains and to secure global markets' operations.[95] After all, this goal aligns with the Commission's recognition that "the ecological transition will reshape geopolitics" in a scenario where "the global climate and environmental challenges are a significant threat multiplier and a source of instability".[96]

---

[91] Sjåfjell (fn. 77) 196-202.

[92] *Ibidem*, 201.

[93] Increased resort to dispute settlement mechanisms, such as the Investor-State Dispute Settlement regime, testifies the merit of these concerns. More concretely, a paradigmatic example of these risks is offered by the case Bear Creek Mining Corporation v Republic of Peru, ICSID Case No ARB/14/21, Award (30 November 2017). The case concerned a Canadian mining company, which failure to achieve its 'social license to operate' from local communities resulted into social unrests and ultimately in Peru shuttering down the project. In return, the company lodged a claim under the Canada-Peru Free-Trade Agreement against Peru for unlawful expropriation. Eventually, the company won and was awarded compensation. Yet, the awarded amount was significantly lower than the one claimed, resulting into a loose-loose scenario.

[94] *Ibidem*, 202.

[95] The corporates' role in affecting social stability and associated financial markets is highlighted in Sjåfjell B. and Bruner C., "Corporations and Sustainability", in Sjåfjell B. and Bruner C. (eds.), *The Cambridge Handbook of Corporate Law, Corporate Governance and Sustainability*, CUP, 2019, 3-12. The CSDDD contributes to the growing attempts to govern global value chain. On this see topic, see, e.g., Salminen J. and Rajavuori M., "Transnational sustainability laws and the regulation of global value chains: Comparison and a framework for analysis", in *Maastricht Journal of European and Comparative Law*, 26(5), 2019, 602.

[96] COM (2019) 640, 21.

Following this line of reasoning, relegating the CSDDD within traditional meanings of sustainable development might minimise its broader contribution to economic transition. The CSDDD's two-faceted understanding of sustainability – as both a limitation and a necessity – qualifies sustainable business as one that proactively engages with sustainable economic models to reduce global unsustainability and thereby secure its own survival. Arguably, this is a more complex qualification than the usual understanding of sustainable development in terms of limits to economic expansion to reduce adverse impacts on human and natural dimensions.[97] In a nutshell, while the CSDDD preserves profit as the corporation's defining end, it innovatively shapes its relationship with sustainability. Specifically, not in terms of economic thriving despite some limitations aimed at reducing corporate harm, i.e., internalising externalities, but rather in the sense of thriving together with – under the necessary condition of – enhancing social and environmental factors to preserve the stability of global markets. Bringing these considerations together, one could infer that the CSDDD underlies an idea of 'sustainable profit', highlighting the convergence of interests between sustainability and business models beyond traditional dichotomies. Recalling the earlier distinction between sustainability and sustainable law, such 'sustainable profit' is found in-between these two paradigms. It does not integrate a sustainable paradigm of law due to its lack of a transformative and critical approach to profit, which remains the core justification for corporate private power.[98] However, it extends beyond the narrow perimeters of reciprocal restraints that characterise sustainability law mirroring the traditional idea of sustainable development. In general terms, 'sustainable profit' could be seen as a model of business governance that tends towards sustainable concepts of law.

By embracing this progressive understanding of corporate sustainable governance, the CSDDD seems to forge a normative convergence, a 'new deal', between public and private spheres to shoulder the economic transition. Specifically, this deal entails a positive commitment, or in the Commission's wording "support", from both private sectors and EU and Member States' public institutions to achieve this transition and reduce global harms.[99]

---

[97] Although the CSDDD explicitly refers to the traditional idea of sustainable economic growth, such as in Recital 9.

[98] On the transformative dimension of the sustainable paradigm of law, see fn. 59 *supra*.

[99] The term 'support' spreads across the CSDDD's Recitals and provisions. For instance, Articles 18, 19, 20 and 31 require public support, from both the EU and Member States to companies. Additional examples include Articles 6 that refers to support

Numerous provisions require corporations to consider those adversely impacted, as well as to identify and assess,[100] prevent[101], bringing to an end actual adverse impacts or terminating the harmful activity as a last resort.[102] In this latter case, remediation of actual adverse impacts is also due.[103] Article 11 is particularly meaningful in this regard. By acknowledging the inherent environmental harm of certain economic activities, it prescribes actions that go beyond a mere 'protection-based' approach, promoting a proactive commitment to reshaping those activities. These measures include obligations to make necessary investments "in adjustments or upgrades of, for example, facilities, production or other operational processes and infrastructures",[104] "make necessary modifications of, or improvements to, the company's own business plan, overall strategies and operations"[105] and to "provide targeted and proportionate support to an SME which is a business partner of the company".[106] Further obligations under Article 11 include: seeking contractual assurances from its indirect partners operating within the companies' value chain; refraining from entering into new or extending existing relations connected with the harmful activities and eventually suspending existing ones; and, ultimately, terminating the business relationship with respect to the activities concerned. For social stability, EU companies should prioritise continuous engagement with their value chain business partners rather than disengagement, using termination only as a last resort to prevent exacerbating adverse impacts, such as in cases involving child labour.[107]

At the same time, EU and national institutions are expected to support the private sector in numerous ways. This includes providing alternatives when companies must terminate business relationships;[108] offering support

---

between parent company and its subsidiary to fulfil due diligence at group level, the role of companies in supporting 'industry or multi-stakeholder initiative' as defined under Article 3 let. (j), and broadly to support from companies to SMEs in preventing and bringing actual adverse impacts to an end, as detailed in Articles 10 and 11. Article 27 §2, let. (b) "Penalties" establishes that any targeted support provided by companies to their partners to prevent adverse impacts ex Article 10 is of relevance to determine the quantum of penalties.

[100] CSDDD Article 8.

[101] *Ibidem*, Article 10.

[102] *Ibidem*, Article 11.

[103] *Ibidem*, Article 12.

[104] *Ibidem*, § 3, let. (d).

[105] *Ibidem*, § 3, let. (e).

[106] *Ibidem*, let. (f).

[107] *Ibidem*, § 7. See also CSDDD's Recital 50.

[108] *Ibidem*, Article 11, § 7 let. (b).

and practical tools for fulfilling due diligence obligations, using relevant international guidelines and standards as references; [109] and providing financial aid and capacity-building assistance to SMEs. [110]

The CSDDD's underlying idea of a convergence between public and private spheres seems to inform the State's obligations to ensure corporations' compliance with this directive's obligations through coercion. [111] In this regard, the CSDDD's administrative sanction regime shares some similarities with, but also differs from, the ECD's criminal one. Both respond to deterrence concerns, as indicated by the common reference to 'effective, proportionate and dissuasive' sanctions. [112] The underlying assumption is that coercion is necessary to promote economic transition, reflecting sustainability as a business limit enforced through top-down sanctions. Additionally, the need for state-centred sanctions under both the ECD and the CSDDD is driven by concern for fair competition, ensuring a level playing field among economic actors. However, while the ECD pursues this goal through a purely negative logic of internalising externalities, [113] the CSDDD reveals a more nuanced sense of coercion. Specifically, it aims to protect and support virtuous corporations that have voluntary invested more in due diligence mechanisms, as opposed to economic actors adhering to harmful 'business as usual' practices. [114] In other terms, the CSDDD, which pertains to the physiological corporate activities, seeks to create a level playing field to shield virtuous companies that opt for proactive approaches in protecting and restoring those adversely impacted by their harmful extractive and productive activities. To this end, the envisaged network of EU

[109] *Ibidem*, Recital 6; Article 19.

[110] *Ibidem*, Article 20 § 2.

[111] *Ibidem*, Article 27 § 1 states: "Member States shall lay down the rules on penalties, including pecuniary penalties, applicable to infringements of the provisions of national law adopted pursuant to this Directive and shall take all measures necessary to ensure that they are implemented. The penalties provided for shall be effective, proportionate and dissuasive".

[112] CSDDD's Article 27 § 1; ECD's Articles 5 and 7.

[113] This was the underlying rationale of Case 68/88 Commission v Greece (Greek Maize) [1989] ECR 2965, that opened the path towards the adoption of duties to criminalize.

[114] CSDDD's Article 27 § 2 states that "In deciding whether to impose penalties and, if such penalties are imposed, in determining their nature and appropriate level, due account shall be taken of": (...) let. (b) any investments made and any targeted support provided pursuant to Articles 10 and 11; let. (c) any collaboration with other entities to address the impacts concerned; (...) let. (f) the extent to which the company carried out any remedial action with regard to the subject matter concerned (...).

and national agencies will likely play a central role in ensuring such a level playing field not only internally within the EU, but also externally at the global level throughout supply chains.[115]

Simultaneously, the CSDDD requires strong support from the public sphere for the operationalization of its robust enforcement regime. This is the essence of the 'deal' promoted by the Commission through the adoption of the CSDDD, necessitating a joint economic effort from both the private economic and public political-institutional spheres. Arguably, the core rationale for moving towards mandatory due diligence law, enforced through top-down sanctions, lies in the Commission's attempt to affirm the role of the State in supporting the Green Deal's goals. In this respect, the Commission's frequent use of 'support' echoes the use of the term 'enable' in the related EU Communication "A New Industrial Strategy for Europe".[116] As Chiti argues, 'enable' is more than 'allowing'. It rather refers to "a technique to mobilise social and economic forces",[117] which indicates the need for synergy between the public and private spheres for the success of the Union's Green Transition.[118]

5. Conclusions: supporting the transition globally?

This Chapter has examined two complementary responses to corporate environmental harm enacted pursuant to the Green Deal, namely the ECD and the CSDDD. As argued, these responses might embody two distinct understandings of sustainability. While the ECD mirrors the traditional dichotomy underpinning sustainable development, the CSDDD unveils a more transformative approach in shaping the relationship between business and sustainability.

---

[115] CSDDD's Articles 24, 25 and 28 relates to this network of agencies.

[116] COM (2020) 102. The connection between the CSDDD and the Industrial Strategy is stated in CSDDD's Recital 11 and emerges multiple times in the body of the CSDDD. This connection appears to be more than coincidental. Industry is among the most environmentally impacting business sectors, thus justifying the CSDDD's focus on it.

[117] Chiti E., "Managing the Ecological Transition of the EU: The European Green Deal as a Regulatory Process", in *CMLRev*, 2022, 59, 41.

[118] Significantly, in COM (2022) 71, Explanatory Memorandum, § 1, the Commission acknowledged the role of States in promoting corporate due diligence facing the shortcomings of mere actions voluntary taken by the private sector. On the evolution of the state paradigm vis-à-vis the current scenarios of global crises, see Mazzucato M., *The Entrepreneurial State: Debunking Public Vs. Private Sector Myths*, Penguin Books, 2018.

In conclusion, this Chapter suggests that the economic transition envisioned by the Green Deal rests upon an improved ability of EU policymakers to enable sustainable business, i.e. to trigger and steer a mobilisation of public-private forces towards this goal. In essence, this requires coupling reactive top-down criminal penalties with proactive regulatory tools that are effective and fit for purpose. In this regard, the CSDDD appears to be moving in the right direction as it deploys a toolkit approach, mixing different regulatory techniques, from traditional CSR ones, such as guidelines, [119] to contracts, [120] and top-down state-centred afflictive measures. [121]

The success of these measures in achieving their intended goals is intrinsically linked to their enforcement. As previously mentioned, the envisaged system of national supervisory authorities is key in safeguarding this transition from unfair competition, both within the EU and, perhaps above all, from outside it. Moreover, geopolitical considerations are inevitable. As Pierre-Henri Conac observes, the CSDDD represents the Commission's ambition to make the EU a global standard giver, not taker, on sustainable governance by leveraging a 'Brussels effects' based on the EU's economic strength and attractiveness. [122] However, the Commission's ambitions could backfire on EU businesses, given the severe costs associated with due diligence obligations. Furthermore, EU companies' capability of compelling indirect partners to comply with harm-reduction strategies, or to terminate harmful business relations, is questionable. Such capability could be undermined by actual relations of dependence on these partners due to lack of alternatives, as seen in sectors like minerals. To succeed, the EU economic transition then necessarily depends on the capability of both the EU and its Member States to 'support the deal', i.e., to strategically protect EU businesses: not only within the internal market, but also – most crucially – in a scenario of global competition.

---

[119] CSDDD, Article 19.

[120] *Ibidem*, Article 18.

[121] *Ibidem*, Article 27.

[122] Conac P.H., "Sustainable Corporate Governance in the EU: Reasonable Global Ambitions?", in *RED-Rethinking Capitalism*, 2022, 4/1, 111, 115-118.

INDEX

www.ingramcontent.com/pod-product-compliance
Lightning Source LLC
LaVergne TN
LVHW021118300926
849160LV00010B/776
9781032932804